CEOE Field 29
Mild-Moderate Disabilities
Teacher Certification Exam

By: Sharon Wynne, M.S
Southern Connecticut State University

"And, while there's no reason yet to panic, I think it's only prudent that we make preparations to panic."

XAMonline, INC.
Boston

Copyright © 2007 XAMonline, Inc.

All rights reserved. No part of the material protected by this copyright notice may be reproduced or utilized in any form or by any means, electronic or mechanical, including photocopying, recording or by any information storage and retrievable system, without written permission from the copyright holder.

To obtain permission(s) to use the material from this work for any purpose including workshops or seminars, please submit a written request to:

XAMonline, Inc.
21 Orient Avenue
Melrose, MA 02176
Toll Free 1-800-509-4128
Email: info@xamonline.com
Web www.xamonline.com
Fax: 1-781-662-9268

Library of Congress Cataloging-in-Publication Data

Wynne, Sharon A.
  Mild-Moderate Disabilities Field 29: Teacher Certification / Sharon A. Wynne. -2nd ed.
  ISBN 978-1-58197-2474
    1. Mild-Moderate Disabilities Field 29   2. Study Guides.   3. CEOE
    4. Teachers' Certification & Licensure.   5. Careers

Disclaimer:

The opinions expressed in this publication are the sole works of XAMonline and were created independently from the National Education Association, Educational Testing Service, or any State Department of Education, National Evaluation Systems or other testing affiliates.

Between the time of publication and printing, state specific standards as well as testing formats and website information may change that is not included in part or in whole within this product. Sample test questions are developed by XAMonline and reflect similar content as on real tests; however, they are not former tests. XAMonline assembles content that aligns with state standards but makes no claims nor guarantees teacher candidates a passing score. Numerical scores are determined by testing companies such as NES or ETS and then are compared with individual state standards. A passing score varies from state to state.

Printed in the United States of America   œ-1

CEOE: Mild-Moderate Disabilities Field 29
ISBN: 978-1-58197-791-2

ACKNOWLEDGEMENTS
Special Education

Recognizing the hard work in the production of our study guides we would like to thank those involved. The credentials and experience fulfilling the making of this study guide, aided by the professionalism and insight of those who expressed the subject mastery in specialized fields, is valued and appreciated by XAMonline. It results in a product that upholds the integrity and pride represented by modern educators who bear the name **TEACHER**.

Providers of foundational material
Founding authors 1996   Kathy Schinerman
   Roberta Ramsey
Pre-flight editorial review   Paul Sutliff
Pre-flight construction :   Brittany Good
   Harris
   Brooks
   Hughes
Authors 2006   Paul Sutliff
Beatrice Jordan

   Marisha Tapera
   Kathy Gibson
   Christi Godard
   Carol Moore
   Twya Lavender
Sample test rational   Sidney Findley

XAMonline Editorial and Production acknowledgements
Project Manager   Sharon Wynne
Project Coordinator   Twya Lavender
Series Editor   Mary Collins
Editorial Assistant   Virginia Finnerty
Marketing Manager   John Wynne
Marketing support   Maria Ciampa
Cover design   Brian Messenger
Sales   Justin Dooley
Production Editor   David Aronson
Typist   Julian
   German
Manufacturing   Chris Morning/Midland Press
E-Books   Kristy Gipson/Lightningsource
Cover Administrator   Jenna Hamilton

*Thank you
for supporting our goals
and accomplishing our aims*

TEACHER CERTIFICATION STUDY GUIDE

About the Test

The purpose of this test is to ensure that the teaching candidates for Oklahoma have the education knowledge, professional knowledge, and subject matter knowledge.

Test Format

Each test includes a section of about 80 multiple-choice questions with four options and one constructed response assignment.

Passing Score

The candidate will receive a total score for each test taken. Total test scores are reported as scaled scores using a range from 100 to 300, with 240 as the minimum passing scaled score.

Location, Fees, Times

For up to date information, please go to
HTTP://WWW.SDE.STATE.OK.US/HOME/DEFAULTIE.HTML

TEACHER CERTIFICATION STUDY GUIDE

Table of Contents

Pre-test 1

SUBAREA I.   **UNDERSTANDING STUDENTS WITH MILD/MODERATE DISABILITIES**

COMPETENCY 1.0   **UNDERSTAND PROCESSES OF HUMAN DEVELOPMENT AND FACTORS, INCLUDING DISABILITY, THAT AFFECT DEVELOPMENT AND LEARNING 50**

Skill 1.1   Understand theories and processes related to ways in which development and learning occur. 50

Skill 1.2   Demonstrate knowledge of the etiologies and effects of various disabilities on development and learning. 57

Skill 1.3   Recognize environmental and other factors that may impede learning in students with mild/moderate disabilities. 63

Skill 1.4   Recognize environmental and other factors that may facilitate learning in students with mild/moderate disabilities. 64

Skill 1.5   Understand how primary language and cultural and familial background can affect the academic, social, and career development of students with mild/moderate disabilities. 67

COMPETENCY 2.0   **UNDERSTAND TYPES AND CHARACTERISTICS OF SPECIFIC LEARNING DISABILITIES AND THEIR SIGNIFICANCE FOR HUMAN DEVELOPMENT AND LEARNING 69**

Skill 2.1   Understand types and characteristics of specific learning disabilities. 69

Skill 2.2   Recognize differences between specific learning disabilities and other types of disabilities. 70

Skill 2.3   Understand the effects of specific learning disabilities on psychomotor, cognitive, social, emotional, and language development. 72

Skill 2.4   Understand the implications of various types of specific learning disabilities for students' educational development. 73

TEACHER CERTIFICATION STUDY GUIDE

COMPETENCY 3.0 UNDERSTAND CAUSES AND CHARACTERISTICS OF MILD/MODERATE MENTAL RETARDATION AND THE SIGNIFICANCE OF MENTAL RETARDATION FOR HUMAN DEVELOPMENT AND LEARNING 81

Skill 3.1 Recognize definitions, causes, and criteria associated with levels of mental retardation...81

Skill 3.2 Understand major cognitive, behavioral, physical, and social characteristics of individuals with mental retardation..........................82

Skill 3.3 Recognize the effects of mental retardation on sensory, motor, adaptive, cognitive, language, social, and emotional development. 82

Skill 3.4 Demonstrate knowledge of learning characteristics of students with mental retardation...82

COMPETENCY 4.0 UNDERSTAND TYPES AND CHARACTERISTICS OF EMOTIONAL DISTURBANCE AND THEIR SIGNIFICANCE FOR DEVELOPMENT AND LEARNING..83

Skill 4.1 Demonstrate knowledge of definitions and identifying criteria of emotional disturbance. 83

Skill 4.2 Recognize major behavioral and social characteristics of students with emotional disturbance. 84

Skill 4.3 Understand the implications of various types of behavioral, social, and emotional disturbances for students' educational development. 85

Skill 4.4 Recognize ways in which emotional disturbance influences personal productivity, interpersonal/intrapersonal effectiveness, communication skills, self-control, and self-monitoring.......................85

COMPETENCY 5.0 UNDERSTAND TYPES AND CHARACTERISTICS OF OTHER CATEGORIES OF DISABILITIES AND THEIR SIGNIFICANCE FOR HUMAN DEVELOPMENT AND LEARNING 86

Skill 5.1 Recognize definitions, causes, and criteria associated with other categories of disabilities 86

Skill 5.2 Understand major cognitive, behavioral, physical, and social characteristics of individuals with other categories of disabilities 86

Skill 5.3 Recognize the effects of other categories of disabilities on sensory, motor, adaptive, cognitive, language, social, and emotional development. 101

TEACHER CERTIFICATION STUDY GUIDE

SUBAREA II. ASSESSING STUDENTS AND DEVELOPING INDIVIDUALIZED EDUCATION PROGRAMS (IEPS) AND INDIVIDUALIZED FAMILY SERVICE PLANS (IFSPS

COMPETENCY 6.0 UNDERSTAND ASSESSMENT INSTRUMENTS AND PROCEDURES FOR EVALUATING THE STRENGTHS AND NEEDS OF STUDENTS WITH MILD/MODERATE DISABILITIES 102

Skill 6.1 Demonstrate knowledge of types and characteristics of formal and informal assessments for students with mild/moderate disabilities. 102

Skill 6.2 Demonstrate knowledge of ways to modify and adapt assessments to accommodate individual abilities and needs. 105

Skill 6.3 Demonstrate knowledge of procedures for screening, prereferral, referral, and classification. 107

Skill 6.4 Demonstrate knowledge of procedures, criteria, personnel, and functions associated with evaluations used to determine eligibility for special education and related services. 113

Skill 6.5 Understand factors in identifying students with exceptional learning needs. 116

Skill 6.6 Understand procedures for using and maintaining ongoing assessment of students with mild/moderate disabilities. 116

Skill 6.7 Understand how to interpret assessment data to evaluate academic progress, revise IEPs and IFSPs, and modify programming for students with mild/moderate disabilities. 117

COMPETENCY 7.0 UNDERSTAND PROCEDURES AND CRITERIA FOR ASSESSING THE COMMUNICATIVE STRENGTHS AND NEEDS OF STUDENTS WITH MILD/MODERATE DISABILITIES 124

Skill 7.1 Demonstrate knowledge of types and characteristics of formal and informal assessments of expressive and receptive language............124

Skill 7.2 Understand how to use assessment results to guide instruction in communication skills. 125

Skill 7.3 Understand how to interpret and communicate the results of assessments of communicative functioning. 126

TEACHER CERTIFICATION STUDY GUIDE

COMPETENCY 8.0 UNDERSTAND PROCEDURES AND CRITERIA FOR ASSESSING THE COGNITIVE AND ACADEMIC STRENGTHS AND NEEDS OF STUDENTS WITH MILD/MODERATE DISABILITIES 128

Skill 8.1 Demonstrate knowledge of types and characteristics of formal and informal assessments of cognitive functioning and academic achievement. 128

Skill 8.2 Understand how to use assessment results to meet students' cognitive and academic needs 128

Skill 8.3 Understand how to interpret and communicate the results of cognitive functioning and academic achievement 130

COMPETENCY 9.0 UNDERSTAND PROCEDURES AND CRITERIA FOR ASSESSING THE SOCIAL AND ADAPTIVE BEHAVIOR OF STUDENTS WITH MILD/MODERATE DISABILITIES 131

Skill 9.1 Understand types and characteristics of formal and informal assessments of social skills and adaptive behavior 131

Skill 9.2 Demonstrate knowledge of procedures for conducting different types of adaptive behavior assessments 132

Skill 9.3 Understand how to interpret and communicate the results of assessments of adaptive behavior and social skills 136

TEACHER CERTIFICATION STUDY GUIDE

COMPETENCY 10.0 UNDERSTAND PROCEDURES FOR DEVELOPING AND IMPLEMENTING INDIVIDUALIZED EDUCATION PROGRAMS (IEPS) AND INDIVIDUALIZED FAMILY SERVICE PLANS (IFSPS) FOR STUDENTS WITH MILD/MODERATE DISABILITIES 137

Skill 10.1 Understand roles and functions of members of IEP and IFSP teams.. 137

Skill 10.2 Recognize components of a comprehensive evaluation used to determine eligibility for early intervention or special education services. 138

Skill 10.3 Demonstrate knowledge of factors and procedures in gathering information, creating and maintaining records, developing IEPs and IFSPs, monitoring progress, and planning transitions from one setting or service delivery system to another.................................... 138

Skill 10.4 Demonstrate awareness of how cultural diversity and linguistic differences may affect evaluation and placement decisions in special education.. 143

Skill 10.5 Understand issues, assurances, and due process rights related to assessment, eligibility, and placement within a continuum of services. 144

SUBAREA III. PROMOTING STUDENT DEVELOPMENT AND LEARNING

COMPETENCY 11.0 UNDERSTAND HOW TO ESTABLISH POSITIVE AND PRODUCTIVE LEARNING ENVIRONMENTS FOR STUDENTS WITH MILD/MODERATE DISABILITIES 147

Skill 11.1 Understand strategies to promote the development and learning of students with mild/moderate disabilities. 147

Skill 11.2 Recognize ways in which disabilities may affect students' progress in the general education curriculum. 154

Skill 11.3 Demonstrate knowledge of factors in the learning environment that affect achievement, self-esteem and attitudes toward learning 155

Skill 11.4 Understand cultural and language diversity and the significance of student diversity for establishing a safe, positive, equitable, and supportive learning environment for all students. 157

Skill 11.5 Demonstrate knowledge of specialized health and safety practices for students with mild/moderate disabilities. 160

Skill 11.6 Demonstrate knowledge of individual and group management strategies for achieving instructional management goals and promoting successful transitions 162

COMPETENCY 12.0 UNDERSTAND EVIDENCE-BASED STRATEGIES AND TECHNIQUES FOR IMPROVING THE EXPRESSIVE AND RECEPTIVE COMMUNICATION SKILLS OF STUDENTS WITH MILD/MODERATE DISABILITIES 167

Skill 12.1 Understand types and characteristics of speaking and writing difficulties associated with various disabilities. 167

Skill 12.2 Understand strategies and techniques for improving students' vocabulary and oral and written communication skills. 168

Skill 12.3 Understand instructional methods, resources, and technologies for promoting students' reading skills and monitoring strategies to students with various types of disabilities. 174

Skill 12.4 Understand augmentative, alternative, and assistive communication strategies. 179

Skill 12.5	Demonstrate knowledge of effective ways to address a broad range of individual communication needs, including the needs of students whose primary language is not English.	180
COMPETENCY 13.0	**UNDERSTAND EVIDENCE-BASED STRATEGIES AND TECHNIQUES FOR IMPROVING THE SOCIAL COMPETENCE OF STUDENTS WITH MILD/MODERATE DISABILITIES**	**183**
Skill 13.1	Understand types and characteristics of social difficulties associated with various disabilities.	183
Skill 13.2	Apply knowledge of social skills needed for educational and other environments.	185
Skill 13.3	Understand strategies and techniques for promoting students' ability to understand expectations and respond appropriately in various social situations.	187
COMPETENCY 14.0	**UNDERSTAND EVIDENCE-BASED STRATEGIES AND TECHNIQUES FOR PROMOTING THE ACADEMIC ACHIEVEMENT AND INDEPENDENT LEARNING OF STUDENTS WITH MILD/MODERATE DISABILITIES**	**193**
Skill 14.1	Understand general and special curricula and types and characteristics of academic difficulties associated with various disabilities.	193
Skill 14.2	Demonstrate knowledge of effective instructional planning and implementation for students with mild/moderate disabilities.	193
Skill 14.3	Demonstrate knowledge of instructional methods and materials.	205
Skill 14.4	Understand instructional methods to strengthen and compensate for deficits in attention, perception, comprehension, memory, and retrieval.	210
Skill 14.5	Understand strategies and activities for helping students organize and manage time, work independently, give and receive feedback, use higher-order thinking skills, and use effective study and test-taking skills.	217
Skill 14.6	Demonstrate knowledge of strategies for teaching students to use self-assessment, problem solving, and other cognitive strategies to meet academic and other needs.	221

| Skill 14.7 | Understand principles and techniques for promoting students' self-confidence, decision-making skills, ownership of tasks and goals, and ability to make successful transitions between grades, schools, and service delivery systems. | 223 |

COMPETENCY 15.0 UNDERSTAND EVIDENCE-BASED STRATEGIES AND TECHNIQUES FOR PROMOTING STUDENTS' ACQUISITION OF FUNCTIONAL SKILLS 228

Skill 15.1	Recognize components of a functional skills curriculum.	228
Skill 15.2	Understand techniques for designing and implementing functional skills instruction	229
Skill 15.3	Understand strategies for teaching functional skills in the major domains	230
Skill 15.4	Understand techniques for promoting skill transfer and generalization.	231

COMPETENCY 16.0 UNDERSTAND THE DEVELOPMENT AND IMPLEMENTATION OF BEHAVIOR INTERVENTIONS FOR STUDENTS WITH MILD/MODERATE DISABILITIES 233

Skill 16.1	Demonstrate knowledge of types, characteristics, strengths, and limitations of various behavior intervention approaches.	233
Skill 16.2	Understand how to develop and implement systematic behavior intervention plans to promote positive social behavior and self-control.	247
Skill 16.3	Understand the use of positive behavior supports and crisis management techniques with students with mild/moderate disabilities.	249
Skill 16.4	Recognize appropriate ways to involve students' families and other school personnel in behavior intervention plans.	251
Skill 16.5	Demonstrate knowledge of strategies for monitoring the effects of behavior interventions and making changes to interventions as necessary.	251
Skill 16.6	Demonstrate knowledge of laws, policies, and ethical principles regarding behavior management planning and implementation.	252

COMPETENCY 17.0 UNDERSTAND PRINCIPLES AND PROCEDURES FOR PROMOTING SUCCESSFUL STUDENT TRANSITIONS 254

Skill 17.1 Demonstrate knowledge of factors that affect student transition across school environments and methods for facilitating transitions. 254

Skill 17.2 Demonstrate knowledge of techniques and settings for promoting career and vocational awareness, exploration, and preparation. 256

Skill 17.3 Understand strategies for providing work experience and career planning services to students. 257

Skill 17.4 Understand strategies for developing goals, benchmarks, activities, programs, and support to promote individuals' transitions to employment and/or postsecondary education. 259

Skill 17.5 Demonstrate knowledge of techniques for promoting students' community living skills; citizenship skills; self-advocacy; multicultural awareness; and participation in social, civic, and recreational activities. 259

Skill 17.6 Recognize how to promote students' self-determination and develop students' understanding of the responsibilities associated with friendships, human sexuality, family life, and parenting. 260

TEACHER CERTIFICATION STUDY GUIDE

SUBAREA IV. WORKING IN A COLLABORATIVE LEARNING COMMUNITY

COMPETENCY 18.0 UNDERSTAND HOW TO ESTABLISH PARTNERSHIPS WITH OTHER MEMBERS OF THE SCHOOL AND THE COMMUNITY TO ENHANCE LEARNING OPPORTUNITIES FOR STUDENTS WITH MILD/MODERATE DISABILITIES 262

Skill 18.1 Demonstrate awareness of consultation, collaboration, and communication strategies for working with others in the school community to solve problems and promote student achievement. 262

Skill 18.2 Understand strategies for providing services in a variety of educational contexts 267

Skill 18.3 Understand strategies for enhancing integration and coordination of related services for educational benefit. 270

Skill 18.4 Demonstrate knowledge of strategies for assisting general education teachers in integrating students with disabilities into general education classes. 271

Skill 18.5 Demonstrate knowledge of local, state, and federal agencies and services that can help meet the needs of students with mild/moderate disabilities 272

Skill 18.6 Understand how to work with community agencies and services to promote students' successful transitions to community living 274

COMPETENCY 19.0 UNDERSTAND HOW TO PROMOTE POSITIVE SCHOOL-HOME RELATIONSHIPS AND ENCOURAGE FAMILIES' INVOLVEMENT IN THEIR CHILDREN'S EDUCATION 275

Skill 19.1 Understand how to establish and maintain effective communication with all families, including culturally and linguistically diverse families, and to overcome communication barriers 275

Skill 19.2 Understand how to design special education programs that are consistent with the beliefs and values of the individuals served and their families. 277

Skill 19.3 Understand the role of families in supporting students' learning and development. 278

Skill 19.4 Understand roles and relationships within families and ways to involve families in the assessment of and service delivery to their children. 280

Skill 19.5 Understand how to provide information, training, support, counseling, and referrals to families of students with mild/moderate disabilities. 281

TEACHER CERTIFICATION STUDY GUIDE

COMPETENCY 20.0 UNDERSTAND THE HISTORY AND PHILOSOPHY OF SPECIAL EDUCATION AND KEY ISSUES AND TRENDS, ROLES AND RESPONSIBILITIES, AND LEGAL AND ETHICAL ISSUES RELEVANT TO SPECIAL EDUCATION 282

Skill 20.1 Demonstrate knowledge of historical, theoretical, and philosophical foundations of and current issues and trends in special education. 282

Skill 20.2 Understand roles and responsibilities of teachers of students with mild/moderate disabilities and relationships of special education to the organization and functions of schools and school systems. 299

Skill 20.3 Demonstrate knowledge of rights and responsibilities of students, parents/guardians, classroom teachers, and other professionals related to exceptional learning needs. 302

Skill 20.4 Demonstrate knowledge of mediation techniques and crisis prevention/intervention. 303

Skill 20.5 Demonstrate knowledge of sources of specialized materials, services, curricula, and resources for individuals with disabilities and organizations and publications relevant to individuals with disabilities. 303

Skill 20.6 Demonstrate knowledge of legal and ethical issues in special education and special-education-related laws, regulations, and guidelines 303

Sample Test 305

Answer Key 329

Rationales with Sample Questions 330

References 372

Resource Guide 388

TEACHER CERTIFICATION STUDY GUIDE

PRE-TEST

1. A ruling pertaining to the use of evaluation procedures later consolidated in Public Law 94 – 142 resulted from which court case listed?
   a. Diana v. the State Board of Education (1970)
   b. Wyatt v. Stickney
   c. Larry P. v. Riles
   d. PASE v. Hannon

Correct answer is "a."
Diana v. the State Board of Education resulted in the decision that all children must be evaluated in their native language.

2. Included in data brought to the attention of Congress regarding the evaluation procedures for education of students with disabilities was the fact that?
   a. There were a large number of children and youths with disabilities in the United States
   b. Many children with disabilities were not receiving an appropriate education
   c. Many parents of children with disabilities were forced to seek services outside of the public realm
   d. All of the above

Correct answer is "d."
All three factors, and many more, have driven Congress to act.

3. The Individuals with Disabilities Education Act (IDEA) was signed into law in and later reauthorized through second revision in what years?
   a. 1975 and 2004
   b. 1980 and 1990
   c. 1990 and 2004
   d. 1995 and 2001

Correct answer is "c."
IDEA, Public Law 101-476 is a consolidation and reauthorization of all prior Special Education mandates, with amendments. It was signed into law by President Bush on October 30, 1990. Revision of IDEA occurred in 2004, IDEA was re-authorized as the Individuals with Disabilities Education Improvement Act of 2004 (IDEIA 2004) is commonly referred to as IDEA 2004. IDEA 2004 (effective July 1, 2005).

4. How was the training of Special Education teachers changed by the No Child Left Behind Act of 2002?
   a. Required all Special Education teachers to be certified in reading and math
   b. Required all Special Education teachers to take the same coursework as general education teachers
   c. If a Special Education teacher is teaching a core subject, he or she must meet the standard of a highly qualified teacher in that subject.
   d. All of the above

Correct answer is "c."

In order for special education teachers to be a students sole teacher of a core subject they must meet the professional criteria of NCLB. They must be *highly qualified*, that is certified or licensed in their area of special education and show proof of a specific level of professional development in the core subjects that they teach. As special education teachers received specific education in the core subject they teach, they will be better prepared to teach to the same level of learning standards as the general education teacher.

5. Which of the following is a specific change of language in the IDEA?
   a. The term "Disorder" changed to "Disability"
   b. The term "Children" changed to "Children and Youth"
   c. The term "Handicapped" changed to "Impairments"
   d. The term "Handicapped" changed to "With Disabilities"

Correct answer is "d."

"Children" became "individuals", highlighting the fact that some students with special needs were adolescents not just "children". The word "handicapped" was changed to "with disabilities", denoting the difference between limitations imposed by society, (handicap) and an inability to do certain things (disability). "With disabilities" also demonstrates that the person is thought of first, and the disabling condition is but one of the characteristics of the individual.

6. Which component changed with the reauthorization of the Education for all Handicapped Children Act of 1975 (EHA) 1990 EHA Amendment?
   a. Specific terminology
   b. Due Process Protections
   c. Non-Discriminatory Reevaluation Procedures
   d. Individual Education Plans

Correct answer is "a."
See Skill 1.1 Question # 5

7. The definition of Assistive technology devices was amended in the IDEA reauthorization of 2004 to exclude what?
   a. iPods other hand-held devices
   b. Computer enhanced technology
   c. Surgically implanted devices
   d. Braille and/or special learning aids

Correct answer is "c."
The definition of Assistive technology devices was amended to exclude devices that are surgically implanted (i.e. cochlear implants), and clarified that students with assistive technology devices shall not be prevented from having special education services. Assistive technology devices may need to be monitored by school personnel, but schools are not responsible for the implantation or replacement of such devices surgically.

8. Which of these factors relate to eligibility for learning disabilities?
   a. A discrepancy between potential and performance
   b. Sub-average intellectual functioning
   c. Social deficiencies or learning deficits that are not due to intellectual, sensory, or physical conditions
   d. Documented results of behavior checklists and anecdotal records of aberrant behavior

Correct answer is "a."
Tests need to show a discrepancy between potential and performance. Classroom observations and samples of student work (such as impaired reading ability) also provide indicators of possible learning disabilities. Eligibility for services in behavior disorders requires documented evidence of social deficiencies or learning deficits that are not due to intellectual, sensory, or physical conditions. Any student undergoing multidisciplinary evaluation is usually given an intelligence test, diagnostic achievement tests, and social and/or adaptive inventories. Answers b, c and d are symptoms displayed before testing for eligibility. Some students who display these symptoms do fail the tests and are not categorized as eligible to receive services.

9. Which is untrue about the Americans with disabilities Act (ADA)?
   a. It was signed into law the same year as IDEA by President Bush
   b. It reauthorized the discretionary programs of EHA
   c. It gives protection to all people on the basis of race, sex, national origin, and religion
   d. It guarantees equal opportunities to persons with disabilities in employment, public accommodations, transportation, government services, and telecommunications.

Correct answer is "b."
EHA is the precursor of IDEA, the Individuals with Disabilities Education Act. ADA, however, is Public Law 101 – 336, the Americans with disabilities Act, which gives civil rights protection to all individuals with disabilities in private sector employment, all public services, public accommodations, transportation and telecommunications. It was patterned after the Rehabilitation Act of 1973.

10. Requirements for evaluations were changed in IDEA 2004 to reflect that no 'single' assessment or measurement tool can be used to determine special education qualification, furthering that a disproportionate representation of what types of students?
    a. Disabled
    b. Foreign
    c. Gifted
    d. Minority and Bilingual

Correct answer is "d."
IDEA 2004 recognized that there exists a disproportionate representation of minorities and bilingual students and that pre-service interventions that are *scientifically based on early reading programs, positive behavioral interventions and support,* and early intervening services may prevent some of those children from needing special education services.

11. IEPs continue to have multiple sections; one section, present levels now addresses what?
    a. Academic achievement and functional performance
    b. English as a second language
    c. Functional performance
    d. Academic achievement

Correct answer is "a."
Individualized Education Plans (IEPS) continue to have multiple sections. One section, present levels, now addresses academic achievement and functional performance. Annual IEP goals must now address the same areas.

12. What is true about IDEA? In order to be eligible, a student must:
    a. Have a medical disability
    b. Have a disability that fits into one of the categories listed in the law
    c. Attend a private school
    d. Be a slow learner

Correct answer is "b."
IDEA is a legal instrument, thus it is defined by law. Every aspect in the operation of IDEA is laid out in law.

13. What determines whether a person is entitled to protection under Section 504?
    a. The individual must meet the definition of a person with a disability
    b. The person must be able to meet the requirements of a particular program in spite of his or her disability
    c. The school, business or other facility must be the recipient of federal funding assistance
    d. All of the above

Correct answer is "d."
To be entitled to protection under Section 504, an individual must meet the definition of a person with a disability, which is: any person who (i) has a physical or mental impairment which substantially limits one or more of that person's major life activities, (ii) has a record of such impairment, or (iii) is regarded as having such an impairment. Major life activities are: caring for oneself, performing manual tasks, walking, seeing, hearing, speaking, breathing, learning, and working. The person must also be "otherwise qualified," which means that the person must be able to meet the requirements of a particular program in spite of the disability. The person must also be afforded "reasonable accommodations" by recipients of federal financial assistance.

14. The Free Appropriate Public Education (FAPE) describes Special Education and related services as?
   a. Public expenditure and standard to the state educational agency
   b. Provided in conformity with each student's individualized education program, if the program is developed to meet requirements of the law.
   c. Include preschool, elementary and/or secondary education in the state involved
   d. All of the above.

Correct answer is "d."
FAPE states that Special Education and related services are provided at public expense; meet the standards of the state educational agency; include preschool, elementary and/or secondary education in the state involved; and are provided in conformity with each student's IEP is the program is developed to meet requirements of the law.

15. Jane is a third grader. Mrs. Smith, her teacher, noted that Jane was having difficulty with math and reading assignments. The results from recent diagnostic tests showed a strong sight vocabulary, strength in computational skills, but a weakness in comprehending what she read. This weakness was apparent in mathematical word problems as well. The multi-disciplinary team recommended placement in a special education resource room for learning disabilities two periods each school day. For the remainder of the school day, her placement will be:
   a. In the Regular Classroom
   b. At a Special School
   c. In a Self-Contained Classroom
   d. In a Resource Room for Mental Retardation

Correct answer is "a."
The resource room is a special room inside the school environment where the child goes to be taught by a teacher who is certified in the area of disability. We hope the accommodations and services provided in the resource room will help her to catch up and perform with her peers in the regular classroom.

16. Legislation in Public Law 94 – 142 attempts to:
    a. Match the child's educational needs with appropriate educational services
    b. Include parents in the decisions made about their child's education
    c. Establish a means by which parents can provide input
    d. All of the above

Correct answer is "d."
Much of what was stated in separate curt rulings and mandated legislation was brought together into what is now considered to be the "backbone" of special education. Public Law 94 – 142, (education for All Handicapped Children Act) was signed into law by President Ford in 1975. It was the culmination of a great deal of litigation and legislation from the late 1960's to the mid 1970's , that included decisions supporting the need to assure an appropriate education to all persons regardless of race, creed, or disability. In 1990, this law was reauthorized and renamed the Individuals with Disabilities education Act, IDEA.

17. Bob shows behavior problems like lack of attention, out of seat and talking out. His teacher has kept data on these behaviors and has found that Bob is showing much better self-control since he has been self-managing himself through a behavior modification program. The most appropriate placement recommendation for Bob at this time is probably:
    a. Any available part-time special education program
    b. The regular classroom solely
    c. A behavior disorders resource room for one period a day
    d. A specific learning disabilities resource room for one period a day

Correct answer is "b."
Bob is able to self-manage himself and is very likely to behave like the other children in the regular classroom. The classroom is the least restrictive environment.

18. Which is an educational characteristic common to students with mild intellectual learning and behavioral disabilities?
    a. Show interest in schoolwork
    b. Have intact listening skills
    c. Require modification in classroom instruction
    d. Respond better to passive than to active learning tasks

Correct answer is "c."
Here are some of the characteristics of students with mild learning and behavioral disabilities are as follows: Lack of interest in schoolwork; prefer concrete rather than abstract lessons; weak listening skills; low achievement; limited verbal and/or writing skills; respond better to active rather than passive learning tasks; Have areas of talent or ability often overlooked by teachers; prefer to receive special help in regular classroom; higher dropout rate than regular education students; achieve in accordance with teacher expectations; require modification in classroom instruction; and are easily distracted.

19. Michael's teacher complains that he is constantly out of his seat. She also reports that he has trouble paying attention to what is going on in class for more than a couple of minutes at a time. He appears to be trying, but his writing is often illegible, containing many reversals. Although he seems to want to please, he is very impulsive and stays in trouble with his teacher. He is failing reading, and his math grades, though somewhat better, are still below average. Michael's psychometric evaluation should include assessment for:
    a. Mild mental retardation
    b. Specific learning disabilities
    c. Mild behavior disorders
    d. Hearing impairment

Correct answer is "b."
Here are some of the characteristics of persons with learning disabilities:
- Hyperactivity: a rate o motor activity higher than normal
- Perceptual difficulties: visual, auditory, and hap tic perceptual problems
- Perceptual-motor impairments: poor integration of visual and motor systems, often affecting fine motor coordination.
- Disorders of memory and thinking: memory deficits, trouble with problem-solving, concept formation and association, poor awareness of own metacognitive skills (learning strategies)
- Impulsiveness: acts before considering consequences, poor impulse control, often followed by remorselessness.
- Academic problems in reading, math, writing or spelling; significant discrepancies in ability levels.

20. In general, characteristics of the learning disabled include:
   a. A low level of performance in a majority of academic skill areas
   b. Limited cognitive ability
   c. A discrepancy between achievement and potential
   d. A uniform pattern of academic development

Correct answer is "c."
The individual with a specific learning disability exhibits a discrepancy between achievement and potential.

21. Zero Reject requires all children with disabilities be provided with what?
   a. Total exclusion of Functional exclusion
   b. Adherence to the annual local education agency (LEA) reporting.
   c. Free, appropriate public education
   d. Both b and c.

Correct answer is "both a and c."
The principle of zero reject requires that all children with disabilities be provided with a free, appropriate public education and the LEA reporting procedure locates, identifies and evaluates children with disabilities within a given jurisdiction to ensure their attendance in public school.

22. Joey is in a mainstreamed preschool program. One of the means his teacher uses in determining growth in adaptive skills is that of observation. Some questions about Joey's behavior that she might ask include:
   a. Is he able to hold a cup?
   b. Can he call the name of any of his toys?
   d. Can he reach for an object and grasp it?
   e. All of the above

Correct answer is "d."
Here are some characteristics of individual with mental retardation or intellectual Disabilities:
- IQ of 70 or below
- Limited cognitive ability; delayed academic achievement, particularly in language-related subjects
- Deficits in memory which often relate to poor initial perception, or inability to apply stored information to relevant situations
- Impaired formulation of learning strategies
- Difficulty in attending to relevant aspects of stimuli: slowness in reaction time or in employing alternate strategies.

23. Individuals with mental retardation ca be characterized as:
    a. Often indistinguishable from normal developing children at an early age
    b. Having a higher than normal rate of motor activity
    c. Displaying significant discrepancies in ability levels
    d. Uneducable in academic skills

Correct answer is "a."
See rationale included in previous question and response.

24. Which of the following statements about children with an motional/behavioral disorder is true?
    a. They have very high IQs
    b. They display poor social skills
    c. They are poor academic achievers
    d. b and c

Correct answer is "d."
Children who exhibit mild behavioral disorders are characterized by:
- Average or above average scores o intelligence tests
- Poor academic achievement; learned helplessness
- Unsatisfactory interpersonal relationships
- Immaturity; attention seeking

Aggressive, acting-out behavior: (hitting, fighting, teasing, yelling, refusing to comply with requests, excessive attention seeking, poor anger control, temper tantrums, hostile reactions, defiant use of language) OR
Anxious, withdrawn behavior: (infantile behavior, social isolation, few friends, withdrawal into fantasy, fears, hypochondria, unhappiness, crying).

25. Which behavior would be expected at the mild level of emotional/behavioral disorders?
    a. Attention seeking
    b. Inappropriate affect
    c. Self-Injurious
    d. Poor sense of identity

Correct answer is "a."
See rationale to question 19.

26. Which of the following is true about autism?
    a. It is caused by having cold, aloof or hostile parents
    b. Approximately 4 out of 10 people have autism
    c. It is a separate exceptionality category in idea
    d. It is a form of mental illness

Correct answer is "c."
In IDEA, the 1990 Amendment to the Education for All Handicapped Children Act, autism was classified as a separate exceptionality category. It is thought to be caused by a neurological or biochemical dysfunction. It generally becomes evident before age 3. The condition occurs in about 4 of every 10,000 persons. Smith and Luckasson, 1992, describe it as a severe language disorder which affects thinking, communication, and behavior. They list the following characteristics:

- **Absent or distorted relationships with people**—inability to relate with people except as objects, inability to express affection, or ability to build and maintain only distant, suspicious or bizarre relationships.
- **Extreme or peculiar problems in communication**—absence of verbal language or language that is not functional such as echolalia (parroting what one hears), misuse of pronouns (e.g. he for you or I for her), neologisms (made-up meaningless words or sentences), talk that bears little or no resemblance to reality.
- **Self-stimulation**—repetitive stereo-typed behavior that seems to have no purposes other than providing sensory stimulation. this may take a wide variety of forms, such as swishing saliva, twirling objects, patting one's cheeks, flapping one's arms, staring,…etc.
- **Self-injury**—repeated physical self-abuse, such as biting, scratching, or poking oneself, head banging, …etc
- **Perceptual anomalies**—unusual responses or absence of response to stimuli that seem to indicate sensory impairment or unusual sensitivity.

27. Autism is a condition characterized by:
    a. Distorted relationships with others
    b. Perceptual anomalies
    c. Self-stimulation
    d. All or the above

d. is correct.
See previous question.

28. As a separate exceptionality category in IDEA, autism:
    a. Includes emotional/behavioral disorders as defined in federal regulations
    b. Adversely affects educational performance
    c. Is thought to be a form of mental illness
    d. Is a developmental disability that affects verbal and non-verbal communication

Correct answer is "d."

29. Which of the following must be provided in a written notice to parents when proposing a child's educational placement?
    a. A list of parental due process safeguards
    b. A list of current test scores
    c. A list of persons responsible for the child's education
    d. A list of academic subjects the child has passed

Correct answer is "a."
Written notice must be provided to parents prior to a proposal or refusal or refusal to initiate or make a change in the child's identification, evaluation or educational placement. Notices must contain:
- A listing of parental due process safeguards.
- A description and a rationale for the chosen action.
- A detailed listing of components (e.g. tests, records, reports) which were
- the basis for the decision.
- Assurance that the language and content of the notices were understood by the parents.

30. Students who receive special services in a regular classroom with consultation, generally have academic and/or social-interpersonal performance deficits at which level of severity?
    a. Mild
    b. Moderate
    c. Severe
    d. Profound

Correct answer is "a."
The majority of students receiving special services are enrolled primarily in regular classes. Those with mild learning and behavior problems exhibit academic and/or social interpersonal deficits that are often evident only in a school-related setting. These students appear no different to their peers, physically.

31. The greatest number of students receiving special services are enrolled primarily in:
    a. The regular classroom
    b. The resource room
    c. Self-contained classrooms
    d. Special schools

Correct answer is "a."
See previous question.

32. The most restrictive environment in which an individual might be placed and receive instruction is that of:
    a. Institutional setting
    b. Homebound instruction
    c. Special schools
    d. Self-contained special classes

Correct answer is "a."
Individuals, who require significantly modified environments for care treatment and accommodation, are usually educated in an institutional setting. They usually have profound/multiple disorders.

33. The law effects required components of the IEP, elements required by the IEP and the law are?
   a. Present level of academic and functional performance; statement of how the disability affects the student's involvement and progress; evaluation criteria and timeliness for instructional objective achievement; modifications of accommodations
   b. Projected dates for services initiation with anticipated frequency, location and duration; statement of when parent will be notified; statement of annual goals
   c. Extent to which child will not participate in regular education program; transitional needs for students age 14.
   d. All of the above.

Correct answer is "d."
IEPs state 14 elements that are required, review them in Skill 1.3 under IEP. Educators must keep themselves apprised of the changes and amendments to laws such as IDEA 2004 with addendums released in October of 2006.

34. The opportunity for persons with disabilities to live as close t the normal as possible describes:
a. Least Restrictive Environment
   b. Normalization
   c. Mainstreaming
   d. Deinstitutionalization

Correct answer is "b."

35. Developmental Disabilities:
   a. Is the categorical name for mental retardation in IDEA
   b. Includes congenital conditions such as severe Spina Bifida, deafness, blindness or profound mental retardation
   c. Includes children who contract diseases such as polio or meningitis, and are left in an incapacitating functional state
   d. b and c

Correct answer is "d."

36. IDEA defines children with a disability as children evaluated in accordance with what?
a. 300.53.0200.4
b. 300.54.0200.6
c. 300.53.0300.5
d. None of the above

Correct answer is "c."
300.53.0300.5 defines disability as children who are mentally retarded, hard of hearing deaf, speech impaired, visually impaired, seriously emotionally disturbed, orthopedic ally impaired, other health impaired, deaf-blind, multi-handicapped, or as having specific learning disabilities, who, because of those impairments, need special education and related services (300.5).

37. Normality in child behavior is influenced by societies?
    a. Attitudes and cultural beliefs
    b. Religious beliefs
    c. Religious and cultural beliefs
    d. Attitudes and Victorian era motto

Correct answer is "a."

38. The CST coordinates and participates in due diligence through what process?
    a. Child study team meets first time without parents
    b. Teachers take child learning concerns to the school counselor
    c. School counselor contact parents for permission to perform screening assessments
    d. All of the above

Correct answer is "d."
The CST coordinates and participates in due diligence through a process that includes teachers or parents concerns about academic or functional development goes to the counselor who then obtain a permission for screening assessments of child's skills And, the results determine need, if needed child study team meets without parents first.

TEACHER CERTIFICATION STUDY GUIDE

39. When a student is identified as being at-risk academically or socially what does Federal law hope for first?
    a. Move the child quickly to assessment
    b. Place child in Special Education as soon as possible
    c. Observe child to determine what is wrong
    d. Perform remedial intervention in the classroom

Correct answer is "d."
Once a student is identified as being at-risk academically or socially, remedial interventions are attempted within the regular classroom. Federal legislation requires that sincere efforts be made to help the child learn in the regular classroom.

40. What do the 9th and 10th Amendments to the U.S. Constitution state about education?
    a. That education belongs to the people
    b. That education is an unstated power vested in the states
    c. That elected officials mandate education
    d. That education is free

41. The IDEA states that child assessment is?
    a. At intervals with teacher discretion
    b. Continuous on regular basis
    c. Left to the counselor
    d. Conducted annually

Correct answer is "b."
Assessments in Special Education are continuous and occur on a regular basis.

42. Safeguards against bias and discrimination in the assessment of children include:
    a. The testing of a child in Standard English
    b. The requirement for the use of one standardized test
    c. The use of evaluative materials in the child's native language or other mode of communication
    d. All testing performed by a certified, licensed, psychologist

Correct answer is "c."
The law requires that the child be evaluated in his native language, or mode of communication. The idea that a licensed psychologist evaluate the child does not meet the criteria if it is not done in the child's normal mode of communication.

43. Which is characteristic of group tests?
    a. Directions are always read to students
    b. The examiner monitors several students at the same time
    c. The teacher is allowed to probe students who almost have the correct answer
    d. Both quantitative and qualitative information may be gathered

Correct answer is "b."
In group tests, the examiner may provide directions for children up to and including fourth grade. Children write or mark their own responses. The examiner monitors the progress of several children at the same time. He cannot rephrase questions or probe or prompt responses. It is very difficult, almost impossible to obtain qualitative information in group tests. Group tests are appropriate for program evaluation, screening, and some types of program planning, such as tracking. Special consideration may need to be given if there is any motivational, personality, linguistic, or physically disabling factors that might impair the examinee's performance. When planning individual programs, individual tests should be used.

44. For which of the following uses are individual tests most appropriate?
    a. Screening students to determine possible need for special education services
    b. Evaluation of special education curricular
    c. Tracking of gifted students
    d. Evaluation of a student for eligibility and placement, or individualized program planning, in special education

Correct answer is "d."
See previous question.

45. Which of the following is an advantage of giving individual, rather than group tests?
    a. The test administrator can control the tempo of an individual test, giving breaks when needed
    b. The test administrator can clarify or rephrase questions
    c. Individual tests provide for the gathering of both qualitative and quantitative results
    d. All of the above

Correct answer is "d."

46. Mrs. Stokes has been teaching her third-grade students about mammals during a recent science unit. Which of the following would be true of a criterion-referenced test she might administer at the conclusion of the unit?
   a. It will be based on unit objectives
   b. Derived scores will be used to rank student achievement.
   c. Standardized scores are effective of national performance samples
   d. All of the above

Correct answer is "a."
Criterion-referenced tests measure the progress made by individuals in mastering specific skills. The content is based on a specific set of objectives rather than on the general curriculum. Criterion-referenced tests provide measurements pertaining to the information a given student needs to know and the skills that student needs to master. Norm-referenced tests have a large advantage over criterion-referenced tests when used for screening or program evaluation. Norm-referenced tests provide a means of comparing a student's performance to the performance typically expected of others of his age.

47. For which of the following purposes is a norm-referenced test least appropriate?
   a. Screening
   b. Individual program planning
   c. Program evaluation
   d. Making placement decisions

Correct answer is "b."

48. Criterion referenced tests can provide information about:
   a. Whether a student has mastered prerequisite skills
   b. Whether a student is ready to proceed to the next level of instruction
   c. which instructional materials might be helpful in covering program objectives
   d. All of the above

Correct answer is "a."
In criterion referenced testing, the emphasis is on assessing specific and relevant behaviors that have been mastered. Items on criterion-referenced tests are often linked directly to specific instructional objectives.

49. Which of the following purposes of testing calls for an informal test?
    a. Screening a group of children to determine their readiness for the first reader
    b. Measure the content of a social studies unit prepared by the classroom teacher covering one aspect of the general curriculum
    c. Evaluating the effectiveness of a fourth-grade math program at the end of its first year of use in a specific school
    d. Determining the general level of intellectual functioning of a class of fifth graders

Correct answer is "b."
Formal tests are commercially prepared standardized tests. Formal tests may be categorized as norm-referenced or as criterion-referenced. Informal tests are usually teacher-prepared. These are usually criterion referenced. b is the only teacher-made test.

50. Which of the following is **not** a true statement about informal tests?
    a. Informal tests are useful in comparing students to others of their age or grade level
    b. The correlation between curriculum and test criteria is much higher in informal tests
    c. Informal tests are useful in evaluating an individual's response to instruction
    d. Informal tests are used to diagnose a student's particular strengths and weaknesses for purposes of planning individual programs

Correct answer is "a."
Informal or teacher-made tests are usually criterion-referenced. Norm-referenced tests are usually group tests given to large populations, rather than individualized, or teacher-made.

51. For which situation might a teacher be apt to select a formal test?
    a. A pretest for studying world religions
    b. A weekly spelling test
    c. To compare student progress with that of peers of same age or grade level on a national basis
    d. To determine which content objectives outlined on the student's IEPs were mastered

Correct answer is "c."
See previous question.

TEACHER CERTIFICATION STUDY GUIDE

52. The extent to which a test measures what its authors or users claim that it measures is called its:
    a. Validity
    b. Reliability
    c. Normality
    d. Acculturation

Correct answer is "a."
Validity: degree or extent to which a test measures what it was designed or intended to measure.
Reliability: the extent to which a test is consistent in its measurements.

53. Which of the following is a factor in determining test validity?
    a. The appropriateness of the sample items chosen to measure a criterion
    b. The acculturation of the norm group as compared to that of the population being tested
    c. The reliability of the test
    d. All of the above

Correct answer is "d."
Validity can be affected by:
- The appropriateness of the sample items chosen to measure a criterion
- The cultural, environmental and language background of the norm group as compared to that of the population being tested
- The accuracy with which a person's performance on a criterion can be predicted from his test score on that criterion
- The consistency in administration and scoring of the test
- The reliability of the test

54. If a scholastic aptitude test is checked against predictive success in academic endeavors, which type of validity is one attempting to establish?
    a. Content
    b. Criterion-related
    c. Construct
    d. Confirmation

Correct answer is "b."
There are different kinds of evidence to support a particular judgment. If the purpose of a test is to measure the skills covered in a particular course or unit, then we would hope to see test questions on all the important topics and not on extraneous topics. If this condition is met, then we would have content validity. Some tests, like the SAT, are designed to predict outcomes. If SAT scores correlate with academic performance in college, as measured by GPA in the first year, then, we have criterion related validity. Construct validity is probably the most important. It is gathered over many years, and is indicated by a pattern of scores e.g. older children can answer more questions on intelligence tests than younger children. This fits with our construct of intelligence.

55. Acculturation refers to the individual's:
    a. Gender
    b. Experiential background
    c. Social class
    d. Ethnic background

Correct answer is "b."
A person's culture has little to do with gender, or social class, or ethnicity. A person is the product of his experiences. Acculturation: differences in experiential background.

56. To which aspect does fair assessment relate?
    a. Representation
    b. Acculturation
    c. Language
    d. All of the above

Correct answer is "d."
All three aspects are necessary and vital for assessment to be fair.

57. Youngsters in regular classrooms receive regular testing primarily related to:
    a. Eligibility for special education
    b. Promotion by grade level
    c. IEP program planning
    d. All of the above

Correct answer is "b."
Promotion by grade level is the only reason for testing of regular students in regular classrooms.

58. Which of the following statements reflects true factors that affect the reliability of a test?
    a. Short tests tend to be more reliable than long tests
    b. The shorter the time length between two administrations of a test, the greater the possibility that the scores will change
    c. Even if guessing results in a correct response, it introduces error into a test score and into interpretation of the results
    d. All of the above

Correct answer is "c."
The reliability of a test is concerned with the extent to which the person tested will receive the same score on repeated administrations of that test. When a person's score fluctuates randomly, the test lacks reliability.

59. Mrs. Freud administered a personality traits survey to her high school psychology class. She readministered the same survey two weeks later. The method which she used to determine reliability was that of:
    a. Test-retest
    b. Split half
    c. Alternate form
    d. Kuder-Richardson formula

Correct answer is "a."
The test-retest reliability is accomplished by do the same test on a second occasion.

60. Children who write poorly might be given tests which allow oral responses that are unless the purpose for giving the test is to:
    a. Assess handwriting skills
    b. Test for organization of thoughts
    c. Answer questions pertaining to math reasoning
    d. Assess rote memory

Correct answer is "a."
It is necessary to have the child write, if we are assessing his skill in that domain.

61. Which of the following types of tests is used to estimate learning potential and to predict academic achievement?
    a. Intelligence tests
    b. Achievement tests
    c. Adaptive behavior tests
    d. Personality tests

Correct answer is "a."
An intelligence test is designed to measure intellectual abilities like memory, comprehension and abstract reasoning. IQ is often used to estimate the learning capacity of a student as well as to predict academic his achievement.

62. Which skills are typically assessed by an intelligence test?
    a. Abstract reasoning, comprehension
    b. Interest, capacity
    c. Math computation, math-reasoning skills
    d. Independent functioning, language development

Correct answer is "a."
See previous question.

63. In which of the following exceptionality categories may a student be considered for inclusion if his IQ score falls more than two standard deviations below the mean?
    a. Mental retardation
    b. Specific learning disabilities
    c. Emotionally/behaviorally disordered
    d. Gifted

Correct answer is "a."
Only about 1 to 1.5% of the population fit the AAMD's definition of mental retardation. They fall outside the 2 standard deviations limit for Special Learning Disabilities and Emotionally/Behaviorally disordered.

64. A test, which measures students' skill development in academic content areas, is classified as an _____ test.
    a. Achievement
    b. Aptitude
    c. Adaptive
    d. Intelligence

Correct answer is "a."
Achievement tests directly assess students' skill development in academic content areas. It measures the degree to which a student has benefited education and/or life experiences compared to others of the same age or grade level. They may be used as diagnostic tests to find strengths and weaknesses of students. They may be used for screening, placement progress evaluation, and curricular effectiveness.

65. The Key Math Diagnostic Arithmetic Test is an individually administered test of math skills. It is comprised of fourteen subtests which are classified into the major math areas of content, operations, and applications for which subtest scores are reported. The test manual describes the population sample upon which the test was normed, and reports data pertaining to reliability and validity. In addition, for each item in the test, a behavioral objective is presented. From the description, it can be determined that this achievement test is:
    a. Individually administered
    b. Criterion-referenced
    c. Diagnostic
    d. All of the above

Correct answer is "d."
The test has a limited content designed to measure to what extent the student has mastered specific areas in math. The expressions "individually administered" and "diagnostic" appear in the description of the test.

66. The best measures of a student's functional capabilities and entry level skills are:
    a. Norm-referenced tests
    b. Teacher-made post-tests
    c. Standardized I Q tests
    d. Criterion referenced measures

Correct answer is "d."
Criterion-referenced measures are useful for assessment of a student's functional capabilities and entry-level skills. unlike norm-referenced tests, which compare an individual with others of the same grade or age level, criterion-referenced tests, measures the level of functions and skills if the individual.

67. A prerequisite skill is:
    a. The lowest order skill in a hierarchy of skills, needed to perform a specific task
    b. A skill which must be demonstrated before instruction on a specific task can begin
    c. A tool for accomplishing task analysis
    d. The smallest component of any skill

Correct answer is "b."
This is an enabling skill that a student needs in order to perform an objective successfully.

68. Presentation of tasks can be altered to match the student's rate of learning by:
    a. Describing how much of a topic is presented in one day and how much practice is assigned, according to the student's abilities and learning style
    b. Using task analysis, assign a certain number of skills to be mastered in a specific amount of time
    c. Introducing a new task only when the student has demonstrated mastery of the previous task in the learning hierarchy
    d. a and c

Correct answer is "d."
Pacing is the term used for altering of tasks to match the student's rate of learning. This can be done in two ways; altering the subject content and the rate at which tasks are presented.

69. All of the following are suggestions for altering the presentation of tasks to match the student's rate of learning except:
    a. Teach in several shorter segments of time rather than a single lengthy session
    b. Continue to teach a task until the lesson is completed in order to provide more time on task
    c. Watch for nonverbal cues that indicate students are becoming confused, bored, or restless
    d. Avoid giving students an inappropriate amount of written work

Correct answer is "b."
This action taken does not alter the subject content; neither does it alter the rate at which tasks are presented.

70. In which of the following ways does an effective teacher cooperate pacing as a means of matching a student's rate of learning?
    a. Selected content is presented based upon prerequisite skills
    b. Task presentations are paced during optimum time segments
    c. Special needs students always require smaller steps and learning segments regardless of the activity or content
    d. a and b

Correct answer is "d."
C is not a true statement. A and B are true statements.

71. Which of the following examples would be considered of highest priority when determining the need for the delivery of appropriate special education and related services?
    a. An eight-year-old boy is repeating first grade for the second time and exhibits problems with toileting, gross motor functions, and remembering number and letter symbols. His regular classroom teacher claims the referral forms are too time-consuming and refuses to complete them. He also refuses to make accommodations because he feels every child should be treated alike.
    b. A six-year-old girl who has been diagnosed as autistic is placed in a special education class within the local school. Her mother wants her to attend residential school next year, even though the girl is showing progress.
    c. A ten-year-old girl with profound mental retardation who is receiving education services in a state institution.
    d. A twelve-year-old boy with mild disabilities who was placed in a behavior disorders program, but displays obvious perceptual deficits (e.g. reversal of letters and symbols, and inability to discriminate sounds). He originally thought to have a learning disability, but did not meet state criteria for this exceptionality category, based on results of standard scores. He has always had problems with attending to a task, and is now beginning to get into trouble during seatwork time. His teacher feels that he will eventually become a real behavior problem. He receives social skills training in the resource room one period a day.

Correct answer is "a."
No modifications are being made, so the child is not receiving any services whatsoever.

72. Which of the following would be classified as direct rather than indirect services that a specially trained special education teacher would provide to regular education teachers?
    a. Answer questions about a particular child's academic or social-interpersonal needs
    b. Teach a math unit on measurement
    c. Assist with selecting special materials for a student
    d. Develop math worksheets tailored to meet a student's needs

Correct answer is "b."
Indirect services are those given when special education personnel consult with regular classroom teachers to assist them in teaching students with mild disabilities who are enrolled fulltime in their regular classrooms. Direct services are those in which personnel work with the students in the classroom to remediate difficulties.

TEACHER CERTIFICATION STUDY GUIDE

73. Which is a less than ideal example of collaboration in successful inclusion?
    a. Special education teachers are part of the instructional team in a regular classroom
    b. Special education teachers assist regular education teachers in the classroom
    c. Teaming approaches are used for problem solving and program implementation
    d. Regular teachers, special education teachers, and other specialists or support teachers co-teach

Correct answer is "b."
In a special education setting, the special education teacher should be the lead teacher.

74. Which of the following is an example of tactile perception?
    a. Making an angel in the snow with one's body
    b. Running a specified course
    c. Identifying a rough surface with eyes closed
    d. Demonstrating aerobic exercises

Correct answer is "c."
Tactile: having to do with touch.

75. Which of the following activities best exemplifies a kinesthetic exercise in developing body awareness?
    a. Touching materials of different textures
    b. Playing a game like "Looby Loo"
    c. Identifying geometric shapes being drawn on one's back
    d. Making a shadow-box project

Correct answer is "b."
Kinesthetic: having to do with body movement.

76. Which of the following teaching activities is least likely to enhance observational learning in students with special needs?
    a. A verbal description of the task to be performed, followed by having the children immediately attempt to perform the instructed behavior
    b. A demonstration of the behavior, followed by an immediate opportunity for the children to imitate the behavior
    c. A simultaneous demonstration and explanation of the behavior, followed by ample opportunity for the children to rehearse the instructed behavior
    d. Physically guiding the children through the behavior to be imitated, while verbally explaining the behavior

Correct answer is "a."
Students are given verbal instructions only. The children are not given a chance to observe, or see, the behavior so that they can imitate it. Some of the students may have hearing deficiencies.

77. The _____ modality is most frequently used in the learning process.
    a. Auditory
    b. Visual
    c. Tactile
    d. All of the Above

Correct answer is "d."
The auditory, visual, and tactile modalities are the ones frequently used in the learning process. We learn through an integration of these modalities (multi-sensory approach).

78. Which of the following is an example of cross-modal perception involving integrating visual stimuli to an auditory verbal process?
    a. Following spoken directions
    b. Describing a picture
    c. Finding certain objects in pictures
    d. b and c

Correct answer is "b."
We see (visual modality) the picture and use words (auditory modality) to describe it.

79. Which of the following is a good example of a generalization?
    a. Jim has learned to add and is now ready to subtract
    b. Sarah adds sets of units to obtain a product
    c. Bill recognizes a vocabulary word on a billboard when traveling
    d. Jane can spell the word "net" backwards to get the word "ten"

Correct answer is "c."
Generalization is the occurrence of a learned behavior in the presence of a stimulus other than the one that produced the initial response. It is the expansion of a student's performance beyond the initial setting. Students must be able to expand or transfer what is learned to other settings (e.g., reading to math word problems, resource room to regular classroom). Generalization may be enhanced by the following:
- Use many examples in teaching to deepen application of learned skills
- Use consistency in initial teaching situations, and later introduce variety in format, procedure and use of examples
- Have the same information presented by different teachers, in different settings, and under varying conditions
- Include a continuous reinforcement schedule at first, later changing to delayed and intermittent schedules as instruction progresses
- Teach students to record instances of generalization and to reward themselves at that time
- Associate naturally occurring stimuli when possible

80. _____ is a method used to increase student engaged learning time by having students teach other students.
    a. Collaborative learning
    b. Engaged learning time
    c. Allocated learning time
    d. Teacher consultation

Correct answer is "a."
Collaborative Learning is a method for increasing student learning time by having students teach other students.

81. Which is NOT included by Henley, Ramsey, and Algozzine (1993) as steps teachers use to establish cooperative learning groups in the classroom? The teacher:
   a. Selects Members of Each Learning Group
   b. Directly Teaches Cooperative Group Skills
   c. Assigns Cooperative Group Skills
   d. Has Students Self-Evaluate Group Efforts

Correct answer is "d."
According to Henley et al, there are four steps to establishing cooperative learning groups:
1. The teacher selects members of each learning group
2. The teacher directly teaches cooperative group skills
3. The teacher assigns cooperative group activities
4. The teacher evaluates group efforts

82. Some environmental elements which influence learning styles include all except:
   a. Light
   b. Temperature
   c. Design
   d. Motivation

Correct answer is "d."
Individual learning styles are influenced by environmental, emotional, sociological, and physical elements. Environmental include sound, light, temperature and design. Emotional elements such as motivation, persistence, responsibility and structure. Motivation is not an environmental element.

TEACHER CERTIFICATION STUDY GUIDE

83. When teaching a student, who is predominantly auditory, to read, it is best to:
    a. Stress sight vocabulary
    b. Stress phonetic analysis
    c. Stress the shape and configuration of the word
    d. Stress rapid reading

Correct answer is "b."
Sensory modalities are one of the physical elements that affect learning style. Some students learn best through their visual sense (sight), others through their auditory sense (hearing) and still others by doing, touching and moving (tactile-kinesthetic). Auditory learners generally listen to people, follow verbal directions, and enjoy hearing records, cassette tapes, and stories. Phonics has to do with sound, an auditory stimulus.

84. If a student is predominantly a visual learner, he may learn more effectively by:
    a. Reading aloud while studying
    b. Listening to a cassette tape
    c. Watching a film strip
    d. Using body movement

Correct answer is "c."
Visual learners use their sense of sight, which is the sense being used to watch a filmstrip.

85. Cognitive learning strategies include:
    a. Reinforcing appropriate behavior
    b. Teaching students how to manage their own behavior in school
    c. Heavily structuring the learning environment
    d. Generalizing learning from one setting to another

Correct answer is "b."
See previous question.

86. The effective teacher varies her instructional presentations and response requirements depending upon:
    a. Student needs
    b. The task at hand
    c. The learning situation
    d. All of the above

Correct answer is "d."

87. In order for a student to function independently in the learning environment, which of the following must be true?
    a. The learner must understand the nature of the content
    b. The student must be able to do the assigned task
    c. The teacher must communicate performance criteria to the learner
    d. All of the above

Correct answer is "d."
Together with the above, the child must be able to ask for and obtain assistance if necessary.

88. Cognitive modeling is an essential component of which self-training approach?
    a. Self-instructional training
    b. Self-monitoring
    c. Self-reinforcing
    d. Self-punishing

Correct answer is "a."
Cognitive modeling: The adult model performs a task while verbally instructing himself
Self-instruction: The child performs the task while instructing himself, silently or overtly
Self-monitoring: Refers to procedures by which the learner records whether or not he is engaging in certain behaviors, particularly those that would lead to increased academic achievement and/or social behavior

89. Strategies specifically designed to move the learner from dependence to independence include:
    a. Assessment, planning, implementation, and reevaluation
    b. Demonstration, imitation, assistance, prompting, and verbal instruction
    c. Cognitive modeling and self-guidance through overt, faded overt and covert stages
    d. b and c

Correct answer is "a."
Both are correct, as demonstration is a form of modeling.

90. Alan has failed repeatedly in his academic work. He needs continuous feedback in order to experience small, incremental achievements. What type of instructional material would best meet this need?
    a. Programmed materials
    b. Audiotapes
    c. Materials with no writing required
    d. Worksheets

Correct answer is "a."
Programmed materials are best suited as Alan would be able to chart his progress as he achieves each goal. He can monitor himself and take responsibility for his successes.

91. After purchasing what seemed to be a very attractive new math kit for use with her SLD (severely learning disabled) students, Ms. Davis discovered her students could not use the kit unless she read the math problems and instructions to them, as the readability level was higher than the majority of the students' functional reading capabilities. Which criterion of the materials selection did Ms. Davis most likely fail to consider when selecting this math kit?
    a. Durability
    b. Relevance
    c. Component Parts
    d. Price

Correct answer is "b."
Relevance is the only cognitive factor, listed. Since her students were severely learning disabled, she almost certainly would have considered the kit's durability and component parts. She did not have to consider price. That would be taken care of by the district.

92. Which of the following questions most directly evaluates the utility of instructional material?
    a. Is the cost within budgetary means?
    b. Can the materials withstand handling by students?
    c. Are the materials organized in a useful manner?
    d. Are the needs of the students met by the use of the materials?

Correct answer is "c."
It is a question of utility or usefulness.

93. Which of the following is descriptive of a good safety precaution when operating equipment?
    a. Reporting malfunctioning of a machine to the school's media specialist
    b. Leaving the room while a filmstrip is being shown in class
    c. Operating a machine with frayed cords
    d. Allowing an overhead projector to remain set up and plugged into a wall receptacle so the next class can view the transparencies too

Correct answer is "a."
All three others are hazardous practices, and should not be allowed to happen.

94. John learns best through the auditory channel, so his teacher wants to reinforce his listening skills. Through which of the following types of equipment would instruction be most effectively presented?
    a. Overhead projector
    b. Cassette player
    c. Microcomputer
    d. Opaque projector

Correct answer is "b."
Audio cassette player would help sharpen and further develop his listening skills as he is an auditory learner.

95. A money bingo game was designed by Ms Johnson for use with her middle grade students. Cards were constructed with different combinations of coins pasted on each of the nine spaces. Ms. Johnson called out various amounts of change (e.g. 30 cents) and students were instructed t cover the coin combinations on their cards which equaled the amount of change (e.g. two dimes and two nickels, three dimes, and so on). The student who had the first bingo was required to add the coins in each of the spaces covered and tell the amounts before being declared the winner. Five of Ms. Johnson's sixth graders played the game the ten minute free activity time following math the first day the game was constructed. Which of the following attributes are present in this game in this situation?
    a. Accompanied by simple, uncomplicated rules
    b. Of brief duration, permitting replay
    c. Age appropriateness
    d. All of the above

Correct answer is "d."
Games and puzzles should also be colorful and appealing, of relevance to individual students, and appropriate for learners at different skill levels, in order to sustain interest and motivational value.

96. For which stage of learning would computer software be utilized that allows for continued drill and practice of a skill to achieve accuracy and speed?
    a. Acquisition
    b. Proficiency
    c. Maintenance
    d. Generalization

Correct answer is "b."
Acquisition: Introduction of a new skill.
Maintenance: Continued practice without further instruction.
Proficiency: Practice under supervision to achieve accuracy and speed.
Generalization: Application of the new skills in new settings and situations.

97. In which way is a computer like an effective teacher?
    a. Provides immediate feedback
    b. Sets the pace at the rate of the average student
    c. Produces records of errors made, only
    d. Programs to skill levels at which students at respective chronological ages should be working

Correct answer is "a."

98. During which written composition stage are students encouraged to read their stories aloud to others?
    a. Planning
    b. Drafting
    c. Revising/editing
    d. Sharing/publication

Correct answer is "c."
It is encouraged at this stage as both the child and the audience will distinguish errors and make corrections. The child also learns to accept constructive criticism.

99. Which recently developed assistive device can "read' aloud sections from a newspaper received electronically?
    a. Soniguide
    b. Personal companion
    c. Closed circuit television
    d. Talking books

Correct answer is "b."
The Personal Companion can "read" aloud sections from newspapers delivered over telephone lines. This machine can maintain a daily appointment book, and turn appliances on and off.

100. Which electronic device enables persons with hearing impairments to make and receive phone calls?
    a. Personal companion
    b. Telecommunication device for the deaf
    c. Deafnet
    d. Hearing aids

Correct answer is "b."

101. Which electronic device can assist by dialing a telephone, turning book pages, and drinking from a cup?
    a. Communication boards
    b. Manipulator robots
    c. Electronic switches
    d. Crutches

Correct answer is "b."
As the name implies, a manipulator robot is a moving, electronic device that can be manipulated or controlled.

102. Behaviorists contend that all behavior is:
    a. Predictable
    b. Observed
    c. Conditioned
    d. Learned

Correct answer is "d."
Behavior modification is based on the premise that all behavior, regardless of its appropriateness, has been learned, and therefore, can be changed.

103. Procedures employed to decrease targeted behaviors include:
    a. Punishment
    b. Negative reinforcement
    c. Shaping
    d. a and b

Correct answer is "a."
Punishment and extinction may be used to decrease target behaviors.

104. Which description best characterizes primary reinforcers of an edible nature?
    a. Natural
    b. Unconditioned
    c. Innately motivating
    d. All of the above

Correct answer is "d."
Primary reinforcers are those stimuli which are of biological importance to an individual. They are natural, unlearned, unconditioned, and innately motivating. The most common and appropriate reinforcer used in the classroom is food.

105. Mrs. Chang is trying to prevent satiation from occurring, so that her reinforcers will be effective, as she is using a continuous reinforcement schedule. Which of the following ideas would be least effective in preventing satiation?
    a. Use only one type of edible rather than a variety
    b. Ask for ten vocabulary words rather than twenty
    c. Give pieces of cereal, bits of fruit, or M&Ms rather than large portions of edibles
    d. Administer a peanut then a sip of water

Correct answer is "a."
Here are some suggestions for preventing satiation:
- Vary reinforcers with instructional tasks
- Shorten the instructional sessions, and presentation of reinforcers will be decreased
- Alternate reinforcers (e.g. food, then juice)
- Decrease the size of edibles presented
- Have an array of edibles available

106. Which tangible reinforcer would Mr. Whiting find to be most effective with teenagers?
    a. Plastic whistle
    b. Winnie-the-Pooh book
    c. Poster of a current rock star
    d. Toy ring

Correct answer is "c."
This tops the list of things that teenagers crave. It is the most desirable.

107. Which is an example of a secondary reinforcer?
    a. Water
    b. Praise
    c. Hug
    d. b and c

Correct answer is "d."
Secondary reinforcers are not necessarily naturally reinforcing to most people. Their value is learned or conditioned through an association, or pairing, with primary reinforcers. Secondary reinforcers include social participation in preferred activities, praise, body language and attention.

108. Which is not a valid reason for using a secondary reinforcer?
    a. The possibility of satiation, using a primary reinforcer
    b. The pairing of a primary reinforcer with a secondary reinforcer, which requires too much time and effort
    c. The inability to assure a state of deprivation when using a primary reinforcer
    d. The possibility of student dependency upon the primary reinforcer

Correct answer is "b."
Some reasons for using secondary reinforcers are:
- The student may become temporarily satiated with the primary reinforcer
- The inability to assure a state of deprivation when using a primary reinforcer
- The possibility of student dependency upon the primary reinforcer

109. Positive reinforcer is generally effective if it is desired by the student and:
    a. Is worthwhile in size
    b. Given immediately after the desired behavior
    c. Given only upon the occurrence of the target behavior
    d. All of the above

Correct answer is "d."
Timing and quality of the reinforcer are key to encourage the individual to continue the targeted behavior.

110. Which of the following is a behavioral rule, which places emphasis on consequential events?
    a. Behavior that is reinforced tends to occur more frequently
    b. Behavior that is no longer reinforced will be extinguished
    c. Behavior that is punished occurs less frequently
    d. All of the above

Correct answer is "d."
The basic rules of behaviorism are stated in a, b, and c.

111. Dispensing school supplies is a component associated with which type of reinforcement system?
    a. Activity reinforcement
    b. Tangible reinforcement
    c. Token reinforcement
    d. b and c

Correct answer is "a."
The Premack Principle states that any activity in which a student voluntarily participates on a frequent basis can be used as a reinforcer for any activity in which the student seldom participates. Running errands, decorating bulletin boards, leading group activities, passing out books or papers, collecting materials, or operating equipment, all provide activity reinforcement.

112. Which type of reinforcement system is most easily generalized into other settings?
    a. Social reinforcement
    b. Activity reinforcement
    c. Tangible reinforcement
    d. Token reinforcement

Correct answer is "a."
There are many advantages to social reinforcement. It is easy to use, takes little of the teacher's time or effort, and is available in any setting. It is always positive, unlikely to satiate, and can be generalized to most situations.

113. Bill talks out in class an average of 15 times an hour. Other youngsters sometimes talk out, but Bill does so as a higher:
    a. Rate
    b. Intensity
    c. Volume
    d. Degree

Correct answer is "a."
Rate or frequency is the number of times the behavior is displayed in a given period.

114. Which category of behaviors would most likely be found on a behavior rating scale?
    a. Disruptive, acting out
    b. Shy, withdrawn
    c. Aggressive (physical or verbal)
    d. All of the above

Correct answer is "d."
These are all possible problem behaviors that can adversely impact the student or the class, thus they may be found on behavior rating scales.

115. The social skills of students in mental retardation programs are likely to be appropriate for children of their mental age, rather than chronological age. This means that the teacher will need to do all of the following except:
    a. Model desired behavior
    b. Provide clear instructions
    c. Expect age appropriate behaviors
    d. Adjust the physical environment when necessary

Correct answer is "c."
Age appropriate means mental age appropriate, not chronological age appropriate.

116. Target behaviors must be:
    a. Observable
    b. Measurable
    c. Definable
    d. All of the above

Correct answer is "d."
Behaviors must be observable, measurable and definable in order to be assessed and changed.

117. The Carrow Elicited Language Inventory is a test designed to give the examiner diagnostic information about a child's expressive grammatical competence. Which of the following language components is being assessed?
    a. Phonology
    b. Morphology
    c. Syntax
    d. b and c

Correct answer is "c."
- Morphology and syntax refer to refer to understanding grammatical structure of language in the receptive channel, and using the grammatical structure of language in the expressive channel.
- Assessment of morphology refers to linguistic structure of words.
- Assessment of syntax includes grammatical usage of word classes, word order, and transformational rules for the variance of word order.

118. In the Grammatic Closure subtest of the Illinois Test of Psycholinguistic Abilities, the child is presented with a picture representing statements such as the following: "Here is one die; here are two ____." This test is essentially a test of:
    a. Phonology
    b. Morphology
    c. Syntax
    d. Semantics

c. is correct.

119. Five-year-old Tom continues to substitute the "w" sound for the "r" sound when pronouncing words; therefore, he often distorts words e.g., "wabbit" for "rabbit" and "wat" for "rat." His articulation disorder is basically a problem in:
    a. Phonology
    b. Morphology
    c. Syntax
    d. Semantics

Correct answer is "a."
Phonology: the study of significant units of speech sounds
Morphology: The study of the smallest units of language that convey meaning.
Syntax: A system of rules for making grammatically correct sentences
Semantics: the study of the relationships between words and grammatical forms in a language, and their underlying meaning

120. Which of the following is untrue about the ending "er?"
    a. It is an example of a free morpheme
    b. It represents one of the smallest units of meaning within a word
    c. It is called an inflectional ending
    d. When added to a word, it connotes a comparative status

Correct answer is "a."
Morpheme: the smallest unit of meaningful language. "Er" on its own, has no meaning.

121. Which component of language involves **language content** rather than the form of language?
    a. Phonology
    b. Morphology
    c. Semantics
    d. Syntax

c. is correct.

122. Matthew's conversational speech is adequate, but when he tries to speak before a group of more than two listeners, his speech becomes mumbling and halting. which of the following activities would be least helpful in strengthening Matthew's self-expression skills?
    a. Having him participate in show-and-tell time
    b. Asking him comprehension questions about a story that was read to the class
    c. Having him recite a poem in front of the class, with two other children
    d. Asking him to tell a joke to the rest of the class

Correct answer is "a."
This exercise helps him to speak before a group larger than two listeners but smaller than the class.

123. Which of the following language skills involve encoding?
    a. Application
    b. Interpretation
    c. Comprehension
    d. Self-Expression

Correct answer is "d."
The child who has difficulty in verbalizing his thoughts and feelings (self-expression) has a problem **encoding** language. The child who has difficulty understanding what is said to him, relating it to situations with which he is familiar, or applying it to a new or different situation, may have a problem **decoding** language.

124. The child who has a problem decoding language, may exhibit difficulty:
    a. Understanding what is said to him
    b. Relating what was said, to familiar situations or objects
    c. Generalizing what was stated to new and appropriate situations
    d. All of the above

Correct answer is "d."
See previous rationale.

125. Which of the following is a language disorder?
    a. Articulation problems
    b. Stuttering
    c. Aphasia
    d. Excessive Nasality

Correct answer is "c."
Language disorders are often considered just one category of speech disorder. The problem is really different, with its own origins and causes. Persons with language disorders exhibit one or more of the following traits:
- Difficulty in comprehending questions, commands or statements (receptive language problems)
- Inability to adequately express their own thoughts (expressive language problems).
- Language that is below the level expected for the child's chronological age (delayed language)
- Interrupted language development (dysphasia)
- Qualitatively different language
- Total absence of language.

126. Which of the following is a speech disorder?
    a. Disfluency
    b. Aphasia
    c. Delayed language
    d. Comprehension difficulties

Correct answer is "a."
Persons with speech disorders exhibit one or more of the following traits:
- Unintelligible speech or speech that is difficult to understand, and articulation disorders (distortions, omissions, substitutions).
- Speech-flow disorders (sequence, duration, rate, rhythm, fluency)
- Unusual voice quality (nasality, breathiness, hoarseness, pitch, intensity, quality disorders)
- Obvious emotional discomfort when trying to communicate (stuttering, cluttering)
- Damage to nerves or brain centers which control muscles used in speech (dysarthria).

127. Children with disabilities can be taught social-interpersonal skills by:
    a. Developing sensitivity to other people
    b. Making behavioral choices in social situations
    c. Developing social maturity
    d. All of the above

Correct answer is "d."
Social-interpersonal skills: the ability to build and maintain interdependent relationships between persons. These skills are considered the domain of affective education and classroom management.

128. Children are engaged in a game of charades. Which type of social-interpersonal skill is the teacher most likely attempting to develop?
    a. Sensitivity to others
    b. Making behavioral choices in social situations
    c. Social maturity
    d. All of the above

Correct answer is "a."
Children with disabilities often perceive facial expressions and gestures differently to their nondisabled peers, due to their impairment. The game of charades, a guessing game, would help them develop sensitivity to others.

129. Social maturity may be evidenced by the student's:
    a. Recognition of rights and responsibilities (his own and others)
    b. Display of respect for legitimate authority figures
    c. Formulation of a valid moral judgment
    d. Demonstration of all of the above

Correct answer is "d."
Some additional evidence of social maturity:
- The ability to cooperate
- Following procedures formulated by an outside party
- Schieving appropriate levels of independence

130. Mrs. Right has noticed that Stevie typically plays alone and is seldom seen playing with other children. Today, Stevie is one of the last children in her room to be chosen by a team captain as a member of his group. One way in which Mrs. Wright can find out how Stevie is accepted by his peers would be to administer:
    a. Burk's behavior rating scale
    b. The walker problem behavior identification checklist
    c. A class play
    d. A self-test

Correct answer is "c."
A class play is the best choice as it gives the teacher a chance to assess the behavior through all of its five phases.

131. The work-study movement:
    a. Evolved primarily during the 1970s
    b. Focused upon the delivery of services within a specific type of interagency agreement
    c. Was declared a top priority by the U.S. Office of Education by Sidney Maryland, the Commissioner of Education
    d. Was implemented in both regular and special education settings

Correct answer is "b."
This program was conducted cooperatively between the schools and the local state rehabilitation services, when it emerged in the 1960s. The general goal was to create an integrated, academic social and vocational curriculum that included appropriate work experience. Programs were to be designed in such a way that students with mild disabilities would become prepared for eventual community adjustment. Cooperative agreements between the schools and the rehabilitation agencies were made in order to administer these programs.

132. The career education movement:
    a. Had its inception during the 1960s
    b. Maintained a cooperative agreement between the schools and the rehabilitation agencies
    c. Was funded by federal monies generated by rehabilitation agencies
    d. Was targeted for the general populace of students but included special education students as well

Correct answer is "d."
This movement had its inception in 1970, and focused upon the integration and of readiness for a life career throughout a student's education, from kindergarten to 12th grade. It targeted the general populace of students, and did not mention students with disabilities. However, when the Career Education Implementation Incentive Act, P.L. 95-207, was passed in 1977, it specifically mentioned people with disabilities as an appropriate target population for services.

133. Effective transition was included in:
    a. President Bush's 1990 State of the Union Message
    b. Public Law 101-476
    c. Public Law 95-207
    d. a and b

Correct answer is "d."
With the enactment of P. L. 101-476, (IDEA) transition services became a right.

134. Vocational training programs are based on all of the following ideas except:
    a. Students obtain career training from elementary through high school
    b. Students acquire specific training in job skills prior to exiting school
    c. Students need specific training and supervision in applying skills learned in school to requirements in job situations
    d. Students obtain needed instruction and field-based experiences that help them to be able to work in specific occupations

Correct answer is "a."
Vocational education programs or transition programs prepare students for entry into the labor force. They are usually incorporated into the work-study at the high school or post-secondary levels. They are usually focused on job skills, job opportunities, skill requirements for specific jobs, personal qualifications in relation to job requirements, work habits, money management, and academic skills needed for specific jobs.

135. In career education specific training and preparation required for the world of work occurs during the phase of:
    a. Career Awareness
    b. Career Exploration
    c. Career Preparation
    d. Daily Living and Personal-Social Interaction

Correct answer is "c."
Curricular aspects of career education include:
- career awareness: diversity of available jobs
- career exploration: skills needed for occupational groups
- career preparation: specific training and preparation required for the world of work

136. What is most descriptive of vocational training in special education?
    a. Trains students in intellectual disabilities solely
    b. Segregates students with and without disabilities in vocational training programs
    c. Only includes students capable of moderate supervision
    d. Instruction focuses upon self-help skills, social-interpersonal skills, motor skills, rudimentary academic skills, simple occupational skills, and lifetime leisure and occupational skills

Correct answer is "d."
Persons with disabilities are mainstreamed with nondisabled students where possible. Special sites provide training for those persons with more severe disabilities who are unable to be successfully taught in an integrated setting. Specially trained vocational counselors monitor and supervise student work sites.

137. An individual with disabilities in need of employability training, as well a job, would go to which community service agency for assistance?
    a. State Health Department
    b. Rehabilitation Services
    c. Social Services Agency
    d. Social Security Administration

Correct answer is "b."

TEACHER CERTIFICATION STUDY GUIDE

SUBAREA I.	UNDERSTANDING STUDENTS WITH MILD/MODERATE DISABILITIES

COMPETENCY 1.0   UNDERSTAND PROCESSES OF HUMAN DEVELOPMENT AND FACTORS, INCLUDING DISABILITY, THAT AFFECT DEVELOPMENT AND LEARNING.

SKILL 1.1   Understand theories and processes related to ways in which development and learning occur

LEARNING THEORIES

There are many factors that affect student learning including: the way in which students learn, how learning is presented, and the background knowledge or experiences that the student's possess. There are several educational learning theories that can be applied to classroom practices. One classic learning theory is Piaget's stages of development which consist of four learning stages: sensory motor stage (from birth to age 2); pre-operation stages (ages 2 to 7 or early elementary); concrete operational (ages7 to 11 or upper elementary); and formal operational (ages 7-15 or late elementary/high school). Piaget believed children passed through this series of stages developing from the most basic forms of concrete thinking to sophisticated levels of abstract thinking.

Two of the most prominent learning theories in education today include: Brain-Based Learning and the Multiple Intelligence Theory. Supported by recent brain research, Brain-Based Learning suggests increased medical knowledge about the way the brain retains information. It enables educators to design the most effective learning environments. As a result, researchers have developed twelve principles relating knowledge about the brain and teaching practices. These twelve principles are:

- The brain is a complex adaptive system
- The brain is social
- The search for meaning is innate
- We use patterns to learn more effectively
- Emotions are crucial to developing patterns
- Each brain perceives and creates parts and whole simultaneously
- Learning involves focused and peripheral attention
- Learning involves conscious and unconscious processes
- We have at least two ways of organizing memory
- Learning is developmental
- Complex learning is enhanced by challenged (and inhibited by threat)
- Every brain is unique

(Caine & Caine, 1994, Mind/Brain Learning Principles)

Educators can use these principles to help design methods and environments in their classrooms to maximize student learning.

The Multiple Intelligence Theory, developed by Howard Gardner, suggests students demonstrate different learning styles in (at least) seven different ways. These include visually/spatially, musically, verbally, logically/mathematically, interpersonally, intrapersonally, and bodily/kinesthetically. Keeping in mind each area overlaps and students may demonstrate strengths in multiple areas, it is important to design instructional procedures and lessons incorporating as many of the above referenced intelligences. In this way, the teacher can reach more students through their individual strengths with each lesson.

Yet another learning theory is that of constructivism. Constructivist learning allows students to build learning through exposure and various opportunities. For constructivist teachers, the belief is that students create their own reality of knowledge and how to process and observe the world around them. Students are constantly constructing new ideas, which serve as frameworks for learning and teaching. Researchers have shown that the constructivist model is comprised of four components:

1. Learner creates knowledge
2. Learner constructs and makes meaningful new knowledge to existing knowledge
3. Learner shapes and constructs knowledge by life experiences and social interactions
4. In constructivist learning communities, the student, teacher and classmates establish knowledge cooperatively on a daily basis.

Kelly (1969) states, " (The idea that) human beings construct knowledge systems based on their observations, parallels Piaget's theory that individuals construct knowledge systems as they work with others who share a common background of thought and processes." Constructivist learning, for students, is dynamic and ongoing. For constructivist teachers, the classroom becomes a place where students are encouraged to interact with the instructional process by asking questions and posing new ideas to old theories. The use of cooperative learning encourages students to work in supportive learning environments using their own ideas to stimulate questions and propose outcomes. This is a major aspect of a constructivist classroom.

The metacognition learning theory deals with "the study of how to help the learner gain understanding about how knowledge is constructed and about the conscious tools for constructing that knowledge" (Joyce and Weil, 1996). The cognitive approach to learning involves the teacher's understanding that teaching the student to process his/her own learning and mastery of skills provides the greatest learning and retention opportunities within the classroom. Students are taught to develop concepts and teach themselves skills in problem solving and critical thinking. The student becomes an active participant in the learning process and the teacher facilitates conceptual and cognitive learning processes.

Finally, social and behavioral theories examine the social interactions that instruct or impact learning opportunities of students in the classroom. The psychological approaches behind both theories are subject to individual variables that are learned and applied either proactively or negatively. The stimulus of the classroom can be conducive for learning or evoke behavior that is counterproductive for both students and teachers. Students are social beings that normally gravitate to action in the classroom, so teachers must be cognizant in planning classroom environments that provide both focus and engagement in maximizing learning opportunities.

UNDERSTANDING THE RELATIONSHIP BETWEEN PROCESSING SKILLS AND COGNITIVE SKILLS OF LEARNERS WITH DISABILITIES

Though questions have been raised concerning the relationship between the perceptual skills of students and academic achievement, it is a fact that learners: must receive information through receptive channels (e.g. visual, auditory, haptic), use integrative skills to organize, store, react to, or retrieve acquired information, and make responses through various expressive channels (i.e. motor, written, spoken). The use of perceptual neuron-pathways through which students acquire, integrate, and express information is referred to as processing skills, and must be well understood by the teacher.

Students with learning problems are frequently found to experience processing deficiencies in academic pursuits. These problems are often a result of some perceptual or neurological deficit that occurs in varying degrees (or combinations). Teachers must understand how students process information, store this knowledge, and express it so they can evaluate or determine in some way whether or not learning has occurred.

The majority of assessment tools used to diagnose processing deficits have been proven inadequate. However, the fact remains these skills are a vital part of the learning process for all students. Educators must know how to identify strengths and weaknesses in their students' processing skills. They must also be familiar with specific activities or teaching strategies that might be used to further develop these skills. It is important to know significant timelines for normal development of language and motor skills. Being able to transfer and generalize these skills is essential as well. Thus, the need for a separate section devoted to the development of these skills seems to be necessary.

Students may experience learning problems when they attempt to process knowledge and information. These problems in learning can occur during any step of the processing sequence: receiving information through the senses (e.g. visual, auditory, and haptic), using integrative skills to organize, store, react to, or retrieve acquired information, and responding through movement or speech.

Processing skills relate directly to cognitive skills. For instance, a problem may occur in one or more of the perceptual neuron-pathways activated during learning. In school, these perceptual neuro-pathways are primarily visual or auditory. Educator's use terms such as visual or auditory: discrimination, memory, closure, sequencing, and blending to describe the interplay between perception and mental processing. Difficulties can occur at any point along the continuum; reception (input), integration (association), or expression (output).

The receptive process utilizes sub skills that are essential to learning. These include attending to task, and being able to discriminate what is heard or seen (Ramsey, 1988). Attending relates to one's knowing what to pay attention to and what to ignore in the environment around them (Tarver, 1986). Distractibility is sometimes confused with attending, as students may appear to be not attending when he or she is actually attending to the distraction. Learners must enhance appropriate attending skills in order to be proficient in the classroom (Tarver, 1986).

Discrimination refers to the ability to differentiate one thing from another (e.g. an object, an item, a sound). When asked to identify the letters "m" and "n" the child must visually perceive that there are two humps in "m" and only one is "n." Children learn to discriminate by color, shape, pattern, size, position, and brightness. Eventually, students must be able to visually discriminate letters and words to learn to read (Ramsey, 1986).

Subskills directly related to the auditory receptive process include auditory attending, auditory awareness, and auditory discrimination. Sometimes it is necessary for the teacher to eliminate auditory distractions within the classroom. In order to read, a child must be able to perceive individual phoneme sounds and correspond these sounds with the correct letter symbols. These skills are necessary for decoding written and spoken language.

Ideas about activities that are useful in helping to develop perceptual skills are given in this section. Though they are primarily associated with students who have learning disabilities, these activities can be used with any student whose information processing skills need further improvement.

Figure 3-1 Information Processing Skills

INPUT	ASSOCIATION	OUTPUT
	Discrimination	
	Integrations	
	Organization	
	Reasoning Skills	
Visual	Inductive Thinking	Movement
Auditory`	Deductive Thinking	Action
Tactile	Analysis	Handwriting
Kinesthetic	Synthesis	Speech
Haptic	Evaluation	
Olfactory	Appreciation	
Gustatory	Storage	
	Long and Short term Memory	
	Transmodal:	
	One modality to another	

IDENTIFY ACTIVITIES FOR EVALUATING AUDITORY PERCEPTION SKILLS

Many teachers operate under the mistaken belief that if a student's hearing is within normal limits, that the student can be expected to process and correctly respond to those sounds heard. The deficiency here it not a problem of auditory acuity (hearing) but of auditory perception, sometimes referred to as a Central Auditory Processing Disorder (CAPD). There is impairment in the ability to recognize or interpret what is heard.

Problems in auditory perception may be manifested in the following auditory processing skills.

1. **Auditory discrimination**. A child with problems in auditory discrimination has difficulty differentiating between the sounds of certain words or letters, such as "big" and "pig," "Men" and "man," "Man" and "mad."
2. **Auditory memory.** A child with an auditory memory problem lacks the ability to store sounds and their meanings efficiently and later recall them. Such a child will have difficulty remembering several steps in a math procedure, or carrying out several directions given him at the same time by the teacher. Auditory memory can also affect a student's ability to decode text.
3. **Auditory sequencing.** An inability to sequence information received through auditory channels renders a child unable to count, say his alphabet or sing the lyrics of a song, even immediately after being exposed to them.
4. **Auditory blending.** A child with a problem in auditory blending has difficulty combining single phonic elements or phonemes into complete words. This child usually experiences difficulty learning to read phonemes into a complete word. This child usually experiences difficulty learning to read phonetically, and may on occasion not be able to perceive accurately what is being said to him.

In trying to determine whether a student can recognize and interpret sounds other than linguistic phonemes, the teacher can simply introduce sounds with which the child should be familiar, such as a telephone ring, a car honk, or a dog's bark, and see if the child can name the source of the sound. Care should be taken to introduce sounds familiar to the student.

UNDERSTAND THOSE VARABLES WHICH INFLUENCE THE STORAGE, REHEARSAL, AND RETRIEVAL OF INFORMATION IN EDUCATIONAL SITUATIONS

Ongoing sensations and perceptions are received into the brain for processing. The ability to store and retrieve experienced sensations and perceptions is referred to as memory. Problems in learning can occur at the stages of reception, storage, or retrieval. There are three types of memory storage systems: (1) the sensory storage or register, where incoming information is first contained: (2) the short-term store, where the information is identified and retained on a temporary basis; and (3) the long-term store, where selected information is assimilated into what is already stored. Information must be focused upon before it can be perceived or entered into the brain and information must be understood in order to be stored. Data must be successfully coded if it is to pass from short-term to long-term storage, or it will slowly fade and be forgotten.

Rehearsal (review and/or practice of what has been learned) is needed to maintain information in short-term storage. Reviewing the learned material and organizing it into meaningful units facilitate speed and efficiency in committing it to memory.

Cues (prompts) and mnemonic strategies (anchoring new knowledge to old knowledge) make newly learned material much more likely to be remembered. For example, this can be done by remembering the name of someone named Carl by picturing his car, or conjuring a term using a real or nonsense word like "peach" to remember the needed groceries such as pears, eggs, apples, corn, and ham. Other strategies making information more memorable include: organizing material into categories, reviewing material at distributed intervals, and increasing recall through associations by highlighting relationships in the material, drawing conclusions, making judgments, and connecting ideas to previously learned information.

The only practical way to determine if material has been stored in a child's memory is for him to retrieve it from storage. When some stimulus reminds the student of what has been previously learned (a cue), is presented to the learner, the ability to recall related material from storage is referred to as retrieval. Teaching test taking tips such as distinguishing between recognition memory (multiple choices) and recall ability (fill in answers, essays) often enables retrieval of education material. Knowledge that cannot be retrieved from memory does a student little good.

UNDERSTAND THE NEED FOR CHANGING THE RATE, LEVEL, AND SEQUENCE AT WHICH NEW CONCEPTS ARE ACQUIRED

All children function with a conceptual level (CL) located at some point on a continuum of ability to handle easy-to-complex information processing under low-to-high task structure. Students who function at a low CL are categorical thinkers, who are dependent upon rules and are less capable of discovering their own concepts and considering alternatives. In other words, they have difficulty directing their own learning. Learners with a higher CL, on the other hand, can discover concepts by themselves. They can make their own rules, consider different views, and make use of alternatives during problem solving.

Students with intellectual disabilities appear to parallel the development of normal children, except at a slower, more delayed rate. This affects their rate of acquisition, ability to amend, memory, and transfer of newly acquired skills. The final level of skill mastery may lack refinement.

Similarly, students with learning disabilities who are of an impulsive nature often approach learning tasks in a global, nondetail oriented way. They tend to ignore details, utilize poor planning strategies, omit portions of tasks, lack in organizational skills, and fail to double-check or self-correct their work.

Teachers sensitive to a child with a lower CL could modify their instruction by presenting material in an organized, straightforward manner, rather than through a discovery method. Visible concrete teaching aids should be incorporated into instructional demonstrations. It would also help to present the rules for problem solving before presenting examples. Asking comprehension questions before, rather than after, a reading selection is usually more beneficial to learners with lower CLs. Structuring the learning environment, as well as the sequence of concepts presented, instead of expecting the students to do it for themselves, is also necessary.

Other cognitive training methods that seem to influence concept formation are: teaching children to stop and think before responding, to verbalize and rehearse what they have been taught, to monitor their own inappropriate behavior, to visually imagine what they must remember, to preplan task approaches, and to organize their time. They can be taught to ask themselves questions about the material (self-questioning techniques) and to compare new information with what they already know (assimilation and accommodation). The use of learned cognitive strategies can facilitate conceptual learning.

SKILL 1.2 Demonstrate knowledge of the etiologies and effects of various disabilities on development and learning

Causes for disabilities can primarily be subdivided into two major categories: organic (biological) and environmental. Figure 2-1 presents common causes of mild disabilities.

Under the organic category-pre-peri, and postnatal factors, genetic factors, biochemical factors, and maturational lag are listed. These contributors originate within the body (i.e. endogenous). Included under environmental reasons for mild learning and behavior disabilities are factors relating to poverty, nutrition, toxins, language differences, sensory deprivation, emotional problems, and inadequate education. Although some environmental factors (e.g. toxins) cause organic dysfunction, the point of origin is outside the body (e.g. exogenous).

Experts in the field have reported about 6 to 12 percent of the special education population are identified as having severe to profound disabilities, an estimated 12 to 25 percent have moderate disabilities, while approximately 75 to 87 percent have mild disabilities (Henly, Ramsey, and Algozzine, 1993). Because of the larger number in this latter group, of those with mild disabilities, it is difficult to trace the origins. Mild learning and behavior difficulties usually remain undetected until children enter school.

Figure 2-1 Common Causes of Mild Disabilities

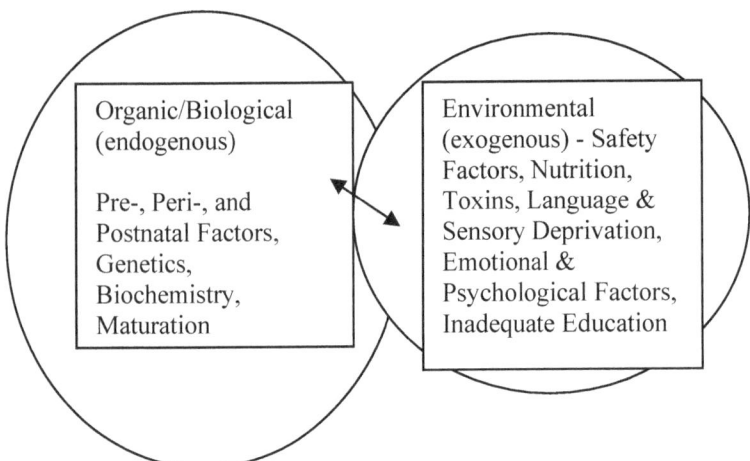

Adapted from: M. Henley, R.S. Ramsey and R. Algozzine, Characteristics of and Strategies for Teaching Students with Mild Disabilities, 1993, Allyn and Bacon p. 43.

THE CAUSATION AND PREVENTION OF A DISABILITY

No one knows exactly what causes learning disabilities. There is a wide range of possibilities that make it almost impossible to pin point the exact cause. Listed below are some factors that can attribute to the development of a disability.

Problems in Fetal Brain Development - During pregnancy things can go wrong in the development of the brain, which alters how the neurons form or interconnect. Throughout pregnancy, brain development is vulnerable to disruptions. If the disruption occurs early, the fetus may die, or the infant may be born with widespread disabilities and possibly mental retardation. If the disruption occurs later, when the cells are becoming specialized and moving into place, it may leave errors in the cell makeup, location, or connections. Some scientists believe that these errors may later show up as learning disorders.

Genetic Factors - Learning disabilities can run in families, which show there may be a genetic link. For example, children who do not have certain reading skills, such as hearing the separate sounds of words, are likely to have a parent with a similar problem. A parent's learning disability can take a slightly different form in the child. Due to this, it is unlikely that specific learning disorders are directly inherited.

Environment - Additional reasons for why learning disabilities appear to run in families stem from the family environment. Parents with expressive language disorders may talk less to their children or their language may be muffled. In this case the lack of a proper role model for acquiring good language skills causes the disability.

Tobacco, Alcohol, and Other Drug Use -- Many drugs taken by the mother pass directly to the fetus during pregnancy. Research shows that a mother's usage of cigarettes, alcohol, or other drugs during pregnancy may have damaging effects on the unborn child. Mothers who smoke during pregnancy are more likely to have smaller birth weight babies. Newborns, who weigh less than 5 pounds, are more at risk for learning disorders.

Heavy alcohol use during pregnancy has been linked to fetal alcohol syndrome, a condition resulting in low birth weigh, intellectual impairment, hyperactivity, and certain physical defects.

Problems During Pregnancy or Delivery -- Complications during pregnancy can also cause learning disabilities. The mother's immune system can react to the fetus and attack it as if it were an infection. This type of problem appears to cause newly formed brain cells to settle in the wrong part of the brain. In addition, during delivery, the umbilical cord can become twisted and temporarily cut off oxygen to the fetus, resulting in impaired brain functions.

Toxins in the Environment -- New brain cells and neural networks are produced for a year after the child is born. These cells are vulnerable to certain disruptions. There are certain environmental toxins that may lead to learning disabilities. Cadmium and lead are becoming a leading focus of neurological research. Cadmium is used in making some steel products. It can get into the soil and then into the foods we eat. Lead was once common in paint and gasoline, and is still present in some water pipes.

Children with cancer who have been treated with chemotherapy or radiation at an early age can also develop learning disabilities. This is very prevalent in children with brain tumors who received radiation to the skull.

In order to prevent disabilities from occurring, information on the causes of disabilities should be widely available so parents can take the necessary steps to safeguard their children from conception up through the early years of life. While some of the causes of disability are unavoidable or incidental, there are many causes that can be prevented.

HEARING LOSS
There are two major types of hearing loss; conductive and sensorineural. A combination of the two is possible and called mixed hearing loss. Conductive hearing loss results from blockages and obstructions as sound moves from the peripheral to the inner ear, and is the most common type of hearing loss. Impacted wax, infections, and fluid in the middle ear - otitis media - are common causes of this type. Sensorineural hearing loss results from damage to the auditory nerve or to the inner ear organ.

AUTISM

In the federal regulations, autism is defined as a developmental disability that affects verbal and nonverbal communication. It is thought to be caused by a neurological or biochemical dysfunction.

TRAUMATIC BRAIN INJURY

Traumatic brain injury is occurring in more children and youth than ever before. Ironically, many of these injuries are preventable. Automobile accidents, falls, high fever, and child abuse are among the most frequent causes.

EFFECTS OF VARIOUS DISABILITIES

CHARACTERISTICS OF EMOTIONALLY DISTURBED CHILDREN

Studies of children with behavioral and emotional disorders, share some general characteristics:

Lower academic performance: While it is true that some emotionally disturbed children have above average IQ scores, the majority are behind their peers in measures of intelligence and school achievement. Most score in the "slow learner" or "mildly mentally retarded" range on IQ tests, averaging about 90. Many have learning problems that exacerbate their acting out or "giving-up" behavior. As the child enters secondary school, the gap between her and nondisabled peers widens until the child may be as many as 2 to 4 years behind in reading and/or math skills. Children with severe degrees of impairment may provide a challenge to obtain an accurate evaluation.

Social Skills deficits: Students with these deficits may be uncooperative, selfish in dealing with others, unaware of what to do in social situations, or ignorant of the consequences of their actions. This may be a combination of lack of prior training, lack of opportunities to interact, and dysfunctional value systems and beliefs learned from their family.

Classroom behaviors: Often, emotionally disturbed children display classroom behavior that is highly disruptive to the classroom setting. Emotionally disturbed children are often out of their seat or running around the room, hitting, fighting, or disturbing their classmates, stealing or destroying property, defiant and noncompliant, and/or verbally disruptive. They do not follow directions and often do not complete assignments.

Aggressive behaviors: Aggressive children often fight or instigate their peers to strike back at them. Aggressiveness may also take the form of vandalism or destruction of property. Aggressive children also engage in verbal abuse.

Delinquency: As emotionally disturbed, acting-out children enter adolescence, they may become involved in socialized aggression (i.e. gang membership) and delinquency. Delinquency is a legal term, rather than a medical, and describes truancy, and actions that would be criminal if adults committed them. Not every delinquent is classified as emotionally disturbed, but children with behavioral and emotional disorders are especially at risk for becoming delinquent because of their problems at school (the primary place for socializing with peers), deficits in social skills that may make them unpopular at school, and/or dysfunctional homes.

Withdrawn behaviors: Children who manifest withdrawn behaviors may consistently act in an immature fashion or prefer to play with younger children. They may daydream or complain of being sick in order to "escape". They may also cry often, cling to the teacher, ignore those who attempt to interact, or suffer from fears or depression.

Schizophrenia and psychotic behaviors: Children may have delusions, hallucinations, incoherent thoughts, and disconnected thinking. Schizophrenia typically manifests itself between the ages of 15 and 45, and the younger the onset, the more severe the disorder. These behaviors usually require intensive treatment beyond the scope of the regular classroom setting.

Gender: Many more boys than girls are identified as having emotional and behavioral problems, especially hyperactivity and attention deficit disorder, autism, childhood psychosis and problems with under control (aggression, socialized aggression). Girls, on the other hand, have more problems with over control (i.e. withdrawal and phobias). Boys are much more prevalent than girls in problems with mental retardation and language and learning disabilities.

Age Characteristics: When they enter adolescence, girls tend to experience affective or emotional disorders such as anorexia, depression, bulimia, and anxiety at twice the rate of boys, which mirrors the adult prevalence pattern.

Family Characteristics: Having a child with an emotional or behavioral disorder does not automatically mean that the family is dysfunctional. However, there are family factors that create or contribute to the development of behavior disorders and emotional disturbance.
- Abuse and neglect
- Lack of appropriate supervision
- Lax, punitive, and/or lack of discipline
- High rates of negative types of interaction among family members
- Lack of parental concern and interest
- Negative adult role models
- Lack of proper health care and/or nutrition
- Disruption in the family

CHILDREN WITH MILD LEARNING, INTELLECTUAL, AND BEHAVIORAL DISABILITIES

Some characteristics of students with mild learning and behavioral disabilities are as follows:
- Lack of interest in schoolwork
- Prefer concrete rather than abstract lessons
- Possess weak listening skills
- Low achievement; limited verbal and/or writing skills
- Respond better to active rather than passive learning tasks
- Have areas of talent or ability often overlooked by teachers
- Prefer to receive special help in regular classroom
- Higher dropout rate than regular education students
- Achieve in accordance with teacher expectations
- Require modification in classroom instruction and are easily distracted.

CHARACTERISTIC OF STUDENTS WHO HAVE A LEARNING DISABILITY

- Hyperactivity: a rate of motor activity higher than normal
- Perceptual difficulties: visual, auditory, and perceptual problems
- Perceptual-motor impairments: poor integration of visual and motor systems, often affecting fine motor coordination.
- Disorders of memory and thinking: memory deficits, trouble with problem-solving, concept formation and association, poor awareness of own metacognitive skills (learning strategies)
- Impulsiveness: acts before considering consequences, poor impulse control, often followed by remorselessness.
- Academic problems in reading, math, writing or spelling; significant discrepancies in ability levels.

CHARACTERISTICS OF INDIVIDUALS WITH MENTAL RETARDATION OR INTELLECTUAL DISABILITIES:

- IQ of 70 or below
- Limited cognitive ability; delayed academic achievement, particularly in language-related subjects
- Deficits in memory which often relate to poor initial perception, or inability to apply stored information to relevant situations
- Impaired formulation of learning strategies
- Difficulty in attending to relevant aspects of stimuli: slowness in reaction time or in employing alternate strategies.

IDENTIFY CHARACTERISTICS OF INDIVIDUALS WITH AUTISM

This exceptionality appears very early in childhood. Six common features of autism are:

- **Apparent sensory deficit** – The child may appear not to see, hear, or react to a stimulus, then react in an extreme fashion to a seemingly insignificant stimulus.
- **Severe affect isolation** — The child does not respond to the usual signs of affection such as smiles and hugs.
- **Self-stimulation** – Stereotyped behavior takes the form of repeated or ritualistic actions that make no sense to others, such as hand flapping, rocking, staring at objects, or humming the same sounds for hours at a time.
- **Tantrums and self-injurious behavior (SIB)** – Autistic children may bite themselves, pull their hair, bang their heads, or hit themselves. They can throw severe tantrums, and direct aggression and destructive behavior toward others.
- **Echolalia** — also known as "parrot talk." The autistic child may repeat what is played on television, for example, or respond to others by repeating what was said to him. Alternatively, he may simply not speak at all.
- **Severe deficits in behavior and self-care skills**. Autistic children may behave like children much younger than themselves.

SKILL 1.3 Recognize environmental and other factors that may impede learning in students with mild/moderate disabilities

There are many factors which can impede the learning of students with mild to moderate disabilities. Many of these factors will be discussed throughout this study guide.

CULTURAL ISSUES
Hispanic children represent the fastest-growing minority and approximately three fourths of the children designated as Limited English Proficiency (LEP). Additionally, culturally diverse students may speak a dialect of a language such as Spanish, which has its own system of pronunciation and rules. It should be stressed that speaking a dialect does not in itself mean that the child has a language problem. Certain English sounds and grammar structures may not have equivalents in some languages, and failure to produce these elements may be a function of inexperience with English, rather than a language delay.

When minority or culturally diverse children are being screened for language problems, learning disabilities, or other exceptional student programs, the tests and assessment procedures must be non-discriminatory. Furthermore, testing should be done in the child's native language; however, if school instruction has not been in the native language, there may appear to be a problem because assessments typically measure school language. Even with native English-speaking children, there are differences between the language that functions at home and community, and the language requirements of school.

Please refer to skill 1.2 for more information.

SKILL 1.4 **Recognize environmental and other factors that may facilitate learning (e.g., parental support and protection, family values and beliefs, early intervention, personal resilience) in students with mild/moderate disabilities**

The student's capacity and potential for academic success within the overall educational experience are products of her or his total environment: classroom and school system; home and family; neighborhood and community in general. All of these segments are interrelated and can be supportive, one of the other, or divisive, one against the other. As a matter of fact, the teacher will become familiar with all aspects of the system, the school and the classroom pertinent to the students' educational experience. This would include not only process and protocols but also the availability of resources provided to meet the academic, health and welfare needs of students. It is incumbent upon the teacher to look beyond the boundaries of the school system to identify additional resources, as well as issues and situations which will effect (directly or indirectly) a student's ability to succeed in the classroom.

Examples of Resources

- Libraries, museums, zoos, planetariums, etc.
- Clubs, societies and civic organizations, community outreach programs of private businesses and corporations and of government agencies. These can provide a variety of materials and media as well as possible speakers and presenters
- Departments of social services operating within the local community. These can provide background and program information relevant to social issues which may be impacting individual students. And this can be a resource for classroom instruction regarding life skills, at-risk behaviors, etc.

Initial contacts for resources outside of the school system will usually come from within the system itself: from administration; teacher organizations; department heads; and other colleagues.

Examples of Issues/Situations

- Students from multicultural backgrounds:

    Curriculum objectives and instructional strategies may be inappropriate and unsuccessful when presented in a single format which relies on the student's understanding and acceptance of the values and common attributes of a specific culture which is not his or her own.

- Parental/family influences: Attitude, resources and encouragement available in the home environment may be attributes for success or failure.

Families with higher incomes are able to provide increased opportunities for students. Students from lower income families will need to depend on the resources available from the school system and the community. This should be orchestrated by the classroom teacher in cooperation with school administrators and educational advocates in the community.

Family members with higher levels of education often serve as models for students, and have high expectations for academic success. And families with specific aspirations for children (often, regardless of their own educational background) encourage students to achieve academic success, and are most often active participants in the process.

A family in crisis (caused by economic difficulties, divorce, substance abuse, physical abuse, etc.) creates a negative environment which may profoundly impact all aspects of a student's life, and particularly his or her ability to function academically. The situation may require professional intervention. It is often the classroom teacher who will recognize a family in a crisis situation and instigate an intervention by reporting this to school or civil authorities.

Regardless of the positive or negative impacts on the students' education from outside sources, it is the teacher's responsibility to ensure that all students in the classroom have an equal opportunity for academic success. This begins with the teacher's statement of high expectations for every student. It develops through planning, delivery and evaluation of instruction, which provides for inclusion and ensures that all students have equal access to the resources necessary for successful acquisition of the academic skills being taught and measured in the classroom.

CULTURAL

Oftentimes, students absorb the culture and social environment around them without deciphering contextual meaning of the experiences. When provided with a diversity of cultural contexts, students are able to adapt and incorporate multiple meanings from cultural cues vastly different from their own socioeconomic backgrounds. Socio-cultural factors provide a definitive impact on a students' psychological, emotional, affective, and physiological development, along with a students' academic learning and future opportunities.

The educational experience for most students is a complicated and complex experience with a diversity of interlocking meanings and inferences. If one aspect of the complexity is altered, it affects other aspects, which may impact how a student or teacher views an instructional or learning experience. With the current demographic profile of today's school communities, the complexity of understanding, interpreting, and synthesizing the nuances from the diversity of cultural lineages can provide many communication and learning blockages that could impede the acquisition of learning for students.

Teachers must create personalized learning communities where every student is a valued member and contributor of the classroom experiences. In classrooms where socio-cultural attributes of the student population are incorporated into the fabric of the learning process, dynamic interrelationships are created that enhance the learning experience and the personalization of learning. When students are provided with numerous academic and social opportunities to share cultural incorporations into the learning, everyone in the classroom benefits from bonding through shared experiences and having an expanded viewpoint of a world experience and culture that vastly differs from their own.

Research continues to show personalized learning environments increase the learning affect for students; decrease drop-out rates among marginalized students; and decrease unproductive student behavior which can result from constant cultural misunderstandings or miscues between students. Promoting diversity of learning and cultural competency in the classroom for students and teachers creates a world of multicultural opportunities and learning. When students are able to step outside their comfort zones and share the world of a homeless student or empathize with an English Language Learner (ELL) student who has just immigrated to the United States, is learning English for the first time, and is still trying to keep up with the academic learning in an unfamiliar language, students grow exponentially in social understanding and cultural connectedness.

Personalized learning communities provide supportive learning environments that address the academic and emotional needs of students. As socio-cultural knowledge is conveyed continuously in the interrelated experiences shared cooperatively and collaboratively in student groupings and individualized learning, the current and future benefits will continue to present the case and importance of understanding the "whole" child, inclusive of the social and the cultural context.

SKILL 1.5 Understand how primary language and cultural and familial background can affect the academic, social, and career development of students with mild/moderate disabilities

The average classroom today is composed of several different cultures. Your understanding of your students' actions and the manner in which you communicate with them now requires your foresight into what cultural influences your students bring with them to the classroom. This knowledge of these areas will help you to serve as both an advocate and interpreter for the student who may appear "odd" when he/she is only doing what is expected in her culture. This is especially true for those who are new to the country or are in the elementary level.

It is possible the next student in your classroom may be Vietnamese, and you may begin to think they are polite, but slow learners, because they are quiet, and do not take part in classroom discussions. Your impression would be different if you had learned that children in Vietnam believe their teachers are never wrong, they are taught through rote memorization and that classroom discussion/open participation, is a foreign concept to them.

Unfortunately, some teachers may think students of a certain culture learn slower in one area, while misunderstanding the fact that they may be learning differently. Therefore, it may be important to complement your instruction with peer tutoring. Sharing of their different cultural strengths may build a unique opportunity for both cultures to grow side by side.

Recognition of cultural differences allows the teacher to build on different cultural strengths at opportune times. This may also give the culturally aware teacher the ability to soar above others in their teaching environment.

> RECOGNIZING HOW CULTURAL PERSPECTIVES INFLUENCE THE
> RELATIONSHIP AMONG FAMILIES, SCHOOLS, AND COMMUNITIES, AS
> RELATED TO EFFECTIVE INSTRUCTION
> FOR STUDENTS WITH DISABILITIES

The teacher should be familiar with the effects of cultural stereotypes and racism on the development of students with disabilities. The teacher should know variations in beliefs, traditions, and values exist across and within cultures.

The teacher should also be familiar with the characteristics and biases of their own culture and how these biases can impact their teaching, behavior, and communication.

The teacher should include multicultural perspectives in his lessons and convey to students how knowledge is developed from the vantage point of a particular culture.

Educators need to ensure they demonstrate positive regard for the culture, religion, gender, and varying abilities of students and their families. This should include showing sensitivity to students with different cultural and ethnic backgrounds when designing the curriculum.

Teachers who use themes with a multicultural perspective should ensure that they are not teaching material that could be considered culturally insensitive or offensive.

For professional development training programs to be successful, it is crucial that teachers develop an in-depth understanding of the influence of culture and language on students' academic performance to differentiate between genuine learning problems and cultural differences.

Culturally sensitive teaching creates a helpful, receptive, and enriched educational setting that permits each student to feel comfortable as they look at their attitudes and share their thoughts.

As members of a culturally pluralistic society, students and educators must develop healthy and open-minded attitudes and interpersonal skills to communicate and collaborate across cultures and to function successfully in many situations.

Multiculturalism is for all students and teachers because in unbiased classrooms students hear the voices of a variety of different cultural groups. This enables students to be able to understand the world from multiple ethnic and cultural perspectives, instead of just agreeing with the point of view of the mainstream culture.

Please refer to skills 1.3 and 1.4 for more information.

COMPETENCY 2.0 UNDERSTAND TYPES AND CHARACTERISTICS OF SPECIFIC LEARNING DISABILITIES AND THEIR SIGNIFICANCE FOR HUMAN DEVELOPMENT AND LEARNING.

SKILL 2.1 Understand types and characteristics of specific learning disabilities

Specific Learning Disability is defined as a disorder in one or more of the basic psychological processes involved in understanding or in using language, spoken or written, which may manifest itself in an imperfect ability to listen, think, speak, read, write, spell, or do mathematical calculations. The term includes such conditions as: perceptual handicaps, brain injury, minimal brain dysfunction, dyslexia, and developmental aphasia. The term does not include children who have learning problems, which are primarily the result of visual, hearing, or motor handicaps, mental retardation, emotional disturbance, or environmental, cultural, or economic disadvantage.

IDENTIFY CHARACTERISTICS OF STUDENTS WITH LEARNING DISABLITIES

The individual with a specific learning disability exhibits a discrepancy between achievement and potential. Deficiencies can occur within a spectrum of skill areas. The youngster typically shows a low level of performance in one of several skill areas, rarely is a uniform pattern of academic development demonstrated. Within the recent reauthorization of the Individual With Disabilities Education Act, additional criteria were approved in regards to the identification of students with learning disabilities. The new regulations discuss a lack of Response To appropriate Intervention (RTI) delivered within the school setting. In this RTI model, students would be identified as having a specific learning disability based upon their lack of response to scientific, well designed and implemented teaching.

The cause of delayed academic performance is not due to limited cognitive ability, sensory and physical impairments, emotional disturbances, or environmental deprivation. The child or youth with a disability is characterized by:

1. Hyperactivity: a rate of motor activity higher than normal.
2. Perceptual difficulties: visual, auditory, and haptic perceptual problems.
3. Perceptual-motor impairments: poor integration of visual and motor systems, often affecting fine motor coordination.
4. General coordination deficits: clumsiness in physical activities.
5. Disorders of memory and thinking: memory deficits, trouble with problem solving, concept formation, and association: poor awareness of own metacognitive skills (learning strategies).

6. Disorders of attention: short attention span, distractibility, lack of selective attention, perseveration.
7. Emotional ability: frequent changes in mood, low tolerance for frustration, and sensitive to others.
8. Impulsiveness: acts before considering consequences, poor impulse control, often followed by remorsefulness.
9. Academic problems in reading, math, writing, or spelling: significant discrepancies in ability levels.
10. Disorders in speech, hearing, and sight: high proportion of auditory and visual perceptual difficulties.
11. Equivocal neurological signs and electroencephalogram (EEG) irregularities, neurological abnormalities (soft signs), which may or may not be due to brain injury.
12. Social adjustment: frequently poor adjustment: low self-esteem, social isolation or reckless and uninhibited, learned helplessness, poor motivation, external focus of control, poor reaction to environmental changes.
13. Interpersonal problems: over-excitable in a group, better relations with limited number of peers, frequently poor judgment exhibited: often overly affectionate and clinging.
14. Problems in achievement: academic disability, poor graphics (wiring), disorganized, slow in finishing work.

SKILL 2.2 Recognize differences between specific learning disabilities and other types of disabilities

Student with a disability means a student with a disability who has not attained the age of 21 prior to September 1st and who is entitled to attend public schools and who, because of mental, physical or emotional reasons, has been identified as having a disability and who requires special services and programs approved by the department. The terms used in this definition are defined as follows:

(1) *Autism* is a developmental disability significantly affecting verbal and nonverbal communication and social interaction, generally evident before age 3, that adversely affects a student's educational performance. Other characteristics often associated with autism are engagement in repetitive activities and stereotyped movements, resistance to environmental change or change in daily routines, and unusual responses to sensory experiences. The term does not apply if a student's educational performance is adversely affected primarily because the student has an emotional disturbance. A student who manifests the characteristics of autism after age 3 could be diagnosed as having autism if the criteria in this paragraph are otherwise satisfied.

(2) *Deafness* is a hearing impairment that is so severe the student is impaired in processing linguistic information through hearing, with or without amplification that adversely affects a student's educational performance.

(3) *Deaf-blindness* is concurrent hearing and visual impairments, the combination of which causes such severe communication and other developmental and educational needs that they cannot be accommodated in special education programs solely for students with deafness or students with blindness.

(4) *Emotional disturbance* is a condition exhibiting one or more of the following characteristics over a long period of time and to a marked degree that adversely affects a student's educational performance:
   (i) An inability to learn that cannot be explained by intellectual, sensory, or health factors.
   (ii) An inability to build or maintain satisfactory interpersonal relationships with peers and teachers;
   (iii) Inappropriate types of behavior or feelings under normal circumstances;
   (iv) A generally pervasive mood of unhappiness or depression; or
   (v) A tendency to develop physical symptoms or fears associated with personal or school problems.
   (vi) The term includes schizophrenia. The term does not apply to students who are socially maladjusted, unless it is determined that they have an emotional disturbance.

(5) *Hearing impairment* is an impairment in hearing, whether permanent or fluctuating, that adversely affects the child's educational performance but is not included under the definition of *deafness* in this section.

(6) *Learning disability* is a disorder in one or more of the basic psychological processes involved in understanding or in using language, spoken or written, which manifests itself in an imperfect ability to listen, think, speak, read, write, spell, or do mathematical calculations. The term includes such conditions as perceptual disabilities, brain injury, minimal brain dysfunction, dyslexia and developmental aphasia. The term does not include learning problems that are primarily the result of visual, hearing or motor disabilities, of mental retardation, of emotional disturbance, or of environmental, cultural or economic disadvantage.

(7) *Mental retardation is* significantly sub-average general intellectual functioning, existing concurrently with deficits in adaptive behavior and manifested during the developmental period, that adversely affects a student's educational performance.

(8) *Multiple disabilities* are concomitant impairments (such as mental retardation-blindness, mental retardation-orthopedic impairment, etc.), the combination of which cause such severe educational needs that they cannot be accommodated in a special education program solely for one of the impairments. The term does not include deaf-blindness.

(9) *Orthopedic impairment* is a severe orthopedic impairment that adversely affects a student's educational performance. The term includes impairments caused by congenital anomaly (*e.g.*, clubfoot, absence of some member, etc.), impairments caused by disease (*e.g.*, poliomyelitis, bone tuberculosis, etc.), and impairments from other causes (*e.g.*, cerebral palsy, amputation, and fractures or burns which cause contractures).

10) *Other health-impairment* is having limited strength, vitality or alertness, including a heightened alertness to environmental stimuli, that results in limited alertness with respect to the educational environment, that is due to chronic or acute health problems, including but not limited to a heart condition, tuberculosis, rheumatic fever, nephritis, asthma, sickle cell anemia, hemophilia, epilepsy, lead poisoning, leukemia, diabetes, attention deficit disorder or attention deficit hyperactivity disorder or Tourettes syndrome, which adversely affects a student's educational performance.

(11) *Speech or language impairment* is a communication disorder, such as stuttering, impaired articulation, a language impairment or a voice impairment, that adversely affects a student's educational performance.

(12) *Traumatic brain injury* is an acquired injury to the brain caused by an external physical force or by certain medical conditions such as stroke, encephalitis, aneurysm, anoxia or brain tumors with resulting impairments that adversely affect educational performance. The term includes open or closed head injuries or brain injuries from certain medical conditions resulting in mild, moderate or severe impairments in one or more areas, including cognition, language, memory, attention, reasoning, abstract thinking, judgment, problem solving, sensory, perceptual and motor abilities, psychosocial behavior, physical functions, information processing, and speech. The term does not include injuries that are congenital or caused by birth trauma.

(13) *Visual impairment including blindness* is an impairment in vision that, even with correction, adversely affects a student's educational performance. The term includes both partial sight and blindness.

SKILL 2.3   Understand the effects of specific learning disabilities on psychomotor, cognitive, social, emotional, and language development

Please refer to Skill 2.1.

SKILL 2.4 Understand the implications of various types of specific learning disabilities for students' educational development

TYPES AND CHARACTERISTICS OF RECEPTIVE AND EXPRESSIVE LANGUAGE DISORDERS ASSOCIATED WITH LEARNING DISABILITIES

Language is the means whereby people communicate their thoughts, make requests and respond to others. Communication Competence is an interaction of cognitive competence, social knowledge, and language competence. Communication problems may result from any or all of these areas, which directly impact the student's ability to interact with others. Language consists of several components, each of which follows a sequence of development. Brown and colleagues were the first to describe language as a function of developmental stages rather than age (Reid, 1988 p 44). He developed a formula to group the mean length of utterances (sentences) into stages. Counting the number of morphemes per 100 utterances, one can calculate a mean length of utterance, MLU. Total number of morphemes / 100 = MLU e.g. 180/100 = 1.8

Summary of Brown's findings about MLU and language development:

Stage	MLU	Developmental Features
L	1.5-2.0	14 basic morphemes (e.g. in, on, articles, possessives)
Ll	2.0-2.5	Beginning of pronoun use, auxiliary verbs
Lll	2.5-3.0	Language form approximate adult forms. Beginning of questions and negative statements
Lv	3.0-3.5	Use of complex (embedded)sentences
V	3.5-4.0	Use of compound sentences.

COMPONENTS OF LANGUAGE
Language learning is composed of five components. Children progress through developmental stages through each component.

Phonology
Phonology is the system of rules about sounds and sound combinations for a language. A phoneme is the smallest unit of sound that combines with other sounds to make words. A phoneme, by itself, does not have a meaning; it must be combined with other phonemes. Problems in phonology may be manifested as developmental delays in acquiring consonants, or reception problems, such as misinterpreting words because a different consonant was substituted.

Morphology

Morphemes are the smallest units of language that convey meaning. Morphemes are root words, or free morphemes that can stand alone (e.g. walk), and affixes (e.g. ed, s, ing). Content words carry the meaning in a sentence, and functional words join phrases and sentences. Generally, students with problems in this area may not use inflectional endings in their words, may not be consistent in their use of certain morphemes, or may be delayed in learning morphemes such as irregular past tenses.

Syntax

Syntax rules, commonly known as grammar, govern how morphemes and words are correctly combined. Wood, (1976) describes six stages of syntax acquisition (Mercer, p 347).

- **Stages 1 and 2** - Birth to about 2 years: Child is learning the semantic system.
- **Stage 3** – Ages 2 – 3 years: Simple sentences contain subject and predicate.
- **Stage 4** - Ages 2 ½ to 4 years: Elements such as question words are added to basic sentences (e.g. where), word order is changed to ask questions. The child begins to use "and" to combine simple sentences, and the child begins to embed words within the basic sentence.
- **Stage 5** - About 3 ½ to 7 years: The child uses complete sentences that include word classes of adult language. The child is becoming aware of appropriate semantic functions of words and differences within the same grammatical class.
- **Stage 6** - About 5 to 20 years: The child begins to learn complex sentences and sentences that imply commands, requests and promises.

Syntactic deficits are manifested by the child using sentences that lack length or complexity for a child that age. The child may have problems understanding or creating complex sentences and embedded sentences.

Semantics

Semantics is language content: objects, actions, and relations between objects. As with syntax, Wood (1976) outlines stages of semantic development:

- **Stage 1** - Birth to about 2 years: The child is learning meaning while learning his first words. Sentences are one-word, but the meaning varies according to the context. Therefore, "doggie" may mean, "This is my dog," or, "There is a dog," or "The dog is barking."
- **Stage 2** - About 2 to 8 years: The child progresses to two-word sentences about concrete actions. As more words are learned, the child forms longer sentences, until about age 7, things are defined in terms of visible actions. The child begins to respond to prompts (e.g. pretty/flower), and at about age 8, the child can respond to a prompt with an opposite (e.g. pretty/ugly).
- **Stage 3** - Begins at about age 8: The child's word meanings relate directly to experiences, operations and processes. Vocabulary is defined by the child's experiences, not the adult's. At about age 12, the child begins to give "dictionary" definitions, and the semantic level approaches that of adults.

Semantic problems take the form of:

- Limited vocabulary
- Inability to understand figurative language or idioms; interprets literally
- Failure to perceive multiple meanings of words, changes in word meaning from changes in context, resulting in incomplete understanding of what is read
- Difficulty understanding linguistic concepts (e.g. before/after), verbal analogies, and logical relationships such as possessives, spatial, and temporal
- Misuse of transitional words such as "although," "regardless"

Pragmatics

Commonly known as the speaker's intent, pragmatic language is used to influence or control actions or attitudes of others. **Communicative competence** depends on how well one understands the rules of language, as well as the social rules of communication such as taking turns and using the correct tone of voice.

Pragmatic deficits are manifested by failures to respond properly to indirect requests after age 8 (e.g. "Can't you turn down the TV"? elicits a response of "No" instead of "Yes" and the child turning down the volume). Children with these deficits have trouble reading cues that indicate the listener does not understand them. Whereas a person would usually notice this and adjust one's speech to the listener's needs the child with pragmatic problems does not do this.

MILD-MODERATE DISABILITIES

Pragmatic deficits are also characterized by inappropriate social behaviors such as interruptions or monopolizing conversations. Children may use immature speech and have trouble sticking to a topic. These problems can persist into adulthood, affecting academic, vocational and social interactions.

Problems in language development often require long-term interventions, and can persist into adulthood. Certain problems are associated with different grade levels:

Preschool and Kindergarten: The child's speech may sound immature, the child may not be able to follow simple directions, and often cannot name things such as the days of the week and colors. They child may not be able to discriminate between sounds and the letters associated with the sounds. The child might substitute sounds and have trouble responding accurately to certain types of questions. The child may play less with his peers or participate in non-play or parallel play.

Elementary School: Problems with sound discrimination persist, and the child may have problems with temporal and spatial concepts (e.g. before/after). As the child progresses through school, he may have problems making the transition from narrative to expository writing. Word retrieval problems may not be very evident because the child begins to devise strategies such as talking around the word he cannot remember, or using fillers, and descriptors. The child might speak more slowly, have problems sounding out words, and get confused with multiple-meaning words. Pragmatic problems show up in social situations such as failure to correctly interpret social cues and adjust to appropriate language, inability to predict consequences, and inability to formulate requests to obtain new information.

Secondary School: At this level, difficulties become more subtle. The child lacks the ability to use and understand higher-level syntax, semantics, and pragmatics. If the child has problems with auditory language, he may also have problems with short-term memory. Receptive and/or expressive language delays impair the child's ability to learn effectively. The child often lacks the ability to organize and categorize the information received in school. Problems associated with pragmatic deficiencies persist but because the child is aware of them, he becomes inattentive, withdrawn or frustrated.

CHARACTERISTICS OF STUDENTS WITH SPEECH/LANGUAGE IMPAIRMENTS

As a group, youngsters with speech and language impairments generally score below normal children on measures of intelligence, achievement, and adaptive social skills. However, this is in part attributable to the fact that a large percentage of children with mental, physical, behavioral and learning disabilities exhibit speech and language disorders secondary to their major disability. Children with markedly deviant or delayed speech and language generally have concurrent difficulties with severe intellectual disabilities, chronic emotionally/behavioral disturbances, or acute hearing problems, and function at a delayed developmental level.

Children with speech impairments who have no observable organic defects perform slightly lower than average on tests of motor proficiency. Problems are most likely to occur in the areas of coordination, application of strength, and rhythm. Children with communication disorders tend to demonstrate less interaction with peers.

In addition to these general characteristics, children with cleft palates tend to be underachieving and to show more personality problems (e.g. shyness, inhibition, and social withdrawal) then normal children. Children who stutter severely exhibit much anxiety and have low self-esteem.

Speech Disorders

IDENTIFICATION AND CHARACTERISTICS

Children with speech disorders are characterized by one or more of the following:

1. Unintelligible speech, or speech that is difficult to understand, and articulation disorders (distortions, omissions, substitutions).
2. Speech-flow disorders (sequence, duration, rate, rhythm, fluency).
3. Unusual voice quality (nasality, breathiness, hoarseness, pitch, intensity, quality disorders).
4. Peculiar physical mannerisms when speaking.
5. Obvious emotional discomfort when trying to communicate (particularly stutterers and clutterers).
6. Damage to nerves or brain centers which control muscles used in speech (dysarthria).

Language Disorders

Language disorders are often considered just one category of speech disorder, but the problem is really a separate one with different origins and causes. Language-disordered children exhibit one or more of the following characteristics.

1. Difficulty in comprehending questions, commands, or statements (receptive language problems).
2. Inability to adequately express their own thoughts (expressive language problems).
3. Language that is below the level expected for the child's chronological age (delayed language).
4. Interrupted language development (dysphasia).
5. Qualitatively different language.
6. Total absence of language (aphasia).

TYPES AND CHARACTERISTICS OF PERCEPTUAL AND MEMORY DISORDERS ASSOCIATED WITH LEARNING DISABILITIES

Perceptual disorders refer to visual processing problems that occur when an individual has problems making sense of information that is seen through the eyes. This is not to be confused with problems that result from sight or sharpness of vision. People that have perceptual disorders have problems processing visual information, not seeing it.

Students with perceptual disorders have problems identifying the position of objects in space. They cannot precisely view objects in space when placed next to other objects.

The problems of spatial relationships are significant in reading and math. Both math and reading require the use of symbols, letters, numbers, punctuation, and signs. Some examples of problems associated with perception include not being able to view words and numbers as separate entities, confusion with letters that resemble each other such as b, d, and p, and having problems with directions in reading and math.

The significance of having perceptual acuity is present throughout math. In order to fully master mathematical concepts, individuals have to be able to ascertain that certain digits go together to create a single number such as 25, and that other digits are single digit numbers and the addition, subtraction, and multiplication signs are separate from the numbers but show a relationship between the numbers.

There are three different types of memories that are significant in the learning process. Working memory is the ability to hold on to parts of information until the pieces come together to formulate a complete thought or concept. An example of this is when you read a sentence and at the end of it are able to comprehend the full context.

Short-term memory is the active process of storing and retaining information for a brief limited period of time. The information is available for a short period of time and is not yet stored for long-term memorization.

Long-term memory is information that has been stored and is available for use over a long period of time. Some people may have problems with auditory or visual memory. Auditory memory is being able to store and recall information that is received verbally. Visual memory is being able to store and recall information that is received visually or through the eyes.

Sequencing problems stem from people having problems learning information in the correct sequence. For example, a student can have problems memorizing the order of the alphabet or the months of the year.

Abstraction problems occur when an individual has problems deducing the meaning of words or concepts. Someone with abstraction problems would have difficulty understanding jokes, sarcasm, idioms, or words with different meanings. Organization problems occur when an individual has problems keeping his things organized. They may constantly lose, forget, or misplace homework, school assignments, and papers. They also have problems keeping their work environment organized and have difficulty with projects that may be due on a particular date.

TYPES AND CHARACTERISTICS OF THINKING DISORDERS ASSOCIATED WITH LEARNING DISABILITIES

Thinking disorders associated with learning disabilities include problems forming concepts and solving problems. Problem solving is the systematic use of a step-by-step system to respond to hard questions. Concept formation is the process of combining a series of features that group together to create a class of ideas or objects.

If there were no formation of concepts people would have to learn and recall the word that stands for every unique thing in the world. For example, each type of chair, flower, or truck would require its own name.

Difficulties with higher order thinking skills are problematic in all academic areas. For brevity of time, one subject area, math, will be used to provide you with more detailed explanations of how these disorders affect a subject. Understanding high order thinking is required in all subject areas in order to successfully progress through the curriculum.

For students studying mathematics these skills are needed for many problems in upper level math classes. Students must determine the solution to questions that are indirect, and without the use of higher order thinking, many students will have difficulty correctly identifying the real problem and how to find the solution. Some students also have difficulty with any sort of problem requiring many steps to complete. Students with disabilities sometimes cannot determine how to begin working on the problem or are unable to finish the problem once they have completed some of the steps, leaving an incomplete resolution.

Underdeveloped processing skills may also lead to problems deducing important information from insignificant information when resolving word problems. Numerous problems presented entail too much or too little information, which then requires the student to deduce what additional information is necessary to solve the problem. This makes it even harder for students who have problems with multi-step problem solving and higher order thinking skills.

TEACHER CERTIFICATION STUDY GUIDE

COMPETENCY 3.0   **UNDERSTAND CAUSES AND CHARACTERISTICS OF MILD/MODERATE MENTAL RETARDATION AND THE SIGNIFICANCE OF MENTAL RETARDATION FOR HUMAN DEVELOPMENT AND LEARNING.**

SKILL 3.1   Recognize definitions, causes, and criteria associated with levels of mental retardation

PLEASE REFER TO SKILL 1.2 FOR POTENTIAL CAUSES OF DISABILITIES.

Characteristics with regard to the degree of retardation fall into four categories.

1. Mild (IQ of 50-55 to 70)
   a. Delays in most areas (i.e. communication, motor, academics).
   b. Often not distinguished from "normal" children until school age.
   c. Acquire both academic and vocational skills: can become self-supporting.

2. Moderate (IQ of 35-40 to 50-55)

   a. Only fair motor development: clumsy.
   b. Poor social awareness.
   c. Can be taught to communicate.
   d. Can profit from training in social and vocational skills: needs supervision, but can perform semi-skilled labor as an adult.

3. Severe (IQ of 20-25 to 35-40)

   a. Poor motor development
   b. Minimal speech and communication.
   c. Minimal ability to profit from training in health and self-help skills: may contribute to self maintenance under constant supervision as an adult.

4. Profound (IQ below 20-25)

   a. Gross retardation, both mental and sensor-motor.
   b. Little or no development of basic communication skills.
   c. Dependency on others to maintain basic life functions.
   d. Lifetime of complete supervision (i.e. institution, home, nursing home).

SKILL 3.2 Understand major cognitive, behavioral, physical, and social characteristics of individuals with mental retardation

Mental retardation, called intellectual disabilities in some states, refers to significantly sub-average general intellectual functioning existing concurrently with impairments in adaptive behavior. Sub-average intellectual functioning is determined by scores of two or more standard deviations below the mean on a standardized test of intelligence. Students exhibiting mental handicaps typically show a flat profile in academic areas.

Adaptive behavior differs according to age and situation. For example, during infancy and early childhood, sensory motor, self-help, communication, and socialization skills are considered important. During middle childhood and early adolescence, abilities involving learning processes and interpersonal social skills are essential. During late adolescence and adulthood, vocational skills, and social responsibilities are important.

SKILL 3.3 Recognize the effects of mental retardation on sensory, motor, adaptive, cognitive, language, social, and emotional development

Please refer to Skill 3.1 for more information.

SKILL 3.4 Demonstrate knowledge of learning characteristics of students with mental retardation.

Please refer to Skill 3.1 and 3.2 for more information.

COMPETENCY 4.0 UNDERSTAND TYPES AND CHARACTERISTICS OF EMOTIONAL DISTURBANCE AND THEIR SIGNIFICANCE FOR DEVELOPMENT AND LEARNING.

SKILL 4.1 Demonstrate knowledge of definitions and identifying criteria of emotional disturbance.

PLEASE REFER TO SKILL 2.2 FOR CURRENT DEFINITION.

Several approaches have been devised in classifying characteristics of students with emotional/behavioral disorders. One such method is that of classifying by dimensions of behaviors or clusters of interrelated traits. Another is that of identifying disturbed behaviors as they relate to the federal definition ("Education of Handicapped Children." 1981; Individuals with Disabilities in Education Act. 1990). This identification continues to be modeled after what was proposed by Eli Bower in 1969.

Several parameters are considered in determining disturbed behavior. These include the departure from acceptable standards, the degree to which behavior deviates from these standards, the length of time the behavior pattern has existed, and the situations in which the behavior most typically occurs. The level of severity is determined from these parameters.

Mild Emotional Disturbance
Children who exhibit mild behavior disorders are characterized by:

1. Average or above average on intelligence tests.
2. Poor academic achievement; learned helplessness.
3. Unsatisfactory interpersonal relationships.
4. Immaturity; attention seeking.
5. Aggressive, acting-out behavior; hitting, fighting, teasing, telling, refusal to comply with requests, excessive attention seeking, poor anger control, temper tantrums, hostile reactions, defiant use of language, or anxious-withdrawn behavior, infantile behavior, social isolation, few friends, withdrawal into fantasy, fears, hypochondria, unhappiness, depression, crying.

Moderate Emotional Disturbance

Behaviors at the moderate level of severity include:
1. Scores on tests of intelligence are often below average.
2. Academic achievement generally below average.
3. Generally excessive, disruptive, inappropriate behaviors, lack of appropriate behaviors may be of concern.

4. Behaviors exhibited are unacceptable to others, and sometimes self.
5. Comparatively high number of problem behaviors.
6. Problem behaviors interfere with expected performance relative to chronological age.

Severe to Profound Emotional Disturbance

Those who exhibit severe to profound behavior disorders are characterized by:
1. Average intelligence quotient (IQ) score in mentally retarded range, and frequently unable to obtain true scores for this population.
2. Cognitive defects; markedly deficient in academic areas.
3. Often are classified by personality categories or conditions[4] (e.g. schizophrenic).
4. Poor sense of identity.
5. Deficient awareness of reality.
6. Unable to relate to other people; excessive resistance.
7. Language and speech deviations; inappropriate speech.
8. Aggression towards others of a serious nature (i.e. unexplained tantrums, aggression towards others of a serious nature (e.g. unprovoked tantrums, scratching, or kicking others).
9. Incoherence; illogical thinking.
10. Inappropriate attachments to objects.
11. Bizarre delusions and hallucinations.
12. Inappropriate affect; variable behavior.
13. Unable to perform basic life skills or functions.
14. Self-mutilations; self-injurious.
15. Repetitive motor behaviors; perseveration.

The law excludes students from services in emotional/behavioral disorders if the problems are those of a social maladjustment. This is true UNLESS the student is also assessed as having an emotional behavioral disturbance.

SKILL 4.2   Recognize major behavioral and social characteristics of students with emotional disturbance

PLEASE REFER TO SKILL 1.2 FOR CHARACTERISTICS OF STUDENTS WITH EMOTIONAL DISTURBANCE.

SKILL 4.3 Understand the implications of various types of behavioral, social, and emotional disturbances for students' educational development

There are many different types of behavioral, social and emotional disorders found in society and schools today. Below you will find brief explanations of the most typical and common found in schools today, it is by no means a completely comprehensive list of all of the possible disorders, which can be found. Additionally, further information can be found under skill 1.2 as to other disorders which affect behavior, social and emotional development of students.

Anxiety Disorders The National Institute of Mental Health divides this area of mental illness into five kinds: generalized anxiety disordered, obsessive-compulsive disorder, panic disorder, post-traumatic stress disorder, and social phobia. Some individuals with anxiety disorders may also have ADHD.

Bipolar Disorder (Manic Depression) The National Institute of Mental Health describes children and adolescents with bipolar disorder as having frequent and severe mood swings between mania and depression. Many individuals with bipolar disorder demonstrate suicidal tendencies. Bipolar disorder is more common in children of individuals who are bipolar, but many bipolar individuals do not have parents who suffer from the illness. This mental illness can also be characterized by aggression and irritability.

Schizophrenia and psychotic behaviors Children may have delusions, hallucinations, incoherent thoughts, and disconnected thinking. Schizophrenia typically manifests itself between the ages of 15 and 45, and the younger the onset, the more severe the disorder. These behaviors usually require intensive treatment beyond the scope of the regular classroom setting.

Any disorder which affects the emotional, behavioral or social development of students will have serious implications on the educational process. Schools are social institutions, where students must have tools available with them to work not only with peers, but also with the adults. Children who have difficulty in these areas will experience significant challenges accessing the information presented in schools. The more outward displayed the behavior issues may result in removal from the classroom for extended periods of time. Every time a child is removed from the classroom, they are missing learning opportunities. On the other end of the spectrum, students who withdraw may be physically present, but are not able to acquire information presented.

SKILL 4.4 Recognize ways in which emotional disturbance influences personal productivity, interpersonal/intrapersonal effectiveness, communication skills, self-control, and self-monitoring

Refer to Skill 4.2.

COMPETENCY 5.0 UNDERSTAND TYPES AND CHARACTERISTICS OF OTHER CATEGORIES OF DISABILITIES (I.E., AUTISM, OTHER HEALTH IMPAIRMENTS, TRAUMATIC BRAIN INJURY, ORTHOPEDIC IMPAIRMENT) AND THEIR SIGNIFICANCE FOR HUMAN DEVELOPMENT AND LEARNING.

SKILL 5.1 Recognize definitions, causes, and criteria associated with other categories of disabilities (i.e., autism, other health impairments, traumatic brain injury, orthopedic impairment.

Please refer to Skills 2.2 and 5.2.

SKILL 5.2 Understand major cognitive, behavioral, physical, and social characteristics of individuals with other categories of disabilities (i.e., autism, other health impairments, traumatic brain injury, orthopedic impairment)

Please refer to Skill 2.4 for information about speech disorders/impairments.

IDENTIFY CHARACTERISTICS OF STUDENTS WITH HEARING IMPAIRMENTS

Similarly, to other physical and sensory impairments, it is not the hearing impairment itself but how significant others respond to the hearing-impaired child that ultimately influences whether the child will show behavioral problems. The possibility of communicative isolation increases the need for social interaction: acceptance is crucial. Adjustment, immaturity, and appearance of self-centeredness are not unusual social problems.

Educationally, hearing- impaired individuals sometimes demonstrate a lower level of achievement than their hearing proficient peers. Speech and language development may be affected. Because most tests of intelligence rely heavily upon verbal skills, it is difficult to assess the true capacities of a deaf child. Generally, the use of nonverbal tests and/or sign language produces more scores in the normal range of intelligence. And those who do score in the range of mental retardation may have other disabling conditions such as learning disabilities, visual impairment, and so forth.

The child with hearing handicaps may exhibit the following behavioral and physical symptoms.

1. Appearance of not paying attention.
2. Turns head or ear toward speaker.
3. Has difficulty following oral directions, and frequently loses place during oral reading.
4. Concentrates on speaker's face or mouth.
5. Exhibits acting-out behavior, and is stubborn, shy, withdrawn, or paranoid.
6. Reluctant to participate in oral activities.
7. Asks teacher or peers to repeat instructions and questions.
8. Best achievement accomplished in small groups.
9. Frequent speech defects, particularly misarticulation.
10. Disparity between expected and actual achievement.
11. Certain medical conditions (frequent colds, earaches, sore throats, sinus congestions, chronic allergies, fluid running from the ears, mouth, breathing, and nose).
12. Complains of ringing or buzzing in the ears.

Table 2-2 Hearing Loss: Effects of Degree and Type

NORMAL RANGE (0-2- dB)

Areas of Concern	Effects
Problematic Causes	Slight fluctuating conductive loss
Ability to hear speech without a hearing aid	No difficulty with normal conversation
Educational Implications	None specifically
Extent of communicative handicaps	None
Auditory rehabilitative consideration	Probably needs no treatment

MILD LOSS (20-40) dB)

Areas of Concern	Effects
Problematic Causes	Most likely conductive from otitis media; sensorineural loss may result from mild illness or disease
Ability to hear speech without a hearing aid	Is able to hear most speech except soft or whispered; hears vowels but may miss unvoiced consonants; often says "huh?" and may turn the television, radio, or stereo volume loud
Educational Implications	Typically has difficulty hearing faint or distant speech. May experience problems in Integrated Language Arts subjects
Extent of communicative handicaps	Mild handicap; possible speech disorder or language delay; may omit final and voiceless consonants
Auditory rehabilitative consideration	Losses that are medically treatable need favorable classroom seating and other environmental accommodations; sensorineural problems may require hearing aid, speech reading, or auditory training

Table 2-2 Hearing Loss: Effects of Degree and Type (cont.)

MODERATE LOSS (40-60 dB)

Areas of Concern	Effects
Problematic Causes	Conductive losses result from otitis media or a middle ear problem; sensorineural losses result from ear disease or illness
Ability to hear speech without a hearing aid	Hearing is a problem in most conversational settings, in groups, or in the presence of background noise; hears louder voiced consonants; turns television, radio, or stereo volume loud and has trouble hearing on the phone
Educational Implications	Understands face-to-face conversational speech. May miss up to 50% of discussion in the classroom if voices are soft or speakers are not in line of vision
Extent of communicative handicaps	Possible difficulty with auditory learning; mild to moderate language delay; articulation problems with final and voiceless consonants; may not pay attention
Auditory rehabilitative consideration	Same as mild loss; may also need special class for the hearing impaired or special tutoring

Table 2-2 Hearing Loss: Effects of Degree and Type (cont.)

SEVERE LOSS (60-80 dB)

Areas of Concern	Effects
Problematic Causes	Most likely sensorineural, although mixed is possible; causes include rubella, meningitis, RH incompatibility, and heredity
Ability to hear speech without a hearing aid	Can only hear very loud speech; cannot carry on a conversation without help; cannot use the telephone without amplification.
Educational Implications	May be able to hear loud voices about one foot from ear and to identify some environmental sounds. Speech and language may deteriorate.
Extent of communicative handicaps	Probable severe language and speech disorders; frequent learning disorders; may have no intelligible speech.
Auditory rehabilitative consideration	Same as in moderate loss; may need placement in school for the deaf.

Table 2-2 Hearing Loss: Effects of Degree and Type (cont.)

PROFOUND LOSS (Greater than 80 dB)

Areas of Concern	Effects
Problematic Causes	Mostly sensorineural, may include mixed; rubella, meningitis, RH compatibility, heredity, and ear diseases are contributing factors.
Ability to hear speech without a hearing aid	Can hear only extremely loud shouts; cannot understand spoken language; cannot hear television, radio, or stereo; cannot use the telephone.
Educational Implications	More aware of vibrations than tonal patterns. Relies on vision as primary avenue for communication. Speech and language may deteriorate further.
Extent of communicative handicaps	Severe and language deficits; no oral speech, or characteristic "deaf-like" speech and voice.
Auditory rehabilitative consideration	Same as severe; will need placement in dear-oral school or school for the deaf.

Adapted from W.W. Green, "Hearing Disorders," Table 5-3, p. 208, in Berdine and Blackhurst, (eds.). An Introduction to Special Education, 2nd ed. Copyright 1985 by W.H. Berdine and A.E. Blackhurst. By permission of Little, Brown, and Company. Also adapted from Report of a Committee for a Comprehensive Plan for Hearing Impaired Children, Office of the Superintendent of Public Instruction. Title VI Elementary and Secondary Act and the Division of Services for Crippled Children May 1968.

INDENTIFY CHARACTERISTICS OF STUDENTS WITH VISUAL IMPAIRMENTS

As a group, visually impaired children tend to develop physically and to understand and use language similarly to their sighted peers. Only a few minor aspects of communication, such as the use of gestures, have been found to differ. Though it wouldn't be expected, blind children tend to use language, which reflects visual experiences, and thus exhibit verbalism or verbal reality. For example, to the word "grass" they are likely to respond with "visual" words such as "green" or "brown." It has been concluded that they learn many words and word meanings from their own use in the language rather than from personal experience.

Studies indicate students with visual impairments tend to have intelligence score distributions similar to those of normal children. But the development of conceptual or cognitive abilities typically lags behind that of sighted peers. Perhaps the only accurate way of comparing intellectual abilities of sighted and sight-impaired children is by examining performance on skills where the visual disorder is not a factor. Typically, students with visual disabilities seem to exhibit a greater attention level than sighted children.

The social adjustment and self-concept development by children with visual handicaps tend to be influenced by association with significant others. Furthermore, restricted mobility and consequently limited experiences, may cause passivity and dependency, resulting ultimately in learned helplessness.

The child with a visual problem often exhibits one or more of the following behaviors:

1. Rubs the eyes excessively.
2. Shuts or covers one eye; tilts the head or thrusts the head forward.
3. Shows sensitivity to light or glare; not able to see things at certain times of the day.
4. Squirms, blinks, frowns, and/or makes facial distortions while reading or doing other close work.
5. Complains of scratchy feeling, burning, or itching of the eyes.
6. Experiences difficulty with reading or other work requiring close visual contact; may experience headaches, dizziness, or nausea following close eye work.
7. Holds reading material too closely or too far away, or frequently changes the distance from near to far or from far to near.
8. Exhibits a tendency to lose place in sentence or on page.
9. Shows poor spacing in writing and has difficulty in staying on the line.
10. Often confuses letters of similar shape (e.g. o/a, c/e, n/m/h, f/t).
11. Frequently reverses letters, syllables, or words.
12. Experiences difficulty in seeing distant objects.
13. Tunes out material written on the chalkboard.

Medically, the visually impaired child often has one or more of the following physical indicators:

1. Red eyelids.
2. Recurring sty's or swollen lids.
3. Crust on lids among the lashes
4. Thick discharges from the eyes
5. Inflamed and watery eyes.
6. Crossed eyes, or eyes that do not appear to be straight.
7. Pupils of uneven size.
8. Eyes that move excessively (nystagmus).
9. Drooping eyelids

IDENTIFY CHARACTERISTICS OF STUDENTS WITH PHYSICAL DISABILITIES AND OTHER HEALTH IMPAIRMENTS

Children with physical impairments possess a variety of disabling conditions. Although there are significant differences among these conditions, similarities also exist. Each condition usually affects one particular system of the body: the cardiopulmonary system (i.e. blood vessels, heart, and lungs), the musculoskeletal system (i.e. spinal cord, brain nerves), etc. Some conditions develop during pregnancy, birth, or infancy because of the known or unknown factors, which may affect the fetus or newborn infant. Other conditions occur later due to injury (trauma), disease, or factors not fully understood.

In addition to motor disorders, individuals with physical disabilities may have multidisabling conditions such as: concomitant hearing impairments, visual impairments, perceptual disorders, speech defects, behavior disorders, mental handicaps, performance, and emotional responsiveness.

Some characteristics which may occur with individuals with physical disabilities and other health impairments are:

1. Lack of physical stamina; fatigue
2. Chronic illness; poor endurance
3. Deficient motor skills; normal movement may be prevented
4. May cause physical limitations or impede motor development; a prosthesis or an orthosis may be required.
5. Mobility and exploration of one's environment may be limited.
6. Limited self-care abilities.
7. Progressive weakening and degeneration of muscles.
8. Frequent speech and language defects; communication may be prevented; echolatia orthosis may be present.
9. May experience pain and discomfort throughout the body.
10. May display emotional (psychological) problems, which require treatment.
11. Social adjustments may be needed; may display maladaptive social behavior.
12. May necessitate long-term medical treatment.
13. May have embarrassing side effects from certain diseases or treatment.
14. May exhibit erratic or poor attendance patterns.

IDENTIFY CHARACTERISTICS OF STUDENTS WITH MULTIDISABILITIES

Children who have multiple disabilities are an extremely heterogeneous population. Their characteristics are determined by the type and severity of their combined disabilities, thus they differ in their sensory, motor, social, and cognitive abilities. Although any number of combinations of disabilities is possible, major dimensions typically include mental retardation, neurological impairments, emotional disturbance, or deafness and blindness.

Those whose impairments combine to form multiple disabilities often exhibit characteristics on a severe level. Low self-esteem and poor social skills often characterize this population. Youngsters with severe disabilities may possess profound language or perceptual-cognitive deprivations. Moreover, they may have extremely fragile physiological conditions. "It is important to understand that the problem of severe/profound disabilities…It is the extent of the disabilities that results in the child's classification, not the type of disabilities," (Blackhurst & Berdine, 1985, pp. 473-474).

Among the characteristics that can be present with youth with severely or profound multi-disabilities are:

1. Multiple disabilities.
2. Often not toilet trained.
3. Frequently non-ambulatory.
4. Aggressiveness toward others without provocation and antisocial behavior.
5. Markedly withdrawn, or unresponsive to others.
6. No attention to even the most pronounced social stimuli.
7. Self-mutilation (i.e. head banging, biting, and scratching or cutting of self.
8. Rumination (i.e. self-induced vomiting, swallowing vomitus.
9. Self-stimulation (i.e. rocking, hand-flapping).
10. Intense temper tantrums of unknown origin.
11. Excessive, pointless imitation, or the total absence of the ability to imitate.
12. Inability to be controlled verbally.
13. Seizures
14. Extremely brittle medical existence (i.e. life-threatening conditions such as congenital heart disease, respiratory difficulties, metabolic disorders, central nervous system disorders, and digestive malfunctions).

KNOW THE CHARACTERISTICS OF AUTISM

In 1981, the condition of autism was moved from the exceptionality category of the seriously emotionally disturbed to that of other health impaired by virtue of a change in language in the original definitions under Public Law 94-142 ("Education of Handicapped Children." Federal Register, 1977). With IDEA, in 1990, autism was made into a separate exceptionality category. Refer to Competency 13 for additional information on autism.

Autism is a severe language disorder, which affects thinking, communication, and behavior (Smith & Luckasson, 1992). The condition occurs in about four out of 10,000 persons. It is characterized by dysfunctional interpersonal relationships, abnormal or no language, extreme withdrawal by some, self-stimulation and other ritualistic movements, and frequently self-injurious behaviors.

When autism was initially identified, it was thought to be a psychosocial problem caused by parents who were either cold and aloof, or hostile to their children. Early on, autism was thought to be a form of mental illness. Some have even associated autism with mental retardation.

In IDEA, the 1990 EHA Amendment, autism was finally classified as a separate exceptionality category. In this federal regulation, autism is defined as a developmental disability that affects verbal and nonverbal communication. It is thought to be caused by a neurological or biochemical dysfunction. The condition is generally evident before age three. Cognitive deficits are present. These and other characteristics are such that educational performance is adversely affected.

Smith and Luckasson (1992, p. 227) list the following characteristics:

1. **Absent or distorted relationship with people** - Inability to relate to people except as objects, inability to express affection, or ability to build and maintain only distant, suspicious, or bizarre relationships.
2. **Extreme or peculiar problems in communications** - Absence of verbal language or language that is not functional, such as echolalia (parroting what one hears), misuse of pronouns (e.g. he for you and I for her), neologisms, (made up, meaningless words or sentences), talk that bears little or no resemblance to reality.
3. **Self-stimulation** - repetitive, stereotyped behavior that seems to have no purpose other than providing sensory stimulation (this may take a wide variety of forms, such as swishing saliva, twirling objects, patting one's cheeks, flapping one's hands, staring, etc.)

4. **Self-injury** - repeated physical self-abuse, such as biting, scratching, or poking oneself, head banging, etc.
5. **Perceptual anomalies** - unusual responses or absence of response to stimuli that seems to indicate sensory impairments or unusual sensitivity.

The term does not include children with characteristics of the exceptionality Serious Emotional Disturbance as it is defined in federal regulations. Treatment is closer to the categories of Emotional/Behavioral Disorders and Language/Communications Impairments. That is because behavioral interventions such as behavior modification and alternative communication devices like communication boards, typewriters, and computers are currently being used to shape behaviors that are more appropriate and to provide avenues for communication to occur.

KNOW THE CHARACTERISTICS OF TRAUMATIC BRAIN INJURY

Traumatic brain injury is occurring to more children and youth than ever before. Ironically, many of these injuries are preventable. Automobile accidents, falls, high fever, and child abuse are among the most frequent causes. Proper use of seat belts, adult supervision, preventive medical care, and parent education are possible ways to prevent many incidents. Traumatic brain injury too often results in brain damage, which can range from mild to profound and be temporary or permanent. The brain injury generally affects the individual physically, cognitively, emotionally, and socially (Hallahan & Kauffman, 1994).

According to the National Head Injury Foundation, there are approximately 500,000 cases of traumatic brain injury each year. Statistics report about 100,000 of those victims die, and another 100,000 are debilitated for life. Traumatic brain injury is the leading killer of persons under thirty-four years old, and the leading cause of the injury is motor vehicle accidents. Child abuse accounts for 64% of head injuries (Smith & Luckasson, 1992).

Like autism, traumatic brain injury became a separate exceptionality category under IDEA in 1990. Educational plans need to be concerned with cognitive, social/behavioral, and sensorimotor domains.

UNDERSTAND THE TRAITS OF ATTENTION DEFICIT DISORDER (ADD) AND HOW TO ACCOMMODATE STUDENTS WITH ADD IN THEIR LEARNING

Of the approximately forty-five million children in the United State under the age of eighteen, it has been conservatively estimated that three to six percent of them have an attention disorder. Attention deficit disorders are a physiological, neurological problem characterized by the inability to pay attention and impulsiveness. Some are overactive, typically referred to as hyperactive. They generate much energy and are frequently restless, fidgety, and easily distracted. Others may be under active or sluggish. Attention disorders occur two to four times more frequently in boys than girls. They occur in persons of all ability levels and in every socioeconomic group.

Attentional problems usually begin in early childhood or in the elementary school years. They often continue into adolescence and adulthood and can last a lifetime. Each child or adolescent with an attention disorder manifests difficulties in an individual manner, although a core of behaviors indicative of attentional disorders has been identified.

In the fall of 1990, Congress inquired of the public whether to add Attention Deficit Disorders as a special education exceptionality category. Early 1991, it was decided not to do so for several reasons. First, many of these students were qualifying for the federally designated categories of Specific Learning Disabilities and Emotionally/Behaviorally Disordered. Second, there is no neurological test that will confirm the condition of ADD; therefore, testing for the disorder might become an ambiguous endeavor.

Since that time, many of these students have been accommodated in the regular classroom without having been declared eligible for any exceptionality category. Legal experts have used the terminology "students with disabilities" stated in Public Law 93-112 (Rehabilitation Act of 1973), since Attention Deficit Disorders is not specifically named as a category in Public Law 94-142 (EHA), or its amendment Public Law 101-476 (IDEA). Special accommodations must be given this youngster in the regular classroom by the general education teacher if the school receives documented evidence that a student has the disorder and needs special accommodations in order to control behavior and learn (e.g. a letter from the physician treating the youngster).

To be diagnosed as having ADHD, a child, adolescent, or adult must demonstrate eight of the following symptoms and they must have occurred before the age of seven. The behavioral symptoms have been coded as to whether they are indicative of inattention, impulsivity, or hyperactivity.

CODE: A=Inattention   B=Impulsivity   C=Hyperactivity

C	1.	Often fidgets with hands or feet or squirms in seat.
C	2.	Has difficulty remaining seated when required doing so.
A	3.	Is easily distracted be extraneous stimuli.
B	4.	Has difficulty waiting turn in games or group situations.
B	5.	Often blurts out answers to questions before they have been completed.
A	6.	Has difficulty following through on instructions from others (not due to oppositional behavior or failure of comprehension), e.g. fails to finish tasks and chores.
A	7.	Has difficulty sustaining attention in tasks or play activities.
B	8.	Often shifts from one uncompleted activity to another.
C	9.	Has difficulty playing quietly.
C	10.	Often talks excessively
B	11.	Often interrupts or intrudes on others, e.g. butts into other children's games.
A	12.	Often doesn't seem to listen to what is being said about him/her.
B	13.	Often loses things necessary for talks or activities at school, or at home like toys, pencils, books, assignments, etc.
C	14.	Often engages in physically dangerous activities without considering possible consequences (not for the purpose of thrill-seeking), e.g. runs into street without looking.

KNOW CHARACTERISTICS OF STUDENTS WITH SOCIAL MALADJUSTMENT

A student with social maladjustment is defined as one whose values and/or behaviors are in conflict with the school, home, or community (Brewton, Undated). Students with ordinary classroom behavior problems and social problems are not included in this category.

According to state and federal law, students with social maladjustment are ineligible for services in Emotional/Behavioral Disorders unless they have an emotional/behavioral disorder as well. Social maladjustment is not defined in the federal guidelines; however, this condition is considered independent of an emotionally based disability.

Youth who exhibit socially maladjusted behaviors are those who persistently refuse to meet what are considered minimum standards of conduct and whose behaviors and values are most often in conflict with society's standards. These students are disruptive and defy teachers. They intimidate and harass other students, and in general, refuse to respect the rights of others. They maintain a consistent pattern of aberrant and antisocial behavior without signs of guilt, remorse, or concern for the feelings of others. Their deviant behavior occurs largely from their tendency to place their own needs above those of others.

Though not in chronic distress, these students may demonstrate situational anxiety, depression, or agitation in response to certain isolated events, like when they are faced with serious consequences for their behavior. They are often motivated to continue their behavior by the approval they receive from a deviant group or gang. The immediate gratification of their behavior outweighs any consideration of long-term consequences. Typically, they are unable to benefit from previously experienced consequences, and lack of motivation to change.

The following characteristics are listed on the Social Maladjustment Checklist by Brewton (undated).

1. Participates in activities of deviant clique or peer group.
2. Projects tough image.
3. Expresses feelings of being unfairly treated.
4. Blames others for difficulties
5. Avoids displays of emotional vulnerability (denies soft, hurt or needful feelings).
6. Engages in early smoking.
7. Engages in early drinking.
8. Engages in substance abuse.
9. Displays precocious (early or excessive) sexual activity.
10. Shows poor frustration tolerance.
11. Shows little or no remorse for violating rules.
12. Exhibits temper outbursts when confronted with wrongdoing.
13. Exhibits reckless behavior, with frequent physical injuries.
14. Initiates fights.
15. Receives school suspensions.
16. Has experienced legal difficulties (delinquency).
17. Displays truancy
18. Has run away from home.
19. Lies.
20. Participates in acts of vandalism
21. Engages in theft.
22. Violates rules at home and at school.

Table 2-3 Differences Between Severely Emotionally Disturbed (SEM) and Socially Maladjusted (SM)

SED	SM
Self-critical, unable to have fun	Little remorse, pleasure seeking
Fantasy, naïve, gullible	Street-wise
Consistently poor	More situationally dependent
Affective disorder	Character disorder
Hurts self or others as an end	Hurts others as a means to an end
Easily hurt	Acts tough; survivor
Tense; fearful	Appears relaxed; "cool"
Ignored or rejected	Accepted by sociocultural group
Law-abiding, younger, no real friends	Bad companions, same age or older
Seen as unable to comply;	Seen as unwilling to comply,
Inconsistent achievements,	Generally low achievement
Good attendance record,	Excessive absences,
Appreciates help	Doesn't want help
Blames self	Blames others
Psychological	Sociological
Wants to trust, feels insecure	Dumb to trust others
Withdrawn, unhappy	Outgoing
Emotional support, likes structure,	Warmth; dislikes structure,
Decrease in anxiety	Needs to increase anxiety
Overly compliant	Non-compliant, hostile
Aware as problem exists	Denies problem
Inappropriate for age	Appropriate for age
Hyperactive; hypoactive	Normal, but acts out
Variable, labile	Relatively stable, even

Adapted from Clarizio, H.F., (1987). Differentiating emotionally impaired from socially maladjusted students. Psychology in the Schools, 24.

SKILL 5.3 Recognize the effects of other categories of disabilities (i.e., autism, other health impairments, traumatic brain injury, orthopedic impairment) on sensory, motor, adaptive, cognitive, language, social, and emotional development

Please refer to Skill 5.2.

SUBAREA II. ASSESSING STUDENTS AND DEVELOPING INDIVIDUALIZED EDUCATION PROGRAMS (IEPS) AND INDIVIDUALIZED FAMILY SERVICE PLANS (IFSPS

COMPETENCY 6.0 UNDERSTAND ASSESSMENT INSTRUMENTS AND PROCEDURES FOR EVALUATING THE STRENGTHS AND NEEDS OF STUDENTS WITH MILD/MODERATE DISABILITIES.

SKILL 6.1 Demonstrate knowledge of types and characteristics of formal and informal assessments for students with mild/moderate disabilities

Formal assessments include standardized, criterion, norm-referenced instruments, and commercially prepared inventories, which are developmentally appropriate for students across the spectrum of disabilities. Criterion-referenced tests compare a student's performance to a previously established criterion rather than to other students from a normative sample. Norm-referenced tests use normative data for scoring which include performance norms by age, gender, or ethnic group.

Informal assessment strategies include non-standardized instruments such as checklists, developmental rating scales, observations, error analysis, interviews, teacher reports and performance-based assessments. Informal evaluation strategies rely upon the knowledge and judgment of the professional and are an integral part of the evaluation process. An advantage of using informal assessments is the ease of design and administration, and the usefulness of information the teacher can gain about the student's strength and weaknesses.

Some instruments can be both formal and informal tools. For example, observation may incorporate structured observation instruments as well as other informal observation procedures, including professional judgment. When evaluating a child's developmental level, a professional may use a formal adaptive rating scale while simultaneously using professional judgment to assess the child's motivation and behavior during the evaluation process.
IDEA requires a variety of assessment tools and strategies are utilized when conducting assessments. Many assessment tools can be used across disabilities. Dependent upon the disability in question, such as blindness, autism, or hearing impaired, some assessment tools will give more information than others.

Some of the informal and formal assessments that can be used across disabilities are curriculum-based assessments, multiple baseline design, norm-referenced test, and momentary time sampling.

Momentary time sampling—This is a technique used for measuring behaviors of a group of individuals or several behaviors from the same individual. Time samples are usually brief, and may be conducted at fixed or variable intervals. The advantage of using variable intervals is increased reliability, as the students will not be able to predict when the time sample will be taken.

Multiple Baseline Design—This may be used to test the effectiveness of an intervention in developing a skill or to determine if the intervention accounted for the observed changes in a target behavior. First, the initial baseline data is collected, followed by the data during the intervention period. To get the second baseline, the intervention is removed for a period of time and data is collected again. The intervention is then reapplied, and data collected on the target behavior.

An example of a multiple baseline design might be ignoring a child who calls out in class without raising his hand. Initially, the baseline could involve counting the number of times the child calls out before applying interventions. During the time the teacher ignores the child's call-outs, data is collected. For the second baseline, the teacher would resume the response to the child's call-outs in the way she did before ignoring. The child's call-outs would probably increase again, if ignoring actually accounted for the decrease. If the teacher reapplies the ignoring strategy, the child's call-outs would probably decrease again.
Multiple baseline designs may also be used with single-subject experiments where:
- The same behavior is measured for several students at the same time. An example would be observing off-task or out-of-seat behavior among three students in a classroom.
- Several behaviors may be measured for one student. The teacher may be observing call-outs, off-task, and out-of-seat, behavior for a particular child during an observation period.
- Several settings are observed to see if the same behaviors are occurring across settings. A student's aggressive behavior toward his classmates may be observed at recess, in class, going to or from class, or in the cafeteria.

Norm-Referenced Test- An individual's performance is compared to the group that was used to calculate the performance standards in this standardized test. Some examples are the CTBS, WISC-R and Stanford-Binet.

Intelligence testing -Intelligence is considered an important attribute of a person and is related to socially valued criteria. The premise intelligence is inheritable has been supported statistically: a strong positive relationship exists between level of intelligence and degree of kinship. However, it is recognized heredity and environmental factors interact to affect cognitive development.

Educationally, intelligence tests [e.g. Wechsler Intelligence Scale for Children - IV (WISC-IV). Slosson Intelligence Test (SIT), System of Multicultural Pluralistic Assessment (SOMPA)] have been used to obtain measures relating to potential and capacity for learning. In special education, scores derived from administering tests of intelligence are called intelligence quotients (IQ). IQ's are used for inclusive as well as exclusive purposes. Along with other measures, the decision to place or include students in special education services or gifted education classes is influenced by obtaining these scores.

Characteristically, intelligence tests sample aptitude, learning, achievement, and current responses in a child's repertoire in a broader sense than achievement tests. Intelligence tests assess learning that occurs in a wide variety of life experiences, and emphasize the ability to apply information in novel ways.

The varied kinds of behaviors sampled by an intelligence test are listed by Salvia and Ysseldyke (1995).

1. **Discrimination.** The examinee identifies items that are different from the others (i.e. figuratively, symbolically, and semantically).
2. **Generalization.** Given a stimulus element (i.e. figuratively, symbolically, and semantically), the examinee is required to identify the one that is like it or that goes with it.
3. **Motor Behavior.** The examinee is required to copy geometric designs, trace paths through a maze, or reconstruct designs from memory.
4. **General Information.** The test taker is sometimes asked to answer specific factual questions.
5. **Vocabulary.** A variety of activities necessitating differing responses are included.
6. **Induction.** Following the presentation of a series of examples, the student is required to induce governing principles.
7. **Comprehension.** The examinee is asked to give evidence of comprehension of directions, printed material, or social customs and mores.
8. **Sequencing.** Given items that comprise a series of stimuli, the student must identify a response, which continues the progressive relationship.
9. **Detail Recognition.** Students must attend to detail in stimulus drawings and reflect this attention to detail in making responses.
10. **Analogies.** The student must identify the response that has the same relationship. (C as to B as to A)
11. **Abstract Reasoning.** Abstract reasoning ability is sampled through identifying the absurdity in verbal statements and pictures, stating essential meanings to a series of proverbs, and in selected scales, answering math-reasoning problems.

12. **Memory.** A variety of tasks assess memory, including repetition of sequences of orally presented digits, reproduction of geometric designs from memory, verbatim repetition of sentences, and reconstruction of the essential meaning of paragraphs or stories.
13. **Pattern Completion.** From an assortment of possibilities, the test taker selects the missing element for a pattern or matrix.

An individual's IQ is purported to be a prediction of one's success in school. In order not to inflate the importance of an IQ score, the following qualifications should be recognized. IQ scores (1) do not measure innate intelligence, (2) are variable and can change, (3) are only estimates of ability, (4) reflect only one part of the spectrum of human abilities, (5) are not necessarily consistent from test to test, and (6) are just one sample of behavior; therefore, they do not give us all the essential information needed about a student. (Sattler, 1982).

SKILL 6.2 Demonstrate knowledge of ways to modify and adapt assessments to accommodate individual abilities and needs

In general, formal assessment (including those used for identification of the adverse effect of a disability on a student's education or for re-evaluation of the student's need for ongoing special education services) should follow the printed directions for administering the test. At times, however, certain modifications and accommodations are made in order to meet the individual needs of the student to complete the assessment. Any time a deviation is made from the specifications for test administration, the modifications and accommodations should be explained in the written report provided for the IEP team and should be explained verbally at the IEP meeting. Although deviations influence the reliability and validity of the exam, they are sometimes unavoidable. If at all possible, an alternative formal assessment that does not require modification or accommodation should be administered.

Additionally, when considering assessment modifications and adaptations, it is important to realize this goes beyond the evaluation process and needs to be considered when administering the state assessments as well as general classroom assessments.

There are some different types of modifications which can be utilized during the assessment procedure to accommodate the needs of specific individuals.

PRESENTATION OF THE ASSESSMENT

It may be necessary to make language accommodations in the presentation of the assessment. This may include the services of an interpreter or translator. It is important for the examiner to meet with the interpreter or translator to discuss the nature of the test components and what is allowed as far as repetition or rewording of directions. Some assessments (such as the Peabody Picture Vocabulary Test – PPVT) are inappropriate for administration in sign language as the motion or position of some signs would be a visual clue to the answer. The result is a greatly inflated score.

If the test is not a reading test and therefore does not test reading per se, some subtests may be read to students in order to insure that the subtest shows the student's knowledge or ability in an area and not his ability to read. An example would be reading a math word problem to a child with a reading disability so the child is tested on his ability to set up and compute the problem's answer and not tested on his ability to read the problem.

LENGTH OF TESTING SESSIONS

Some formal assessments specify a length of time for completion. Unless completing a subtest in the allotted time is actually what is being tested, some students may need additional time to complete a subtest. Again, this should be noted in the examiner's written report.

Many students with a disability need more testing sessions that are shorter in length. If possible, a subtest should not be interrupted, but the examiner may decide to break the subtests into more testing sessions than commonly used.

METHOD OF STUDENT RESPONSE

Obviously a test that asks a student to point to a specified picture may be difficult or impossible for a student with a physical disability. The student response may be verbal in this situation.

Many hearing impaired students or ESL (English as a Second Language) students may communicate answers through an interpreter or translator.

Again, it should be emphasized that the first responsibility of the examiner is to locate a test that is normed on students with a similar disability and does not require accommodations or modifications. When such a test is not an option, all variances from the directions for administration should be noted in the examiner's written report and consideration should be given on the effect on the student's scores.

SKILL 6.3 Demonstrate knowledge of procedures for screening, prereferral, referral, and classification

The following information is helpful to an educator candidate, but this skill's information can be found on the state website at
HTTP://WWW.SDE.STATE.OK.US/HOME/DEFAULTIE.HTML

Intervention/Prereferral

Once a student is identified as being at-risk academically or socially, remedial interventions are attempted within the regular classroom. Federal legislation requires that sincere efforts be made to help the child learn in the regular classroom.

In some states, school-based teams of educators are formed to solve learning and behavior problems in the regular classroom. These informal problem-solving teams have a variety of names that include concepts of support (school support teams, student support teams), assistance (teacher assistance teams, school assistance teams, or building assistance teams), and appraisal (school appraisal teams - Pugach & Johnson 1989).

Regardless of what the teams are called, their purpose is similar. Chalfant, Pysh, and Moultrie (1979) state that teacher assistance teams are created to make professional suggestions about curricular alternatives and instructional modifications. These teams may be composed of a variety of participants, including regular education teachers, building administrator, guidance counselor, special education teacher, and the student's parent(s). The team composition varies based on the type of referral, the needs of the student, and availability of educational personnel and state requirements. (Georgia Department of Education 1986.)

Instructional modifications or interventions are tried in an attempt to accommodate the student in the regular classroom. Effective instruction is geared toward individual needs and recognizes differences in how students' learn. Modifications are tailored to individual student needs. Some strategies for modifying regular classroom instruction shown on Table 1-1 are effective with at-risk students with disabilities, and students without learning or behavior problems.

Table 1-1 Strategies for Modifying Classroom Instruction

Strategy 1 Provide active learning experiences to teach concepts. Student motivation is increased when students can manipulate, weigh, measure, read, or write using materials and skills that relate to their daily lives.

Strategy 2 Provide ample opportunities for guided practice of new skills. Frequent feedback on performance is essential to overcome student feelings of inadequacy. Peer tutoring and cooperative projects provide non-threatening practice opportunities. Individual student conferences, curriculum-based tests, and small group discussions are three useful methods for checking progress.

Strategy 3 Provide multisensory learning experiences. Students with learning problems sometimes have sensory processing difficulties; for instance, an auditory discrimination problem may cause misunderstanding about teacher expectations. Lessons and directions that include visual, auditory, tactile, and kinesthetic modes are preferable to a single sensory approach.

Strategy 4 Present information in a manner that is relevant to the student. Particular attention to this strategy is needed when there is a cultural or economic gap between the lives of teachers and students. Relate instruction to a youngster's daily experience and interests.

Strategy 5 Provide students with concrete illustrations of their progress. Students with learning problems need frequent reinforcement for their efforts. Charts, graphs, and check sheets provide tangible markers of student achievement.

Referral

Referral is the process through which a teacher, parent, or some other person formally requests an evaluation of a student to determine eligibility for special education services. The decision to refer a student may be influenced by: (1) student characteristics, such as the abilities, behaviors, or skills students exhibit (or lack of them): (2) individual differences among teachers, in their beliefs, expectations, or skill in dealing with specific kinds of problems: (3) expectations for assistance with a student who is exhibiting academic or behavioral learning problems: (4) availability of specific kinds of strategies and materials: (5) parents' demand for referral or opposition to referral: and (6) institutional factors which may facilitate or constrain teachers in making referral decisions. Fewer students are referred when school districts have complex procedures for referral, psychological assessments are backlogged for months, special education classes are filled to capacity, or principals and other administrators do not fully recognize the importance of special services.

It is important that referral procedures be clearly understood and coordinated among all school personnel. All educators need to be able to identify characteristics typically exhibited by special needs students. Also, the restrictiveness of special service settings must be known and the appropriateness of each clearly understood. The more restrictive special education programs tend to group students with similar disabilities for instruction. Last, the specialized services afforded through equipment, materials, teaching approaches, and specific teacher-student relations should be clearly understood.

Evaluation

If instructional modifications in the regular classroom have not proven successful, a student may be referred for multidisciplinary evaluation. The evaluation is comprehensive and includes norm and criterion-referenced tests (e.g. IQ and diagnostic tests), curriculum-based assessment, systematic teacher observation (e.g. behavior frequency checklist), samples of student work, and parent interviews. The results of the evaluation are twofold: to determined eligibility for special education services and to identify a student's strengths and weaknesses in order to plan an appropriate educational program

The wording in federal law is very explicit about the manner in which evaluations must be conducted, and about the existence of due process procedures that protect against bias and discrimination. Provisions in the law include the following as listed.

1. The testing of children in their native or primary language unless it is clearly not feasible to do so.
2. The use of evaluation procedures selected and administered to prevent cultural or ethnic discrimination.
3. The use of assessment tools validated for the purpose for which they are being used (e.g. achievement levels, IQ scores, adaptive skills).
4. Assessment by a multidisciplinary team utilizing several pieces of information to formulate a placement decision.

Furthermore, parental involvement must occur in the development of the child's educational program. According to the law, parents must:

1. Be notified before initial evaluation of any change in placement by a written notice in their primary language describing the proposed school action, the reasons for it, and the available educational opportunities.
2. Consent, in writing, before the child is initially evaluated.

Parents may:

1. Request an independent educational evaluation if they feel the school's evaluation is inappropriate.
2. Request an evaluation at public expense if a due process hearing decision is that the public agency's evaluation was inappropriate.
3. Participate on the committee that considers the evaluation, placement, and programming of the student.

All students referred for evaluation for special education should have on file the results of a relatively current vision and hearing screening. This will determine the adequacy of sensory acuity and ensure that learning problems are not due to a vision and/or hearing problem.

Eligibility

Eligibility is based on criteria defined in federal law or state regulations (see skill 1.2 for more information), which vary from state to state. Evaluation methods correspond with eligibility criteria for the special education classifications. For example, a multidisciplinary evaluation for a student being evaluated for intellectual disabilities would include the individual's intellectual functioning, adaptive behavior, and achievement levels. Other tests are based on developmental characteristics exhibited (e.g. social, language, and motor).

A student evaluated for learning disabilities is generally given reading, math, and/or spelling achievement tests, an intelligence test to confirm average or above average cognitive capabilities, and tests of written and oral language ability. Tests need to show a discrepancy between potential and performance. Classroom observations and samples of student work (such as impaired reading ability or impaired writing ability) also provide indicators of possible learning disabilities.

Eligibility for services in behavior disorders requires documented evidence of social deficiencies or learning deficits that are not due to intellectual, sensory, or physical conditions. Therefore, any student undergoing multidisciplinary evaluation for this categorical service is usually given an intelligence test, diagnostic achievement tests, and social and/or adaptive inventories. Results of behavior frequency lists, direct observations, and anecdotal records collected over an extended period often accompany test results.

Additional information frequently used when making decisions about a child's eligibility for special education include:

- Developmental history
- Past academic performance
- Medical history or records
- Neurological reports
- Classroom observations
- Speech and language evaluations
- Personality assessment
- Discipline reports
- Home visits
- Parent interviews
- Samples of student work

If considered eligible for special education services, the child's disability should be documented in a written report stating specific reasons for the decision.

See skill 2.1 for a brief explanation of RTI as a means of determining eligibility for services.

Three-year re-evaluations of a student's progress are required by law and serve the purpose of determining the growth and changing needs of the student. During the re-evaluation, continued eligibility for services in special education must be assessed using a range of evaluation tools similar to those used during the initial evaluation. All relevant information about the student is considered when making a decision about continued eligibility or whether the student no longer needs the service and is ready to begin preparing to exit the program. If the latter is transition, additional planning must occur.

Individual Education Plan

Before placement can occur, the multidisciplinary team must develop an Individualized Education Plan (IEP), a child-centered educational plan that is tailored to meet individual needs. IEPs acknowledge each student's requirement for a specially designed educational program. Three purposes are identified by Holloway, Patton, Payne, and Payne (1989):

1. IEPs outline instructional programs. They provide specific instructional direction, which eliminates any pulling together of marginally related instructional exercises.
2. IEPs function as the basis for evaluation
3. IEPs facilitate communication among staff members, teachers, and parents, and to some extent, teachers, and students.

Development of the IEP follows initial identification, evaluation, and classification. The educational plan is evaluated and rewritten at least annually.

Please refer to skill 10.3 for more information about IEPs.

Placement

The law defines special education and identifies related services that may be required if special education is to be effective. By law, placement in a special education delivery service must be the student's least restrictive environment. Special education services occur at a variety of levels, some more restrictive than others. The largest numbers of students (i.e. mild disabilities) are served in settings closest to normal educational placements. Service delivery in more restrictive settings is limited to students with severe or profound disabilities, who comprise a smaller population within special education. The exception is correctional facilities, which serve a limited and restricted populace.

Options for placement of special education students are given on what we call a "cascade of services," a term coined by Deno (1970). The multidisciplinary team must be able to match the needs of the student with an appropriate placement in the cascade system of services (see Figure 1-2). According to Polloway, et al. (1994), two assumptions are made when we place students using the cascade of services as a guide. First, a child should be placed in an educational setting as close to the regular classroom as possible, and placed only as far away from this least restrictive environment as necessary to provide an appropriate education.

Second, program exit should be a goal. A student's placement may change when the team obtains data suggesting the advisability of an alternative educational setting. As adaptive, social, cognitive, motor, and language skills are developed, the student may be placed in a less restrictive environment. The multidisciplinary team is responsible for monitoring and recommending placement changes when appropriate.

Figure 1-2 Cascade System of Special Education Services

Level 1	Regular classroom, including students with disabilities able to learn with regular class accommodations, with or without medical and counseling services.
Level 2	Regular classroom with supportive services (i.e. consultation, inclusion).
Level 3	Regular class with part-time special class (i.e. itinerant services, resource room).
Level 4	Full-time special class (i.e. self-contained).
Level 5	Special stations (i.e. special schools).
Level 6	Homebound
Level 7	Residential (i.e. hospital, institution)

SKILL 6.4 **Demonstrate knowledge of procedures, criteria, personnel, and functions associated with evaluations used to determine eligibility for special education and related services**

Please refer to Skill 6.3.

The special educator is trained to work in a team approach. This occurs from the initial identification of students who appear to deviate from what is considered normal performance or behavior for particular age- and grade-level students. The special education teacher serves as a consultant (or as a team member, depending on the school district) to the student support team. If the student is referred, the special education teacher may be asked to collect assessment data for the forthcoming comprehensive evaluation. This professional then generally serves on the multidisciplinary eligibility, individualized educational planning and placement committees. If the student is placed in a special education setting, the special educator continues to coordinate and collaborate with regular classroom teachers and support personnel at the school-based level.

Support professionals are available at both the district- and school-based levels, and they contribute valuable services and expertise in their respective areas. A team approach between district ancillary services and local school-based staff is essential.

1. **School psychologist.** The school psychologist participates in the referral, identification, and program planning processes. She contributes to the multidisciplinary team by adding important observations, data, and inferences about the student's performance. As she conducts an evaluation, she observes the student in the classroom environment, takes a case history, and administers a battery of formal and informal individual tests. The psychologist is involved as a member of a professional team throughout the stages of referral, assessment, placement, and program planning.
2. **Physical therapist.** This person works with disorders of bones, joints, muscles, and nerves following medical assessment. Under the prescription of a physician, the therapist applies treatment to the students in the form of heat, light, massage, and exercise to prevent further disability or deformity. Physical therapy includes the use of adaptive equipment, and prosthetic and orthotic devices to facilitate independent movement. This type of therapy helps individuals with disabilities to develop or recover their physical strength and endurance.
3. **Occupational therapist.** This specialist is trained in helping students develop self-help skills (e.g., self-care, motor, perceptual, and vocational skills). The students are actively involved in the treatment process to quicken recovery and rehabilitation.
4. **Speech and language pathologist.** This specialist assists in the identification and diagnosis of children with speech or language disorders. In addition, she makes referrals for medical or habilitation needs, counsels family members and teachers, and works with the prevention of communicative disorders. The speech and language therapist concentrates on rehabilitative service delivery and continuing diagnosis.

5. **Administrators.** Building principals and special education directors (or coordinators) provide logistical as well as emotional support. Principals implement building policy procedures and control designation of facilities, equipment, and materials. Their support is crucial to the success of the program within the parameters of the base school. Special education directors provide information about federal, state, and local policy which is vital to the operation of a special education unit. In some districts the special education director may actually control certain services and materials. Role clarification, preferably in writing, should be accomplished to ensure effectiveness of program services.

6. **Guidance counselors, diagnosticians and others.** These persons often lead individual and group counseling sessions, and are trained in assessment, diagnostic, and observation skills, as well as personality development and functioning abilities. They can apply knowledge and skills to multidisciplinary teams, and assist in the assessment, diagnosis, placement, and program planning process.

7. **Social worker.** The social worker is trained in interviewing and counseling skills. This person possesses knowledge of available community and school services, and makes these known to parents. She often visits homes of students, conducts intake and assessment interviews, counsels individuals and small groups, and assists in district enforcement policies.

8. **School nurse.** This person offers valuable information about diagnostic and treatment services. She is knowledgeable about diets, medications, therapeutic services, health-related services, and care needed for specific medical conditions. Reports of communicable diseases are filed with the health department to which a health professional has access. A medical professional can sometimes obtain cooperation with the families of children with disabilities in ways that are difficult for the special education teacher to achieve.

9. **Regular teachers and subject matter specialists.** These professionals are trained in general and specific instructional areas, teaching techniques, and overall child growth and development. They serve as a vital component to the referral process, as well as in the subsequent treatment program, if the student is determined eligible. They work with the students with special needs for the majority of the school day and function as a link to the children's special education and medical programs.

10. **Paraprofessional.** This staff member assists the special educator and often works in the classroom with the special needs students. She helps prepare specialized materials, tutors individual students, leads small groups, and provides feedback to students about their work.

SKILL 6.5 Understand factors in identifying students with exceptional learning needs, including those from culturally and linguistically diverse background

Please refer to skill 6.3 and the state website at

HTTP://WWW.SDE.STATE.OK.US/HOME/DEFAULTIE.HTML

SKILL 6.6 Understand procedures for using and maintaining ongoing assessment of students with mild/moderate disabilities

Assessment skills should be an integral part of teacher training, where teachers are able to monitor student learning using pre and post assessments of content areas; analyze assessment data in terms of individualized support for students and instructional practice for teachers; and designing lesson plans that have measurable outcomes and definitive learning standards. Assessment information should be used to provide performance-based criteria and academic expectations for all students in evaluating whether students have learned the expected skills and content of the subject area.

For example in an Algebra I class, teachers can use assessments to see whether students have learned the prior knowledge to engage in the subject area. If the teacher provides students with a pre-assessment on algebraic expression and ascertains whether the lesson plan should be modified to include a pre-algebraic expression lesson unit to refresh student understanding of the content area, then the teacher can create if needed, quantifiable data to support the need of additional resources to support student learning. Once the teacher has taught the unit on algebraic expression, a post assessment test can be used to test student learning and a mastery exam can be used to test how well students understand and can apply the knowledge to the next unit of math content learning.

Teachers can use assessment data to inform and impact instructional practices by making inferences on teaching methods and gathering clues for student performance. By analyzing the various types of assessments, teachers can gather more definitive information on projected student academic performance. Instructional strategies for teachers would provide learning targets for student behavior, cognitive thinking skills, and processing skills that can be employed to diversify student learning opportunities.

SKILL 6.7 Understand how to interpret assessment data to evaluate academic progress, revise IEPs and IFSPs, and modify programming for students with mild/moderate disabilities.

Results from norm-referenced tests compare the performance of an individual with the performance of other individuals possessing similar characteristics on the same test or measure. The content of norm-referenced tests reflects some area of the general curriculum, and is focused upon skill acquisition by age or grade level.

Norm-referenced tests are standardized on groups of individuals (also referred to as population samples of norm group) with scores derived from similar age and grade levels. These tests are designed to separate the performance of individuals so that there is a distribution of scores. Students are ranked in order, from those who have mastered many skills to those who have learned few.
In contrast, results from criterion-referenced tests give measures of progress made by individuals in learning specific skills in terms of level of mastery. The content of criterion-referenced tests is based on a specified set of objectives rather than on general curriculum content. Criterion-referenced testing provides measurements pertaining to the information a given student needs to know and the skills that student's need to master.

For purposes of screening or program evaluation, norm-referenced tests have a large advantage over criterion-referenced tests in that they provide a means of comparing a student's performance to the performance typically expected of others his age. Norm-referenced tests are also useful in making placement decisions.

When tests are administered for assisting the teacher in planning appropriate programs for children, criterion-referenced tests are recommended. When planning an individual education program (IEP), a teacher needs to be more concerned with identifying the specific and relevant behaviors that have been mastered. Items on criterion-referenced tests are often linked directly to specific instructional objectives. Therefore, this type of test assists with the writing of instructional objectives by enabling the teacher to determine the specific point at which to begin instruction, and to plan the instructional content that follows in sequence in the curriculum.

Formal tests can be norm- or criterion-referenced, or both, while informal tests are usually criterion-referenced. Norm-referenced tests are produced commercially, whereas criterion-referenced tests may be constructed by the teacher. Norm-referenced tests should always be standardized upon groups of individuals presumed to have similar acculturation to the group proposed to be tested. Both norm-referenced and criterion-referenced tests have predetermined answers and scoring standards.

In order to interpret results one must understand the terminology involved in assessments.

The following terms are frequently used in behavioral as well as academic testing and assessment. They represent basic terminology and not more advanced statistical concepts.

Baseline—(Also known as establishing a baseline) This procedure means collecting data about a target behavior or performance of a skill before certain interventions or teaching procedures are implemented. Establishing a baseline will enable a person to determine if the interventions are effective.

Criterion-Referenced Test – A test in which the individual's performance is measured against mastery of curriculum criteria rather than comparison to the performance of other students. Criterion-referenced tests may be commercially or teacher made. Since these tests measure what a student can or cannot do, results are especially useful for identifying goals and objectives for IEPs and lesson plans.

Curriculum-Based Assessment—Assessment of an individual's performance of objectives of a curriculum, such as a reading or math program. The individual's performance is measured in terms of what objectives were mastered.

Duration recording-- Measuring the length of time a behavior lasts (i.e. tantrums, time out of class, or crying).

Error Analysis—The mistakes on an individual's test are noted and categorized by type. For example, an error analysis in a reading test could categorize mistakes by miscues, substituting words, omitted words or phrases, and miscues that are self corrected.

Event recording—The number of times a target behavior occurs during an observation period.

Formal Assessment—Standardized tests have specific procedures for administration, norming, scoring and interpretation. These include intelligence and achievement tests.

Frequency—The number of times a behavior occurs in a time interval, such as out-of-seat behavior, hitting, and temper tantrums.

Frequency Distribution—Plotting the scores received on a test and tallying how many individuals received those scores. A frequency distribution is used to visually determine how the group of individuals performed on a test, illustrate extreme scores, and compare the distribution to the mean or other criterion.

Informal Assessment—Non-standardized tests such as criterion referenced tests and teacher-prepared tests. There are no rigid rules or procedures for administration or scoring.

Intensity—The degree of a behavior as measured by its frequency and duration.

Interval recording—This technique involves breaking the observation into an equal number of time intervals, such as 10-second intervals during a 5-minute period. At the end of each interval, the observer notes the presence or absence of the target behavior. The observer can then calculate a percentage by dividing the number of intervals in which the target behavior occurred by the total number of intervals in the observation period. This type of recording works well for behaviors that occur with high frequency or for long periods of time, such as on or off-task behavior, pencil tapping, or stereotyped behaviors. The observer does not have to constantly monitor the student, yet can gather enough data to get an accurate idea of the extent of the behavior.

Latency—The length of time that elapses between the presentation of a stimulus (e.g. a question), and the response (e.g. the student's answer).

Mean—The arithmetic average of a set of scores, calculated by adding the set of scores and dividing the sum by the number of scores. For example, if the sum of a set of 35 scores is 2935, dividing that sum by 35, (the number of scores), yields a mean of 83.9.

Median—The middle score: 50% of the scores are above this number and 50% of the scores are below this number. In the example above, if the middle score were 72, 17 students would have scored less than 72, and 17 students would have scored more than 72.

Mode: The score most frequently tallied in a frequency distribution. In the example above, the most frequently tallied score might be 78. It is possible for a set of scores to have more than one mode.

Momentary time sampling—This is a technique used for measuring behaviors of a group of individuals or several behaviors from the same individual. Time samples are usually brief, and may be conducted at fixed or variable intervals. The advantage of using variable intervals is increased reliability, as the students will not be able to predict when the time sample will be taken.

Norm-Referenced Test- An individual's performance is compared to the group that was used to calculate the performance standards in this standardized test. Some examples are the CTBS, WISC-R and Stanford-Binet.

Operational Definition-The description of a behavior and its measurable components. In behavioral observations, the description must be specific and measurable so that the observer will know exactly what constitutes instances and non-instances of the target behavior. Otherwise, reliability may be inaccurate.

Pinpoint- Specifying and describing the target behavior for change in measurable and precise terms. "On time for class" may be interpreted as arriving physically in the classroom when the tardy bell has finished ringing or it may mean being at the pencil sharpener or it may mean being in one's in seat and ready to begin work when the bell has finished ringing. Pinpointing the behavior makes it possible to accurately measure the behavior.

Profile-Plotting an individual's behavioral data on a graph.

Rate-The frequency of a behavior over a specified time period, such as 5 talk-outs during a 30-minute period, or typing 85 words per minute.

Raw Score-The number of correct responses on a test before they have been converted to standard scores. Raw scores are not meaningful because they have no basis of comparison to the performance of other individuals.

Reliability—The consistency (stability) of a test over time to measure what it is supposed to measure. Reliability is commonly measured in four ways:
- Test-retest method—The test is administered to the same group or individual after a short period of time and the results are compared.

- Alternate form (equivalent form)—measures reliability by using alternative forms to measure the same skills. If both forms are administered to the same group within a relatively short period of time, there should be a high correlation between the two sets of scores if the test has a high degree of reliability.
- Interrater—This refers to the degree of agreement between two or more individuals observing the same behaviors or observing the same tests.

- Internal reliability—is determined by statistical procedures or by correlating one-half of the test with the other half of the test.

Standard Deviation—The standard deviation is a statistical measure of the variability of the scores. The more closely the scores are clustered around the mean, the smaller the standard deviation will be.

Standard Error of Measurement—This statistic measures the amount of possible error in a score. If the standard error of measurement for a test is + or - 3, and the individual's score is 35, then, the actual score may be 32 to 35.

Standard Score—A derived score with a set mean, (usually 100) and a standard deviation. Examples are T-scores (mean of 50 and a standard deviation of 10), Z-scores (mean of 0 and standard deviation of 1), and scaled scores. Scaled scores may be given for age groups or grade levels. IQ scores, for instance, use a mean of 100 and a standard deviation of 15.

Task Analysis --Breaking an academic or behavioral task down into its sequence of steps. Task analysis is necessary when preparing criterion-referenced tests and performing error analysis. A task analysis for a student learning to do laundry might include:
1. Sort the clothes by type (white, permanent press, delicate)
2. Choose a type and select the correct water temperature and setting
3. If doing a partial load, adjust the water level
4. Measure the detergent
5. Turn on the machine
6. Load the clothes
7. Add bleach, fabric softener at the correct time
8. Wait for the machine to stop spinning completely before opening it
9. Remove the clothes from the machine and place in a dryer (A task analysis could be done for drying and folding as well)

Validity—The degree to which a test measures what it claims to measure, such as reading readiness, self-concept, or math achievement. A test may be highly reliable but it will be useless if it is not valid. There are several types of validity to examine when selecting or constructing an assessment instrument.

- Content –examines the question of whether the types of tasks in the test measure the skill or construct the test claims to measure. That is, a test, which claims to measure mastery in algebra, would probably not be valid if the majority of the items involved basic operations with fractions and decimals.
- Criterion – referenced validity involves comparing the test results with a valid criterion. For example, a doctoral student preparing a test to measure reading and spelling skills may check the test against an established test such as the WRAT-T or another valid criterion such as school grades.
- Predictive validity - refers to how well a test will relate to a future criterion level, such as the ability of a reading test administered to a first-grader to predict that student's performance at third or fifth grade.
- Concurrent validity – refers to how well the test relates to a criterion measure given at the same time. The test results are compared using statistical measures. The recommended coefficient is .80 or better.
- Construct validity – refers to the ability of the test to measure a theoretical construct, such as intelligence, self-concept, and other non-observable behaviors. Factor analysis and correlation studies with other instruments that measure the same construct are ways to determine construct validity.

Having the knowledge of interpreting and applying formal and informal assessment data is very important to deciding placement. An educator must have knowledge of interpreting formal and informal assessment data to assist him in determining some of those strengths and weaknesses.

Results of formal assessments are given in derived scores, which compare the student's raw score to the performance of a specified group of subjects. Criteria for the selection of the group may be based on characteristics such as age, sex, or geographic area. The test results of formal assessments must always be interpreted in light of what type of tasks the individual was required to perform. The most commonly used derived scores follow.

Age and Grade Equivalents are considered developmental scores because they attempt to convert the student's raw score into an average performance of a particular age or grade group.

 -**Age equivalents** are expressed in years and months, i.e. 7-3. In the standardization procedure, a mean is calculated for all individuals of the particular age who took the test. If the mean or median number of correct responses for children 7 years and 3 months were 80, then an individual whose raw score was 80 would be assigned an age-equivalent of 7 years and 3 months.

-**Grade Equivalents** are written as years and tenths of years, e.g., 6.2 would read sixth grade, second month. Grade equivalents are calculated on the average performance of the group, and have been criticized for their use to measure gains in academic achievement and to identify exceptional students.

-**Quartiles, Deciles, and Percentiles** indicate the percentage of scores that fall below the individual's raw score. Quartiles divide the score into four equal parts; the first quartile is the point at which 25% of the scores fall below, the full score. Deciles divide the distribution into ten equal parts; the seventh decile would mark the point below which 70% of the scores fall. Percentiles are the most frequently used, however. A percentile rank of 45 would indicate that the person's raw score was at the point below which 45% of the other scores fell.

B. Standard Scores are raw scores with the same mean (average) and standard deviation (variability of asset of scores). In the standardization of a test, about 68% of the scores will fall above or below 1 standard deviation of the mean of 100. About 96% of the scores will fall within the range of 2 standard deviations above or below the mean. A standard deviation of 20, for example, will mean that 68% of the scores will fall between 80 and 120, with 100 as the mean. The most common are T scores, z scores, stanines, and scaled scores. Standard scores are useful because they allow for direct comparison of raw scores from different individuals. In interpreting scores, it is important to note what type of standard score is being used.

C. Criterion Referenced Tests and Curriculum-based Assessments are interpreted on the basis of the individual's performance on the objectives being measured. Such assessments may be commercially prepared or teacher-made, and can be designed for a particular curriculum or a scope and sequence. These assessments are made by selecting objectives, task analyzing those objectives, and selecting measures to test the skills necessary to meet those tasks. Results are calculated for each objective, such as Cindy was able to divide 2-digit numbers by 1-digit numbers 85% of the time and was able to divide 2-digit numbers by 2-digit numbers 45% of the time. These tests are useful for gaining insight into the types of error patterns the student makes. Because the student's performance is not compared to others in a group, results are useful for writing IEPs as well as deciding what to teach.

COMPETENCY 7.0 UNDERSTAND PROCEDURES AND CRITERIA FOR ASSESSING THE COMMUNICATIVE STRENGTHS AND NEEDS OF STUDENTS WITH MILD/MODERATE DISABILITIES.

SKILL 7.1 Demonstrate knowledge of types and characteristics of formal and informal assessments of expressive and receptive language

When a child is demonstrating difficulty with receptive (understanding) language or expressive (speaking or otherwise communicating) language an assessment of his strengths and weaknesses and resulting educational needs may be done informally or formally. Informal language assessments may be used as part of the district's regular screening process. For example, every child entering kindergarten may be routinely screened by the speech and language pathologist to determine which students may need to be referred on for more formal assessments.

For initial placement in services for language (such as services with a Speech and Language Pathologist, SLP, or in a special education program that focuses on language) a formal assessment will be done. Components of a formal language assessment may be completed by a psychologist. In cases where language is a significant component, the assessment would be completed by the SLP.

Components of a language assessment could include the following:

- Vocabulary
- Concepts
- Expression of wants and needs
- Use of words, phrases, and complete sentences
- Length of utterance
- Ability to follow single step directions
- Ability to follow multiple step directions
- Ability to list the steps needed to complete a task
- Ability to answer simple *yes/no* questions
- Ability to answer simple *Wh* questions
- Ability to answer questions involving inference or cause/effect
- Ability to carry on basic conversation

In each instance, the student would be assessed on his ability to understand (receptive) and to use the language through self-initiated communication or by answering a question (expressive). For example, consider the following.

Teacher: *Where is the ball?* (Student must understand – receptive language- what is being asked.)

Student: *Under.* (Expressive language that shows concept of where, but does not give indication of the child's ability to use the concept in extended language such as a phrase or complete sentence.)

Informal assessment of the student's expressive and receptive language may be done in the classroom with the psychologist, speech and language pathologist, teacher or assistant, charting or keeping a written log of communication. This gives valuable information about how the student uses language in his natural educational setting. If difficulty with language is noted, the student will probably also be pulled for a more formal evaluation outside of the classroom.

Commonly used tests for evaluation of language:

- REEL – The Receptive-Expressive Emergent Language Test is designed to identify language difficulty in infants and toddlers (birth through age three).
- PPVT – The Peabody Picture Vocabulary Test is often used to assess a student's vocabulary. The student is presented with a field of four pictures and is told a word. He must then point to the correct picture.
- TOLD – The Test of Language Development is available in a primary test and an intermediate test. The TOLD has nine subtests: *Picture Vocabulary, Relational Vocabulary, Oral Vocabulary, Grammatic Understanding, Sentence Imitation, Grammatic Completion, Word Articulation, Phonemic Analysis, and Word Discrimination.*

SKILL 7.2 Understand how to use assessment results to guide instruction in communication skills

The results of informal and formal language testing assist the IEP team in planning an appropriate special education program. The resulting instruction may take place in a therapy setting with a speech and language pathologist or a social worker. It may occur in the special education classroom or in the inclusion classroom. Parents will be asked to practice carryover skills at home. Any member of the educational team may be asked to reinforce or monitor skills once the student reaches a certain level of competence/mastery. Consider the following communication-needs cases.

Example 1: Sara is unable to use words to communicate basic wants and needs due to a physical impairment. She may be taught to use an augmentative device to communicate. This device may be a communication board with four picture choices which Sara pushes to communicate. Different picture templates may be used in different situations. For example, there may be a template for snack time which includes pictures of crackers, pudding, juice, and water. The template for free time may include movie, computer, swing, or book.

Example 2: Jason has difficulty participating in basic social conversations because of Asperger's syndrome. He does not face the speaker in conversations and does not show interest in what is happening with other people. Jason may be a part of a social language group with a speech and language pathologist or with a social worker to practice these conversational skills. He will also be encouraged and later expected to use the learned skills in other school settings such as the special education or inclusion classroom, at lunch, or on the playground, etc.

Example 3: Isabelle had a low score for grammatical understanding. This is also evidenced in her fourth grade science class where she has difficulty answering verbal and written questions on the presented lessons. Isabelle sees the resource teacher for reading and language. In those subjects, considerable emphasis is placed on understanding what the question is asking, finding information in print text, and saying or writing an appropriate answer. In the inclusion setting, Isabelle is monitored and prompted as needed to use the same skills to answer science questions.

SKILL 7.3 Understand how to interpret and communicate the results of assessments of communicative functioning

The special educator should be knowledgeable of the components of receptive and expressive language evaluation as outlined in skill 7.1. She should be able to explain how these may be manifested in the school and home setting. Because communication includes a wide range of sequential skills in the receptive and expressive areas, the special educator has the task of understanding the student's educational needs in the area of communication.

With test results, classroom observation, and knowledge of the sequence of language development, the special educator (often in conjunction with the speech language pathologist, social worker, or technology consultant) will formulate possible IEP goals and objectives based on the student's individual needs. The special educator will communicate ways that other school staff and parents can assist in developing/practicing those language skills with the student.

For example, the student may be lacking in basic vocabulary (naming of objects). Because of this he is unable to communicate his basic wants and needs at home and at school. The special educator must be able to explain that the child needs a way to communicate those needs (reducing frustration and tantrums) while increasing his ability to use words for communication. The child may be given a picture card of two items that he may point to tell his parents what he wants (blanket or juice). As the parent gets the cup of juice, she will reinforce the word juice by saying it. Later, the child will be encouraged to say the word to express his request.

When explaining the language needs and programming for a student, the special educator should differentiate between the receptive and expressive components of language skills. Receptive language at any given level *always* precedes expressive language as it is impossible to communicate (expressive) what one does not yet understand (receptive).

The special educator should also be able to explain the manner in which the child's disability will impact language. For example, a deaf child will not hear language incidentally as he enters the classroom, plays on the playground, and even watches TV at home. For this reason, each sequential step of language development (i.e. sentence structures) must be isolated, taught, and then expected to be used in communication (first receptively and then expressively).

In the case of the child with a cognitive impairment, language is understood at a very basic, concrete level. The special educator's task is to explain that idioms (for example) must be taught. If someone says that it is raining cats and dogs, it is likely that the child may look to see if that is indeed the case. The educator, therapist, or parent can introduce the idiom by saying: *It is raining hard! It is raining cats and dogs – not real cats and dogs. I mean it is raining hard. We say it is raining cats and dogs.*

The more clearly parents and other educational team members understand the specific students level of language functioning and ideas for remediation and practice, the more successful the special education program will be. Often special educators use the following ways to communicate language skills that are currently being taught: email, newsletter, passbook between parent and school, phone call, or language practice folder.

COMPETENCY 8.0 UNDERSTAND PROCEDURES AND CRITERIA FOR ASSESSING THE COGNITIVE AND ACADEMIC STRENGTHS AND NEEDS OF STUDENTS WITH MILD/MODERATE DISABILITIES.

SKILL 8.1 Demonstrate knowledge of types and characteristics of formal and informal assessments of cognitive functioning and academic achievement

Please refer to Skill 6.1.

SKILL 8.2 Understand how to use assessment results to meet students' cognitive and academic needs (e.g., identifying learning styles, selecting appropriate instructional materials)

The assessment information gathered from various sources is key to identifying the strengths and the weaknesses of the student. Each test and each person will have something to offer about the child, therefore increasing the possibility of creating a well-developed plan to assist in the success of the student. The special education and general education teacher along with other professionals will use the assessment data to make appropriate instructional decisions and to modify the learning environment that it is conducive to learning.

The information gathered can be used to make some of the following instructional decisions:

I **Classroom Organization:** The teacher can vary grouping arrangements (e.g. large group, small group, peer tutoring, or learning centers) and methods of instruction (teacher directed, student directed)

II **Classroom Management:** The teacher can vary grading systems, reinforcement systems, and rules (differentiate for some students).

III **Methods of Presentation:** Variation of methods include--
   A. Content: Amount to be learned, time to learn, and concept level
   B. General Structure: advance organizers, immediate feedback, memory devices, and active involvement of students.
   C. Type of presentation: verbal or written, transparencies, audiovisual

IV **Methods of Practice:**
   A. General Structure: amount to be practiced, time to finish, group, individual or teacher-directed, and, varied level of difficulty
   B. Level of response: copying, recognition, or recall with and without cues
   C. Types of materials: worksheets, audiovisual, texts

V **Methods of Testing:**
  A   Type: verbal, written, or demonstration
  B. General Structure: time to complete, amount to complete, group or individual testing
  C. Level of response: multiple choice, essay, recall of facts

Instructional Decisions:

PRESENTATION OF SUBJECT MATTER

Subject Matter should be presented in a fashion that helps students <u>organize, understand,</u> and <u>remember</u> important information. Advance organizers and other instructional devices can help students to:

- Connect information to what is already known
- Make abstract ideas more concrete
- Capture students' interest in the material
- Help students to organize the information and visualize the relationships.

Organizers can be visual aids such as diagrams, tables, charts, guides, or verbal cues that alert students to the nature and content of the lesson. Organizers may be used:

- **Before the lesson** to alert the student to the main point of the lesson, establish a rationale for learning, and activate background information.
- **During the lesson** to help students organize information, keep focused on important points, and aid comprehension.
- **At the close of the lesson** to summarize and remember important points.

Examples of organizers include:

- Question and graphic-oriented study guides.
- Concept diagramming: students brainstorm a concept and organize information into three lists (always present, sometimes present, and never present).
- Semantic feature analysis: students construct a table with examples of the concept in one column and important features or characteristics in the column opposite.
- Semantic webbing: The concept is placed in the middle of the chart or chalkboard and relevant information is placed around it. Lines show the relationships.
- Memory (mnemonic) devices. Diagrams, charts, and tables.

See also Skill 6.3.

SKILL 8.3 Understand how to interpret and communicate the results of assessments of cognitive functioning and academic achievement

Please refer also to Skill 6.7.

ABILITY TO INTERPRET TEST RESULTS INTO LAYMAN'S TERMS

The special educator must be able to communicate assessment results into understandable language for a variety of individuals. These individuals may include parents or guardians, paraprofessionals, professionals in general education, administration, and (in the case of older students) even the student himself.

A review of assessment and evaluation results may be done during an IEP meeting in which the formal test lingo is used but paired with an interpretation in layman's terms. Results may also be done in the form of a written report.

ABILITY TO REPRESENT TEST RESULTS AND EDUCATIONAL IMPLICATIONS IN WRITTEN FORMAT

Although the school psychologist most often completes student evaluations and writes a report, this may sometimes be the task of the special educator. In the case of annual reviews, the special education teacher will be asked to write a report summarizing assessment findings and educational implications. The teacher should be able to organize the data in a concise, readable format. Some components of such a report include:

- Identifying information (student name, age, date of birth, address, gender)
- Reason for Assessment
- Test administration information (date, time, duration of test, response of student)
- Test results
- Summary of Educational Recommendations

COMPETENCY 9.0 UNDERSTAND PROCEDURES AND CRITERIA FOR ASSESSING THE SOCIAL AND ADAPTIVE BEHAVIOR OF STUDENTS WITH MILD/MODERATE DISABILITIES

SKILL 9.1 Understand types and characteristics of formal and informal assessments of social skills and adaptive behavior

"Adaptive behavior has been defined by the American Association on Mental Deficiency (Grossman, 1973) as behavior that is effective in meeting the natural and social demands of one's environment." (Sattler, 1982, p. 308). Assessment in adaptive behavior focuses upon two main premises: (1) the extent to which an individual is able to function and maintain independence, and (2) the degree to which this person satisfactorily meets society's demands within his or her environment. In brief, adaptive behavior reflects the functional ability of the individual to exercise personal independence and social responsibility. It is a measure of personal and social competence.

Adaptive behavior is so encompassing that it is impossible for any one scale to measure all of the relevant domains. Adaptive behavior scales (e.g. Vineland Social Maturity Scale, AAMD Adaptive Behavior Scale) have been designed to provide information about individuals, particularly those who score in the sub-average intellectual range on intelligence tests, that is helpful in making decisions about qualifications, placement, and treatments. Adaptive behavior is considered a compilation of complex personal, social, cognitive, and situational variables. Therefore, caution is given in the use of a sole adaptive behavioral scale in evaluating an individual's adaptive abilities. In addition, consideration must be given to the societal and parental expectations that are active in the person's environment.

The assessment of adaptive behavior is typically performed by interviewing significant adults (i.e. parent, teacher) who know the child. Adaptive rating scales are somewhat subjective because behaviors may be viewed differently by differing persons, and the judgments the informants are required to make about the child's functioning may be subject to bias.

Other uses for adaptive behavior scales include: (1) using scale items as criterion-referenced items in educational planning: (2) identifying behavioral strengths and weaknesses; (3) comparing an individual's ratings over time in order to plot progress or evaluate the effectiveness of a program: (4) comparing ratings on the same individual in different situations (e.g. between societal institutions like home and school, within school settings, and so on: (5) comparing the ratings of different raters: (6) providing a standardized reporting system between and within organizations: and (7) stimulating the design and implementation of new training programs. (Sattler, 1982)

SKILL 9.2 Demonstrate knowledge of procedures for conducting different types of adaptive behavior assessments

Adaptive behavior refers to the knowledge, behavior, and daily living skills that are required to function effectively and independently in a number of different settings.

Adaptive behaviors commonly include communication and social, daily living, personal care, and other skills that are needed to function at home, school, and in the community.

Adaptive behavior measurement is important for pinpointing specific areas that need to be taught or further developed. Most students acquire adaptive behavior skills through practical experiences. Students with disabilities may need direct instruction in order to acquire them.

Measurement of adaptive behaviors should take into account the student's behavior in a number of settings including the classroom, school, home, and neighborhood. In order to get an accurate assessment, the adaptive behavior should be measured by a variety of different people in different settings.

The primary method of measuring adaptive behavior is via structured interviews with teachers and parents. A person trained to administer an adaptive behavior rating scale, such as a school counselor, interviews the student's parents and teachers. The responses are recorded on a rating scale that assesses the student's skills and abilities in various settings. The information obtained from the interview is more valid when the people being interviewed are familiar with the student. It is important that parents and teachers provide the most accurate and objective assessment as possible.

Additional methods of measuring adaptive behavior include analyzing the student's records from schools, observing the student in specific circumstances, and testing the student's skills by giving him specific tasks to complete.

The rating scales are created to address the following areas:
- Communication—communicating with others, talking, writing
- Self-care—toileting, eating, dressing, hygiene, and grooming
- Home-living—clothing care, housekeeping, property maintenance, food preparation and cooking, planning and budgeting for shopping
- Social—getting along with others in social situations, interacting with others, forming relationships
- Community use—travel within community, shopping, obtaining services in community (doctor, dentist, setting up utilities), public transportation
- Self-direction—making choices in allocation of time and effort, following a schedule, seeking assistance, deciding what to do in new situations

- Health and safety—making choices about what to eat, illness identification and treatment, avoiding danger, and relationships
- Functional academics—skills taught in school that are used every day including reading, writing, computation, telling time, and using numbers
- Leisure—using available time when not working or in school, choosing age-appropriate activities
- Work—employment skills, including work related attitudes and social behaviors, completion of tasks, and persistent effort.

Some of the most common adaptive behavior instruments include the following:

Measure	Format	Useful Derived Information
American Association of Mental Retardation (AAMR) 1993	Rating scale or interview	Factor scores of Personal, Social, and Community plus 2 Maladaptive Domains
Adaptive Behavior Assessment System – second edition 2003– school, parent, and adult forms	Multiple formats including rating scale, interview, and self report for adults; multiple formats encouraged	Composite, plus scores in 10 adaptive skills areas.
Comprehensive Test of Adaptive Behavior (Revised 2000)	Rating scale with behavioral composite plus "tests" that are used if the behavior has not been observed	7 domains, self-help, home, independence, social, sensory, motor, and language/academic
Scales of Independent Behavior – Revised (1996)	Highly structured interview conducted by professional or paraprofessional.	Composite plus motor, social interaction and communication, personal living, and community living; maladaptive behaviors included
Vineland Adaptive Behavior Scales (1984)	Semi-structured interview requiring well-trained professional; school form uses a rating scale format.	Composite plus Communication, Daily Living, Motor (0-6 yrs), and Socialization. No maladaptive behavior content

DEMONSTRATE UNDERSTANDING OF THE DEVELOPMENT AND USE OF A TASK ANALYSIS

After completing an adaptive behavior scale, it is important to look specifically at the skills which are shown at a deficit level for the student and complete a task analysis. This task analysis can then be used to provide IEP goals and objectives in order to have the deficit areas become part of the student's instructional content.

A teacher can use the set of behavioral specifications that are the result of the task analysis to prepare tests that will measure the student's ability to meet those specifications. These tests are referred to as criterion measurements. If task analysis identifies which skills will be needed to perform a task successfully, then the criterion measurements will further identify whether the student possesses the necessary skills or knowledge for that task. The level of performance that is acceptable is the "criterion level."

Criterion measurements must be developed along certain guidelines if they are to accurately measure a task and its sub-areas. Johnson and Morasky (1977) give the following guidelines for establishing criterion measurement:

1. Criterion measurement must directly evaluate a student's ability to perform a task.
2. Criterion measurements should cover the range of possible situations in order to be considered an adequate measure.
3. Criterion measurements should measure whether or not a student can perform the task without additional or outside assistance. They should not give any information that the student is expected to possess.
4. All responses in the criterion measurement should be relevant to the task being measured.

Behavioral objectives offer descriptive statements defining the task that the student will perform, state the conditions under which the task will occur, and show the criterion measurement required for mastery. The criterion measurement is the process for evaluating what the student can do. For the instruction to be meaningful there must be a precise correspondence between the capabilities determined in a criterion measurement and the behavioral demands of the objective.

Learning should be logically sequenced, presenting lower order skills and concepts before moving on to higher order or more complex ones. By considering the structure of the task to be learned and using task analysis to specify the sub-skills and concepts necessary for reaching the goal, or target behavior, a learning hierarchy can be developed. Successful learning depends on presentation in a logically sequenced curriculum.

Task sequences may be forward chained or backward chained. Backward chaining is called descending task analysis, because it begins with a target task, the terminal behavior and works backwards to prerequisite sub-skills. Descending task analysis works backward to subsidiary tasks on the theory that the successful mastery of those easier skills that precede them in the learning hierarchy is more effective

In forward chaining or ascending task analysis, the teacher initiates instruction on the first sub-skill of a task sequence. Once the designated criterion mastery is reached, instruction continues on the next sub-skill, linking it to the previously mastered response that now serves as a prerequisite. More complex ones in the learning hierarchy are introduced, as preceding ones are mastered.

Effectiveness of instruction is linked to the teacher's ability to know when mastery criterion has been reached on each one in ascending order. If instruction begins before mastery of a lower level skill is achieved, performance gaps will weaken the chances of that student reaching the target task, or terminal behavior. Too slow a pace creates boredom and may lessen the student's enthusiasm for progressing through subsequent steps. Therefore, successful learning depends not only on presentation of skills in a logically sequenced learning hierarchy, but also upon the responsiveness to criteria mastery and appropriate movement through levels of difficulty.

Figure 6-1 Descending Task Analysis

TEACHER DOES	TEACHER ASKS
Step 1 Statement of Target Task	Is it significant? Is it relevant?
Step II Statement of Sub-Skills SA SB SC etc.	Are these sub-skills necessary for performing target tasks? Are these sub-skills sufficient for performing target tasks? Are these sub-skills relevant for performing target tasks? Are there any missing or redundant sub-skills? Can the child perform any of these tasks?
Step III Statement of Sub-Skills SA SB SC etc SSA SSAA SSB SSBB SSC SSCC	Are these sub-skills necessary for performing target tasks? Are these sub-skills sufficient for performing target tasks? Are these sub-skills relevant for performing target tasks? Are there any missing or redundant sub-skills? Can the child perform any of these tasks?

Please also refer to skill 6.7 for more information.

SKILL 9.3   Understand how to interpret and communicate the results of assessments of adaptive behavior and social skills

Please refer to Skill 6.7.

COMPETENCY 10.0 UNDERSTAND PROCEDURES FOR DEVELOPING AND IMPLEMENTING INDIVIDUALIZED EDUCATION PROGRAMS (IEPS) AND INDIVIDUALIZED FAMILY SERVICE PLANS (IFSPS) FOR STUDENTS WITH MILD/MODERATE DISABILITIES.

SKILL 10.1 Understand roles and functions of members of IEP and IFSP teams

According to IDEA 2004, the IEP/IFSP team includes: the parents of a child with a disability; not less than one regular education teacher of such child (if the child is, or may be, participating in the regular education environment); not less than one special education teacher, or where appropriate, not less than one special education provider of such child; a representative of the local educational agency; an individual who can interpret the instructional implications of evaluation results; at the discretion of the parent of the agency, other individuals who have knowledge or special expertise regarding the child, including related services personnel as appropriate; and whenever appropriate, the child with a disability.

The role of the representative of the local education agency is to provide or supervise the provision of specifically designed instruction to meet the unique needs of the child. This is usually the school principal if this is the first time the child has been evaluated. If the representative is not an expert on evaluations, then one of the people who participated in the actual testing of the child must be present.

The role of the teacher is to identify the short and long term goals for the student and to give the student's current progress including strengths and weaknesses. The school must allow any other individual whom the parent wants to invite to attend the meeting. This may be a caseworker involved with the student's family, people involved with the day-to-day care of the student or any person whom the parent feels can contribute vital information to the meeting.

The parent or guardian can also bring someone to help them understand the IEP/IFSP or the process, such as a lawyer experienced with educational advocacy or parent advocate.

There are lists of related services that may be considered during an IEP meeting. The related services are developmental, corrective, and other supportive services that are required to help a child with special needs benefit from special education. These related services can include speech pathology and audiological, psychological services, physical and occupational therapy, recreation and extracurricular activities, counseling services, and medical services for diagnostic or evaluation purposes.

The IEP should specify the services to be provided, the extent to which they are necessary, and who will provide the services. If a specialist such as a speech teacher or occupational therapist will provide specific services, they should be included in the IEP team so they can give input on the types of services required, available, and what may be beneficial to the student in question. Information on how they are doing in particular specialist areas will also be included with an evaluation of student progress with speech therapy and occupational therapy.

SKILL 10.2 Recognize components of a comprehensive evaluation used to determine eligibility for early intervention or special education services

Although skill 6.3's section on evaluation is quite helpful in answering this skill, for state specific information please refer to:

HTTP://WWW.SDE.STATE.OK.US/HOME/DEFAULTIE.HTML

SKILL 10.3 Demonstrate knowledge of factors and procedures in gathering information, creating and maintaining records, developing IEPs and IFSPs, monitoring progress, and planning transitions from one setting or service delivery system to another

INDIVIDUALIZED EDUCATION PROGRAMS

It is important to understand how much the law effects the required components of the IEP/IFSP. Educators must keep themselves apprised of the changes and amendments to laws such as IDEA and the required manner in which it must be completed. At present the following elements are required of an IEP/IFSP:

1. The student's present level of academic performance and functional performance.

2. A statement of how the disability affects the student's involvement and progress in the general education curriculum. Preschool children must have a statement explaining how the disability effects the child's participation in appropriate activities (IFSP).

3. A statement of annual goals, or anticipated attainments.

4. Short-term objectives are no longer required on every IEP. Students with severe disabilities or those taking an alternative assessment may need short- term objectives, which lead to the obtainment of annual goals.

5. A statement of when the parent will be notified of their child's progress which must be at least as often as the regular education student.

6. Modifications or accommodations for participation in statewide or citywide assessments; or if it is determined that the child cannot participate, why the assessment is inappropriate for the child and how the child will be assessed.

7. Specific educational services, assistive technology, and related services, to be provided, and those who will provide them.

8. Evaluate criteria and timeliness for determining whether instructional objectives have been achieved.

9. Projected dates for initiating services with their anticipated frequency, location and, duration.

10. The extent to which the child will not participate in the regular education program.

11. Transition

    i. Beginning when a student is 14, and annually thereafter, the student's IEP must contain a statement of his or her transition service needs under the various components of the IEP that focus upon the student's courses of study (e.g., vocational education or advanced placement); and when appropriate include interagency responsibilities and links for possible future assistance.
    ii. Beginning at least one year before the student reaches the age of majority under state law, the IEP must contain a statement that the student has been informed of the rights under the law that will transfer to him or her upon reaching the age of majority.

TRANSITION PLANNING

Transition services will be different for each student. They must take into account the student's interests and preferences. An evaluation of career interests, aptitudes, necessary and obtained skills, and training may be considered.

The transition activities that have to be addressed, unless the IEP team finds it uncalled for, are:

1. Instruction – The instruction part of the transition plan deals with school instruction. The student should have a portfolio completed upon graduation. They should research and plan for further education and/or training after high school. Education can be in a college setting, technical school, or vocational center. Goals and objectives created for this transition domain depend upon the nature and severity of the student's disability, the students interests in further education, plans made for accommodations needed in future education and training, identification of post-secondary institutions that offer the requested training or education.
2. Community experiences – this part of the transition plan investigates how the student utilizes community resources. Resources entail places for recreation, transportation services, agencies, and advocacy services. It is essential for students to deal with the following areas:
    - Recreation and leisure - examples: movies, YMCA, religious activities.
    - Personal and social skills - examples: calling friends, religious groups, going out to eat.
    - Mobility and transportation - examples: passing a driver's license test or utilizing Dial-A-Ride.
    - Agency access - examples: utilizing a phone book and making calls.
    - System advocacy- example: have a list of advocacy groups to contact.
    - Citizenship and legal issues - example: registering to vote.
3. Development of employment -This segment of the transition plan investigates becoming employed. Students should complete a career interest inventory. They should have chances to investigate different careers. Many work skill activities can take place within the classroom, home, and community. Classroom activities may concentrate on employability, community skills ,mobility, and vocational training. Home and neighborhood activities may concentrate on personal responsibility and daily chores. Community based activities may focus on part-time work after school and in the summer, cooperative education or work-study, individualized vocational training, and volunteer work.

4. <u>Daily living skills</u> – This segment of the transition plan is also important although not essential to the IEP. Living away from home can be an enormous undertaking for people with disabilities. Numerous skills are needed to live and function as an adult. In order to live as independently as possible, a person should have an income, know how to cook, clean, shop, pay bills, get to a job, and have a social life. Some living situations may entail independent living, shared living with a roommate, supported living or group homes. Areas that may need to be looked into include: personal and social skills; living options; income and finances; medical needs; community resources and transportation.

REQUIREMENTS FOR CREATING AND MAINTAINING RECORDS AND PRESERVING CONFIDENTIALITY

One of the most important professional practices a teacher must maintain is student confidentiality. This extends far beyond paper records, and goes into the realm of oral discussions. Teachers are expected not to mention the names of students and often the specifics of their character in conversations with those who are not directly involved with them, inside and outside of school.

In the school environment, teacher record keeping comes in three main formats with specific confidentiality rules. All of the records stated below should be kept in a locked place within the classroom or an office within the school:

1) *Teacher's personal notes on a student.*

When a teacher takes notes on a student's actions including behaviors and/or grade performance that are not intended to be placed in a school recorded format, such as a report card, the teacher may keep this information private and confidential to his/her own files. Teachers may elect to share this information or not.

2) *Teacher daily recorded grades and attendance of the student.*

Teacher's grade books and attendance records are to be open to the parent/guardian of that child who wishes to check on their child. Only that child's information may be shared not that of others.

3) *Teacher recorded/notation on records that appear in the student cumulative file.*

There are specific rules regarding the sharing of the cumulative records of students.

- a) Cumulative files will follow a student that transfers within the school district and from school to school.
- b) All information placed in a cumulative file may be examined by a parent at any time it is requested. If a parent shows up to review their child's cumulative file, the file should be shown as it is in its current state. (This includes IEPs.)
- c) When information from a cumulative file is requested by another person/entity outside of the parent/guardian, the information may not be released without the express written consent of the parent/guardian. The parental consent must specify which records may be shared with the other party of interest.
- d) A school which a student may intend to enroll may receive the student's educational record without parental consent. However, the school sending that information must make a reasonable attempt to notify the parent/guardian of the request. (FERPA)

Today's world is quickly becoming a digital environment. Teacher's now communicate often with Email and are keeping records in digital formats, often within a district mandated program. Teachers should keep in mind that Emails and other electronic formats can be forwarded and are as "indelible" as permanent ink and should maintain a professional decorum just as when they are writing their own records that will be seen outside of their personal notations.

SKILL 10.4 Demonstrate awareness of how cultural diversity and linguistic differences may affect evaluation and placement decisions in special education

Please refer to Skills 6.2 and 10.2.

FAIR ASSESSMENT PRACTICES

The issue of fair assessment for individuals from minority groups has a long history in the law, philosophy, and education. Slavia and Ysseldyke, 1995 point out three aspects of this issue that is particularly relevant to the assessment of students.

1. **Representation** - Individuals from diverse backgrounds need to be represented in assessment materials. It is essential that persons from different cultures be represented fairly. Of equal importance is the presentation of individuals from differing genders in non-stereotypical roles and situations.

2. **Acculturation** - It is important that individuals from different backgrounds receive opportunities to acquire the tested skills, information, and values. When students are tested with standardization instruments, they are compared to a set of norms in order to gain an index of their relative standing, and to make comparisons. We assume that the students tested are similar to those on whom the test was standardized. That is, it is assume that their acculturation is comparable. Acculturation is a matter of educational, socioeconomic, and experiential background rather than of gender, skin color, race, or ethnic background. When it is said that a child's acculturation differs from that of the group used as a norm, what is really meant is that the experiential background differed, not simply that the child is of a different ethnic origin (Slavia & Ysseldyke, 1991). Differences in experiential background should therefore be accounted for when administering tests.

3. **Language** - The language and concepts that comprise test items should be unbiased. Students should be familiar with terminology and references to which the language is being made when they are administered tests, especially when the results of the tests are going to be used for decision- making purposes. Many tests given in regular grades relate to decisions about promotion and grouping of students for instructional purposes. Tests and other assessment instruments that relate to special education are generally concerned with two types of decisions: (1) eligibility, and (2) program planning for individualized education.

SKILL 10.5 Understand issues, assurances, and due process rights related to assessment, eligibility, and placement within a continuum of services

LEAST RESTRICTIVE ENVIRONMENT

A continuum of educational services (Please refer to the continuum of services table in skill 6.3) must be made available by the LEA. Children must be placed in their least restrictive environment and, insofar as possible, with regular classmates.

Placement decisions must be made based upon the student's IEP, and the stipulated goals and objectives must be reviewed and rewritten on an annual basis. Thus, progress revisions may suggest the need for a change in placement to a less (or more) restrictive environment.

All individuals with disabilities should participate in academic and non-academic (i.e. extracurricular) services to the maximum extent appropriate, considering the individual needs of the child. If skills (e.g. self-help, social, physical education) need to be acquired by a youngster with disabilities in order to participate successfully in these services or activities, then the skills should be included as goals or objectives in the student's IEP.

DUE PROCESS

"Due process is a set of procedures designed to ensure the fairness of educational decisions and the accountability of both professionals and parents in making these decisions" (Kirk and Gallagher, 1986, p. 24). These procedures serve as a mechanism by which the child and his family can voice their opinions or concerns, and sometimes dissents. Due process safeguards exist in all matters pertaining to identification, evaluation, and educational placement.

Due process occurs in two realms, substantive and procedural. Substantive due process is the content of the law (e.g. appropriate placement for special education students). Procedural due process is the form through which substantive due process is carried out (.e. parental permission for testing). The federal law provides many specific aspects of due process with which to be aware including:

1. A due process hearing may be initiated by parents of the LEA as an impartial forum for challenging decisions about identification, evaluation, or placement. Either party may present evidence, cross-examine witnesses, obtain a record of the hearing, and be advised by counsel or by individuals having expertise in the education of individuals with disabilities. Findings may be appealed to the State Education Agency (SEA) and if still dissatisfied, either party may bring civil action in Federal District Court. Hearing timelines are set by legislation.
2. Parents may obtain an independent evaluation if there is disagreement about the education evaluation performed by the LEA. The results of such an evaluation:
   a. Must be considered in any decision made with respect to the provision of a free, appropriate public education for the child
   b. May be presented as evidence at a hearing.
   c. Further, the parents may request this evaluation at public expense:
      i. If a hearing officer requests an independent educational evaluation
      ii. If the decision from a due process hearing is that the LEA's evaluation was inappropriate. If the final decision holds, the evaluation performed is appropriate, the parent still has the right to an independent educational evaluation, but not at public expense.
3. Written notice must be provided to parents prior to a proposal or refusal to initiate or make a change in the child's identification, evaluation, or educational placement.
   a. A listing of parental due process safeguards.
   b. A description and a rationale for the chosen action.
   c. A detailed listing of components (e.g. tests, records, reports) which was the basis for the decision.
   d. Assurance that the language and content of notices were understood by the parents.
4. Parental consent must be obtained before evaluation procedures can occur, unless there is a state law specifying otherwise.
5. Sometimes parents or guardians cannot be identified to function in the due process role. When this occurs, a suitable person must be assigned to act as a surrogate. This is done by the LEA in full accordance with legislation.

PARENTAL PARTICIPATION

The involvement of parents, though included directly or indirectly in other major provisions (i.e. principles) under Public Law 94-142 (and subsequent reauthorizations of said special education law), is presented as a separate category. Parental participation specific to this section assures access to educational records and participation in developing educational policy.

The Family Educational Rights and Privacy Act (1974), also known as the Buckley Amendment, assures confidentiality of student records. Parents are afforded the right to examine, review, request changes in information deemed inaccurate, and stipulate persons who might access their child's records.

The development and approval of educational policy is another means for involving parents. Membership on advisory boards, participation at public hearings, and review of local and state special education plans are examples of ways in which parents might participate in the formulation of policy and later monitoring of these guidelines.

DOMAIN III. PROMOTING STUDENT DEVELOPMENT AND LEARNING

COMPETENCY 11.0 UNDERSTAND HOW TO ESTABLISH POSITIVE AND PRODUCTIVE LEARNING ENVIRONMENTS FOR STUDENTS WITH MILD/MODERATE DISABILITIES.

SKILL 11.1 Understand strategies for structuring the physical environment, establishing and managing routines, selecting appropriate learning materials and technologies, monitoring behavior, and providing activities to promote the development and learning of students with mild/moderate disabilities

PHYSICAL ENVIRONMENT (SPATIAL ARRANGEMENTS)

The physical setting of the classroom contributes a great deal toward the propensity for students to learn. An adequate, well-built, and well-equipped classroom will invite students to learn. This has been called "invitational learning." Among the important factors to consider in the physical setting of the classroom are the following:

a) <u>Adequate physical space</u> - A classroom must have adequate physical space so students can conduct themselves comfortably. Some students are distracted by windows, pencil sharpeners, doors, etc. Some students prefer the front, middle, or back rows.

b) <u>Repair status</u> - The teacher has the responsibility to report any items of classroom disrepair to maintenance staff. Broken windows, falling plaster, exposed sharp surfaces, leaks in ceiling or walls, and other items of disrepair present hazards to students.

c) <u>Lighting adequacy</u> - Report any inadequacies in classroom illumination. Florescent lights placed at acute angles often burn out faster. A healthy supply of spare tubes is a sound investment.

d) <u>Adequate entry/exit access (including handicap accessibility)</u> - Local fire and safety codes dictate entry and exit standards. In addition, all corridors and classrooms should be wheelchair accessible for students and others who use them. Older schools may not have this accessibility.

e) <u>Ventilation/climate control</u> - Some classrooms in some states use air conditioning extensively. Sometimes it is so cold as to be considered a distraction. Specialty classes such as science require specialized hoods for ventilation. Physical Education classes have the added responsibility for shower areas and specialized environments that must be heated such as pool or athletic training rooms.

f) <u>Coloration</u> - Classrooms with warmer subdued colors contribute to students' concentration on task items. Neutral hues for coloration of walls, ceiling, and carpet or tile are generally used in classrooms so distraction due to classroom coloration may be minimized.

In the modern classroom, there is a great deal of furniture, equipment, supplies, appliances, and learning aids to help the teacher teach and students learn. The classroom should be provided with furnishings that fit the purpose of the classroom. The kindergarten classroom may have a reading center, a playhouse, a puzzle table, student work desks/tables, a sandbox, and any other relevant learning/interest areas.

Whatever the arrangement of furniture and equipment may be, the teacher must provide for adequate traffic flow. Rows of desks must have adequate space between them for students to move and for the teacher to circulate. All areas must be open to line-of-sight supervision by the teacher.

In all cases, proper care must be taken to ensure student safety. Furniture and equipment should be situated safely at all times. No equipment, materials, boxes, etc. should be placed where there is danger of falling over. Doors must have entry and exit accessibility at all times.

Noise level should also be considered as part of the physical environment. Students vary in the degree of quiet that they need and the amount of background noise or talking that they can tolerate without getting distracted or frustrated. The teacher must maintain an environment that is conducive to the learning of each child.

The major emergency responses include two categories for student movement: tornado warning response and building evacuation, which includes most other emergencies (fire, bomb threat, etc.). For tornadoes, the prescribed response is to evacuate all students and personnel to the first floor of multi-story buildings, and to place students along walls away from windows. All persons, including the teacher, should then crouch on the floor and cover their heads with their hands.

Most other emergency situations require evacuation of the school building. Teachers should be thoroughly familiar with evacuation routes established for each classroom in which they teach. Teachers should accompany and supervise students throughout the evacuation procedure, and check to see that all students under their supervision are accounted for. Teachers should then continue to supervise students until the building may be reoccupied (upon proper school or community authority), or until other procedures are followed for students to officially leave the school area and cease to be the supervisory responsibility of the school. Elementary students evacuated to another school can wear nametags and parents or guardians should sign them out at a central location.

TRANSFER BETWEEN CLASSES AND SUBJECTS

Effective teachers use class time efficiently. This results in higher student subject engagement and will likely result in more subject matter retention. One way teachers use class time efficiently is through a smooth transition from one activity to another; this activity is also known as "management transition." Management transition is defined as "teacher shifts from one activity to another in a systemic, academically oriented way." One factor that contributes to efficient management transition is the teacher's management of instructional material. Effective teachers gather their materials during the planning stage of instruction. Doing this, a teacher avoids flipping through things looking for the items necessary for the current lesson. Momentum is lost and student concentration is broken when this occurs.

Additionally, teachers who keep students informed of the sequencing of instructional activities maintain systematic transitions because the students are prepared to move on to the next activity. For example, the teacher says, "When we finish with this guided practice together, we will turn to page twenty-three and each student will do the exercises. I will then circulate throughout the classroom helping on an individual basis. Okay, let's begin." Following an example such as this will lead to systematic smooth transitions between activities because the students will be turning to page twenty-three when the class finishes the practice without a break in concentration.

Another method that leads to smooth transitions is to move students in groups and clusters rather than one by one. This is called "group fragmentation." For example, if some students do seat work while other students gather for a reading group, the teacher moves the students in pre-determined groups. Instead of calling the individual names of the reading group, which would be time consuming and laborious, the teacher simply says, "Will the blue reading group please assemble at the reading station. The red and yellow groups will quietly do the vocabulary assignment I am now passing out." As a result of this activity, the classroom is ready to move on in a matter of seconds rather than minutes.

Additionally, the teacher may employ academic transition signals, defined as "teacher utterance that indicate[s] movement of the lesson from one topic or activity to another by indicating where the lesson is and where it is going." For example, the teacher may say, "That completes our description of clouds, now we will examine weather fronts." Like the sequencing of instructional materials, this keeps the student informed on what is coming next so they will move to the next activity with little or no break in concentration.

Therefore, effective teachers manage transitions from one activity to another in a systematically oriented way through efficient management of instructional matter, sequencing of instructional activities, moving students in groups, and by employing academic transition signals. Through an efficient use of class time, achievement is increased because students spend more class time engaged in on-task behavior.

Transition refers to changes in class activities that involve movement. Examples are:
- (a) Breaking up from large group instruction into small groups for learning centers and small-group instructions
- (b) Classroom to lunch, to the playground, or to elective classes
- (c) Finishing reading at the end of one period and getting ready for math the next period
- (d) Emergency situations such as fire drills

Successful transitions are achieved by using proactive strategies. Early in the year, the teacher pinpoints the transition periods in the day and anticipates possible behavior problems, such as students habitually returning late from lunch. After identifying possible problems with the environment or the schedule, the teacher plans proactive strategies to minimize or eliminate those problems. Proactive planning also gives the teacher the advantage of being prepared, addressing behaviors before they become problems, and incorporating strategies into the classroom management plan right away. Transition plans can be developed for each type of transition and the expected behaviors for each situation taught directly to the students.

STRATEGIES AND TECHNIQUES FOR ENSURING THE EFFICIENT AND EFFECTIVE USE OF INSTRUCTIONAL TIME

Schedule development depends upon the type of class (elementary or secondary) and the setting (regular classroom or resource room). There are, however, general rules of thumb that apply to both types and settings:

1. Allow time for transitions, planning, and setups.
2. Aim for maximum instructional time by pacing the instruction quickly and allotting time for practice of new skills.
3. Proceed from short assignments to long ones, breaking up long lessons or complex tasks into short sessions or step-by-step instruction
4. Follow a less preferred academic or activity with a highly preferred academic or activity.
5. In settings where students are working on individualized plans, do not schedule all the students at once in activities that require a great deal of teacher assistance. For example, have some students work on math or spelling, while the teacher works with the students in reading, which usually requires more teacher involvement.
6. Break up a longer segment into several smaller segments with a variety of activities.

SPECIAL CONSIDERATIONS FOR ELEMENTARY CLASSROOMS

1. Determine the amount of time that is needed for activities such as P.E., lunch, or recess.
2. Allow about 15 to 20 minutes each for opening and closing exercises. Spend this time for "housekeeping" activities such as collecting lunch money, going over the schedule, cleaning up, reviewing the day's activities, getting ready to go home.
3. Schedule academics for periods when the students are more alert and motivated, usually in the afternoon.
4. Build in time for slower students to finish their work; others may work at learning centers or other activities of interest. Allowing extra time gives the teacher time to give more attention where it is needed, conduct assessments, or for students to complete or correct work.

SPECIAL CONSIDERATIONS FOR SECONDARY CLASSES

Secondary school days are usually divided into five, six, or seven periods of about 50 (or 90 if using a 4 class block scheduling system) minutes, with time for homeroom and lunch. Students cannot stay behind and finish their work, since they have to leave for a different room. Resource room time should be scheduled so that the student does not miss academic instruction in his classroom or miss desirable nonacademic activities. In schools where special education teachers also co-teach or work with students in the regular classroom coordination and consultation time will also have to be budgeted into the schedule.

ASSISTIVE TECHNOLOGY

1. **Determination of Student Need for Assistive Technology**-Often the special educator will identify the need for consultation or testing in an area that a student is having difficulty. Testing or other professional evaluation may result in the trial or ongoing use of some form of assistive technology as listed on the student's IEP.

2. **Development of Student Skill Using Specific Assistive Technology-** Students who have been identified as needing assistive technology require training in the use of the equipment. Sometimes a therapist or consultant will "push in" to the classroom providing training for the student in the classroom setting. Other times the student will practice using the assistive technology in a separate setting until a level of experience/expertise is reached. Then the assistive technology may be used in the special education or inclusion classroom.

3. **Communication of Expected Skill Level in Classroom** - As students begin to use assistive technology in the classroom, the desired use (Including activity, location, and time) should be outlined for the special educator so that misunderstanding does not result in a student misusing or under using the technology. The student, then, will have a level of accountability and be functioning to the best of his abilities.

4. **Training of School Personnel on Use of Assistive Technology-** Although special educators are often trained in using a variety of assistive devices, advances in technology make it necessary for professionals to participate in ongoing training for new or unfamiliar equipment. This training may be conducted by a knowledgeable therapist or consultant in the school district, or school personnel may need to attend a workshop off campus.

5. **Evaluation of Student Independent Management of Assistive Technology in Various Settings** - Ongoing evaluation of the student's use of the equipment is vital. This may be monitored through observation by the therapist or consultant, anecdotal records of the special educator, or some type of checklist. Often an IEP goal will address how the use and evaluation of the student's performance with the equipment will be implemented.

6. **How to incorporate instructional and assistive technologies into IEPs**-Many students with disabilities require assistive technologies in order to be successful within the regular curriculum or environment. As with any form of technology, assistive devices are constantly being changed and updated, therefore it is important to stay as up-to-date as possible. It is also essential to search out within your district, who to contact to provide help in finding the necessary technologies to allow student success.

    When considering adding technology for students with special needs it is important to conduct a multi-disciplinary evaluation to ensure the specific student strengths are utilized in providing appropriate technology. This might include people such as: an assistive technology specialist, an occupational therapist, a physical therapist, a speech pathologist, or other designated people with specific training.

    Consider the needs of the student and those working with the device. For instance, an augmentative communication device is only as good as it is easy for the student to use and access and for the person in school and at home to program. If the device is so complicated to program with phrases or to make changes to when necessary, it will be less than ideal in the school setting.

    Also, always start with the least restrictive device. If, for example a student requires information to be visually presented at the same time it is orally presented, an overhead/ smart board might be your best bet. There are also other students in the classroom who will benefit from this type of modification as well, and the student with special needs will not have to be isolated or pointed out to his classmates.

    If any form of assistive technology, even simply typing assignments instead of handwriting them, is required it is essential to include it in the child's IEP. While many teachers and parents will follow the special educator's word and implement what is best for the child with no difficulties, it can provide future teachers with beneficial information. The IEP is legally binding and therefore mandates the users to implement it with that child.

Teachers in future years can look back and see what worked in previous years, or if the student moves, the new personnel will understand what specific devices and needs the student has and better service those needs from the beginning. In the end, the IEP is an important document where all information pertaining to the student, including assistive technology needs should be conveyed.

SKILL 11.2 Recognize ways in which disabilities may affect students' progress in the general education curriculum

The role of the special education teacher and the general education teacher is to work together to ensure that students with disabilities are able to attain their educational objectives in the least restrictive environment. Some students are best served in the general education setting with additional accommodations, while other students may be best served in the special education setting. The educators must work together to decide what educational program is best suited for the student and where the student can best meet his goals and objectives.

These decisions should be made during the student's IEP meeting. It is important that the special education teacher, the general education teacher, and other interested professionals, such as speech teacher, are in attendance at the meeting so they can discuss and collaborate on their role in helping the student. Students with disabilities often experience insufficient access to and a lack of success in the general education curriculum.

To promote improved access to the general curriculum for all learners, information should be presented in various formats using a variety of media forms; students should be given numerous methods to express and demonstrate what they have learned; and students should be provided with multiple entry points to engage their interest and motivate their learning.

Printed reading materials can be challenging to individuals with disabilities. Technology can help alleviate some of these difficulties by providing a change from printed text to electronic text that can be modified, enhanced, programmed, linked, and searched.

Text styles and font sizes can be changed as required by readers with visual disabilities. Text can be read aloud with computer-based text-to-speech translators and combined with illustrations, videos, and audio. Electronic text provides alternative formats for reading materials that can be tailored to match learner needs, and structured in ways that enhance the learning process and expand both physical and cognitive access.

When a child has a disability, he or she learns differently than others so the format of instruction should be a little different than usual. A teacher should incorporate a variety of teaching techniques throughout her class. There should be small group instruction, direct instruction, hands on activities, one on one instruction, and peer tutoring.

SKILL 11.3 Demonstrate knowledge of factors in the learning environment that affect achievement, self-esteem and attitudes toward learning

The attitude of the teacher can have both a positive or negative impact on student performance. A teacher's attitude can impact the expectations the teacher may have toward the student's potential performance, as well as how the teacher behaves toward the student. This attitude combined with expectations can impact the students self image as well as their academic performance. Negative teacher attitudes toward students with disabilities are detrimental to the handicapped students mainstreamed in general education classrooms.

The phenomenon of a self-fulfilling prophecy is based on the attitude of the teacher. A self-fulfilling prophecy means what we expect to happen is usually what ends up happening. In the context of education, this can mean the predictions of a teacher about the ability of a student to achieve or not to achieve educational objectives are always proven to be correct.

In subtle ways, teachers communicate their expectations of individual students. In turn, the student may adjust their behavior to match the teacher's expectations. Based on this, the teacher's expectations of what will happen is indeed true, which is a self-fulfilling prophecy.

Researchers in psychology and education have investigated this occurrence and discovered many people are sensitive to verbal and nonverbal cues from others regarding how they expect to be treated. As a result, they may consciously and subconsciously change their behavior and attitudes to conform to another person's hopes. Depending on the expectation, this can be either advantageous or detrimental.

The teacher's attitude toward a student can be shaped by a number of variables including race, ethnicity, disability, behavior, appearance, and social class. All of these variables can impact the teacher's attitude toward the student and how the student will achieve academically.

The premise of the self-fulfilling prophecy is the prediction and expectation of a teacher, which in turn impacts on the attitude of the teacher towards that student. Researchers question whether the fact that a teacher believes the prediction to be correct, means that the teacher will behave in a certain manner towards that student. The teacher has a responsibility to not allow her negative attitudes toward the student to impact how she perceives the student or interacts with him. If the teacher is able to communicate to all of her students that they all have great potential and is optimistic regarding this, then the student should excel in some aspect of his educational endeavors, as long as the teacher is able to make the student believe in himself.

It can be hard for teacher's to maintain a positive attitude at all times with all students, but it is important to be encouraging to all students at all times as every student has the potential to be successful in school. Consistent encouragement can help turn a C student into a B or even A student. While negative feedback can lead to failure and loss of self esteem.

Teachers should utilize their verbal communication skills to ensure the things they communicate to students are said in the most positive manner possible. For example, instead of saying, 'You talk to much' it would be more positive to state, 'you have excellent verbal communication skills and are very sociable.

Teachers have a major influence on what happens in the classrooms because they are the primary decision makers and they set the tone for how the information distributed is absorbed. In order for teachers to rise above their prejudices and preset attitudes it is important teachers are given training and support services to enable them to deal with students who come from challenging backgrounds or present challenging behaviors.

SOCIAL ISSUES

The most significant group any individual faces is their peers. Pressure to appear normal and not "needy" in any area is still intense from early childhood to adulthood. During teen years when young people are beginning to express their individuality, the very appearance of walking into a Special Education classroom often brings feelings of inadequacy, and labeling by peers that the student is different.

Many students with disabilities lack adequate social skills, which hinders them from making and keeping friends. Being considered normal is the desire of all individuals with disabilities regardless of the age or disability. People with disabilities today, as many years ago, still measure their successes by how their achievements mask/hide their disabilities.

The most difficult cultural/community outlook on those who are disabled comes in the adult work world where disabilities of persons can become highly evident often causing those with special needs difficulty in finding work and keeping their jobs. This is a particularly difficult place for those who have not learned to self advocate or accommodate for their area/s of special needs.

SKILL 11.4 Understand cultural and language diversity and the significance of student diversity for establishing a safe, positive, equitable, and supportive learning environment for all students

All special education classrooms need to be as spacious and fully equipped with desks, tables, bulletin boards, bookshelves, and activity centers, similar to regular classrooms. Room arrangement should facilitate the instructional and functional needs of the students who are served. Classrooms should be attractive, comfortable, safe, and inviting so that students are motivated to learn and teachers are eager to guide the students in their learning experiences.

See skill 11.1 for things to consider when setting up your classroom.

SAFE
In working with a special population composed of students with a variety of needs and disabling conditions, the assurance of a safe learning environment is paramount. The special education classroom, as well as regular classroom and support areas that are utilized by all students, should be set up and maintained so students can move about freely without incurring physical harm.

Included in Abraham Maslow's hierarchy of basic human needs is the requirement for safety and security. Children have the need to feel safe from dangers while at school and during transit to and from school. Educators must respond to this basic need by providing adequate supervision and by developing appropriate safety procedures.

Psychological safety can be heightened by employing instructional approaches that include tasks that students are able to master and complete successfully. Learning environments that children feel threatened and put on the defensive reduce psychological safety.

The avoidance of physical barriers and the formulation of appropriate procedures for emergencies are necessary conditions for students with disabilities. Children with sensory impairments (who are not able to hear audible alarms or to see danger signals), with limited intellectual capabilities (who may not respond well in atypical situations) may need to be protected with preestablished, well thought out procedural regulations. Further, school personnel need to be trained in handling and positioning students with physical impairments so that risk of further physical disability is minimized.

Vocational training programs involve the use of specialized machines and equipments, thus presenting modification and teaching techniques can be of benefit, such as (1) Ensuring a stable and predictable training environment; (2) Outlining concrete, step-by-step procedures; (3) Posting a list of classroom and laboratory safety rules; and (4) Reacting calmly to inappropriate behavior while firmly enforcing set procedures and regulations.

MOTIVATING

Many unmotivated students are unenthusiastic about learning because of the problems they experience in attempting to achieve. The use of multisensory and programmed instructional packages can help these students become motivated to learn. A student who is unmotivated in a conventional setting may become interested in learning through an individualized program. Such a system enables him to make choices, learn in accordance with his preferred learning style, and participate in paired or teamed peer group studies, as well as by himself at his own pace. Apathetic students may exhibit interest and enjoyment in educational games, puzzles, task cards, learning centers, computers, and multimedia learning experiences.

Research has uncovered a number of needs that when fulfilled, enable a student to become more involved and eager to participate in academic endeavors. Among these needs are: being actively involved in the setting of goals in the learning process, relating subject matter to personal experiences, following personal interests, experiencing success, receiving instruction corresponding to personal skill levels and learning styles, and receiving realistic and immediate feedback. In summary, students are more highly motivated to learn when they understand and are involved in determining what they are expected to do, how they should do it, and what rewards they will receive if they respond.

CULTURAL DIVERSITY

Effective teaching and learning for students begins with teachers who can demonstrate sensitivity for diversity in teaching and relationships within school communities. Student portfolios include work that has a multicultural perspective and inclusion where students share cultural and ethnic life experiences in their learning. Teachers are responsive to including cultural and diverse resources in their curriculum and instructional practices. Exposing students to culturally sensitive room decorations and posters that show positive and inclusive messages is one way to demonstrate inclusion of multiple cultures. Teachers should also continuously make cultural connections that are relevant and empowering for all students and communicate academic and behavioral expectations. Cultural sensitivity is communicated beyond the classroom with parents and community members to establish and maintain relationships.

Diversity can be further defined as the following:
- Differences among learners, classroom settings and academic outcomes
- Biological, sociological, ethnicity, socioeconomic status psychological needs, learning modalities and styles among learners
- Differences in classroom settings that promote learning opportunities such as collaborative, participatory, and individualized learning groupings
- Expected learning outcomes that are theoretical, affective and cognitive for students

Teachers establish a classroom climate that is culturally respectful and engaging for students. In a culturally sensitive classroom, teachers maintain equity and fairness in student interactions and curriculum implementation. Assessments include cultural responses and perspectives that become further learning opportunities for students. Other artifacts that could reflect teacher/student sensitivity to diversity might consist of the following:

- Student portfolios reflecting multicultural/multiethnic perspectives
- Journals and reflections from field trips/ guest speakers from diverse cultural backgrounds
- Printed materials and wall displays from multicultural perspectives
- Parent/guardian letters in a variety of languages reflecting cultural diversity
- Projects that include cultural history and diverse inclusions
- Disaggregated student data reflecting cultural groups
- Classroom climate of professionalism that fosters diversity and cultural inclusion

The target of diversity allows teachers a variety of opportunities to expand their experiences with students, staff, community members and parents from culturally diverse backgrounds, so that their experiences can be proactively applied in promoting cultural diversity inclusion in the classroom. Teachers are able to engage and challenge students to develop and incorporate their own diversity skills in building character and relationships with cultures beyond their own. In changing the thinking patterns of students to become more culturally inclusive in the 21st century, teachers are addressing the globalization of our world.

SKILL 11.5 Demonstrate knowledge of specialized health and safety practices for students with mild/moderate disabilities

TYPES AND TRANSMISSION ROUTES OF INFECTIOUS DISEASES AND DEMONSTRATING KNOWLEDGE OF UNIVERSAL SAFETY PRECAUTIONS FOR AVOIDING TRANSMISSION OF SUCH DISEASES.

In schools today as with any workplace, it is important all personnel take care when working to avoid exposing themselves or others to infectious diseases. Any body fluid should be considered as having an infectious disease, in this way, the employee can use a standardized set of procedures to insure no chance of spread occurs. This standardized set of procedures are known as universal safety precautions.

Infectious disease can be spread through contact with spilled body fluids, including blood. Small playground scrapes, a weeping sore, or any other spilled body fluid should be avoided unless using universal precautions. Body fluids which can transmit infectious disease include: blood, body fluids with blood visible cerebrospinal, synovial, pleural, peritoneal, pericardial, and amniotic fluids, semen and vaginal secretions.

Before attending to or helping someone where there is blood or other spilled body fluid, you should take time to protect yourself. Barrier protection is the first stage. Use of gloves is a must. Be careful with the use of latex gloves, as there are many people with severe latex allergies. Sometimes, it may be necessary to wear protective clothing or eye protection as well.

Hand washing is also important. If any of the blood or body fluids comes in contact with your skin, be sure to wash the area as soon as possible lathering and washing for fifteen or more seconds. It is also imperative to wash your hands after removing the gloves. In fact, hand washing is the best germ reducer.

In some cases, the local district may ask/require you to have vaccinations to prevent you from some disease transmission. An example of this may be the Hepatitis B vaccine. Typically, teachers are required to be tested for tuberculosis as well. There are usually procedures for the disposal of hazardous waste or biohazardous waste. The employee should check with the building/school nurse or administrator to understand the specific procedures within their school.

If someone is exposed to blood or other body fluids on the job, it is important to report such an incident to their immediate supervisor as soon as they can. There may be steps in place that need to be followed in order to be protected.

LEGISLATION INVOLVING HEALTH AND SAFETY

Irving Independent School District v. Tatro 1984. IDEA lists health services as one of the "related services" that schools are mandated to provide to exceptional students. Amber Tatro, who had spina bifida, required the insertion of a catheter on a regular schedule in order to empty her bladder. The issue was specifically over the classification of clean, intermittent catheterization (CIC) as a medical service (not covered under IDEA) or a "related health service", which would be covered. In this instance, the catheterization was not declared a medical service, but a "related service" necessary for the student to have in order to benefit from special education. The school district was obliged to provide the service. The Tatro case has implications for students with other medical impairments who may need services to allow them to attend classes at the school.

School Board of Nassau County v. Arline, 1987. Established that contagious diseases are a disability under Section 504 of the Rehabilitation Act and that people with them are protected from discrimination, if otherwise qualified (actual risk to health and safety of others may unqualify said individuals).

SKILL 11.6 Demonstrate knowledge of individual and group management strategies for achieving instructional management goals (e.g., maintaining standards of behavior, maximizing time spent in learning) and promoting successful transitions (e.g., from one activity, class, teacher, or level to another)

See skill 11.1 for additional information on transitioning and classroom arrangement.

Five basic types of grouping arrangements are typically used in the classroom. They are:

1. **Large Group with Teacher**-Examples of appropriate activities include show and tell, discussions, watching plays or movies, brainstorming ideas, and playing games. Science, social studies, and most other subjects, except for reading and math are taught in large groups. The advantage of large-group instruction is that it is time-efficient and prepares students for higher levels of secondary and post-secondary education settings. However, with large groups, instruction cannot be as easily tailored to high or low levels of students, who may become bored or frustrated. Mercer and Mercer recommend guidelines for effective large-group instruction:
    a. Keep instruction short, ranging from 5 to 15 minutes for first grade to seventh grade; 5 to 40 minutes, for grades 8 to 12.
    b. Use questions to involve all students, use lecture-pause routines, and encourage active participation among the lower-performing students.
    c. Incorporate visual aids to promote understanding, and maintain a lively pace
    d. Break up the presentation with different rates of speaking, giving students a "stretch" break", varying voice volume, etc…
    e. Establish rules of conduct for large groups and praise students who follow the rules

2. **Small Group Instruction**-Small group instruction usually includes 5 to 7 students and is recommended for teaching basic academic skills such as math facts or reading. This model is especially effective for students with learning problems. Composition of the groups should be flexible to accommodate different rates of progress through instruction. The advantages of teaching in small groups is that the teacher is better able to provide feedback, monitor student progress, and give more instruction, praise and feedback. With small groups the teacher will need to make sure to provide a steady pace for the lesson, provide questions and activities that allow all to participate, and include lots of positive praise.

3. **One Student with Teacher**-One –to-one tutorial teaching can be used to provide extra assistance to individual students. Such tutoring may be scheduled at set times during the day or provided as the need arises. The tutoring model is typically found more in elementary and resource classrooms rather than secondary settings.

4. **Peer Tutoring**-In an effective peer tutoring arrangement, the teacher trains the peer tutors and matches them with students who need extra practice and assistance. In addition to academic skills, the arrangement can help both students work on social skills such as cooperation and self-esteem. Both students may be working on the same material or the tutee may be working to strengthen areas of weakness. The teacher determines the target goals, selects the material, sets up the guidelines, trains the student tutors in the rules and methods of the sessions, and monitors and evaluates the sessions.

5. **Cooperative Learning**-Cooperative learning differs from peer tutoring in that students are grouped in teams or small groups and the methods are based on teamwork, individual accountability and team reward. Individual students are responsible for their own learning and share of the work, as well as the group's success. As with peer tutoring, the goals, target skills, materials, and guidelines, are developed by the teacher. Teamwork skills may also need to be taught. By focusing on team goals, all members of the team are encouraged to help each other as well as improve their individual performance.

CLASSROOM MANAGEMENT TECHNIQUES

Classroom management plans should be in place when the school year begins. Developing a management plan takes a proactive approach—that is, decide what behaviors will be expected of the class as a whole, anticipate possible problems, and teach the behaviors early in the school year.

Behavior management techniques should focus on positive procedures that can be used at home as well as at school. Involving the students in the development of the classroom rules lets the students know the rationale for the rules, and allows them to assume responsibility in the rules because they had a part in developing them. When students get involved in helping establish the rules, they will be more likely to assume responsibility for following them. Once the rules are established, enforcement and reinforcement for following the rules should begin right away.

Consequences should be introduced when the rules are introduced, clearly stated, and understood by all of the students. The severity of the consequence should match the severity of the offense and must be enforceable. The teacher must apply the consequence consistently and fairly, so the students will know what to expect when they choose to break a rule.

Like consequences, students should understand what rewards to expect for following the rules. The teacher should never promise a reward that cannot be delivered, and follow through with the reward as soon as possible. Consistency and fairness is also necessary for rewards to be effective. Students will become frustrated and give up if they see rewards and consequences are not delivered timely and fairly.

About four to six classroom rules should be posted where students can easily see and read them. These rules should be stated positively, and describe specific behaviors, so they are easy to understand. Certain rules may also be tailored to meet target goals and IEP requirements of individual students. (For example, a new student who has had problems with leaving the classroom may need an individual behavior contract to assist him or her with adjusting to the class rule about remaining in the assigned area.) As the students demonstrate the behaviors, the teacher should provide reinforcement and corrective feedback. Periodic "refresher" practice can be done as needed, for example, after a long holiday or if students begin to "slack off." A copy of the classroom plan should be readily available for substitute use, and the classroom aide should also be familiar with the plan and procedures.

The teacher should clarify and model the expected behavior for the students. In addition to the classroom management plan, a management plan should be developed for special situations, (i.e., fire drills) and transitions (i.e., going to and from the cafeteria).

Procedures that use social humiliation, withholding of basic needs, pain, or extreme discomfort should never be used in a behavior management plan. Emergency intervention procedures used when the student is a danger to himself or others are not considered behavior management procedures. Throughout the year, the teacher should periodically review the types of interventions being used, assess the effectiveness of the interventions used in the management plan, and make revisions as needed for the best interests of the child. There are several types of intervention techniques a teacher can use to help with discipline issues within the classroom. Some include:

- **Classroom interventions**-Classroom interventions anticipate student disruptions and nullify potential discipline problems. Every student is different and each situation is unique; therefore, student behavior cannot be matched to specific interventions. Good classroom management requires the ability to select appropriate interventions strategies from an array of alternatives. The following non-verbal and verbal interventions were explained in Henley, Ramsey, and Algonzzine (1993).
- **Nonverbal Intervention -** The use of nonverbal interventions allows classroom activities to proceed without interruption. These interventions also enable students to avoid "power struggles" with students.
- **Body Language -** Teachers can convey authority and command respect through body language. Posture, eye contact, facial expressions, and gestures are examples of body components that signal leadership to students.
- **Planned Ignoring -** Many minor classroom disturbances are best handled through planned ignoring. When teachers ignore attention-seeking behaviors, often students do likewise.
- **Signal Interference -** There are numerous non-verbal signals that teachers can use to quiet a class. Some of these are eye contact, snapping fingers, a frown, shaking the head, or making a quieting gesture with the hand. A few teachers present signs like flicking the lights, putting a finger over their lips, or winking at a selective student.
- **Proximity Control -** Teachers who move around the room merely need to stand near a student or small group of students, or gently place a hand on a student's shoulder to stop a disturbing behavior. Teachers who stand or sit as if rooted are compelled to issue verbal directions in order to deal with student disruptions.
- **Removal of Seductive Objects -** Some students become distracted by objects. Removing seductive objects eliminates the need some students have to handle, grab, or touch objects that distract their attention.
- **Verbal Interventions**-Because non-verbal interventions are the least intrusive, they are generally preferred. Verbal Interventions are useful after it is clear that non-verbal interventions have been unsuccessful in preventing or stopping disruptive behavior.
- **Humor -** Some teachers have been successful in dispelling discipline problems with a quip or an easy comment that produces smiles or gentle laughter from students. This does not include sarcasm, cynicism, or teasing, which increase tension and often creates resentment.
- **Sane Messages**. Sane messages are descriptive and model appropriate behavior. They help students understand how their behavior affects others. "Karol, when you talk during silent reading, you disturb everyone in your group," is an example of a sane message.
- **Restructuring.** When confronted with student disinterest, the teacher makes the decision to change activities. This is an example of an occasion when restructuring could be used by the teacher to regenerate student interest.

- **Hypodermic Affection.** Sometimes students get frustrated, discouraged, and anxious in school. Hypodermic affection lets students know they are valued. Saying a kind word, giving a smile, or just showing interest in a child gives the encouragement that is needed.
- **Praise and Encouragement.** Effective praise is directed at student behavior rather than at the student personally. "Catching a child being good," is an example of an effective use of praise that reinforces positive classroom behavior. Comments like, "you are really trying hard," encourages student effort.
- **Alerting.** Making abrupt changes from one activity to another can bring on behavior problems. Alerting helps students to make smooth transitioning by giving them time to make emotional adjustments to change.
- **Accepting Student Feelings.** Providing opportunities for students to express their feelings, even those that are distressful, helps them to learn appropriate expression techniques. Role playing, class meetings or discussions, life space interviews, journal writings, and other creative modes help students to channel difficult feelings into constructive outlets.

Please refer to skill 11.1 about transition.

COMPETENCY 12.0 UNDERSTAND EVIDENCE-BASED STRATEGIES AND TECHNIQUES FOR IMPROVING THE EXPRESSIVE AND RECEPTIVE COMMUNICATION SKILLS OF STUDENTS WITH MILD/MODERATE DISABILITIES.

SKILL 12.1 Understand types and characteristics of speaking and writing difficulties associated with various disabilities

Please refer to Skill 2.4 for information on types and characteristics of speaking difficulties.

Written expression is one of the highest forms of communication. It reflects a person's level of comprehension, concept development, and abstraction (Mercer & Mercer, 1993). Handwriting is primarily a visual-motor process that includes the writing or copying of word forms, whereas written expression reflects a person's cognitive abilities.

Prerequisite to developing skills in written expression is the need for experiences in listening, reading, spelling, handwriting, and oral expression. Activities in written expression should begin as early as kindergarten and first grade, with skills developed concurrently with prerequisite experiences. Typically, problems in written expression are not identified until the upper elementary grade levels when the student is required to use language arts skills in written composition.

Problems in written expression can be diagnosed by the teacher through formal and informal means. Written expression produces a tangible product that may be evaluated by the teacher using a criterion-referenced tool. Students with deficits in reading and spelling typically exhibit difficulties in written expression. Particular areas of difficulty include: limited vocabulary, immature topic selections, spelling errors, inaccurate syntax, poor organization of thoughts, and obvious stylistic errors. Inadequate cognitive abilities and grammatical inaccuracies may be detected.

Children who are lacking in the development of comprehension skills may be unable to reflect upon the subject and use reasoning skills in the development of content. Likewise, children with hyperactive or impulsive traits are often unable to focus upon details of content and subdivide materials. Deficits may be identified at any point where visual, motor, and cognitive abilities come into play in the production of written expression.

Instruction in written expression should culminate in independently written prose by students. Teacher prompting and feedback will vary, based on the degree of dependency individual students exhibit. For example, the language experience approach, largely a teacher directed group - sometimes individual - activity, is typically used as a form of initial instruction in written expression. The benefit of this activity is in the development of a topic of high interest, the use of students' thoughts and the students' speaking vocabulary, and, of course, the immediate prompting, and feedback of an encouraging and motivating nature from the teacher.

SKILL 12.2 Understand strategies and techniques for improving students' vocabulary and oral and written communication skills

Objectives for oral language development are a part of many IEPs. The designated individuals to address such objectives are often speech and language pathologists, teachers, and parents. Although speech and language pathologists work with students one-on-one or in small groups, this is often in a pull out type of environment. Most often, the student's progress and actual practice with staff and peers is monitored in the classroom by the special education teacher.

STRATEGIES FOR DEVELOPING CONTENT AREA VOCABULARY

- Instruction in how to identify vocabulary in text (highlighted, colored text or bold-faced word)
- Instruction in using context clues and reference to synonyms/antonyms in test.
- Instruction in how to use a glossary or dictionary.
- Practice with study cards (word on one side and definition on the other)
- Practice completing close activities in which student must fill in the correct vocabulary word.

STRATEGIES FOR DEVELOPING GENERAL VOCABULARY

Students will encounter new vocabulary in reading and in conversation. Some school districts use general vocabulary building programs (such as Tampa Reads) for this purpose. Additional strategies may include:

- Have students keep a notebook or word box of new vocabulary, the word's definition in natural language, and an example sentence.
- Develop a class word wall of new vocabulary. This is sometimes done according to theme. For example, using a barn-shaped poster board to display farm related words or a flower-shaped board for spring words.
- Reward students for use of their new vocabulary by tracking on a chart for a reward/reinforcer.

STRATEGIES FOR DEVELOPING SOCIAL LANGUAGE VOCABULARY

- Identification and understanding of social slang.
- Identification and understanding of idioms and expressions.
- Understanding of personal space.
- Understanding the use of eye contact when speaking to others.
- Understanding of social oral language skills such as turn taking in conversations.

METHODS FOR PRACTICING ORAL LANGUAGE

- Model the target oral language.
- Practice the target skill in structured situations.
- Expect and reinforce the use of the target oral language in the classroom setting.
- Communicate the student's progress with the target oral language to parents for carry over at home.

METHODS OF SELF-MONITORING ORAL LANGUAGE

- **Note or Checklist on Desk-**As a student shows a fair level of proficiency using a target oral language skill, he should be expected to use it in the classroom, elsewhere in the school setting, and eventually at home. One way to help the student remember to use his newly learned skills is to attach a note or checklist to his desk.
- **PECS Symbols-**Many students (particularly many autistic students) use the Picture Exchange Communication System. Some students use these small cards with icons to express wants and needs. However, more verbal students may use the picture cards as a visual prompt to use a certain word, phrase, or sentence structure.

EFFECTIVE COMMUNICATION SKILLS BETWEEN THE SENDER AND THE RECEIVER

Communication occurs when one person sends a message and gets a response from another person. In fact, whenever two people can see or hear each other they are communicating. The sender is the person who communicates the message; the receiver is the person who ultimately responds to the message. The receiver changes roles and becomes the sender, once the response is given. The communication process may break down if the receiver's interpretation differs from that of the sender.

Effective teaching depends on communication. By using good sending skills, the teacher has more assurance she is getting her message across to her students. By being a model of a good listener, a teacher can help her students learn to listen and respond appropriately to others.

ATTENDING SKILLS

Attending skills are used to receive a message. Some task-related attending skills that have been identified include: (1) looking at the teacher when information or instructions are being presented, (2) listening to assignment directions, (3) listening for answers to questions, (4) looking at the chalkboard, (5) listening to others speak when appropriate.

For some students, special techniques must be employed to gain and hold attention. For example, the teacher might first call the student by name when asking a question to assure attending by that individual, or she may ask the question before calling the name of a student to create greater interest. Selecting students at random to answer questions helps to keep them alert and listening. Being enthusiastic and keeping lessons short and interactive assists in maintaining the attention of those students who have shorter attention spans. Some students may be better able to focus their attention when environmental distractions are eliminated or at least reduced, and non-verbal signals can be used to draw students' attention to the task. Finally, arranging the classroom so that all students can see the teacher helps direct attention to the appropriate location.

CLARITY OF EXPRESSION

Unclear communication between the teacher and special needs students sometimes contributes to problems in academic and behavioral situations. In the learning environment, unclear communication can add to the student's confusion about certain processes or skills he is attempting to master.

There are many ways in which the teacher can improve the clarity of her communication. Giving clear, precise directions is one. Verbal directions can be simplified by using shorter sentences, familiar words, and relevant explanations. Asking a student to repeat directions or to demonstrate understanding of them by carrying out the instructions is an effective way of monitoring the clarity of expression. In addition, clarification can be achieved by the use of concrete objects, multidimensional teaching aids, and by modeling or demonstrating what should be done in a practice situation.

Finally, a teacher can clarify her communication by using a variety of vocal inflections. The use of intonation juncture can help make the message clearer, as can pauses at significant points in the communication. For example, verbal praise should be spoken with inflection that communicates sincerity. Pausing before starting key words, or stressing those that convey meanings, helps students learn concepts being taught.

PARAPHRASING

Paraphrasing, that is, restating what the student says using one's own words, can improve communication between the teacher and the student. First, in restating what the students has communicated, the teacher is not judging the content - she is simply relating what she understands the message to be. If the message has been interpreted differently from the way intended, the student is asked to clarify. Clarification should continue until both parties are satisfied that the message has been understood.

The act of paraphrasing sends the message the teacher is trying to better understand the student. Restating the student's message as fairly and accurately as possible assists the teacher in seeing things from the student's perspective.

Paraphrasing if often a simple restatement of what has been said. Lead-ins such as "Your position is..." or "it seems to you that..." are helpful in paraphrasing a student's messages. A student's statement, "I am not going to do my math today" might be paraphrased by the teacher as, "Did I understand you to say that you are not going to do your math today?" By mirroring what the student has just said, the teacher has telegraphed a caring attitude for that student and a desire to respond accurately to his message.

To paraphrase effectively a student's message, the teacher should: (1) restate the student's message in her own words; (2) preface her paraphrasing with such remarks as, "You feel..." or "I hear you say that..." (3) avoid indicating any approval or disapproval of the student's statements. Johnson (1978) states the following as a rule to remember when paraphrasing: "Before you can reply to a statement, restate what the sender says, feels, and means correctly and to the sender's satisfaction." (p.139)

Descriptive feedback is a factual, objective (i.e. unemotional) recounting of a behavioral situation or message sent by a student. Descriptive feedback has the same effect as paraphrasing, in that: (1) when responding to a student's statement, the teacher restates (i.e. paraphrases) what the student has said, or factually describes what she has seen, and (2) it allows the teacher to check her perceptions of the student and his message. A student may do or say something but because of the teacher's feelings or state of mind, the student's message or behavior might be totally misunderstood. The teacher's descriptive feedback, which Johnson (1972) refers to as "understanding," indicates that the teacher's intent is to respond only to ask the student whether his statement has been understood, how he feels about the problem, and how he perceives the problem. The intent of the teacher is to more clearly "understand" what the student is saying, feeling, or perceiving, in relation to a stated message or a behavioral event.

Evaluative feedback is verbalized perception by the teacher that judges, evaluates, approves, or disapproves of the statements made by the student. Evaluative feedback occurs when the student makes a statement and the teacher responds openly with "I think you're wrong," "That was a dumb thing to do," or "I agree with you entirely." The tendency to give evaluative responses is heightened in situations where feelings and emotions are deeply involved. The stronger the feelings, the more likely it is that two persons will each evaluate the other's statements solely from their own point of view.

Since evaluative feedback intones a judgmental approval or disapproval of the student's remark or behavior in most instances, it can be a major barrier to mutual understanding and effective communication. It is a necessary mechanism for providing feedback of a quantitative (and sometimes qualitative) instructional nature (e.g. test scores, homework results, classroom performance). In order to be effective, evaluative feedback must be offered in a factual, constructive manner. Descriptive feedback tends to reduce defensiveness and feelings of being threatened because it will most likely communicate that the teacher is interested in the student as a person, has an accurate understanding of the student and what he is saying, and encourages the students to elaborate and further discuss his problems.

To summarize, in the learning environment, as in all situations, effective communication depends upon good sending and receiving skills. Teaching and managing students involves good communication. By using clear, non-threatening feedback, the teacher can provide students with information that helps them to understand themselves better, while at the same time providing a clearer understanding of each student on the teacher's part.

THE SEQUENCE OF DEVELOPMENT OF WRITTEN EXPRESSION SKILLS

Composition should be taught as a process rather than a product. The first step in learning composition is having access to literature and writing materials. When adults read aloud to children, the children learn about styles of literature and the function of print and pictures in a book. Having access to paper and writing materials give children opportunities to experiment with drawing and writing. When children enter school, they can learn to write notes, label pictures, and keep journals.

Most of the writing children do at school is business related, or transactional writing. Transactional writing includes expository (explaining subjects or procedures), descriptive (helps the reader visualize the topic), or persuasive (explaining a point of view). Students may also do expressive writing or poetic writing, which requires knowledge of formal literary style. Initially, students may be resistant to writing, especially expressive writing, because they may be afraid to show their feelings or make mistakes. Journals are especially helpful to encourage students to practice expressive writing.

Free writing will help reduce writing anxiety. Having children participate in journals and free writing will help build confidence. Writing should be integrated in all subject areas, and the atmosphere should be positive. Writing should be fun, and include a variety of types of writing. Children's writing should be shared with others for feedback and enjoyment.

Each phase of the writing process has strategies that help the student develop metacognitive skills and proficiency. Instruction should not just focus on the mechanics (grammar, punctuation, spelling) of writing, but also on developing fluency and positive feelings about the process.

1. *Prewriting:* the planning phase. During preplanning, the student must decide on a purpose, find a topic, establish an audience, decide how the paper will be organized, and experiment with ideas. Strategies for generating ideas can be done individually or as a group activity and include:
    - Listing
    - Brainstorming—gathering ideas about the topic
    - Interest inventories
    - Free writing
2. *Organizing content:* includes graphic approaches that represent the relationships of ideas visually
    - Mapping
    - Webbing
    - Clustering

3. *Drafting:* In this phase, ideas are developed and the writer makes connections between the ideas. During this phase, mechanics should not be considered, and the student should not spend too much time in this phase. Learner activities include:
   - Focus on the ideas, not the content
   - Consult the teacher or peer about the content
   - Read the piece or a portion to defocus and generate new ideas
4. *Revising:* After the drafts have been written, the student may reorganize ideas, select ideas for further development, and edit the paper for mistakes in grammar and spelling. Sections of the paper may be removed or reorganized. Strategies include:
   - Putting the paper aside for a day or two
   - Asking the teacher or a peer for feedback
   - Use scissors and tape to reorganize sections of the paper
   - Use the computer to aid in revision
5. *Final Draft:* The writer gives the paper a final editing, reads the paper to see that everything makes sense, and makes last minute corrections before turning the paper in. Some of the things that a student can do to prepare the final draft are:
   - Use a checklist to check the final copy for errors.
   - Read the story into a tape-recorder and play it back with a written copy to listen for grammatical errors and pauses where punctuation marks should be.
   - Read the paper one sentence at a time to identify sentence fragments.

SKILL 12.3 Understand instructional methods, resources, and technologies for promoting students' reading skills, including the use of systematic instruction to teach various aspects of reading and monitoring strategies to students with various types of disabilities

WORD PROCESSORS

Word processors are used to assist students with written composition. Students with learning disabilities often have difficulty organizing thoughts. Problems with writing are compounded by handwriting difficulties. Many teachers report that use of a word processor has enabled them to motivate students to write. Most are less resistant to rewriting texts when they can do it on a word processing program that erases and replaces text quickly. Printed texts in typewritten form are easier to read. Spelling checkers, built into many word processing programs, assist those who may not be able to spell words correctly. Another option is a thesaurus which provides synonyms and in so doing helps to build vocabulary. The overall quantity and quality of written work improves when word processing programs are used in conjunction with computers.

When working on the word processor, each student needs a data disk so that his work can be evaluated over time and stored electronically. Having a portfolio of printouts enables students to take work home to show parents.

BEGINNING READING APPROACHES

Methods of teaching beginning reading skills may be divided into two major approaches—code emphasis and meaning emphasis. Both approaches have their supporters and their critics. Advocates of code emphasis instruction point out that reading fluency depends on accurate and automatic decoding skills, while advocates of meaning emphasis favor this approach for reading comprehension. Teachers may decide to blend aspects of both approaches to meet the individual needs of their students.

Bottom-up or Code-Emphasis Approach
- Letter-sound regularity is stressed.
- Reading instruction begins with words that consist of letter or letter combinations that have the same sound in different words. Component letter-sound relationships are taught and mastered before introducing new words.
- Examples—phonics, linguistic, modified alphabet, and programmed reading series such as the Merrill Linguistic Reading Program and DISTAR Reading.

Top-down or Meaning Emphasis Model
- Reading for meaning is emphasized from the first stages of instruction.
- Programs begin with words that appear frequently, which are assumed to be familiar and easy to learn. Words are identified by examining meaning and position in context and are decoded by techniques such as context, pictures, initial letters, and word configurations. Thus, a letter may not necessarily have the same sound in different words throughout the passage.
- Examples: whole language, language experience, and individualized reading programs.

Other approaches that follow beginning reading instruction are available to help teachers design reading programs. Choice of approach will depend on the student's strengths and weaknesses. No matter what approach or combination of approaches is used, the teacher should encourage independent reading and build activities into the reading program that stimulate students to practice their skills through independent reading.

DEVELOPMENTAL READING APPROACHES

Developmental reading programs emphasize daily, sequential instruction. Instructional materials usually feature a series of books, often basal readers, as the core of the program.

Basal Reading

Basal reader series form the core of many widely used reading programs from preprimers to eighth grade. Depending on the series, basal readers may be meaning-emphasis or code-emphasis. Teacher manuals provide a highly structured and comprehensive scope and sequence of lesson plans and objectives. Vocabulary is controlled from level to level and reading skills cover word recognition, word attack, and comprehension.

The advantage of basal readers is the structured, sequential manner in which reading is taught. The teacher manuals have teaching strategies, controlled vocabulary, assessment materials and objectives. Reading instruction is in a systematic, sequential, and comprehension-oriented manner.

Many basal reading programs recommend the directed reading activity procedure, for lesson presentation. Students proceed through the steps of preparing for new concepts and vocabulary, guided reading, answering questions that give a purpose or goal for the reading, development of strengths through drills or workbook, application of skills, and evaluation.

A variation of the directed reading method is direct reading-thinking, where the student must generate the purposes for reading the selection, form questions, and read the selection. After reading, the teacher asks questions designed to get the group to think of answers and justify their answers.

A disadvantage of basal readers is the emphasis on teaching to a group rather than the individual. Critics of basal readers claim the structure may limit creativity and not provide enough instruction on organizational skills and reading for secondary content levels. Basal readers, however, offer the advantage of a prepared comprehensive program, and may be supplemented with other materials to meet individual needs.

Phonics Approach

Word recognition is taught through grapheme-phoneme associations, with the goal of teaching the student to independently apply these skills to new words. Phonics instruction may be synthetic or analytic. In the synthetic method, letter sounds are learned before the student goes on to blend the sounds to form words. The analytic method teaches letter sounds as integral parts of words.

The sounds are usually taught in the sequence: vowels, consonants, consonant blends at the beginning of words (e.g. bl and dr), and consonant blends at the end of words (e.g. ld and mp), consonant and vowel digraphs (e.g. ch and sh) and diphthongs (e.g. au and oy).

Critics of the phonics approach point out that the emphasis on pronunciation may lead to the student focusing more on decoding than comprehension. Some students may have trouble blending sounds to form words, and others may become confused with words that do not conform to the phonetic "rules". However, advocates of phonics say that the programs are useful with remedial reading and developmental reading. Examples of phonics series are *Science Research Associates, Merrill Phonics* and DML's *Cove School Reading Program.*

Linguistics Approach

In many programs, the whole-word approach is used. This means that words are taught in families as a whole (e.g. cat, hat, pat, and rat). The focus is on words instead of isolated sounds. Words are chosen on the basis of similar spelling patterns and irregular spelling words are taught as sight words. Examples of programs using this approach are *SRA Basic Reading Series* and *Miami Linguistic Readers* by D.C. Heath.

Some advantages of this approach are that the student learns reading is talk written down, and develops a sense of sentence structure. The consistent visual patterns of the lessons guide students from familiar words to less familiar words to irregular words. Reading is taught by associating with the student's natural knowledge of his own language. Disadvantages are extremely controlled vocabulary, in which word-by-word reading is encouraged. Others criticize the programs for the emphasis on auditory memory skills and the use of nonsense words in the practice exercises.

Whole Language Approach

In the whole language approach, reading is taught as a holistic, meaning-oriented activity and is not broken down into a collection of skills. This approach relies heavily on literature or printed matter selected for a particular purpose. Reading is taught as part of a total language arts program, and the curriculum seeks to develop instruction in real problems and ideas. Two examples of whole language programs are *Learning through Literature* (Dodds and Goodfellow) and *Victory!* (Brigance). Phonics is not taught in a structured, systematic way. Students are assumed to develop their phonetic awareness through exposure to print. Writing is taught as a complement to reading. Writing centers are often part of this program as students learn to write their own stories and read them back, or follow along an audiotape of a book while reading along with it.

While the integration of reading with writing is an advantage of the whole language approach, the approach has been criticized for the lack of direct instruction in specific skill strategies. When working with students with learning problems, instruction that is more direct may be needed to learn the word-recognition skills necessary for achieving comprehension of the text.

Language Experience Approach
The language experience approach is similar to whole language in that reading is considered as a personal activity, literature is emphasized, and students are encouraged to write about their own life experiences. The major difference is that written language is considered a secondary system to oral language, while whole language treats the two as parts of the same structure.

The language experience approach is used primarily with beginner readers, but can also be used with older elementary and with other older students for corrective instruction. Reading skills are developed along with listening, speaking and writing skills. The philosophy of language experience includes:

- What students think about, they can talk about.
- What students say, they can write, or have someone write.
- What students write or have someone write for them, they can read.

Students dictate a story to a teacher as a group activity. Ideas for stories can originate from student artwork, news items, personal experiences, or they may be creative. Topic lists, word cards, or idea lists can also be used to generate topics or ideas for a class story. The teacher writes down the story in a first draft and the students read them back. The language patterns come from the students and they read their own written thoughts.

The teacher provides guidance on word choice, sentence structure and the sounds of the letters and words. The students edit and revise the story on an experience chart. The teacher provides specific instruction in grammar, sentence structure, and spelling, if the need arises, rather than using a specified schedule. As the students progress, they create their individual storybooks, adding illustrations if they wish. The storybooks are placed in folders to share with others. Progress is evaluated in terms of the changes in the oral and written expression as well as in mechanics. There is no set method of evaluating student progress. That is one disadvantage of the language experience approach. However, the emphasis on student experience and creativity stimulates interest and motivates the students.

Individualized Reading Approach
Students select their own reading materials from a variety, according to interest and ability, and they are more able to progress at their own individual rates. Word recognition and comprehension are taught, as the student needs them. The teacher's role is to diagnose errors and prescribe materials, although the final choice is made by the students. Individual work may be supplemented by group activities with basal readers and workbooks for specific reading skills. The lack of systematic check and developmental skills and emphasis on self-learning may be a disadvantage for students with learning problems.

SKILL 12.4 Understand augmentative, alternative, and assistive communication strategies

Other uses of technology allow students to access material they may otherwise be unable to utilize. Students, who are unable to speak, may use technology devices to communicate. These augmentative communication systems are crucial to the participation and success of these learners. In other incidences, there are programs that will read text to students unable to see or read the text independently. Programs are available that will allow the student to dictate written assignments and then the program will translate the spoken words into a word processing document which can be edited.

Smart boards, similar to wipe boards that are connected to a computer, provide a more interactive nature to oral presentations within the classroom. Students are able to use special markers or their hands to activate the display, allowing them to be more active participants in lectures. You can write on the board and then save the information to your computer for use later.

Digital cameras and digital video recorders can be wonderful enhancements to the instructional process. They allow students to add pictures to their assignments making them more personal and real. Another use is to provide the students with authenticity to daily routines. For example, a student who is in need of appropriate behavioral reminders could be photographed completing the proper task. This picture reminder can be used within the classroom to provide the student with a visual cue to the behavior the child should be exhibiting.

Whether the technology is digital clocks, computers, digital cameras, or the more complex smart boards, it is imperative educators take full advantage of the resources available to them. Technology is a part of our daily lives and in order to prepare students, they need to feel comfortable using technology. The flexibility of the inherent nature of technology allows teachers to meet the needs of more students at an individual level than ever before.

SKILL 12.5 Demonstrate knowledge of effective ways to address a broad range of individual communication needs, including the needs of students whose primary language is not English

The No Child Left Behind legislation includes students with Limited English Proficiency and students with disabilities in the accountability system and judges them by the same standard used for all other students. In the past, students with Limited English Proficiency (LEP) were often excluded from high-stakes, large-scale assessments because educators believed it was not in the best interest of students to take the tests. Students who have LEP and a disability have an even greater chance of their educational needs not being met. In many cases educators will have to assess whether their problem in the classroom can be attributed to their language difficulties or to their disability, or a combination of both.

The NCLB legislation was designed to make sure that students in subgroups with low percentages of students meeting standards would receive attention in schools. Educators are concerned excluding students from testing may be detrimental to students because it allows their needs to remain unknown. Students who are not tested may not get the services they need to improve their academic achievement. Many educational researchers now believe that LEP students and students with disabilities should be included in the assessments, when practical, to ensure the needs of these students are not ignored.

The policies for LEP students and students with disabilities under the No Child Left Behind legislation were changed in February 2004. One change was that schools were no longer required to give students with limited English proficiency their state's reading test if the students were enrolled in a U.S. school for less than a year. Schools are still required to give those students the state's math test, but they may substitute an English-proficiency test for the reading test during the first year of enrollment.

As was the case before this change, states have a one-year grace period before they must include scores of students with limited English proficiency in the calculations for adequate yearly progress. The second rule change permits states to count students who have become proficient in English within the past two years in their calculations of adequate yearly progress.

From high school and college, most of us think learning a language strictly involves drills, memorization, and tests, and this is a common method used (some people call it a structural, grammatical, or linguistic approach). While this works for some students, it certainly does not work for all.

Although there are dozens of methods that have been developed to help people learn additional languages, we will focus on some of the more common approaches used in today's K-12 classrooms.

Cognitive approaches to language learning focus on concepts. While words and grammar are important, when teachers use the cognitive approach, they focus on using language for conceptual purposes—rather than learning words and grammar for the sake of simply learning new words and grammatical structures. This approach focuses heavily on students' learning styles, and it cannot necessarily be pinned down as having specific techniques. Rather, it is more of a philosophy of instruction.

There are many approaches that are noted for their motivational purposes. In a general sense, when teachers work to motivate students to learn a language, they do things to help reduce fear and to assist students in identifying with native speakers of the target language. A very common method is often called the functional approach. In this approach, the teacher focuses on communicative elements. For example, a first grade ESOL teacher might help students learn phrases that will assist them in finding a restroom or asking for help on the playground, etc. Many functionally-based adult ESOL programs help learners with travel-related phrases and words.

Another very common motivational approach is Total Physical Response. This is a kinesthetic approach that combines language learning and physical movement. In essence, students learn new vocabulary and grammar by responding with physical motion to verbal commands. Some people say it is particularly effective because the physical actions create good brain connections with the words.

In general, the best methods do not treat students as if they have a language deficit. Rather, the best methods build upon what students already know, and they help to instill the target language as a communicative process rather than a list of vocabulary words that have to be memorized.

In addition to these methods, it is important that teachers communicate and collaborate in order to provide greater consistency, particularly when second language learners have multiple teachers, such as in middle or high school. It is particularly difficult for second language learners to go from one class to the next, with different sets of expectations and varied methods of instruction, to focus on the more complex elements of learning language. When students have higher levels of anxiety regarding the learning of a second language, they will be less likely to focus on the language; rather, they will be focusing on whatever it is that is creating that anxiety. This does not mean that standards and expectations should not be held for students in all classes; it just means that teachers should have common expectations so that students know what to expect in each class and don't have to think about the differences between classes.

Another important reason for teachers to collaborate, particularly with the ESL specialists, is to ensure students are showing consistent development across classes. Where there is inconsistency, teachers should work to uncover what it is that is keeping the student from excelling in a particular class.

The most important concept to remember regarding the difference between learning a first language and a second one is that if the learner is approximately age seven or older, learning a second language will occur very differently in the learner's brain than it will had the learner been younger. The reason for this is that there is a language-learning function that exists in young children that appears to go away as they mature. Learning a language prior to age seven is almost guaranteed, with relatively little effort. The mind is like a sponge, and it soaks up language very readily. Some theorists, including the famous linguist Noam Chomsky, argue that the brain has a "universal grammar" and that only vocabulary and very particular grammatical structures, related to specific languages, need to be introduced in order for a child to learn a language. What this really means is that, in essence, there are slots into which language gets filled in a child's mind. This is definitely not the case with learning a second language after about seven years old.

Learning a second language as a pre-adolescent, adolescent, or adult requires quite a bit of translation from the first language to the second. Vocabulary and grammar particulars are memorized, not necessarily internalized (at least, as readily as a first language). In fact, many (though not all) people who are immersed in a second language never fully function as fluent in the language. They may appear to be totally fluent, but often there will be small traits that are hard to pick up and internalize.

It is fairly clear that learning a second language successfully does require fluency in the first language. This is because, as stated above, the second language is translated from the first in the learner's mind. First language literacy is also a crucial factor in second language learning, particularly second language literacy.

When helping second language learners make the "cross-over" in language fluency or literacy from first language to second language, it is important to help them identify strategies they use in the first language and apply those to the second language. It is also important to note similarities and differences in phonetic principals in the two languages. Sometimes it is helpful to encourage students to translate; other times, it is helpful for them to practice production in the target language. In either case, teachers must realize that learning a second language is a slow and complicated process.

Please refer to Skill 12.2 for more information.

COMPETENCY 13.0 UNDERSTAND EVIDENCE-BASED STRATEGIES AND TECHNIQUES FOR IMPROVING THE SOCIAL COMPETENCE OF STUDENTS WITH MILD/MODERATE DISABILITIES.

SKILL 13.1 Understand types and characteristics of social difficulties associated with various disabilities

Many youngsters with disabilities have difficulty in developing social behavior that follows accepted norms. While non-disabled children learn most social behaviors from family and peers, children with disabilities are the product of a wide, complex range of different social experiences. When coupled with one or more of the disabilities, this experience adds up to a collective deficit in interpersonal relationships.

There is an irreducible philosophical issue underlying the realm of social behavior among children with disabilities. To some extent, the disability itself causes maladaptive behaviors to develop. Regardless whether social skill deficits are seminal or secondary among youth with disabilities; it is the task of the special education professional to help each child develop as normally as possible in the social-interpersonal realm.

Children with disabilities can be taught social-interpersonal skills through developing sensitivity to other people, through making behavioral choices in social situations, and through developing social maturity.

SENSITIVITY TO OTHERS

Central to the human communication process is the nonverbal domain. Children with disabilities may perceive facial expressions and gestures differently than their nondisabled peers, due to their impairment. There are several kinds of activities to use in developing a child's sensitivity to other people. Examples of these activities follow.

1. Offer a selection of pictures with many kinds of faces to the child. Ask the child to identify or classify the faces according to the emotion that appears in the picture. Allow the child to compare his reactions to those of the other students.
2. Compare common gestures through a mixture of acting and discussion. The teacher can demonstrate shaking her head in the negative, and then ask the students for the meaning of the gesture. Reactions can be compared, and then a game can be started in which each student performs a gesture while others tell what it means.
3. DVDs, videotapes, and movies are available in which famous people and cartoon characters utilize gestures. Children can be asked what a particular gesture means.
4. Tape recording with playback can be used to present social sounds. Again, a game is possible here, and the activity focuses the student's attention on one narrow issue - the sound and its precise social meaning.
5. Pairs of students can be formed for exercises in reading each other's gestures and nonverbal communications. Friendships of a lasting nature are encouraged by this activity.

SOCIAL SITUATIONS

Inherent differences in appearances and motions among children with disabilities cause some of them to develop behavior problems in social situations. It is necessary to remediate this situation in order to provide as normal a life as possible.

Here are some activities that strengthen a child's social skills, in social situations.

1. Anticipate the consequence of social actions. Have the students act out roles, tell stories, and discuss the consequences that flow from their actions.
2. Gain appropriate independence. Students can be given exercises in going places alone. For the very young, and for those with development issues, this might consist of finding a location within the room. Go on a field trip into the city. Allow older students to make purchases on their own. Using play money in the classroom for younger children would be beneficial.
3. Make ethical and/or moral judgments. The unfinished story, requiring the pupil to finish it at the point where a judgment is required, makes an independent critique of the choices made by the characters in the play.
4. Plan and execute. Children with disabilities can be allowed to plan an outing, a game, a party, or an exercise.

Having the teacher set an example is always a good way to teach social maturation. If the classroom is orderly, free of an oppressive atmosphere, and full of visibly rational judgments about what is going on, the students absorb the climate of doing things in a mature manner.

SKILL 13.2 Apply knowledge of social skills needed for educational and other environments

Please also refer to Skill 13.4.

Social skill deficits may compound academic problems because time spent engaged in negative encounters with others, or maladaptive behavior takes valuable time away from learning. Many children with behavior disorders display deficits in such areas as popularity with others, ability to adapt to changes, and demands of different situations. Social skills instruction also includes survival skills (such as asking for assistance), communication skills, and problem-solving skills.

Possible reasons for social skills deficits:
- Lack of suitable role models (e.g. family members who constantly use aggression to resolve conflicts)
- Lack of opportunity to observe and practice certain social skills (e.g. a young child who has not had much interaction with children may find it difficult to allow his peers to take turns in games
- Lack of previous instruction in certain skills (e.g. a child who has never had to travel on public transportation will probably not know how to read schedules and ask for help in using public transportation)
- Cultural differences which may create conflicts but may not in themselves be maladaptive (i.e. differences in "personal space" boundaries between persons having a conversation)

Methods of identifying and assessing social skills deficits include:

1. Social Skills Checklists: Examples of commercial checklists include the Walker Problem Behavior Identification Checklist, Revised Behavior Problem Checklist, and the Deveraux Scales for Elementary and Adolescent Children. Checklists are used to report the presence or absence of a behavior, while rating scales indicate the frequency of a particular behavior and often include teacher as well as parent report forms.

2. Direct Observation: Direct observations of the child in various settings to identify problem behaviors across settings. The child's behavior can also be compared to that of his or her peers in similar settings. Observations should include the components of the child's environment as well as how others interact with the child. It is possible that adjustments in the environment can decrease or eliminate the undesirable behavior.

3. Role Playing: In this type of observation, a social situation is staged, and the teacher observes the student's behavior. The teacher can determine if the student does not know or knows but is not putting into use the skill. Role plays may be part of a commercially prepared training activity or designed by the teacher.

4. Self-Reports: The student may complete a checklist, a questionnaire, (questions with open-ended statements), or a direct interview with the teacher.

5. Sociometric Measures: Three basic formats are (a) peer nominations based on nonbehavioral criteria such as preferred playmates, (b) peer ratings, where students rate all of their peers on nonbehavioral criteria such as work preferences, and (c) peer assessments, where peers are rated with respect to specific behaviors.

SKILL 13.3 Understand strategies and techniques for promoting students' ability to understand expectations and respond appropriately in various social situations

Social skills training is an essential part of working with students who exhibit academic and social problems. Often these two problem areas, academic and social deficits, appear together. This issue presents a "chicken-and-egg" situation: Does the learning problem cause the behavior problem, or does the behavior problem cause the learning problem?

Typically, social skills are taught within the academic setting in special education. This is accomplished through classroom rules and contingency point systems that focus upon both areas at the same time. Rules, few in number, written in a positive direction, and designed jointly with students, help to set standards for acceptable behavior within the classroom. Contingency point systems are established to reinforce the occurrence of these behaviors, as well as other academic and social behaviors that are considered appropriate. Reinforcement contingencies are an important means of encouraging their use.

It is important that the physical environment be arranged so that preventive discipline can occur. This means the teacher assumes responsibility for creating and maintaining an environment in which the needs of her charges are met. She may modify the physical aspects of the room create a warm, motivating atmosphere; adapt instructional materials to the respective functioning levels of the students; and deliver specialized services through the use of systematic, reinforcing methods and techniques. When instructional environments, materials, and techniques are implemented that responds to the academic needs of students, often the personal needs of the student are met as well, with a parallel effect of increased learning and appropriate social behaviors.

According to Henley, Ramsey, and Algozzine (1993, 1995), positive student behavior is facilitated by the teacher through techniques such as the following:

1. Provide students with cues about expected behavior. Both verbal and non-verbal signals may become a part of the general classroom routine. The teacher provides cues about acceptable and unacceptable behavior in a consistent manner.
2. Provide appropriate and necessary structure. Based upon individual differences and needs, structure should be built into the environment. Children with aggressive and anxious traits may need a high degree of structure, while others with less significant conditions will require lesser, but varied, amounts of structure. (Structure relates to teacher direction, physical arrangement of environment, routine and scheduling, and classroom rules)
3. Involve each student in the learning process. Allow them to manipulate things, to explore surroundings, to experiment with alternative solutions, to compare findings with those of classmates, and to pose questions and seek answers. This helps to instill an internal focus of control while meaningfully involving the child in the learning process.
4. Enable the student to experience success. If the student is not provided tasks or activities in which success can be experienced, the teacher can expect misbehavior or withdrawal. Having successful experiences are vital in developing feelings of self-worth and confidence in attempting new activities. (Jones & Jones, 1986).
5. Use interest boosting. If signs of disinterest or restlessness occur, the teacher quickly shows interest in the student. Conversing with the student may stimulate renewed interest or enthusiasm.
6. Diffuse tension through humor. A humorous comment may bring forth laughter that lessens the tension in a stressful situation.
7. Help the student hurdle lessons that produce difficulty. The teacher can get a student back on track by assisting in the answering of difficult problems. Thus, the hurdle is removed and the student is back on task.
8. Use signal interference. Cue the student with signals so that a potential problem can be extinguished. Individualized signals may be designed and directed toward specific students.
9. Incorporate antiseptic bouncing when it is obvious that a student needs to be temporarily removed from the classroom situation. This technique is useful in dispelling uncontrollable laughter or hiccups and in helping the student get over feelings of anger, or disappointment. This approach involves no punishment, and removal may be in the form of delivering a message, getting a drink of water, or other chores that appear routine.
10. Use teacher reinforcing. The teacher "catches the child engaged in appropriate behavior" and reinforces him at that time. For example, the teacher praises the student's task-oriented behavior in an effort to keep him from getting off task.

11. Employ planned ignoring. Unless the behavior is of a severe, harmful, or self-injurious nature, the teacher purposefully ignores the child. This strategy helps to extinguish inappropriate behavior by removing a viable reinforcer, that of teacher attention. The key is to deliver substantial reinforcement for appropriate behavior.
12. Use teacher commanding. The teacher uses direct verbal commands in an effort to stop the misbehavior. This technique should not be continued, however, if the student does not stop the inappropriate behavior upon the first instance he is told to do so. Inappropriate behavior will probably worsen upon repeated verbal commands.
13. Try teacher focusing. The teacher expresses empathy or understanding about the student's feelings, situation, or plight. The teacher uses inquiry to obtain information from the student, and then offers reasons or possible solutions to the problem.
14. Utilize teacher redirecting. The student exhibiting an inappropriate behavior is brought back on-task by having him performing an action that is compatible to the previous appropriate behavior. For example, the child who stops singing and starts poking a peer might be asked to play a musical instrument.

INTERVENTIONS THAT PROMOTE AGE APPROPRIATE SOCIAL SKILLS FOR INDIVIDUALS OR GROUPS

Mercer and Mercer (1993) recommend five general teaching techniques to build positive self-concepts in students, which can do much to eliminate the frustration, anxiety and resulting acting-out behaviors in children. These suggestions are:
- Incorporate learning activities that provide opportunities for success
- Establish goals and expectations
- Monitor progress and provide regular feedback
- Provide a positive and supportive learning environment
- Teach students to be independent learners

There are commercial programs to teach specific social skills, but the teacher can take advantage of opportunities throughout the day to teach them. Examples of such opportunities include:
- Teacher modeling of positive social behaviors throughout the day
- Reinforcing instances when students display positive behaviors
- Planning instances for students to practice social behaviors
- Assigning responsibilities to students
- Assisting students in identification of their strengths and in finding behaviors to be targeted for change
- Assist students in setting goals and in making plans to achieve those goals

Teaching techniques that have been used to teach social skills include:

1. *Bibliotherapy:* Selected children's books are used to help the child identify with the problems faced with the main character, release emotions regarding the problems, and develop insight into his own behavior. Through reading about others with similar problems, the child can discuss the situation in the book, relate them to his own situation and analyze the problem-solving methods used in the story.

2. *Attribution Retraining:* Often, students with learning and behavior problems attribute their success or failure to outside causes rather than their own ability or lack of effort. Through attribution retraining, students are taught to attribute success to their own efforts (i.e. studying rather than the test being "too easy") and failure to ineffective strategies, rather than being "dumb". Students are taught study skills and other learning strategies to help them become better learners.

3. *Modeling:* The teacher gives positive reinforcement to students who exhibit desirable behaviors. For example, if the teacher wants students to learn how to initiate a conversation, he can select the student models, set up a demonstration of appropriate ways to initiate a conversation, and have the other students observe the model. The teacher should provide opportunities for the students to practice, and consistently reinforce students who perform the behavior.

4. *Behavior Modification:* Behavior modification is a systematic approach toward the modification of behavior. Its use has the effect of strengthening, maintaining, or weakening target behaviors. Concerns that have surfaced over the use of behavior modification pertain primarily to the concept of free will versus control by external forces.

5. *Cognitive Behavior Modification:* Meichenbaum's research in this technique is well known in the field of learning disabilities. CBM involves a three-step process to teach academic as well as social skills. The goal of CBM is to encourage the student to think through his or her actions before acting. As part of this process, the teacher should build in errors or obstacles in order to teach students how to deal with mistakes and setbacks. In the CBM process,

   a. The teacher or another adult performs the task or social skill while verbalizing the thinking process aloud,
   b. The student performs the task or social skill while verbalizing the process aloud, while the teacher reinforces and provides feedback,
   c. The student performs the task while thinking to himself, and the teacher provides reinforcement and feedback.

6. *Self-management*: Self-management is an important part of social skills training, especially for older students preparing for employment. Components of self-management include:
   a. Self-monitoring: choosing behaviors and alternatives and monitoring those actions.
   b. Self-evaluation: deciding the effectiveness of the behavior in solving the problem.
   c. Self-reinforcement: telling oneself that one is capable of achieving success.

7. *Interview techniques* such as Life-Space Interviewing and Reality Therapy. These techniques assist the student in solving interpersonal problems and manage crisis situations through discussing the problem and the maladaptive behaviors, generating alternatives, and assuming responsibility for one's actions.

8. *Commercial Programs*: Examples of these programs include:
   - Asset: A Social Skills Program for Adolescents
   - CLASS: Contingencies for Learning Academic and Social Skills
   - Getting Along with Others
   - Skill Streaming the Elementary School Child and Skill Streaming the Adolescent
   - Social Skills for Daily Living
   - Coping With Series
   - Walker Social Skills Curriculum, which includes ACCEPTS and ACCESS

These programs teach skills such as friendship (i.e. giving compliments) problem-solving (asking for help), successful classroom behaviors (complying with rules), conversation (asking questions), and other skills for difficult situations (rejection by peers, criticism from an employer). Teaching is usually done through a process of:
- Providing a description of the behavior and rationale for learning the appropriate behavior
- Modeling of the behavior
- Rehearsal and practice
- Feedback
- Generalization

For many students, generalizing skills learned in class to other situations on campus, on the job, or in the home and community, is the most difficult part of training. Thus, the teacher should periodically review the areas with the students and encourage them to learn the skills outside class. By recruiting others on campus to help with reinforcement (such as setting up situation where students must ask the media teacher for assistance in finding a reference, or asking the administrators to reinforce and reward them when they observe students exhibiting social skills), students can have additional instances to use and experience the value of using the skill(s) they learned in class.

COMPETENCY 14.0 UNDERSTAND EVIDENCE-BASED STRATEGIES AND TECHNIQUES FOR PROMOTING THE ACADEMIC ACHIEVEMENT AND INDEPENDENT LEARNING OF STUDENTS WITH MILD/MODERATE DISABILITIES.

SKILL 14.1 Understand general and special curricula and types and characteristics of academic difficulties associated with various disabilities

Please refer to Skills 1.1, 1.2, 2.1, 3.1, and 5.2 for characteristics of academic difficulties.

Please refer to the state website for information specifically about general and special curricula at

HTTP://WWW.SDE.STATE.OK.US/HOME/DEFAULTIE.HTML

SKILL 14.2 Demonstrate knowledge of effective instructional planning and implementation for students with mild/moderate disabilities, including the use of modeling, guided practice, ongoing monitoring progress, collaboration, individualized transition plans, and appropriate technologies.

Please refer to skill 6.6 for information about ongoing monitoring.

ASSESSMENTS USED TO MONITOR ONGOING PROGRESS

The assessment of academic achievement is an essential component of a psychoeducational evaluation. Achievement tests are instruments that directly assess students' skill development in academic content areas. This type of test measures the extent to which a student has profited from educational and/or life experiences compared to others of same age or grade level. Emphasis needs to be placed upon the kinds of behaviors each tests samples, the adequacy of its norms, the test reliability, and its validity.

An achievement test may be classified as a diagnostic test, because the strengths and weaknesses in skill development can be defined. Typically, when used as a diagnostic tool, an achievement test measures one basic skill and its related components. For example, a reading test may measure reading recognition, reading comprehension, reading fluency, decoding skills, and sound discrimination. Each skill measured is reported in sub-classifications.

In order to render pertinent information, achievement tests must reflect the content of the curriculum. Some achievement tests assess development in many subject areas, while others focus upon single content areas. Within similar content areas, the particular areas assessed and how they are measured, differ from test to test. The more prominent areas assessed by achievement tests include math, reading, and spelling.

Achievement test usages include screening, placement, progress evaluation, and curricula effectiveness. As screening tests, these instruments provide a wide index of academic development and may be used to pinpoint students for whom educational interventions may be necessary for purposes of remediation or enrichment. They offer a general idea of where to begin additional diagnostic assessment.

Achievement tests are routinely given in school districts across the nation as a means of evaluating progress. Scores of students can be compared locally, statewide, and with national norms. Accountability and quality controls can be kept in check through the reporting of scores.

Lastly, teachers can be provided with measures showing the effectiveness of their instruction. Progress reflected by student scores should be used to review, and often revise, instructional techniques and content. Alternative methods of delivery (i.e. presentations, worksheets, tests) can be devised to enhance instruction provided students.

TYPES OF ASSESSMENT

It is useful to consider the types of assessment procedures that are available to the classroom teacher. The types of assessment discussed below represent many of the more common types, but the list is not comprehensive.

Anecdotal records-These are notes recorded by the teacher concerning an area of interest or concern with a particular student. These records should focus on observable behaviors and should be descriptive in nature. They should not include assumptions or speculations regarding effective areas such as motivation or interest. These records are usually compiled over a period of several days to several weeks.

Rating scales & checklists-These assessments are generally self-appraisal instruments completed by the students or observation-based instruments completed by the teacher. The focus of these is frequently on behavior or effective areas such as interest and motivation.

Portfolio assessment-The use of student portfolios for some aspect of assessment has become quite common. The purpose, nature, and policies of portfolio assessment vary greatly from one setting to another. In general, a student's portfolio contains samples of work collected over an extended period of time. The nature of the subject, age of the student, and scope of the portfolio, all contribute to the specific mechanics of analyzing, synthesizing, and otherwise evaluating the portfolio contents.

In most cases, the student and teacher make joint decisions as to which work samples go into the student's portfolios. A collection of work compiled over an extended time period allows teacher, student, and parents to view the student's progress from a unique perspective. Qualitative changes over time can be readily apparent from work samples. Such changes are difficult to establish with strictly quantitative records typical of the scores recorded in the teacher's grade book.

Questioning-One of the most frequently occurring forms of assessment in the classroom is oral questioning by the teacher. As the teacher questions the students, she collects a great deal of information about the degree of student learning and potential sources of confusing for the students. While questioning is often viewed as a component of instructional methodology, it is also a powerful assessment tool.

Formal/Informal testing-Please refer to Skill 8.1 for definitions and descriptions.

PURPOSES FOR ASSESSMENT

There are a number of different classification systems used to identify the various purposes for assessment. A compilation of several lists identifies some common purposes such as the following:

1. Diagnostic assessments are used to determine individual weakness and strengths in specific areas.
2. Readiness assessments measure prerequisite knowledge and skills.
3. Interest and Attitude assessments attempt to identify topics of high interest or areas in which students may need extra motivational activities.
4. Evaluation assessments are generally programmed or teacher focused.
5. Placement assessments are used for purposes of grouping students or determining appropriate beginning levels in leveled materials.
6. Formative assessment provides on-going feedback student progress and the success of instructional methods and materials.
7. Summative assessment defines student accomplishment with the intent to determine the degree of student mastery or learning that has taken place.

For most teachers, assessment purposes vary according to the situation. It may be helpful to consult several sources to help formulate an overall assessment plan. Kellough and Roberts (1991) identify six purposes for assessment. These are:

1. To evaluate and improve student learning
2. To identify student strengths and weaknesses
3. To assess the effectiveness of a particular instructional strategy
4. To evaluate and improve program effectiveness
5. To evaluate and improve teacher effectiveness
6. To communicate to parents their children's progress (p.341)

LIMITATIONS OF VARIOUS TYPES OF ASSESSMENT

The existence of various types of assessment stems from the unique needs of children with disabilities and the environments in which the disabilities are most troublesome. A student who demonstrates difficulty interacting with peers and acts impulsively may not be effectively evaluated with a portfolio. Anecdotal records, questioning and certain checklists may give a better picture of the extent to which such peer interactions are detrimental to the student's (and others') well being and success. Conversely, a student who displays academic difficulty is better assessed with samples of work (portfolio) and carefully chosen formal tests. In short, assessments are as valuable as their appropriate choice and use.

ALTERNATE ASSESSMENTS

Test taking is not a pleasant experience for many students with behavioral and/or learning problems. The skills necessary to be successful vary with the type of test. Certain students have difficulty with writing answers, but may be able to express their knowledge of subject matter verbally. Therefore, modifications of content area material may be extended to methods and modifications for evaluation and assessment of student progress.

Information about the student's achievement is gathered in a variety of ways including assessments such as intelligence tests and various achievement tests. In addition to those assessments other information is gathered through alternate assessments such as observations, performance-based assessments, interviews, and portfolios.

Observations - Observations are the recording of information about the student as the behavior occurs.

Performance-Based Assessments - Performance assessment is a form of testing that requires students to perform a task rather than select an answer from a ready-made list. The teacher then judges the quality of the student's work based on a predetermined set of criteria.

Portfolios - Portfolios are selected collections of a variety of the student's work. It includes work samples that are demonstrative of the students strengths and weaknesses.

Interview - Formal or informal interviews are often conducted of persons who have a close relationship to the student and can offer valuable information about the student's progress socially and academically.

TRANSITION PLANNING

Transition planning is mandated in the Individuals with Disabilities Education Act (IDEA). The transition planning requirements ensure planning is begun at age 14 and continued through high school. Transition planning and services focus on a coordinated set of student-centered activities designed to facilitate the student's progression from school to post-school activities. Transition planning should be flexible and focus on the developmental and educational requirements of the student at different grades and times.

Transition planning is a student-centered event that necessitates a collaborative endeavor. In reference to secondary students, the responsibilities are shared by the student, parents, secondary personnel, and postsecondary personnel, who are all members of the transition team.

In most cases when transition is mentioned, it is referring to a child 14 or over, but in some cases children younger than 14 may need transition planning and assistance. Depending on the child's disability and its severity, a child may need assistance with transitioning to school from home, or to school from a hospital or institution or any other setting. In those cases the members of the transition team may also include doctors or nurses, social workers, speech therapist, and physical therapists.

It is important that the student play a key role in transition planning. This will entail asking the student to identify preferences and interests and to attend meetings on transition planning. The degree of success experienced by the student in postsecondary educational settings depends on the student's degree of motivation, independence, self-direction, self-advocacy, and academic abilities developed in high school. Student participation in transition activities should be implemented as early as possible, and no later than age 16.

In order to contribute to the transition planning process, the student should: Understand his learning disability and the impact it has on learning and work; implement achievable goals; present a positive self-image by emphasizing strengths, while understanding the impact of the learning disability; know how and when to discuss and ask for needed accommodations; be able to seek instructors and learning environments that are supportive and establish an ongoing personal file that consists of school and medical records, individualized education program (IEP), resume, and samples of academic work.

The primary function of parents during transition planning is to encourage and assist students in planning and achieving their educational goals. Parents also should encourage students to cultivate independent decision-making and self-advocacy skills.

Transition planning involves input from four groups: the student, parents, secondary education professionals, and postsecondary education professionals. The result of effective transition from a secondary to a postsecondary education program is a student with a learning disability who is confident, independent, self motivated, and striving to achieve career goals. This effective transition can be achieved if the team consisting of the student, parents, and professional personnel work as a group to create and implement effective transition plans. The transition team of a student entering the workforce may also include community members, organizations, company representatives, vocational education instructors, and job coaches.

Please refer to skill 10.3 about transition planning.

LESSON PLAN COLLABORATION

According to Walther-Thomas et al (2000), "Collaboration for Inclusive Education," ongoing professional development providing teachers with opportunities to create effective instructional practice is vital and necessary, "A comprehensive approach to professional development is perhaps the most critical dimension of sustained support for successful program implementation." The inclusive approach incorporates learning programs that include all stakeholders in defining and developing high quality programs for students. Figure 1 below shows how an integrated approach of stakeholders can provide the optimal learning opportunity for all students.

Figure 1-Integrated Approach to Learning

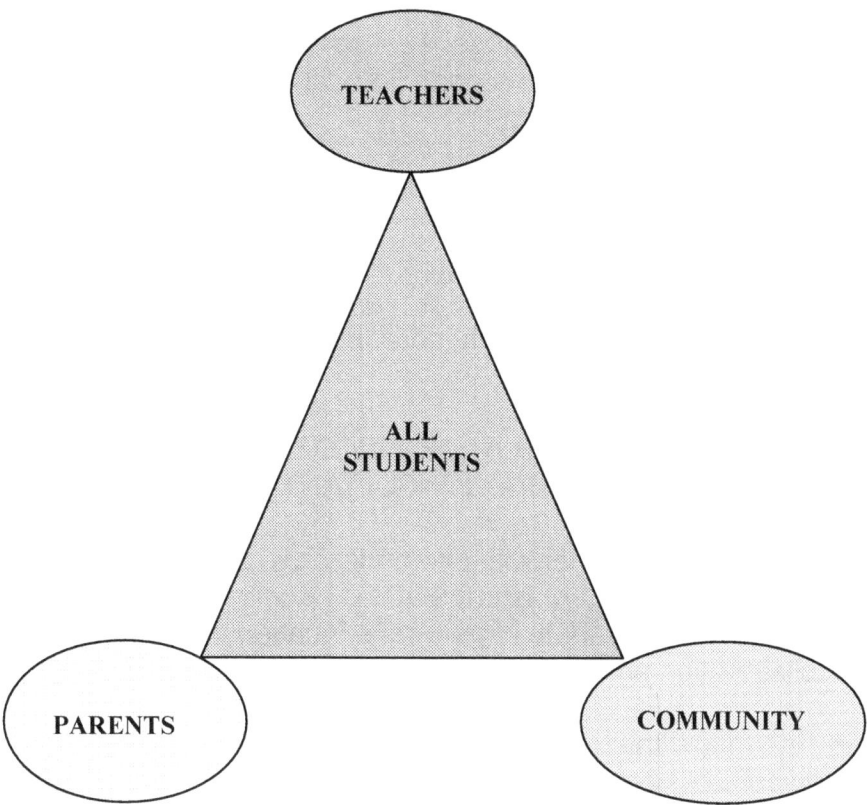

In the integrated approach to learning, teachers, parents, and community support become the integral apexes to student learning. The focus and central core of the school community is triangular as a representation of how effective collaboration can work in creating success for student learners. The goal of student learning and achievement now become the heart of the school community. The direction of teacher professional development in constructing effective instruction is clearly articulated in a greater understanding of facilitating learning strategies that develop skills and education equity for students.

Teachers need diversity in their instructional toolkits, which can provide students with clear instruction, mentoring, inquiry, challenge, performance-based assessment, and journal reflections on their learning processes. For teachers, having a collaborative approach to instruction fosters for students a deeper appreciation of learning, subject matter and knowledge acquisition. Implementing a consistent approach to learning from all stakeholders will create equitable educational opportunities for all learners.

Research has shown that educators who collaborate become more diversified and effective in implementation of curriculum and assessment of effective instructional practices. The ability to gain additional insight into how students learn and modalities of differing learning styles can increase a teacher's capacity to develop proactive instruction methods. Teachers who team teach or have daily networking opportunities can create a portfolio of curriculum articulation and inclusion for students.

People in business are always encouraged to network in order to further their careers. The same can be said for teaching. If English teachers get together and discuss what is going on in their classrooms, those discussions make the "whole" much stronger than the parts. Even if there are not formal opportunities for such networking, it's wise for schools or even individual teachers to develop them and seek them out.

INSTRUCTIONAL PLANNING FOR A VARIETY OF INCLUSIVE MODELS (E.G., CO-TEACHING, PUSH-IN, CONSULTANT TEACHING [CT])

According to IDEA 2004, students with disabilities are to participate in the general education program to the extent that it is beneficial for them. As these students are included into a variety of general education activities and classes, the need for collaboration among teachers grows.

Co-teaching One model that is used for general education and special education teachers to collaborate is co-teaching. In this model, both teachers actively teach in the general education classroom. Perhaps both teachers will conduct a small science experiment group at the same time, switching groups at some point in the lesson. Perhaps in social studies, one teacher will lecture while the other teacher writes notes on the board or points out information on a map.

In the co-teaching model, the general education teacher and special educator often switch roles back and forth within a class period or perhaps at the end of a chapter or unit.

Push-in Teaching In the push-in teaching model, the special educator is teaching parallel material in the general education classroom. When the regular education teacher is teaching word problems in math, for example, the special educator may be working with some students on setting up the initial problems and then having them complete the computation. Another example would be in science when the general education teacher is asking review questions for a test, and the special educator is working with a student who has a review study sheet to show the answer from a group of choices.

In the push-in teaching model, it may appear that two versions of the same lesson are being taught or two types of student responses / activities are being monitored on the same material. The push-in teaching model would be considered one type of differentiated instruction in which two teachers are teaching simultaneously.

Consultant Teaching In the consultant teaching model, the general education teacher conducts the class after planning with the special educator about how to differentiate activities so that the needs of the student with a disability are met.

In a social studies classroom using the consultant teaching model, both teachers may discuss what the expectations will be for a student with a learning disability and fine motor difficulty when the class does reports on states. They may decide that doing a state report is appropriate for the student, however, he may use the computer to write his report so that he can utilize the spell check feature and so that is his work is legible.

DEMONSTRATING KNOWLEDGE OF INSTRUCTIONAL METHODS, TECHNIQUES, AND CURRICULA, INCLUDING ASSISTIVE AND INSTRUCTIONAL TECHNOLOGIES, USED WITH STUDENTS TO ACCOMMODATE SPECIFIC DISABILITIES

No two students are alike. It follows, then, that no two students *learn* alike. To apply a one dimensional instructional approach and a strict tunnel vision perspective of testing is to impose learning limits on students. All students have the right to an education, but there cannot be a singular path to that education. A teacher must acknowledge the variety of learning styles and abilities among students within a class (and, indeed, the varieties from class to class) and apply multiple instructional and assessment processes to ensure that every child has appropriate opportunities to master the subject matter, demonstrate such mastery, and improve and enhance learning skills with each lesson.

It has been traditionally assumed that a teacher will use direct instruction in the classroom. The amount of time devoted to it will vary according to the age of the class as well as other factors. Lecturing can be very valuable because it's the quickest way for transferring knowledge to students and they can also learn note-taking and information-organizing Skills in this way. However, having said that, there are many cautions to using an excessive amount of lecturing in a class of any age. In the first place, attention span even of senior high-school students is short when they are using only one sense—the sense of hearing. Teachers should limit how much lecturing they do as compared to other methods and how long the lectures last.

Most teachers find students enjoy the learning process when lecturing is limited and the students themselves become active in and responsible for their own learning. Students' attitudes and perceptions about learning are the most powerful factors influencing academic focus and success. When instructional objectives center on students' interests and are relevant to their lives, effective learning occurs. Learners must believe that the tasks that they are asked to perform have some value and that they have the ability and resources to perform them. If a student thinks a task is unimportant, he/she will not put forth much effort. If a student thinks he lacks the ability or resources to successfully complete a task, even attempting the task becomes too great a risk. Not only must the teacher understand the students' abilities and interests, she must also help students develop positive attitudes and perceptions about tasks and learning. Below are a few examples of instructional styles that actively involve the students.

DIFFERENTIATED INSTRUCTION

The effective teacher will seek to connect all students to the subject matter through multiple techniques, with the goal that each student, through their own abilities, will relate to one or more techniques and excel in the learning process. Differentiated instruction encompasses several areas:

- Content: What is the teacher going to teach? Or, perhaps better put, what does the teacher want the students to learn? Differentiating content means that students will have access to content that piques their interest about a topic, with a complexity that provides an appropriate challenge to their intellectual development.
- Process: A classroom management technique where instructional organization and delivery is maximized for the diverse student group. These techniques should include dynamic, flexible grouping activities, where instruction and learning occurs both as whole-class, teacher-led activities, as well as peer learning and teaching (while teacher observes and coaches) within small groups or pairs.
- Product: The expectations and requirements placed on students to demonstrate their knowledge or understanding. The type of product expected from each student should reflect each student's own capabilities.

ALTERNATIVE ASSESSMENTS

Alternative assessment is an assessment where students create an answer or a response to a question or task, as opposed to traditional, inflexible assessments where students choose a prepared response from among a selection of responses, such as matching, multiple-choice or true/false.

When implemented effectively, an alternative assessment approach will exhibit these characteristics, among others:
- Requires higher-order thinking and problem-solving
- Provides opportunities for student self-reflection and self-assessment
- Uses real world applications to connect students to the subject
- Provides opportunities for students to learn and examine subjects on their own, as well as to collaborate with their peers.
- Encourages students to continue learning beyond the requirements of the assignment
- Clearly defines objective and performance goals

Teachers are learning the value of giving assignments that meet the individual abilities and needs of students. After instruction, discussion, questioning, and practice have been provided, rather than assigning one task to all students—teachers are asking students to generate tasks that will show their knowledge of the information presented. Students are given choices and thereby have the opportunity to demonstrate more effectively the skills, concepts, or topics that they as individuals have learned. It has been established that student choice increases student originality, intrinsic motivation, and higher mental processes.

Please refer to skill 11.6 for information about grouping arrangements.

CURRICULUM DESIGN

Effective curriculum design assists the teacher from teacher demonstration to independent practice. Components of curriculum design include:
- Quizzes or reviews of the previous lesson
- Step-by-step presentations with multiple examples
- Guided practice and feedback
- Independent practice that requires the student to produce faster responses

The chosen curriculum should introduce information in a cumulative sequence and not introduce too much new information at a time. New vocabulary and symbols should be introduced one at a time, and the relationships of components to the whole should be stressed. Students' background information should be recalled to connect new information to the old. Finally, teach strategies or algorithms first and then move on to tasks that are more difficult.

Course objectives may be obtained from the department head at the local school. District program specialists also have lists of objectives for each course provided in the local school system. Additionally, publishers of textbooks will have scope and sequence lists in the teacher's manual.

ADDRESSING STUDENTS' NEEDS

There are a number of procedures teachers can use to address the varying needs of the students. Some of the more common procedures are:

1. Vary assignments-A variety of assignments on the same content allows students to match learning styles and preferences with the assignment. If all assignments are writing assignments, for example, students who are hands-on or visual learners are at a disadvantage unrelated to the content base itself.

2. Cooperative learning-Cooperative learning activities allow students to share ideas, expertise, and insight with a non-threatening setting. The focus tends to remain on positive learning rather than on competition.

3. Structure environment-Some student's need and benefit from clear structure that defines the expectation and goals of the teacher. The student knows what is expected and when, and can work and plan accordingly.

4. Clearly stated assignments-Assignments should be clearly stated along with the expectation and criteria for completion. Reinforcement and practice activities should not be a guessing game for the students. The exception to this is, of course, those situations in which a discovery method is used.

5. Independent practice-Independent practice involving application and repetition is necessary for thorough learning. Students learn to be independent through practicing independent learning. These activities should always be within the student's abilities to perform successfully without assistance.

6. Repetition-Very little learning is successful with a single exposure. Learners generally require multiple exposures to the same information for learning to take place. However, this repetition does not have to be dull and monotonous. In conjunction with number one above, varied assignments can provide repetition of content or skill practiced without repetition of specific activities. This helps keep learning fresh and exciting for the student.

7. Overlearning-As a principle of effective learning, overlearning recommends students continue to study and review after they have achieved initial mastery. The use of repetition in the context of varied assignments, offers the means to help students pursue and achieve overlearning.

Please refer to skill 11.1 for information about assistive technology.

Skill 14.3 Demonstrate knowledge of instructional methods and materials, including adapted materials and assistive technologies, for promoting the academic achievement of students with mild/moderate disabilities, including those whose primary language is not English

Please refer to Skill 14.2 and 11.1 for more information about assistive technology.

ASSISTIVE DEVICES

Sensory Impairments: Vision and Hearing- The use of electronic devices is nothing new to persons with vision and hearing impairments. For many years, people with sensory impairments have utilized various kinds of technologies to help them learn and function in society (Smith & Luckasson, 1992).

Other technology users who have, and continue to benefit from modern scientific advances, are those with physical and health impairments, and speech/communication disorders. Though the assistive devices are presented in categories, overlap occurs. For example, communication boards can be used to facilitate sound and communication, and when in raised symbols, can facilitate visually impaired persons. Computers and television screens can be adapted to assist persons with visual, auditory, physical, and speech /communication problems.

Visual Impairments –
- **Visual Aids.** For those with visual disorders, the Laser Cane and Sonicguide are two examples of electronic devices that have been in use for some time. These devices operate on the principle that people can learn to locate objects by hearing their echoes. For instance, the Laser Cane emits three beams of infrared light (one up, one down, and one straight ahead) that are converted into sound when they strike objects in the path of the person. The Sonicguide functions as an ultrasonic aid that helps children born blind to gain an awareness of their environment and objects in it. The device is worn on the head, emits ultrasound, and converts reflections from objects into audible sounds.

A newly developed machine, the Personal Companion, can respond to human voice and answer with synthesized voice. It can look up someone's telephone number from an internal directory and dial the telephone. Even though it cannot write a check, it can balance someone's checkbook. The Personal Companion can "read" aloud sections from a morning newspaper delivered through telecommunications over telephone lines. This machine can maintain a daily appointment book, and turn on and off appliances such as radio or lights.

Advances in computer technology are providing access to printed information for many people with visual impairments. Book will soon be available on computer disks, allowing for a variety of outputs: voice, enlarged print, or Braille. Organizations such as the Visually Impaired and Blind User Group (VIBUG) of the Boston Computer Society are exchanging information to expand computer literacy among persons with visual impairments (Smith & Luckasson, 1992). Personal computers with special printers can transform print to Braille. By attaching a specially designed Braille printer to a computer, standard text can be converted into Braille, allowing teachers to produce copies of handouts, worksheets, tests, maps, charts, and other class materials in Braille.

Closed-circuit television (CCTV) can be used to enlarge the print found in printed texts and books. By using a small television camera with a zoom lens and a sliding reading stand upon which the printed materials are placed, the greatly enlarged printed material can be viewed on a television monitor. All types of printed materials can be enlarged, such as magazines, textbooks, and photocopied handouts.

Computers with special word processing programs can produce large print displays that enable persons to adjust the size of the print with their visual capabilities. Not only can different size print be selected for individual students on the viewing monitor, but hard copy printouts can be printed in different sizes for individual uses.

> **Audio Aids.** Talking books have been available through the Library of Congress since 1934, using specially designed record players and tape cassette machines developed by the American Printing House for the Blind. Regional resource and materials centers disseminate these records, tapes, and machines. Audiotape versions of many classic books and current best-sellers are available in most bookstores.

Newly devised systems that allow printed materials to be synthesized into speech are available. They can be purchased at a much lower cost and with higher quality sound than older devices such as the Kurzwell Reader. One of these newer systems uses a small sensor attached to a computer. When the sensor is moved along a line of type, information is passed to the computer, which in turn translates the print to speech. The person listening can select how fast they want the speech to be delivered (rate), the pitch, and the gender of the voice/sound the computer generates. This enables students with visual impairments to use the same books and materials as their regular classmates. They do not have to wait for orders to be prepared or mailed to them.

For those who listen to television, but cannot see what is happening, new technology is being piloted at the present time which adds a sound track. By using the added sound track available in stereo televisions, descriptive videos tell the listener the nonverbal messages others see on the screen.

Hearing Impairments-

- **Visual aids.** Telecommunications and alerting devices are two types of assistive devices that use sight and touch. Captions are like subtitles that appear at the bottom of a television screen that can be read. Open captions appear on the screen for all viewers to see (e.g., foreign films translations), and have been available for some time. Closed captions are relatively new, and are somewhat expensive. In this system, captions can be seen on the screen, only if a decoder is accessible.

The Telecommunication Device for the Deaf (TDD) enables persons who have hearing impairments to make and receive telephone calls. A teletypewriter connected to the telephone prints out a voice message. The teletypewriter can also print out messages, but the receiver must have a teletypewriter as well in order to do this. A TDD can be used in a relay system, where the operator places the call on a voice line and reads the typed message to the non-TDD user. A full conversation can be made using a relay system (Smith & Luckasson, 1992).

DeafNet and Disabilities Forum are computer networks that provide electronic mail for persons with hearing impairments. These network systems function like other kinds of electronic mail where individuals or groups can subscribe to a communication system that transfers printed messages to subscribers. Electronic mail enables individuals and groups with common interests to communicate by using computers and information sent by telephone lines.

- **Audio Aids.** Hearing aids and other equipment that help people make better use of their residual hearing are referred to as assistive listening devices (ALDs). For those with hearing impairments, the hearing aid is the most commonly used electronic device. Other types of ALDs help individuals with hearing impairments use their residual hearing.

Hearing aids differ in size, cost, and efficiency. Types range from wearable hearing aids to group auditory training units that can be used by several children at the same time. Wearable hearing aids can be inserted into the external auditory canal, built into glasses, and worn behind glasses, behind the ear, and on clothing.

FM (frequency-modulated) transmission deices (auditory trainers) are used in some classrooms by teachers and students. To use an auditory trainer, the teacher speaks into a microphone, and the sound is received directly by each student's receiver or hearing aid. This system reduces background noise, allows teachers to move freely around the room, and help students benefit more from lectures.

The audio loop is an ALD that directs sound from its source directly to the listener's ear through a specially equipped hearing aid or earphone. Sound travels through a wire connection or by radio waves. Audio loops can be built into the walls of a classroom or some smaller area like a conference room.

Physical and Health Impairments - Technology has helped individuals with physical and health impairments to gain access to and control the environment around them, communicate with others, and take advantage of health care. There are high-tech devices such as computers, but also low-tech devices like built-up spoons and crutches. Electric typewriters, computer keyboards, and automated language boards provide means for communication to occur.

Mobility has been assisted by use of lightweight or electric specialized wheelchairs. These include motorized chairs, computerized chairs, chairs in which it is possible to rise, wilderness sports chairs, and racing chairs (Smith & Luckasson, 1992). Electronic switches allow persons with only partial movement (e.g., head, neck, fingers, toes) to be more mobile. Even driving a car is possible.

Mobility is also enhanced by use of artificial limbs, personalized equipped vans, and electrical walking machines. Myoelectric (or bionic) limbs contain a sensor that picks up electric signals transmitted from the person's brain through the limb. Robotic arms can manipulate objects by at least three directional movements: extension/retraction, swinging/rotating, and elevation/depression. Manipulator robots can assist by dialing a telephone, turning book pages, and drinking from a cup.

Speech/Communication- A communication board is a flat surface on which words, pictures, or both can be placed. The student is encouraged to point to the symbols of what he or she wants to communicate. Simple boards can be made from magazine or newspaper pictures. Others can be written on to display messages. More sophisticated boards incorporate an attachment that synthesizes a "voice." Communication books function like a board and assist communication.

Media Equipment - Many types of media equipment are available for use in the classroom. Multidimensional teaching approaches are possible with machines that provide instruction through various sensory modality channels. Individual receptive strengths can be matched with equipment directing learning through visual, auditory, haptic, or multidimensional input channels.

The compact disc player and the cassette player are particularly of benefit to students who learn best by auditory input. Both frequently accompany commercial instructional programs (e.g., reading kits, programmed workbooks) and can be operated by students trained to do so. Both can accommodate earphones or headsets for single or group listening opportunities.

Compact disc and cassette players offer the additional benefit of being lightweight for transporting, relatively inexpensive, and adaptable for recording information or responses by teachers or students. Teacher recorded tapes offer the opportunity for students to read along with or follow story sequences with accompanying pictures, listen to stories for pleasure, practice spelling words, and learn to follow instructions. They can also be used to answer comprehension questions, discriminate auditory sounds, perform word study exercises, and in general, maintain and motivate student interest.

Record players offer instructional uses similar to those of cassette players, with the exception of the recording capacity. However, records are often the medium by which foreign languages are taught, motor coordination is developed, and background mood setting music is obtained.

Equipment such as DVD players, television, and videocassette players provide unlimited opportunities for visual and auditory input. Machines of this type offer the capability of presenting instructional content to individuals or groups of students in a format that readers and nonreaders alike can understand. Special effects (e.g., flashbacks, fades, close-ups, quick and slow pans) can be obtained by use of videocassettes. Selected pauses and review of material are easily achieved by means of DVDs and videocassettes.

DVD players, special television programs, and videocassettes are often used to supplement and enhance instructional material already introduced. On occasion, instructional material is introduced by these means. Reinforcement may also be delivered through the showing of entertaining visual material.

Students may be allowed to go to a media center and view a DVD or video for pleasure. Another alternative is to show a part of a selected video and ask students to hypothesize what preceded the viewed portion, or what followed the action they saw. Students can be asked to write a narrative for a film, which they have only seen in silence. A videocassette dealing with a social problem can be stopped before the solutions are offered; students may offer their own solutions. A videocassette portraying a dramatic story can be ended prematurely. Students are directed to write endings and act them out.

The slide projector is used to project visual images on a screen for supplementary types of instructional processes. Slides may be shown singularly, or in a multiple sequence, and accompanied by a cassette tape, synchronized with the showing of a slide.

The overhead projector is an easy-to-use and maintain visual communication device. A bright lamp source transmits light through the translucent material to a screen close to the machine. Transparencies can be purchased commercially or made from clear photocopies of materials.

Flat, printed, drawn pictures, or other materials can be projected with an opaque projector. This machine operates with reflected light; the lamp illuminates the material, and the image is reflected by a mirror through the lens to the screen. Visual images or instruction is provided to learners by this means. Materials in a book may be projected without removing the pages.

Computers and software- Microcomputers are valuable teaching tools. Software programs and adaptations enable learners with disabilities (i.e., physical, cognitive, and sensory) to profit from instruction in the classroom, which they might not be able to receive otherwise. For example, tutorial programs simulate the teaching function of presentations, questions, and feedback. By this means, children are provided learning exercises on an appropriate level of difficulty, and in an interesting manner. Other programs can be used which allow drill and practice (with correct answers shown) on previously learned material. Games are effective as motivators and reinforcers. In addition, use of computer software provides a way of testing students that is more appealing to many than a written test.

Teachers can acquire the skills needed to program the computer so that tasks provided by software correspond with students' individualized education programs. Teaching students to program will develop problem-solving and discovery skills, and also foster reasoning comprehension skills.

SKILL 14.4 Understand instructional methods to strengthen and compensate for deficits in attention, perception, comprehension, memory, and retrieval

Please refer to the "Understand the relationship between processing skills and cognitive skills of disabled learners" for additional information in skill 1.1.

IDENTIFY ACTIVITIES FOR STRENGTHENING VISUAL PERCEPTION SKILLS

"Visual perception plays a significant role in school learning, particularly in reading" (Lerner, 1989, p. 286). Reading and math are both language symbol systems, and are considered to be essential content areas. Authorities purport some visual perception tasks significantly contribute to the establishment of a predictive reading index. Other skill areas included in visual perception are:

Visual Attending-Distractible children are often unable to attend to the most important features of a task. Impulsive children tend to under focus and relinquish concentration too quickly. This phenomenon may be characterized by premature decisions, as well as by responding too rapidly. Impulsivity tends to be directly related to decreased performance in areas requiring sustained attention (e.g. visual memory). Educators need to clarify important task features and to teach appropriate task strategies to help children improve attention and learning.

Other variables that characterize poor attention in students with learning problems include:
1. Slow to notice stimuli
2. Take longer to react to stimuli
3. Experiences difficulty shifting attention between visual and auditory modalities
4. Show inadequate physiological indices associated with attending

Visual Discrimination-Visual discrimination refers to the ability to differentiate one object from another. To test a child's ability to discriminate visually, the teacher may ask him to find a rabbit that is different, and he will have to point out the rabbit with one ear in a row of rabbits with two ears. When asked to distinguish visually between the letters "m" and "n," the child must perceive the number of humps in each letter. The skill of matching identical pictures, designs, shapes, letters, and words is another visual discrimination task. Objects may be discriminated by color, shape, pattern, size, position, or brightness. The ability to visually discriminate letters and words is essential to learning to read.

Spatial Relations - This refers to the ability to distinguish an object or symbol from its surrounding background. Some students have difficulty focusing on the object apart from its background. These students are having trouble reading or doing mathematical problems because they are distracted by irrelevant stimuli.

Visual Closure - When a student is asked to identify an object with part of it missing, visual closure must be made. For example, if a person were to lay a straight-edged ruler across the upper portion of the letters on this line of print, he or she would need to be able to make visual closure in order to know the words presented in print.

Object Recognition - Object recognition is the ability to recognize the nature of objects when viewing them. Being able to identify geometric patterns, letters, and numbers is related to being able to learn to read (Lerner, 1989).
Some techniques designed to improve visual perception include:

1. Pegboard designs. Using colored pegs, have students reproduce colored visual geometric patterns to form the design shown on the pegboard.
2. Parquetry blocks. Using parquetry blocks, have student's copy patterns.
3. Block designs. Using one or more colors, instruct children to replicate model constructions or designs.
4. Finding shapes in pictures. Children are asked to identify round objects, squares, or other designs in a picture.
5. Bead designs. Students are asked to reproduce designs with beads on a string.
6. Puzzles. Have students put together puzzles made by the teacher or produced commercially. Subjects such as people, animals, numbers, or letters can be cut into pieces to show functional parts.
7. Classification. Students are asked to group or to classify geometric shapes in varying sizes and colors. The figures may be three-dimensional objects or may be pictures placed on cards or cardboard backings.
8. Rubber-band designs. Ask students to reproduce geometric configurations with colored rubber bands stretched between rows of nails on a board.
9. Matching shapes. Have children play games that require the matching of shapes on cards. Collect containers with lids and ask students to match lids with jars.
10. Letters and numbers. Provide opportunities for students to march, sort, or name shapes that can be adapted to letters or numbers.
11. Visual perception of words. Have students play word games that involve matching, sorting, grouping, tracing, and drawing geometric shapes and letters.
12. Finding missing parts. Using pictures from newspaper, comics, or magazines and have children find or fill in missing parts.
13. Rate of perception. Use a tachistoscope or window box to pace the length of time a student requires recognizing pictures, figures, numbers, and words.
14. Letter bingo. Make bingo cards with letters. As letters are called, have students cover them. As a variation, make bingo cards of numbers or geometric shapes.
15. Worksheets. Students are directed to find objects or shapes that are different, match same objects, locate objects in varying spatial positions, and identify the shapes and figures from the background.

IDENTIFY ACTIVITIES FOR STRENGTHENING INTEGRATIVE SKILLS

The auditory, visual, and tactile modalities are the ones frequently used in the learning process. The strength of these modalities depends upon intact functioning of channels of communication through which stimuli are received (e.g. speech, writing, movement). A major difficulty in learning has been identified within the integrative (or association) process. Some information that is received requires storage, which involves the memory process. Other information necessitates the neurological process of conversion from one modality to another. That is, information received through one perceptual system must be transferred to or integrated with another sensory channel.

Problems in cross-model perception (or intersensory integration) are often discovered in the reading process, where visual symbols must correspond to phoneme sounds. The student who is unable to make this conversion can identify the letters, but cannot associate them with their sound equivalents. Conversely, the student who has difficulty convening from the auditory to the visual modality is able to learn the sounds of letters, but has problems associating sounds with corresponding graphemes (letter symbols). Another example of a deficit in cross-modal perception is that of planning and executing motor movements. For instance, to speak, a student must convert auditory memory of words to a motor system in order to say the words.

Techniques for strengthening associative tasks include the following activities from Lerner (1989). The suggested activities are categorized by integrative skills.

Visual Memory

1. Identifying missing objects. A collection of objects is shown. The collection is covered while one object is removed. Again, the collection is shown with the student asked to identify the missing object. An alternative is to use an overhead projector, have students view designs or objects, remove one without students looking, and have them recall what is missing.
2. Drawing from memory. Following exposure of a simple design, have the student reproduce the design on paper. A variation would be to make a pattern of objects (i.e. beads, blocks). After viewing, have students reproduce the pattern from memory.
3. Stories from pictures. Pictures of activities that tell a story are placed on a flannel board. Remove the pictures and have the students recall the story based on their visual memory of the pictures.
4. Enumerating see objects. Students are asked to recall objects previously viewed (i.e. looking out window, taking a field trip).

Auditory Memory

1. <u>Do this.</u> Place several objects in front of the students and ask them to follow a series of directions. Gradually increase the number of objects.
2. <u>Number series.</u> Given a series of numbers, ask students to answer questions. For example, "write the number closest to your age" (or first one, last one, fourth, largest, or smallest).
3. <u>Nursery rhymes.</u> The memorizing of rhymes, poems, and finger plays may be helpful.
4. <u>Films, videos.</u> Have students recall certain things, like countries shown or types of transportation.
5. <u>Going to the moon.</u> The teacher begins by saying, "I went on a trip to the moon and took my space suit." The first student repeats the statement and adds one item. Trips may be made to other destinations as a variation.
6. <u>Repetition of Sequences.</u> Read short sentences and have students repeat them. Advance from short, simple sentences to more complex clauses.

Cross-Modal Perception

1. <u>Visual to auditory.</u> Ask the student to look at a pattern of dots and dashes and translate them into rhythmical form.
2. <u>Auditory to visual.</u> Have the student listen to a rhythmical beat and select the matching visual pattern of dots and dashes, given several alternatives.
3. <u>Auditory to visual-motor.</u> Ask the student to listen to a rhythmical beat and transfer it to a visual form by writing corresponding dots and dashes.
4. <u>Auditory-verbal to motor.</u> Play a game like "Simon Says," Have the student listen to commands and transfer the commands to movements of body parts.
5. <u>Tactile to visual-motor.</u> Student is directed to feel shapes in a concealed container and draw the shapes on a piece of paper.
6. <u>Visual to auditory-verbal.</u> Have the child look at several pictures. Ask, "Which one begins with G? Which rhymes with toy?"
7. <u>Auditory-verbal to visual.</u> Describe a picture and have students select the picture from several alternatives presented.

UNDERSTAND THAT STUDENTS RECEIVE AND ATTACH PERSONAL MEANING TO AUDITORY AND VISUAL INFORMATIONAL STIMULI, WHICH MAY BE DIFFERENT FROM THE INTENDED MEANING

Auditory and visual stimuli may be received (1) by intact sensory mechanisms, and (2) through perceptual processing. Due to differing maturational levels and experiential backgrounds (e.g. geographical, socioeconomic, and cultural), the auditory or visual information received may be interpreted differently from the initially intended message. Once a verbal utterance is heard and received by the listener, another function comes into play, and that is deriving meaning from the spoken words.

The ages and background experiences among senders and receivers may be important factors in effective communication. Factors such as where one lives geographically (e.g. farm, city, southern state, northern state), or socioeconomically (e.g. ghetto, affluent, suburban neighborhood) are significant. Attitudes, beliefs, and mores may influence what is communicated.

The cognitive, social, emotional, and linguistic developmental levels of the sender (e.g. speaker, writer) and receiver (e.g. listener, viewer) make a difference in language usage and interpretation. How advanced are the sender/receiver in semantic/syntactic aspects of language? is the sender taking into consideration the perspective of the receiver? Is the message coded for the sender (egocentric), or for the receiver? Is the language being used to send or receive ideas, thoughts, feelings, needs, or to ask or answer questions?

The physical setting, the specific context of the language exchange, and the topic may influence one's understanding of what is being communicated. Different interpretations influence one's understanding of what is being communicated. Different interpretations may also be the result of the way in which word meaning are expressed by the speaker. In addition, the stress, pitch, and intonation used during communication can determine meaning and impact upon interpretation of spoken language.

The good reader is encouraged to bring mental imagery to the printed page. The child who has been exposed to enriched activities, travel, and broadening experiences is better able to formulate mental images and draw upon background experiences. The child who lacks these enabling experiences may be unable to conjure mental imagery, which will assist with memory, vocabulary, comprehension, and effective language experiences.

DISCUSS TECHNIQUES FOR IMPROVING OBSERVATIONAL LEARNING

Learning a behavior by observing a model's performance of that behavior is called observational (or imitative) learning. Children who require special educational services often have problems learning incidental skills.

In imitation training, a target behavior is modeled by the trainer, the learner imitates the demonstrated behavior, and the imitation is reinforced. For example, imitation training occurs when the teacher makes the short vowel /a/ sound, the student imitates the sounds, and the teacher says, "Good job."

Effective models can be parents, teachers, peers, or significant others. For example, parents serve as models during preschool years, teachers often teach through demonstration, children imitate the behavior of their classmates, and hero figures often serve as role models for impressionable youth.

Students are most apt to imitate models that (1) have high status, (2) are perceived as competent; (3) possess physical characteristics similar to observers (e.g. age, gender), and (4) are reinforced for the modeled behavior. Providing handicapped children with opportunities to observe behaviors demonstrated by nonhandicapped peers is one of the primary goals of mainstreaming.

There are several activities a teacher modeling instructional behavior can use to enhance the observational learning of such children.

1. Demonstrate appropriate behaviors
2. Repeat the learning experience several times, to the point of producing over-learning.
3. Verbally explain and emphasize the process while it is being modeled.
4. Emphasize and exaggerate the sequential steps to be imitated.
5. Use physical prompting when necessary and appropriate.
6. Allow children ample opportunity to rehearse and participate.
7. Use stories to exemplify appropriate behavior.
8. Provide immediate feedback.
9. Give plenty of positive reinforcement.
10. Clearly state the concepts and processes involved in the modeled instruction before, during, and after the modeling.

Please refer to skill 1.1 about variables which influence the storage, rehearsal, and retrieval of information in educational situations and the need for changing the rate, level, and sequence at which new concepts are acquired.

SKILL 14.5 Understand strategies and activities for helping students organize and manage time, work independently, give and receive feedback, use higher-order thinking skills, and use effective study and test-taking skills

IDENTIFY TEACHING STRATEGIES DESIGNED TO ASSIST THE STUDENT IN BECOMING AN INDEPENDENT LEARNER

Many students with learning and behavior problems are characterized as poor independent workers. Too frequently these students do not know how to study or work without adult supervision, nor do they view themselves as responsible for their own learning or behavior.

In order that self-sufficiency can occur in the academic arena, teacher must set the environment and make assurances that the child can function independently. Several concerns must be addressed prior to expecting independent functioning. First, the child must understand the nature of the assignment and the context on which they are based. Next, it must be determined whether the child cannot, rather than will not, do the work. Then it needs to be determined whether the child is able to ask for help in a positive, appropriate manner. Finally, the task expectations held by the teacher need to be accurately conveyed to the student (i.e. how they should be done and criteria for successful completion).

Modeling is often used as a mechanism for moving the learner from dependence to independence. Modeling refers to the use of significant adults or peers to demonstrate to the learner appropriate performance behaviors. Initially the teacher models the appropriate performance, which is a form of demonstration. She may then encourage the student to copy her; thus imitation occurs. Next, she might encourage the learner to undertake the task himself, but with her guidance, assistance, and prompting if necessary. Finally, she would provide verbal instruction, without prompting, hopefully leading him to the point at which he can perform the task himself upon request.

Training in self-instruction can be combined with modeling. The underlying purpose for this approach is to encourage the learner to develop verbal control of behavior. Meichenbaum (1975) advocates the use of the following components:

1. Cognitive Modeling. The adult model performs a task while verbally instructing himself.
2. Overt, Self-Guidance. The child performs the same task, imitating instructions spoken by the model.
3. Faded, Overt, Self-Guidance. The child softly repeats the instructions while repeating the task.
4. Covert Self-Instruction. The child performs the task while silently instructing himself.

Self-monitoring refers to procedures by which the learner records whether he is engaging in certain behaviors, particularly those that would lead to increased academic achievement and/or social behavior. Self-reinforcement is important to the success of self-monitoring and may be administered as verbal self-acknowledgment or as tangible rewards. Checklists, or other means of keeping track, may be faded upon evidence of progress. This system encourages self-responsibility and independence.

STRATEGIES FOR PROMOTING STUDENTS' USE OF CRITICAL-THINKING AND PROBLEM SOLVING SKILLS

Most educators recognize comprehension covers a wide continuum of lower-to-higher level thinking skills. The following is one way of displaying the continuum, beginning on the low side of the spectrum:

1. **Literal** indicates an understanding of the primary, direct (literal) meaning of words, sentences, or passages.
2. **Inferential** involves an understanding of the deeper meanings that are not literally stated in a phrase, sentence, or passage.
3. **Evaluation** signifies a judgment made by comparing ideas or information presented in the written passage with other experiences, knowledge, or values.
4. **Appreciation** involves an emotional response to the written selection.

Using Barrett's Taxonomy of Cognitive and Affective Dimensions of Reading Comprehension[1], the teacher can determine the student's level of comprehension and stimulate thinking across a continuum of comprehension levels, by asking questions similar to these about the story of The Three Bears.

    I.   **Literal Comprehension** focuses on ideas and information that are explicitly stated in the selection.
        A.   *Recognition* requires the student to locate or identify ideas or information explicitly stated in the reading selection.
           1.   **Recognition of details.** Where did the three bears live?
           2.   **Recognition of main ideas.** Why did the three bears go out for a walk?
           3.   **Recognition of sequence.** Whose porridge was too hot? Whose porridge did Goldilocks taste first?
           4.   **Recognition of comparisons.** Whose porridge was too hot? Too cold? Just right?
           5.   **Recognition of cause-and-effect relationships.** Why didn't Papa Bear and Mama Bear's chair break into pieces like Baby Bear's chair?
           6.   **Recognition of character traits.** Which words can you find to describe Goldilocks?

In any of the above cases, the teacher may provide the answers herself; or she may state the answer without the question and have the child show her in the pictures, or read in the text, the part of the story pertaining to her statement. The objective is to test the child's literal comprehension and not his memory.

        B.   *Recall* requires the student to produce from memory ideas and information explicitly stated in the reading selection.
           1.   **Recall of details.** What were the names of the three bears?
           2.   **Recall of main ideas.** Why did Goldilocks go into the bears' house?
           3.   **Recall of a sequence.** In order, name the things belonging to the three bears that Goldilocks tried.
           4.   **Recall of comparisons.** Whose bed was too hard? Too soft? Just right?
           5.   **Recall of cause-and-effect relationships.** Why did Goldilocks go to sleep in Baby Bear's bed?
           6.   Recall of character traits. What words in the story described each of the three bears?

In the above cases, the teacher does not give the answer unless the student cannot provide it himself. The purpose is to test the child's recall of stated facts.

II. **Reorganization** requires the student to analyze, synthesize, and/or organize ideas or information explicitly stated in the selection.
   A. *Classifying*. List the things Goldilocks discovered to be "just right" in the story.
   B. *Outlining*. Outline each thing Goldilocks tried, whether it was just right or did not suit her.
   C. *Summarizing*. Tell me in just a few sentences what happened in the story.
   D. *Synthesizing*. Predict what other things Goldilocks might have tried if the bears had had a daughter.

III. **Inferential comprehension** is demonstrated by the student when he "uses the ideas and information explicitly stated in the selection, his intuition, and his personal experiences as a basis for conjectures and hypotheses," according to Barrett (cited in Ekwall & Shanker, 1983, p. 67).
   A. *Inferring supporting details*. Why do you think Goldilocks found Baby Bear's things to be just right?
   B. *Inferring main ideas*. What did the bear family learn about leaving their house unlocked?
   C. *Inferring sequence*. At what point did the bears discover that someone was in their house?
   D. *Inferring comparisons*. Compare the furniture mentioned in the story. Which was adult size and which was a child's size?
   E. *Inferring cause-and-effect relationships*. What made the bears suspect that someone was in their house?
   F. *Inferring character traits*. Which of the bears was the most irritated by Goldilock's intrusion?
   G. *Predicting outcomes*. Do you think Goldilocks ever went back to visit the bears' house again?
   H. *Interpreting figurative language*. What did the author mean when he wrote, "The tress in the deep forest howled a sad song in the wind?"

IV. **Evaluation** requires the student to make a judgment by comparing ideas presented in the selection with external criteria provided by the teacher, or by some other external source, or with internal criteria provided by the student himself.
   A. *Judgment of reality or fantasy.* Do you suppose that the story of The Three Bears really happened? Why or why not?
   B. *Judgment of fact or opinion.* Judge whether Baby Bear's furniture really was just right for Goldilocks. Why or Why not?
   C. *Judgment of adequacy and validity.* Give your opinion as to whether it was a good idea for the bears to take a walk while their porridge cooled.
   D. *Judgment of appropriateness.* Do you think it was safe for Goldilocks to enter an empty house?
   E. *Judgment of worth, desirability, and acceptability.* Was Goldilocks a guest or an intruder in the bears' home?

V. **Appreciation** deals with the psychological and aesthetic impact of the selection on the reader.

   A. *Emotional response to the content.* How did you feel when the three bears found Goldilocks asleep in Baby Bear's bed?
   B. *Identification with characters or incidents.* How do you suppose Goldilocks felt when she awakened and saw the three bears?
   C. *Reaction to the author's use of language.* Why do you think the author called the bears Papa, Mama, and Baby instead of Mr. Bear, Mrs. Bear, and Jimmy Bear?
   D. Imagery. What is meant by "his bed is as hard as a rock?"

SKILL 14.6 Demonstrate knowledge of strategies for teaching students to use self-assessment, problem solving, and other cognitive strategies to meet academic and other needs

Cognitive strategies are useful tools for students with learning difficulties. They use the mind to solve a problem or complete a task. Cognitive strategies may also be referred to as procedural facilitators or scaffolds.

Cognitive strategies provide a structure for learning when an assignment cannot be done through a sequence of steps. For example, algorithms in math provide a series of steps to solve a problem. Attention to the steps results in successful completion of the problem.

Cognitive strategies help support the student as they develop internal procedures that help them to complete assignments that are difficult. Reading comprehension is a subject where cognitive strategies are crucial. A self-questioning strategy can help students understand what they read.

The use of cognitive strategies can increase the efficiency with which the student approaches a learning task. These academic tasks can include remembering and applying information from course content, constructing sentences and paragraphs, editing written work, paraphrasing, and classifying information to be learned.

The teacher fills a key role in providing cognitive strategies. The teacher must understand the assignment that is to be completed as well as understand how to approach doing the assignment and communicate this to the student.

The student should take charge and become self-regulated learners. The student should define learning goals and problems that are meaningful to them and understand how specific activities relate to these goals. Students are also involved in self-assessment, which entails using standards of excellence to evaluate whether they have achieved their goals.

Students discuss learning goals with their teacher, are given a range of options for assignments, take some responsibility for monitoring progress, and are aware of assessment standards. Students work with their teacher to set learning goals and assessment standards and have a range of options for assignments and opportunities to design learning activities. They are responsible for setting timelines and monitoring progress toward completion of their goals.

Assessments are meaningful, challenging experiences that involve presenting students with an authentic task, project, or investigation, and then observing, interviewing and/or examining their artifacts and presentations to assess what they actually know and can do.

The teacher should be comfortable with the content they are teaching so they know which parts are the most important to learn, and which parts may be hard or easy to understand. When a teacher is comfortable with the content she is teaching, she knows which parts are the most important, the most interesting and the easiest (or hardest) to learn.

The teacher then focuses on the student's characteristics such as intellectual ability, interest in the subject, and general motivation to learn. The teacher selects learning approaches that complement the student's characteristics while ensuring success with the content. A strategy should be selected that takes into account the student's learning style as well as the content that needs to be mastered.

SKILL 14.7 Understand principles and techniques for promoting students' self-confidence, decision-making skills, ownership of tasks and goals, and ability to make successful transitions between grades, schools, and service delivery systems

The personal and social development dimensions of a child's education belong to the realm of affective behavior. While all children require conscious instruction in this realm, children with disabilities, for several reasons, appear to require more work and more directed effort by the teacher, to acquire a set of socially acceptable behaviors. Poor self-concept is normative among many of these children, and, since self-concept is central to behavior development, the teacher of students with special needs will need to direct special attention to this issue.

Self Concept-Self-concept may be defined as the collective attitudes or feelings that one holds about oneself. Children with disabilities perceive, early in life, that they are deficient in skills that seem easier for their peers without disabilities. They also receive expressions of surprise or even disgust from both adults and children in response to their differing appearance and actions, again resulting in damage to the self-concept. The special education teacher, for these reasons, will want to direct special and continuing effort to bettering each child's own perception of himself.

1. The poor self-concept of a child with disabilities causes that student at times to exhibit aggression or rage over inappropriate things. The teacher can ignore this behavior unless it is dangerous to others or too distracting to the total group, thereby reducing the amount of negative conditioning in the child's life. Further, the teacher can praise this child, quickly and frequently, for the correct responses he makes, remembering that these responses may require special effort on the student's part to produce. Further, correction, when needed, can be done tactfully, in private.
2. The child whose poor self-concept manifests itself in withdrawn behavior should be pulled gently into as many social situations as possible by the teacher. This child must be encouraged to share experiences with the class, to serve as teacher helper for projects, and to be part of small groups for tasks. Again, praise for performing these group and public acts is most effective if done immediately.

3. The teacher can plan, in advance, to structure the classroom experiences so that aversive situations will be avoided. Thus, settings that stimulate the aggressive child to act out can be redesigned and situations that stimulate group participation can be set up in advance for the child who acts in a withdrawn manner.

    Frequent, positive, and immediate are the best terms to describe the teacher feedback required by children with disabilities. Praise for very small correct acts should be given immediately, and repeated when each correct act is repeated. Criticism or outright scolding should be done, whenever possible, in private. The teacher should first check the total day's interactions with students to ensure that the number and qualitative content of verbal stimuli is heavily on the positive side. While this trait is desirable in all good teaching, it is fundamental and utterly necessary to build the fragile self-concept of youngsters with disabilities.

4. The teacher must have a strategy for use with the child who persists in negative behavior outbursts. One system is to intervene immediately and break the situation down in to three components. First, the teacher requires the child to identify the worst possible outcome from the situation, the thing that he fears. To do this task, the child must be required to state the situation in the most factual way he can. Second, he is required to state what would really happen if this worst possible outcome happened, and to evaluate the likelihood of it happening. Third, he is asked to state an action or attitude that he can take, after examining the consequences in a new light. This process has been termed rational emotive therapy.

Decision Making-The youngster with a disability lacks self-confidence to a high degree, a fact that makes it difficult for him to make decisions. Most of these children consider that they have little real control over their lives, which, in psychology, is termed as an external focus of control. Making this situation more difficult is the fact that some, but not all, children with disabilities genuinely lack the cognitive ability to render a correct decision from a set of perceived facts.

The decision-making capabilities of all children with disabilities can be strengthened with the following techniques.

1. The teacher might read a short story in which someone made a decision based on a set of facts. Then, she could ask a child to say whether the decision was a good one, and why.
2. To achieve comparison with the previous activity, the teacher can read a story in which someone makes a poor decision, again seeking student evaluation.
3. A more complex developmental activity in decision-making is to present a situation in which a decision is strongly required, and then give several possible options. The students are then asked to pick out the best options, and to defend their choices.
4. The teacher can create situations where the student is making a choice over his own destiny. She might offer one of three different games, knowing in advance that all three are acceptable. Most sophisticated choices can be allowed, provided the teacher is careful not to include one in which she will have to overrule the student, which would tend to undercut his decision-making process.
5. The teacher can invent story scenarios that allow the students to act out decision-making roles.
6. When a child makes a poor or unacceptable decision, instead of simply saying "no" or criticizing the decision, the teacher asks the student to analyze it. By talking through the content, the student may be able to discern on his own the unacceptable part, and reach a new decision without the ego damaging process of once again being wrong.

Autonomy-A child with a sense of independence may be said to possess autonomy. Such a child develops feelings of responsibility for his own well-being and actions. The poor self-concept that is normative with so many children with disabilities tends to retard the development of autonomy. Also, the need for externalized controls has the same effect, a process that tends to become self-perpetuating with these children. As they feel bad about themselves, they act out in some manner. Someone imposes external authority, and the growth of autonomy is frustrated at that time. As the child perceives that external authority will be employed, he tends to give up or delay the strengthening of his autonomy, and to feel bad about himself again.

There is a paradox in this process that is difficult to explain. Research shows that the child with a disability who is able to develop a close emotional relationship with at least one significant adult figure in his life is more likely to develop autonomy. An explanation may be found in the quality and content of that external relationship. Apparently, the significant adult figure exercises some controls, but also allows and encourages positive self-concept with a corresponding growth in autonomy.

Here are some activities that encourage the growth of autonomy.

1. Use all the self-concepts building strategies previously listed and look for ways to reinforce their effectiveness.
2. Place the child in charge of a small unit of his environment. Reward successful completion of the task to a degree that would seem inappropriate with other children (i.e. lavish praise). Then, gradually increase the autonomous tasks while simultaneously normalizing the positive recognition to a degree more likely to be done by others outside the classroom.
3. Set up role-playing situations in which the child actors form some decisions that make a difference. Get the children to discuss and evaluate.
4. Read and discuss stories in which children take responsibility for their actions. For example, if there is no adult in the house, can you turn on the television? Can you answer the phone? What do you say? Use practical examples that relate to the life styles of the children's families.

Morality-Morality, in the educational setting, manifests itself in the ability of a child to select right from wrong. It becomes the task of the educator to teach these values. Children with disabilities present their own special ethical dilemmas for the teacher, but they do not usually involve themselves in some of the more abstract philosophical issues that create problems for the general educator.

It is helpful to lay out taxonomy for moral development among all children, and then to apply it to the special needs of children with disabilities.

1. At the pre-conventional level, right and wrong are viewed by children in the light of consequences. Thus, hitting a sibling draws a parental slap and is, per se, wrong because of the relative unpleasantness of the punishment.
2. At the conventional level, the child is passing through adolescence. He begins to make abstract associations through such things as social approval, psychological payoff, and personal gain. Thus, he can visualize that shoplifting is wrong because one gets arrested and punished, but also because parents disapprove, you feel bad about yourself, and the stores raise the price of things if too much gets stolen.

3. The post-conventional level of morality emphasizes abstract principles and extends beyond concern for social rules and enforcement powers. Issues are viewed as right or wrong based upon substantive judgments about their content. Thus, one supports a foreign policy decision because it contains inherent right, or opposes its inherent wrongness but does not experience any personal difference in daily life from the decision. Following ones' conscience takes precedence over obeying laws or doing things just to please other persons.

The special education teacher should introduce concepts of right and wrong at an abstract level, but she must always remember the level of perception at which her students are functioning. Thus, a developmentally disabled 10-year-old boy may not think it morally wrong to hit and will only learn not to hit via the administration of a penalty that seems worse. A hearing impaired ten year old might become upset over the hitting behavior of a peer because he thinks it isn't right to hit.

The following activities help children develop their skills in the area of making moral judgments:

1. Use role reversal play acting and stories. Billy is the hitter. Mary is the one getting hit. Immediately afterwards, the two children change roles. Does Billy now feel the same about hitting as when he was the doer?
2. Films, tapes, and videos are available in which actors show their feelings about a behavior. A film may show the complete process of shoplifting in a store: interception, arrest, detention, family involvement, trial, and sentence. Be sure that the students can grasp appropriately the content of such a film.
3. Make up brief moral judgment exercises and call upon the students for decisions. These can be used to develop social studies awareness, language, and numbers if the content is planned.
4. Develop role-playing situations that a child actor becomes the victim of hitting, lying, or stealing. Stop the action and have the victim actor tell how it feels.

Materials have been developed in the form of classroom kits. One is the Developing Understanding of Self and Others (DUSO) kit, for grades K-4. A slightly more advanced kit is Toward Affective Development (TAD) that serves grades 3-6. These particular kits are published by American Guidance Services, Inc.

Please refer to skill 11.1 for information about transition.

TEACHER CERTIFICATION STUDY GUIDE

COMPETENCY 15.0 UNDERSTAND EVIDENCE-BASED STRATEGIES AND TECHNIQUES FOR PROMOTING STUDENTS' ACQUISITION OF FUNCTIONAL SKILLS.

SKILL 15.1 Recognize components of a functional skills curriculum

UNDERSTAND THE NEED FOR A FUNCTIONAL CURRICULUM

A functional curriculum approach focuses upon what students need to learn and what will be useful to them and prepare them for functioning in society as adults. With this approach, concepts and skills needed for personal-social, daily living, and occupational readiness are taught students. The specific curriculum content needs to be identified in a student's individualized educational program (IEP), and be considered appropriate for his chronological age and current intellectual, academic, or behavioral performance levels (Clark, 1994).

The need for a functional curriculum has been heightened by the current focus upon transition, movement from one level to another, until the individual is prepared to live a life in a self-sufficient manner. The simplest form includes movement from school to the world of work. But like career education, life preparation includes not only occupational readiness, but also personal-social and daily living skills.

Halpern (1992) contends special education curriculum tends to focus too much on remedial academics and not enough on functional skills.

A functional curriculum includes life skills and teaches them in the classroom and in the community. When using this approach, basic academic skills are reinforced in an applied manner. For instance, math may be taught in budgeting, balancing checkbooks, and/or computing interest payments for major purchases.

The Adult Performance Level (APL) has been adapted for secondary level students in special education in a number of school districts in Texas and Louisiana. The APL serves as a core curriculum blending practical academic development with applications to the various demands of community living in adulthood.

Functional competence, as addressed in PAL, is conceptualized as two-dimensional. Major skill areas are integrated into general content/knowledge domains. The major skills that have been identified by this curriculum model as requisite for success are reading, writing, speaking, listening, viewing, problem solving, interpersonal relations, and computation.

SKILL 15.2 Understand techniques for designing and implementing functional skills instruction (e.g., observation, task analysis, establishing behavioral outcomes, teaching in context)

Students use basic skills to understand things that are read such as a reading passage, a math word problem, or directions for a project. However, students apply additional thinking skills to fully comprehend how what was read could be applied to their own life, or how to make comparatives or choices based on the factual information given. These critical thinking skills require students to think about thinking. Teachers are instrumental in helping students use these skills in everyday activities by:

- Analyzing bills for overcharges
- Comparing shopping ads or catalogue deals
- Finding the main idea from readings
- Applying what's been learned to new situations
- Gathering information/data from a diversity of sources to plan a project
- Following a sequence of directions
- Looking for cause and effect relationships
- Comparing and contrasting information in synthesizing information

Attention to learner needs during planning is foremost and includes identification of that which the students already know or need to know; the matching of learner needs with instructional elements such as content, materials, activities, and goals; and the determination of whether or not students have performed at an acceptable level, following instruction.

The ability to create a personal and professional charting of student's academic and emotional growth from within the performance-based assessment of individualized portfolios becomes a toolkit for both students and teachers. Teachers can use semester portfolios to gauge student academic progress and personal growth of students who are constantly changing their self-images and world views on a daily basis. When a student is studying to master a math concept and is able to create a visual of the learnings that transcend beyond the initial concept to create a bridge connecting a higher level of thinking and application of knowledge, then the teacher can share a moment of enjoyable math comprehension with the student.

The idea of using art concepts as visual imagery in helping students process conceptual learning of reading, math and science creates a mental mind mapping of learning for students processing new information. Using graphic organizers and concept web guides that center around a concept and the applications of the concept is an instructional strategy that teachers can use to guide students into further inquiry of the subject matter. Imagine the research of the German chemist Fredrich August Kekule when he looked into a fire one night and solved the molecular structure of benzene and you can imagine fostering that same creativity in students. Helping students understand the art of "visualization" and the creativity of discovery may impart a student visualizing the cure for AIDS or cancer or how to create reading programs for the next generation of readers.

Helping students become effective note-takers and stimulating a diversity of perspectives for spatial techniques that can be applied to learning is a proactive teaching strategy in creating a visual learning environment where art and visualization become natural art forms for learning. In today's computer environment, students must understand that computers cannot replace the creative thinking and skill application that comes from the greatest computer on record, the human mind.

Please refer to Skill 9.2 about task analysis.

SKILL 15.3 Understand strategies for teaching functional skills in the major domains (e.g., self-help skills, daily living skills)

Behavioral chaining is a procedure where individual responses are reinforced for occurring in sequence to form a complex behavior. Each link is subsequently paired with its preceding one, thus each link serves as a conditioned reinforcer for the link immediately preceding it. Behavior chains can be acquired by having each step in the chain verbally prompted or demonstrated. The prompts can then be faded and the links combined, with reinforcement, occurring after the last link has been performed.

In backward chaining, the components of the chain are acquired by reversing the order of the steps (like sub-skills) necessary to complete successfully the target task.

An example of backward chaining would be teaching a child to dress himself. The child is given the instruction, "Jimmy, take your jacket off," and his jacket is unzipped and lifted off the shoulders and down the arms until only the cuffs remain on Jimmy's wrists. If he does not pull the jacket the rest of the way off, he is physically guided to do so. He is given a reinforcer following removal of the garment. During the next session, the procedure is repeated, but the sleeve is left on his arms. In subsequent sessions, both arms are left in the sleeves, and then the jacket is left zipped. The instruction, "Jimmy, take your jacket off" is always presented, and a reinforcer is given only when the task is completed. The removal of each garment is taught in this manner; and the component steps are combined until as instruction like "Jimmy, take your jacket off" has acquired stimulus.

Backward chaining may be used to teach other self-help skills such as toileting, grooming, and eating. Many academic and preacademic readiness areas could be effectively taught using this procedure as well. Each step in the program is prompted until the student can perform the entire sequence by himself. The backward chaining procedure may be of greatest assistance when a student experiences limited receptive abilities or imitative behavior.

See skill 9.2 for more information on forward and backward chaining

SKILL 15.4 Understand techniques for promoting skill transfer and generalization

Transfer of Learning-Transfer of learning occurs when experience with one task influences performance on another task. Positive transfer occurs when the required responses are about the same and the stimuli are similar, such as moving from handball, to racquetball, or field hockey to soccer. Negative transfer occurs when the stimuli remain similar, but the required responses change, such as shifting from soccer to football, tennis to racquetball, and boxing to sports karate. Instructional procedures should stress the similar features between the activities and the dimensions that are transferable. Specific information should emphasize when stimuli in the old and new situations are the same as or similar, and when responses used in the old situation apply to the new.

To facilitate learning, instructional objectives should be arranged in order according to their patterns of similarity. Objectives involving similar responses should be closely sequenced; thus, the possibility for positive transfer is stressed. Likewise, learning objectives that involve different responses should be programmed within instructional procedures in the most appropriate way possible. For example, students should have little difficulty transferring handwriting instruction to writing in other areas; however, there might be some negative transfer when moving from manuscript to cursive writing. By using transitional methods and focusing upon the similarities between manuscript and cursive writing, negative transfer can be reduced.

Generalization-Generalization is the occurrence of a learned behavior in the presence of a stimulus other than the one that produced the initial response (e.g. novel stimulus). It is the expansion of a student's performance beyond conditions initially anticipated. Students must be able to generalize what is learned to other settings (e.g. reading to math, word problems; resource room to regular classroom).

Generalization training is a procedure in which a behavior is reinforced in each of a series of situations until it generalizes to other members of the same stimulus class. Stimulus generalization occurs when responses, which have been reinforced in the presence of a specific stimulus, the discriminative stimulus (SD), occur in the presence of related stimuli (e.g. bathrooms labeled women, ladies, dames). In fact, the more similar the stimuli, the more likely it is that stimulus generalization will occur. This concept applies to intertask similarity, in that the more one task resembles another; the greater the probability the student will be able to master it. For example, if Johnny has learned the initial consonant sounds of "b" and "d," and he has been taught to read the word "dad," it is likely that when he is shown the word "bad," he will be able to pronounce this formerly unknown word upon presentation.

Generalization may be enhanced by the following:

1. Use many examples in teaching to deepen application of learned skills.
2. Use consistency in initial teaching situations, and later introduce variety in format, procedure, and use of examples.
3. Have the same information presented by different teachers, in different settings, and under varying conditions.
4. Include a continuous reinforcement schedule at first, later changing to delayed, and intermittent schedules as instruction progresses.
5. Teach students to record instances of generalization and to reward themselves at that time.
6. Associate naturally occurring stimuli when possible.

COMPETENCY 16.0 UNDERSTAND THE DEVELOPMENT AND IMPLEMENTATION OF BEHAVIOR INTERVENTIONS FOR STUDENTS WITH MILD/MODERATE DISABILITIES.

SKILL 16.1 Demonstrate knowledge of types, characteristics, strengths, and limitations of various behavior intervention approaches

Please refer to skill 11.6 for classroom interventions and strategies to prevent discipline problems.

DISCIPLINE APPROACHES THAT ARE TRADITIONALLY USED WITH STUDENTS WITH BEHAVIOR DISORDERS

Several approaches to student discipline are offered in this review. Examples are given to demonstrate principles of each. Teachers need to know these well-known approaches so that they can be used selectively when particular student behaviors and situations occur.

Life Space Interview (Redl)-The life-space interview is a here-and-now intervention built around the child's life experience. It is applied in an effort toward increasing conscious awareness of distorted perceptions. These perceptions may be directed toward how one reacts to the behaviors and pressures of other persons. It is sometimes referred to as emotional first aide.

Example

Jack, a 10-year old fifth grader, is enrolled in Mr. Bird's resource room for students with behavior disorders. Jack's social behavior is creating difficulties for him, his classmates, and his teachers. Jack's unacceptable social behaviors have caused him to be ignored by some students, overly rejected by others, and used as a scapegoat by a few.

Essentially Jack believes he is unacceptable to his peers. He feels that others are making fun of him or rejecting him even when they are being friendly. When Jack feels he is being rejected, he immediately attempts to escape his discomfort. He tried to isolate himself by placing his backpack over his head, walking the hallways sideways with his face to the wall, and so on.

Mr. Bird recognizes that eventually this behavior will affect all facets of Jack's functioning including his academics. Involved staff discussed and agreed that life-space interviewing was an appropriate intervention in Jack's case. Each time Jack engaged in the behavior, he was immediately removed by a supportive adult from the setting in which the behavior occurred.

The incident was reconstructed and discussed, and a plan for a more acceptable response by Jack to a classmate's smile, wave, and so on, was agreed on by Jack and the supportive adult. Jack returned to the setting in which the behavior occurred and continued his daily schedule.

Over time and after many life-space interviews. Jack increased his capacity to differentiate between social acceptance and rejection.

Interview Guidelines:

1. Be polite to the individual. If you don't have control of your emotions, do not begin the interview.
2. Sit, kneel, or stand to establish eye contact. Talk with, never at, the individual being interviewed.
3. When you are unsure about the history of the incident, investigate. <u>Do not conduct an interview on the basis of second-or third-hand information or rumors.</u>
4. <u>Ask appropriate questions</u> to obtain a knowledgeable grasp of the incident. However, do not probe areas of unconscious motivation; limit the use of "why" questions.
5. <u>Listen to the individual</u> and attempt to comprehend his or her perception of the incident.
6. <u>Encourage the individual to ask questions.</u> Respond to the child's questions appropriately.
7. When the individual is suffering from apparent shame and/or guilt because of the incident, <u>attempt to reduce and minimize these feelings.</u>
8. <u>Facilitate the individual's efforts to communicate</u> what s/he wishes.
9. Work carefully and patiently with the individual to develop a mutually acceptable plan of action for immediate or future implementation.

Reality Therapy-In reality therapy, the therapist or teacher takes present behavior and confronts students about whether their behavior is helping them or hurting them. Confrontational questions assist the individual in taking responsibility for his or her behavior. Responsibility is seen as the ability to fulfill one's personal needs in a manner that does not deprive other individuals of their ability to fulfill their needs. The teacher acts as a facilitator as they assist the individual in developing a plan by which to resolve troublesome behavior. The person generally feels more responsible for enacting the plan if it is written and signed. In summary, reality therapy is the process of teaching an individual to face existing reality, to function responsibly, and, as a result, to fulfill personal needs.

Example

Kyle, a tenth-grade student at Greenwood High School, had superior academic potential. However, he was flunking several subjects. It became evident that Kyle's future relative to graduation and college was being affected by his behavior.

Mr. Scott, Kyle's favorite teacher, decided he needed to help the boy. He did not want Kyle to jeopardize his future. Mr. Scott decided to use the reality therapy approach with Kyle. After all, he and Kyle were friends; he cared about the boy; and he knew Kyle could improve with help.

In their first session, Mr. Scott confronted Kyle with questions like "What are you doing?" "Is it helping you?" "If not, what else could you do to help yourself?" It was found that Kyle would not work in any subject area if he did not like the teacher. If the teacher was too demanding, unfriendly, and so on, Kyle just gave up - he refused to study.

Kyle recognized that his behavior was only harmful to himself. He and Mr. Scott developed a plan of action. During the next few months, they met regularly to monitor Kyle's progress and to write the revise the plan as needed. Kyle learned to accept responsibility for his behavior. His grades improved dramatically.

Guidelines for teachers engaged in the interview.

1. Be personal. Demonstrate to the individual that you are a friend who cares about the individual and who is interested in his or her welfare.
2. Focus the therapeutic process on the individual's present behavior, not his past behavior. Accept the individual's expressed feelings, but do not probe into unconscious motivators. Confront by asking "what," "how," and "who" questions. Limit asking "why" questions.
3. Do not preach, moralize, or make value judgments about the individual's behavior.
4. Help the individual formulate a practical plan to increase responsible behavior.
5. Encourage the individual to overtly make a commitment to the mutually agreed-on plan.
6. Do not accept the individual's excuses for irresponsible behavior. When a plan fails or cannot be implemented, develop another.
7. Do not punish the individual for irresponsible behavior. As a general principle, allow the individual to realize the logical consequences of irresponsible behavior unless the consequences are unreasonably harmful.
8. Provide the individual with emotional support and security throughout the therapeutic process.

Transactional Analysis (Berne & Harris)-Transactional analysis is considered to be a rational approach to understanding human behavior. It is based on the assumption that individuals can learn to have trust in themselves, think for themselves, make their own decisions, and express personal feelings. According to this approach, there are different persons within us. Our day-to-day experiences serve as stimuli that evoke memories of past situations and cause a person to relive the events with recorded images and feelings.

This behavioral intervention provides the teacher with a framework for viewing what is said to and by students. The principles of this intervention can be applied on the job, in the home, in the classroom, and in the neighborhood - wherever people deal with people. Although transactional analysis procedures are primarily intellectual or cognitive, the person using them gains emotional as well as intellectual insight into self and others.

The personality is composed of three ego states: (1) the parent, (2) the child, (3) the adult. Individuals are in the parent state when acting, thinking, and feeling as they observed their parents doing. Individuals are in the adult ego state when dealing with current reality, gathering facts, and computing objectively. Individuals are in the child ego state when they are feeling and acting as they did when they were children. Ego states are most evident and observable in an individual's transactions (interactions, exchanges) with others. The process of transactional analysis is primarily the examination of exchanges between the individual and others in the environment. Although there are many specific types of transaction, there are three major ones:

1. <u>Complementary transaction.</u> These are predictable reactions received from a person in response to an act. For example, the usual response of a child to a parent requesting him or her to clean his room is that the child grumbles a little but he does it.
2. <u>Cross - transactions</u>. These transactions occur when an individual receives an unpredictable response from another individual. For example, an unexpected response from a child who usually cleans his room might be: "No way, I won't do it. You're the mother, and it's your job." An unexpected response from a colleague who is usually helpful in emergencies when requested to substitute might be: "Forget it. I have enough to do. It's your emergency, your class, and your problem, not mine."
3. <u>Ulterior transactions.</u> These transactions have a hidden message in which what is stated is not the real message being sent. For example, a man who is both husband and a father is painting his large family house. He would like and needs help. Instead of saying, "Hey, people, I need help," he complains about the work, his tiredness and muscle aches, his age, the size of the house, and so on. His purpose is really to obtain help, not sympathy.

All humans have a personality composed of the three ego states, which are found to be a result of our reactions to stimulation from others in the environment. This reaction is a result of reinforcement, or strokes, from others in the environment. A stroke is a form of recognition, or attending to, that is necessary for all human beings. Strokes may be verbal or physical, positive or negative.

Four life positions that predominate in a person's personality are:

1. I'm not okay; you're okay.
2. I'm not okay; you're not okay.
3. I'm okay; you're not okay.
4. I'm okay; you're okay.

The fourth position - we are both okay - is only entered because of a conscious and verbal decision. Transactional analysis is designed to help the individual attain this position.

Role-playing and Psychodrama (Moreno & Raths)-Psychodrama was originally developed for therapeutic purposes. Role playing can help an individual clarify feelings and emotions as they relate to existing reality in three ways.

1. It can focus on real occurrences. An incident may be reenacted and the participants told to attend to the feelings aroused, or an incident may be reenacted with the participants changing roles and attending the feelings of the aroused by these new roles. An individual may be directed to deliver a soliloquy (monologue) to recreate an emotionally loaded event. Emphasis here is on expressing feelings that were hidden or held back when the event first occurred.
2. It can focus on significant others. The individual may portray a significant person in his or her life about whom a great amount of conflict is felt.
3. It can focus on processes and feelings occurring in new situations. Directions for this type of role playing may be very specific, with the participants provided with special characters and actions, or directions may be vague, allowing the participants to form their own characters.

Role playing and psychodrama techniques have been incorporated into several effective education programs concerned specifically with clarification of values and standards.

    Example:

        George, a 13-year old eighth grader, was shorter than the other boys in his grade. First the girls and then the boys grew several inches while George's height seemed to stay the same. His classmates were constantly making fun of his size. They called him "runt," "shorty," "midget," and "dwarf." Each day someone came up with a new name to call him.

        George was a sensitive person, and whenever he was called a name, he withdrew. More and more, the teacher began seeing George sitting alone while the others played. Mrs. Wright was very concerned about George's mental well-being and his classmate's lack of consideration and empathy for George and the other children who were different. She believed that role playing might be a method of helping the whole class, including George, gain insight into their behavior.

        As the students began to empathize with the feelings of the characters they were role playing, George became more accepted and less a target of their hurtful behavior. George began playing with the others more readily during free time.

KNOW CONCEPTS UTILIZED IN BEHAVIOR MODIFICATION PROCEDURES

Behavior modification is a systematic approach toward the modification of behavior. Its use has the effect of strengthening, maintaining, or weakening target behaviors. Concerns that have surfaced over the use of behavior modification pertain primarily to the concept of free will versus control by external forces. In addition, misunderstanding of behavioral procedures and misclassification of other types of treatment (e.g. electroconvulsive therapy) have perpetuated doubts about ethical use.

Factors that should be taken into consideration by educators who desire to use behavior modification in a responsible manner are as follows:

1. **Competency of teacher.** A responsible teacher who attempts to use behavior modification will have an understanding of the principles and techniques she is applying.
2. **Selection of appropriate goals.** Behaviors targeted for change should be those that will benefit the students, and are able to be achieved by the student as well.
3. **Accountability.** This implies the necessity of being able to evaluate behaviorally stated goals, clearly described procedures, and results defined in terms of direct, functional relationships between interventions and behaviors.

Behavior modification is based on the premise that all behavior, regardless of its appropriateness, has been learned, therefore, it can be changed. The behavioral model deals with behaviors we can see, hear, or measure. After the behavior that is targeted for change has been identified and the reinforcers located, behavior can be systematically modified through behavior modification procedures.

Some of these procedures are used to increase behaviors (e.g. positive reinforcement, negative reinforcement, shaping and token economy), and other procedures are used to decrease behaviors (e.g. punishment, extinction). A procedure can be used to increase the rate of a desirable behavior while decreasing the rate of related but undesirable behaviors (i.e. differential reinforcement).

The ABCs of behavior modification are specified as the antecedent, the behavior, and the consequence. Stimuli that precede the behavior are referred to as antecedents; stimuli that follow the behavior are known as consequential events. All three are interactive components.

Certain environmental conditions or events become linked to particular behaviors over time. Any behavior is more likely to occur in the presence of stimuli that accompanied the behavior when it was reinforced in the past. This is the principle of stimulus control, that describes a relationship between behavior and its antecedent stimuli (events or condition occurring before the behavior is performed). Antecedent stimuli have a controlling effect upon behavior when the student is able to discriminate that specific consequent stimuli will follow certain behavior.

Following the occurrence of behaviors, consequential events occur. These events (i.e. reward, punishment) control behavior of their effects. Behavior that is followed by a pleasant consequence tends to be increased or repeated. Behavior followed by an unpleasant consequence tends to show a decrease.

Consequential events have a functional relationship with behavior. Similarly, behavior that avoids or terminates an aversive stimulus will show an increase. For example, Jim avoids having his teacher frown at him by finishing his work, or on another occasion, terminates her disapproving scowl by returning to his desk and finishing his work.

UNDERSTAND THE USE OF PRIMARY REINFORCERS AND KNOW THE LIMITATIONS OF THEIR USAGE IN AN EDUCATIONAL SETTING

Primary reinforcers may be referred to as those stimuli that have biological importance to an individual. They may be described as natural, unlearned, unconditioned, and innately motivating. The most common and appropriate reinforcers for use in the classroom are food and liquids. Edible reinforcers have been found to be strong motivators for students with low functioning abilities, for younger students, and for students who are learning a new behavior.

The necessity for the student to be in a state of deprivation is a major drawback in the use of primary reinforcers. However, a state of hunger is not required in order for treats or special foods to be effective as reinforcers.

The opposite condition of deprivation is satiation. The deprivation state that existed before the instructional session may no longer exist, thus the stimulus may cease to be an effective motivator.

Some suggestions for preventing satiation include:

1. Vary reinforcers with instructional tasks.
2. Shorten the instructional sessions, and presentations of reinforcers will therefore be decreased.
3. Alternate reinforcers (e.g. food, then juice).
4. Decrease the size of edibles presented
5. Have an array of edibles available

Teachers must be cautious in the administration of edibles. Parents and children's medical records may need to be consulted. In addition, a student may be on a special diet, have lactose intolerance or allergic reactions to certain foods, or may be susceptible to diabetic reactions. Liquid reinforcers increase the necessity for toileting breaks. Certain cereals or bite size fruits may be better reinforcers than candy. The sugar content and size are easier to control. Finally, teachers need to remember that what is reinforcing for one student is not necessarily reinforcing for another.

DISCUSS THE ADVANTAGES AND DISADVANTAGES OF USING VARIOUS TYPES OF REINFORCERS IN THE SCHOOL SETTING

It is a generally accepted fact that teachers need to create positive learning environment that will meet special needs and accommodate individual learning styles. The need to develop appropriate antecedent stimuli is considered to be of much importance (i.e. classroom arrangement, task assignments, instructions preceding performance); however, emphasis is placed heavily upon the consequential events that follow a behavior. This can be seen in the basic rules of behaviorism: (1) behavior that is reinforced tends to occur more frequently; (2) behavior that is no longer reinforced will be extinguished; (3) behavior that is punished will occur less often. Thus, teachers must systematically be able to use reinforcers that are available to all children during the normal course of a school day.

Social Reinforcement-Social reinforcement refers to the behaviors of others that directly influence the increase in a child's behavior. The range of potential social reinforcers includes verbal expressions that convey approval of the students' accomplishments (e.g. praise such as "I like the way you have stayed at your desk," or "You did a great job!"), nonverbal expressions (e.g. winking, smiling), teacher proximity to student (e.g. hug, pat on the back), and the granting of privileges that carry status for the student among his peers. Social reinforcement can be used as a planned teaching technique or can be given spontaneously.

The advantages for using social reinforcement are many. First, it is easy to use, absorbing little of the teacher's time and effort, and is available in any setting. The fact that teachers are persons who possess high status in the students' eyes makes it especially appropriate for the teacher's use. Social reinforcement rarely incurs criticism, is unlikely to satiate, and can be generalized to most situations. The main disadvantage is that it may not be a strong enough reinforcer, thus may need to be paired with a tangible reinforcer.

Activity Reinforcement-Activity reinforcement refers to the involvement in preferred activities. The systematic use of activity reinforcers is described by the Premack Principle. It states that any activity that a student voluntarily participates on a frequent basis (e.g. high interest activity) can be used as a reinforcer for any activity that the student seldom participates (e.g. running errands, decorating a bulletin board, leading a group activity, earning free time).

Major advantages in using activity reinforcers include their ready availability and unlimited accessibility, thus preventing satiation. If a student tires of one activity, there are many others that can be used. Special needs children are less likely to be seen as different when engaged in earned activity time, and activity reinforcers can be combined with social reinforcers. Furthermore, once activity reinforcers are identified with the learning environment, they can be acquired with little effort. Disadvantages in the use of activity reinforcers are few, but might include the need for handling delayed gratification and the possibility of interrupting other classroom activities.

Token Reinforcement-A system whereby children are given immediate reinforcement by means of an object that can be exchanged for a reinforcer of value as a future time is called token reinforcement. In using this system, the token is delivered contingent on a desired response. Tokens should be durable, practical, and easily dispensed. They can be in the form of objects (e.g. poker chips, play money, stars, or tickets), or they can be symbols like happy faces, check marks or points.

Used alone, tokens have little or no value or power. Their reinforcing value is attained by virtue of their being exchanged for a variety of reinforcing rewards like backup reinforcers). Among the backup reinforcers there must be items desired by all students using the token reinforcement system. An array of items needs to be available for selection, such as tangible objects such as trinkets, school supplies), edibles and activities.

Use of a token economy system has advantages, such as providing a concrete means for immediate reinforcement and an observable record of accomplishments. Tokens can be given without interfering with classroom activities, and their use is generally acceptable by teachers, peers, and parents. Use of this system necessitates a well-organized management system that does require time and energy to operate successfully. Other considerations include dependency upon receiving concrete, immediate reinforcement, the need to acquire an assortment of desirable backup reinforcers, and the inability to readily generalize this system into another environment. However, many teachers have found the token reinforcement system to be of great benefit in modifying student behavior and report that the advantages far outweigh required efforts on their part.

Tangible Reinforcement-The use of tangible items as consequential reinforcement for desired behavior is called tangible reinforcement. This system can be used by itself or as a part of another system, such as token reinforcement. Tangible items dispensed in the educational setting are typically those that can be used or consumed in the classroom for academic activities, such as pencils, paper, erasers, or during free activity time like giving baseball cards, game items, trinkets, or posters.

Tangible reinforcers are seen as desirable by children because they are concrete items. Therefore, their high reinforcing value enhances their effectiveness. This primary advantage, however, must be weighed in relation to possible disadvantages. Tangible reinforcers can be costly and hard to acquire, must be age appropriate, and, if given only to special needs students, may make them appear different from their peers. Children must receive this type of reinforcement less frequently, or else satiation will occur. The less frequent aspect, however, means that immediate reinforcement based on contingent behavior is unlikely to occur. Many teachers pair tangible reinforcers with activity or social reinforcers, and therefore eventually fade the tangible rewards in lieu of using intangible means of reinforcement.

UNDERSTAND EFFECTS OF PUNISHMENT TECHNIQUES USED AS A MEANS OF BEHAVIOR CHANGE

Punishment is a procedure in which a punisher is administered contingent on any undesirable behavior. A punisher is a consequential stimulus that has the following characteristics: (1) it decreases the future rate or probability of the occurrence of the behavior; (2) it is administered contingent upon the production of an undesired behavior, and (3) it is administered immediately following the production of the undesired behavior.

A punisher such as aversive stimulus, aversive consequence, is defined based on the consequent decrease in behavior. This is called a functional definition since, like a reinforcer, what may have an effect upon one student may not necessarily affect another. For example, Timmy continually comes up to the teacher's desk. If the teacher's reprimand results in a reduction or cessation of Timmy's behavior, then the reprimand is a punisher. If Timmy's behavior continues, or even increases, the reprimand will have functioned as a reinforcer.

Most teachers discover that the use of aversive consequences has the following effects: (1) it quickly stops the occurrence of a behavior at least temporarily, (2) it provides a clear discrimination between acceptable and non-acceptable behavior and between safe and harmful behavior, and (3) it models consequential results to other students.

Continuum of Punishers-The continuum of punishers includes aversive consequences such as verbal reprimands, response cost, over correction, corporal punishment, and suspension or expulsion. The type selected should depend upon the situation, the child's offense, and the behavioral strategies previously used with the child.

Verbal reprimands have been found to reduce undesired behavior when delivered privately and firmly. Two points that should be considered when using verbal reprimands are (1) be certain they are not serving as reinforcers for attention, and (2) avoid public reprimand that makes a child defensive.

Response cost is a punishment procedure that involves the loss of reinforcer upon occurrence of an undesired behavior. The reinforcer lost may be an activity like a privilege, or free time, tokens, or tickets, and trinkets. Reinforcers should be delivered in such proportions that cost penalties do not outweigh them. Motivation for earning reinforcers will be negatively affected if this occurs.

Two types of over-correction are frequently used, restitutional and positive practice. The former requires that students restore the effect of their behavior on the environment such as wash or repaint a marred surface, and the latter requires students to practice an incompatible (appropriate) behavior instead of the one demonstrated.

More severe forms of punishment ought to be used only as a last resort, that is, when other strategies based on reinforcement, extinction, or removal of desired stimuli have been proven unsuccessful, or when safety is jeopardized. The use of corporal punishment should follow due process procedures, and be administered in a restrained, businesslike manner. Though corporeal punishment typically brings about an immediate cessation of inappropriate behavior, the change is usually of short duration. For more long-term results, teacher acceptance should be demonstrated following its application, and reinforcement must be given on the first instance of the desired behavior.

Suspension is considered another form of severe punishment, and involves removal from the school environment for relatively short time periods. Many schools have incorporated the use of in-house suspension in an effort to ensure supervision. Family supervision cannot always be provided, especially when parents are employed, thus removal from the school to the home setting may become reinforcing if the student is allowed to watch television, wander the street, or engage in activities contrary to the purpose of the removal. Expulsion, the next step after suspension, is the official denial of a child's right to a free, appropriate instruction. This step is very serious and it is governed by elaborate substantive and procedural due process safeguards.

Extinction-Two procedures are used to decrease behavior in behavior analysis: punishment and extinction. Extinction is based on the fact that behavior is extinguished when consequences that have been maintaining it are removed. Knowledge of which consequences are reinforcing the behavior is essential. For example, if teacher attention through such means as aversive reprimands has been reinforcing John's out-of-seat behavior, then ignoring John by removing teacher attention may help to weaken his out-of-seat behavior. It is important that the incompatible behavior be reinforced immediately and on each occurrence.

Time-out involves removal of the child from an environment in which he has been able to earn positive reinforcement. Time-out, used appropriately, is a form of extinction in that removal from the environment makes it impossible to earn reinforcers. Physical restraint is used to physically prevent the student from behaving in a dangerous way toward himself or others, or in an uncontrollable manner. It is a means of stopping the behavior until the student has regained enough self-control to be responsible for his own actions.

Unconditioned and Conditioned Aversive Stimuli-Aversive stimuli may be categorized as unconditional aversive stimuli and conditioned aversive stimuli. Unconditioned aversive stimuli result in physical pain or discomfort to the student. This class of stimuli includes naturally occurring circumstances such as contact with a hot stove burner, cuts, or sprains from falls or contrived consequences like application of electric shock, loud noises, and unpleasant smells.

Conditioned aversive stimuli are learned because of being paired with unconditioned aversive stimuli. This class of stimuli includes consequential presentations such as words spoken, vocal tones, and non-verbal signals. A student may have experienced being yelled at with being paddled. Past experiences have paired yelling with pain. The pain associated with a conditioned aversive stimulus may also be psychological or social discomfort like embarrassment, ridicule, or teasing.

It is vital for those involved in any program that includes punishment to be certain that it is always used in association with reinforcement for inappropriate behavior. All the student learns from punishment is the behavior in which he should not be engaged. The reinforcement of appropriate behaviors serves as an instruction to the student about appropriate behaviors for which he may find successful experiences.

The term contingency refers to the planned, systematic relationship that is established between a behavior and a consequence. Thus, contingency management is an approach that teachers attempt to modify behavior by managing the contingencies, or consequences, for those behaviors. Contingency management incorporates the systematic use of reinforcement and punishment to develop, maintain, or change behavior. The following guidelines may be used in developing a contingency management plan.

1. Decide what to measure. A desired target behavior is specified and defined.
2. Select a measurement strategy. The behavior must be observable and measurable as in frequency, and duration.
3. Establish a baseline. The level of the behavior prior to implementing a treatment plan or an intervention must be established.
4. Design a contingency plan. Reinforcers or punishers are selected that correspond with behavioral consequences.
5. Implement the contingency plan. Collect data, provide reinforcement or punishment for the behavioral occurrences in accordance with the schedule selected for use and record behavioral measurements on a graph.
6. Evaluate the program. Modify the contingency management plan as needed. Modifications can be achieved by (1) a reversal to baseline to determine effect of treatment on behavior, (2) changing the reinforcer or punisher if needed, or (3) implementing a new treatment.

A contingency management plan can be very useful in the classroom setting. In most classrooms, teachers specify what behaviors are expected and the contingencies for performing those behaviors. Contingencies are stated in the form of "If…then…" statements. Contingency management may take the form of various treatment techniques, such as token economies, contingency contracting, and precision teaching.

Students may be involved in the process of designing, implementing, and evaluating a contingency management plan. They can decide on behaviors that are in need of modification, select their reinforcers, assist in data collection, record the data on graphs, and evaluate the effectiveness of the contingency or treatment plan. The ultimate goal in allowing students to participate in contingency management is to encourage their use of the procedures that they have been taught to manage their own behavior. As with self-recording, the transition from teacher-managed to student-managed programs must be gradual, and students should be explicitly taught how to use self-reinforcement or self-punishment.

SKILL 16.2 Understand how to develop and implement systematic behavior intervention plans (e.g., using behavioral contracts, teaching new behaviors to replace problem behaviors) to promote positive social behavior and self-control

A Functional Behavior Assessment (FBA) is a method of gathering information. The information that is collected is utilized to assess why problem behaviors occur. The data will also help in pinpointing things to do that will help alleviate the behaviors. The data from a functional behavioral assessment is used to create a positive behavioral intervention plan.

The Individuals with Disabilities Education Act (IDEA) specifically calls for a functional behavior assessment when a child with a disability has their present placement modified for disciplinary reasons. IDEA does not elaborate on how an FBA should be conducted as the procedures may vary dependent on the specific child. Even so, there are several specific elements that should be a part of any functional behavior assessment.

The first step is to identify the particular behavior that must be modified. If the child has numerous problem behaviors then it is important to assess which behaviors are the primary one's that should be addressed. This should be narrowed down to one or two primary behaviors. The primary behavior is then described so that everyone is clear as to what the behaviors consist of. The most typical order of procedures is as follows:

Identify and come to an agreement about the behaviors that need to be modified. Find out where the behaviors are most likely to happen and where they are not likely to happen. Identify what may trigger the behavior to occur.

The team will ask these types of questions: What is unique about the surroundings where behaviors are not an issue? What is different in the locations where the problem conduct occurs? Could they be linked to how the child and teacher get along? Does the amount of other students or the work a child is requested to do trigger the difficulty? Could the time of day or a child's frame of mind affect the behaviors? Was there a bus problem or an argument in the hallway? Are the behaviors likely to happen in a precise set of conditions or a specific location? What events seem to encourage the difficult behaviors?

Assemble data on the child's performance from as many resources as feasible. Develop a hypothesis about why difficult behaviors transpire (the function of the behaviors). A hypothesis is an educated deduction, based on data. It helps foretell in which location and for what reason problem behaviors are most likely to take place, and in which location and for what reason they are least likely to take place. Single out other behaviors that can be taught that will fulfill the same purpose for the child.

Test the hypothesis. The team develops and utilizes positive behavioral interventions that are written into the child's IEP or behavior intervention plan. Assess the success of the interventions. Modify or fine-tune as required.

If children have behaviors that place them or others at risk, they may require a crisis intervention plan. Crisis interventions should be developed before they are required. The team should determine what behaviors are crises and what they (and the child) will do in a crisis. By having a plan that guides actions, teachers can assist children through difficult emotional circumstances.

Essential Elements of Behavior Intervention Plan

A Behavior Intervention Plan (BIP) is utilized to reinforce or teach positive behavior skills. It is also known as a behavior support plan or a positive intervention plan. The child's team normally develops the Behavior Intervention Plan. The essential elements of a behavior intervention plan are as follows:
- Skills training to increase the likelihood of appropriate behavior
- Modifications that will be made in classrooms or other environments to decrease or remove problem behaviors
- Strategies to take the place of problem behaviors and institute appropriate behaviors that serve the same function for the child
- Support mechanisms for the child to utilize the most appropriate behaviors

The IEP team determines whether the school discipline procedures need to be modified for a child, or whether the penalties need to be different from those written into the policy. This decision should be based on an assessment and a review of the records, including the discipline records or any manifestation determination review(s) that have been concluded by the school. A child's IEP or behavior intervention plan should concentrate on teaching skills. Sometimes school discipline policies are not successful in rectifying problem behaviors. That is, the child does not learn what the school staff intended through the use of punishments such as suspension. The child may learn instead that problem behaviors are useful in meeting a need, such as being noticed by peers. When this is true, it is difficult to defend punishment, by itself, as effective in changing problem behaviors. One of the most useful questions parents can ask when they have concerns about the discipline recommendations for their child is "Where are the data that support the recommendations?" Special education decisions are based on data. If school staff wants to use a specific discipline procedure, they should check for data that support the use of the procedure.

SKILL 16.3 Understand the use of positive behavior supports and crisis management techniques with students with mild/moderate disabilities

According to the Center for Effective Collaboration and Practice, most schools are safe, but the violence from the surrounding communities have begun to make their way into the schools. Fortunately there are ways to intervene and prevent crises in our schools.

First administrators, teachers, families, students, support staff, and community leaders must be trained and/or informed on early warning signs. It should also be emphasized not to use these warning signs to inappropriately label or stigmatize individual students because they may display some of the following warning signs.

Early Warning Signs- Early warning signs are as follows:
- Social withdrawal
- Excessive feelings of isolation and being alone
- Excessive feelings of rejection
- Being a victim of violence
- Feelings of being picked on and persecuted
- Low school interest and poor academic performance
- Expression of violence in writings and drawings
- Uncontrolled anger
- Patterns of impulsive and chronic hitting, intimidating, and bullying behaviors
- History of discipline problems
- Past history of violent and aggressive behavior
- Intolerance for differences and prejudicial attitudes
- Drug use and alcohol use
- Affiliation with gang**s**
- Inappropriate access to, possession of, and use of firearms
- Serious threats of violence

Imminent Warning Signs -Early warning signs and imminent warning signs differ because imminent warning signs require an immediate response. Imminent warning signs indicate that a student is very close to behaving in a way that is potentially dangerous to self and/or to others.

Imminent warning signs may include:
- Serious physical fighting with peers or family members.
- Severe destruction of property.
- Severe rage for seemingly minor reasons.
- Detailed threats of lethal violence.
- Possession and/or use of firearms and other weapons.
- Other self-injurious behaviors or threats of suicide.

When imminent signs are seen school staff must follow the school board policies in place, which typically includes reporting it to a designated person or persons before handling anything on your own.

Intervention and prevention plan-Every school system's plans may be different but the plan should be derived from some of the following suggestions:

• *Share responsibility by establishing a partnership with the child, school, home, and community.* Schools should coordinate with community agencies to coordinate the plan, in addition to rendering services to students who may need assistance. The community involvement should include child and family service agencies, law enforcement and juvenile justice systems, mental health agencies, businesses, faith and ethnic leaders, and other community agencies.
• *Inform parents and listen to them when early warning signs are observed.* Effective and safe schools make persistent efforts to involve parents by: informing them routinely about school discipline policies, procedures, and rules, and about their children's behavior (both good and bad); involving them in making decisions concerning school-wide disciplinary policies and procedures; and encouraging them to participate in prevention
• *Maintain confidentiality and parents' rights to privacy.* Parental involvement and consent is required before personally identifiable information is shared with other agencies, except in the case of emergencies or suspicion of abuse.
• *Develop the capacity of staff, students, and families to intervene.* Schools should provide the entire school community-teachers, students, parents, support staff-with training and support in responding to imminent warning signs, preventing violence, and intervening safely and effectively. Interventions must be monitored by professionals who are competent in the approach.
• *Support students in being responsible for their actions.* Schools and members of the community should encourage students to see themselves as responsible for their actions, and actively engage them in planning, implementing, and evaluating violence prevention initiatives.
• *Simplify staff requests for urgent assistance.* Many school systems and community agencies have complex legalistic referral systems with timelines and waiting lists. This should be a simple process that does not prevent someone from requesting assistance.

Drill and practice-Most schools are required to have drills and provide practice to ensure that everyone is informed of proper procedure to follow if emergencies occur. In addition to violence caused by a student, the emergency can also be an intruder in the builder, bomb threat, or fire.

SKILL 16.4 Recognize appropriate ways to involve students' families and other school personnel in behavior intervention plans

In order for students to be successful in following a behavior intervention plan, students may need support to help them use appropriate behavior. Supports are created to address factors beyond the immediate context in which the inappropriate behavior occurs. The student may benefit from assistance from school counselors, psychologists, or school social workers to help them focus on academic or personal issues that may add to the problem behaviors.

Families can help by assisting the student in developing a homework schedule and by positively reinforcing their child for appropriate behavior in school. They can also assist by keeping in contact with the teacher on a regular basis and responding to feedback given by the teacher and administering appropriate punishments or rewards when necessary to supplement the behavior interventions in school.

Family members participate in planning teams, learn how to teach their children the importance of school-wide expectations at home and in the community, and volunteer to participate in related school activities including school celebrations, public relations, and the search for donations and free resources in the community.

Speech and Language therapist's can assist by helping to improve the student's expressive and receptive language skills, which should give the student alternative methods to respond to stressful situations.

SKILL 16.5 Demonstrate knowledge of strategies for monitoring the effects of behavior interventions and making changes to interventions as necessary

Regular monitoring and evaluation are needed to prevent ineffective practices from wasting time and resources, improve the efficiency and effectiveness of current procedures, eliminate parts of the process that don't work, and make changes before problem behavior patterns become too hard to modify.
The behavior intervention plan should be monitored to determine whether the plan is being followed and implemented according to the written guidelines. The behavior intervention plan should list specifically who is responsible for implementing each component and the various elements of the plan should be listed. A checklist should be created to correspond with each element of the plan. Written scripts or lists can be created that show the responsibilities of each person participating in the implementation of the plan. The script can indicate both verbal and non-verbal responses categorized according to events. Monitoring should take place every week to assess the faithfulness with which the behavior intervention plan is implemented.

IDEA states that a behavioral intervention plan must be reviewed and revised whenever the IEP team feels that a change is necessary. The situations that may call for such a review include: the student no longer demonstrates behavior problems; the situation has changed and the plan no longer addresses the student's needs; the IEP team determines that the behavior intervention strategies are inconsistent with the student's IEP or placement; or the original plan is not fostering positive changes in the student's behavior.

SKILL 16.6 Demonstrate knowledge of laws, policies, and ethical principles regarding behavior management planning and implementation

The following information is helpful information but, state specific information can be found on **HTTP://WWW.SDE.STATE.OK.US/HOME/DEFAULTIE.HTML**

Positive behavioral interventions and supports (PBS) is IDEA's preferred strategy for handling challenging behaviors of students with disabilities. IDEA requires PBS to be considered in all cases of students whose behavior impedes their learning or the learning of others.

IDEA also requires that "in the case of a child whose behavior impedes his or her learning or that of others," a student's IEP team, while developing an IEP (initial development, review, or revision), is required to "consider, when appropriate, strategies, including positive behavioral interventions, strategies, and supports to address that behavior."

PBS involves the use of positive behavioral interventions and systems to attain socially significant behavior change. PBS has four interrelated components. The components are as follows: systems change activities, environmental alterations activities, skill instruction activities, and behavioral consequence activities.

These come together to form a behaviorally based systems approach which enhances the ability of schools, families, and communities to create effective environments that improve the link between research-validated practices and the environments in which teaching and learning occurs.

In most states a student can be removed from school for disciplinary reasons for a period of time not exceeding ten consecutive school days. Removals less than ten consecutive days may be implemented as long as those removals do not represent an alteration of placement for the student.

The IEP team and additional qualified staff must assess whether the behavior in question is part of the student's disability before a disabled student's placement can be modified, as a result of disciplinary action.

If the student's behavior is assessed to be part of the student's disability, then the student's placement cannot be modified as part of a disciplinary tactic. The IEP team may assess that a modification of placement is required in order to provide a free, appropriate public education (FAPE) in the least restrictive environment.

The district has to give services to a student with a disability who has been taken from his current placement for more than ten school days in the school year as a result of disciplinary action. School staff can place a student in an interim alternative educational setting (IAES) without the consent of the parent for the same time frame that a student without a disability could be placed, but not more than forty-five calendar days, if the student brings a weapon or firearm to school, or knowingly possesses or used illegal drugs or sells or solicits the sale of a controlled substance while at school.

After the functional behavioral assessment is performed, the IEP team must convene to create the positive behavior intervention plan that addresses the behavior in question and makes sure that the plan is put into place. Information from the FBA is utilized to create meaningful interventions and plan for instruction in replacement behaviors. The IEP team must review the positive behavior intervention plan and how it is implemented to decide if changes are needed to make the plan more effective.

COMPETENCY 17.0 UNDERSTAND PRINCIPLES AND PROCEDURES FOR PROMOTING SUCCESSFUL STUDENT TRANSITIONS (E.G., FROM ONE SCHOOL SETTING TO ANOTHER, FROM SCHOOL TO EMPLOYMENT AND/OR POSTSECONDARY EDUCATION AND TRAINING, FROM SCHOOL TO ADULT LIFE ROLES).

SKILL 17.1 Demonstrate knowledge of factors that affect student transition across school environments and methods for facilitating transitions

As mentioned throughout this study guide children with exceptionalities oftentimes have difficulty with academics, social skills, and generalization of skills. These deficits will cause difficulty in transitioning across school environments. A way to facilitate transition would be to teach appropriate socialization, generalization, self advocacy, communication, and job exploration. Methods for teaching these topics are found throughout this study guide.

A major focus of special education is to prepare students to become working, independent members of society. IDEA 2004 (Individuals with Disabilities Education Act) also includes preparing students for *further education*. Certain skills beyond academics are needed to attain this level of functioning.

Affective and Social Skills transcend to all areas of life. When an individual is unable to acquire information on expectations and reactions of others or misinterprets those cues, he is missing an important element needed for success as an adult in the workplace and community in general.

Special education should incorporate a level of instruction in the affective/social area as many students will not develop these skills without instruction, modeling, practice, and feedback.

Affective and social skills taught throughout the school setting might include: social greetings; eye contact with a speaker; interpretation of facial expression, body language, and personal space; ability to put feelings and questions into words; and use of words to acquire additional information as needed.

Career/Vocational Skills including responsibility for actions, a good work ethic, and independence should be incorporated into the academic setting. If students are able to regulate their overall work habits with school tasks, it is likely that the same skills will carry over into the work force. The special education teacher may assess the student's level of career/vocational readiness by using the following list.

- Being prepared by showing responsibility for materials/school tools such as books, assignments, study packets, pencils, pens, assignment notebook.
- Knowing expectations by keeping an assignment notebook completed.
- Asking questions when unsure of the expectations.
- Use of additional checklists as needed.
- Use of needed assistive devices.
- Completing assignments on time to the best of their ability.

An additional responsibility of the special educator when teaching career/vocational skills is recognition that a variety of vocations and skills are present in the community. If academics, per se, are not an area in which students excel, other exploratory or training opportunities should be provided.

Such opportunities might include art, music, culinary arts, childcare, technical, or building instruction. These can often be included (although not to the exclusion of additional programs) within the academic setting. For example, a student with strong vocational interest in art may be asked to create a poster to show information learned in a science or social studies unit. While addressing a career/vocational interest this way, the teacher would also be establishing a program of differentiated instruction.

SKILL 17.2 Demonstrate knowledge of techniques and settings for promoting career and vocational awareness, exploration, and preparation

Career development is the complex process of acquiring the knowledge, skills, and attitudes necessary to create a plan of one's choosing and being successful in a particular career field. Career development typically has four different stages. The stages of career development are awareness, exploration, preparation, and placement.

1. **Career Awareness** -Career awareness activities focus on introducing students to the broad range of career options. First, students must be provided with current, in-depth information about careers, which includes job-related skills, necessary education and training, and a description of typical duties, responsibilities, and tasks. Students must be instructed on how to access the variety of available resources, such as Internet, professional magazines, newspapers, and periodicals. Guest speakers and career fairs are provided for students to speak with and interview workers with first hand experiences.
2. **Career Exploration** -Career exploration focuses on learning about careers through direct, hands on activities. This stage is also important to gain insight into the characteristics of these occupations as well as personal interests and strengths. These activities can be provided through in-school and work-based experiences. In-school activities include contextual learning activities, simulated work experiences, and career fairs. Work-based experiences range from non-paid to paid activities. These activities include job shadowing, mentors, company tours, internships, service learning, cooperative education, and independent study.
3. **Career Preparation**-Career preparation provides students with the specific academic and technical knowledge and skills needed in order to be successful at a particular occupation. This may include Career and Technical Education programs or postsecondary education. They include the core activities of career assessments (formal and informal) and work-readiness (soft-skills development, computer competency and job search skills). Community organizations, employers, and professional organizations are also available to provide trainings and insight on accommodations that may be provided for students with special needs.
4. **Career Placement**-Students transitioning from high school need to work collaboratively with involved parents, teachers, and guidance counselors to successfully enter either the workplace or post-secondary education. Placement should depend on the student's aptitude, skills, experiences, and interest.

SKILL 17.3 Understand strategies for providing work experience and career planning services to students

Vocational training is an important element in transition programs. One of the first steps in determining the appropriate vocational program entails performing a functional vocational evaluation. This evaluation gives information about a student's aptitudes, interests, and abilities in relation to employment. It concentrates on practical skills related to a specific job or goal that a student has. It entails information that is collected through situational assessments while a student is on the job. It may include surveys, observations, interviews and other methods. The information obtained during the evaluation is utilized to define the transition activities needed for the students.

It also provides information on the student's strengths and weaknesses in the vocational area. It includes suggestions regarding potential career paths and training programs that are deemed appropriate for the student. This will make the preparation for vocational education more precise and eliminate students entering vocational programs that are ill suited and don't reflect the students likes or strengths.

Vocational educators that have knowledge of vocational training and job requirements can help provide career information to students. They can also help develop realistic assessment activities for students to determine if they have the aptitude or abilities necessary to complete a particular program.

The transitional plan in the IEP should reflect appropriate vocational training that appeals to both the students aptitude, skills, strengths, and likes. It should be based on decisions involving a variety of people including the student, their family, teacher's, vocational educators, and other interested parties.

Vocational Training-Vocational education programs prepare students for entry into occupations in the labor force. Through these programs, it is intended that they become self-sufficient, self-supporting citizens. This training has typically incorporated work-study programs at the high school and post-secondary levels. These programs include training while students are in school and on-the-job training after leaving school. Instruction focuses on particular job skills and on integral activities such as job opportunities, skill requirements for specific jobs, personal qualifications in relation to job requirements, work habits, money management, and academic areas needed for particular jobs. Such vocational training programs are based on three main ideas (Blake, 1976):

1. Students need specific training in job skills. They must acquire them prior to exiting school.
2. Students need specific training and supervision in applying information learned in school to requirements in job situations.
3. Vocational training can provide instruction and field-based experience, which will meet these needs and help the student become able to work in specific occupations.

Career Education -Curricular aspects of career education include the phases of (1) career awareness (diversity of available jobs); (2) career exploration (skills needed for occupational groups); and (3) career preparation (specific training and preparation required for the world of work). The concept of career education (1) extended this training into all levels of public school education (i.e. elementary through high school); (2) emphasized the importance of acquiring skills in the areas of daily living and personal-social interaction, as well as occupational training and preparation; and (3) focused upon integrating these skills into numerous areas of academic and vocational curricula. In general, career education attempts to prepare the individual for all facets of life.

Vocational Training in Special Education-Vocational training in special education has typically focused upon the exceptionality area of intellectual disabilities. Special guidance and training services have more recently been directed toward students with learning disabilities, emotional behavior disorders, physically disabled, visually impaired, and hearing impaired. Individuals with disabilities are mainstreamed with non-disabled students in vocational training programs when possible. Special sites provide training for those persons with more severe disabilities who are unable to be successfully taught in an integrated setting. Specially trained vocational counselors monitor and supervise student work sites.

Regardless of the disabling condition, aptitude testing is considered an important component in vocational training for the students in a mild or moderate setting. This assessment is necessary in order to identify areas of interest and capability. Many prospective employers deem attitudes and work habits important, and so these competencies are included in the training.

Training provisions for individuals with severe intellectual disabilities have expanded. They include special programs for school-aged children and secondary-level adolescents, and sheltered workshop programs for adults. Instruction focuses upon self-help, social-interpersonal, motor, rudimentary academic, simple occupational, and lifetime leisure and recreational skills.

In addition, secondary-level programs offer on-the-job supervision, and sheltered workshop programs provide work supervision and pay a small wage for contract labor. Some persons with moderate to severe intellectual disabilities can be trained for employment in supervised unskilled occupations, while others are only able to perform chores and other simple tasks in sheltered workshops.

SKILL 17.4 Understand strategies for developing goals, benchmarks, activities, programs, and support to promote individuals' transitions to employment and/or postsecondary education

Please refer to Skill 17.3.

SKILL 17.5 Demonstrate knowledge of techniques for promoting students' community living skills; citizenship skills; self-advocacy; multicultural awareness; and participation in social, civic, and recreational activities

In order for students with disabilities to be prepared to live and work in their communities after graduation, they need practice in independent living and employment skills in the settings in which they will be used while under the supervision of teachers.

Community based instruction is a reality based training program conducted in the community, with the ultimate goal being competitive employment and independent living. Community based training should be offered in several skill areas: vocational, community service utilization, activities of daily living, residential, and recreation. Some students may need community-based instruction in all areas, while other students may need training in one or two areas.

In a community-based approach, students may initially learn and practice a skill, such as buying food, in the classroom setting but eventually practice it in a community or home setting. Many students will have difficulty transferring what they have learned in the classroom to the actual setting in which the information is normally used. The student may be able to perform the activity in class, but unable to do it in the real world environment where the skill is actually needed. Community environments utilized by the student and his family should be the environments used to directly teach the skills.

When conducting community based training, students should have frequent opportunities to interact with people without disabilities. Students should be given a wide range of occupational areas so that they can make career decisions. They should have access to rehabilitation engineering and assistive technology. The training should reflect the local labor market needs and include employment areas that have the potential of providing future meaningful work for decent salaries. Parents should be informed and involved in the planning of community based training for their child. The community-based instruction should be ongoing throughout secondary transition services. The school personnel should also be actively involved in the supervision of the training.

SKILL 17.6 Recognize how to promote students' self-determination and develop students' understanding of the responsibilities associated with friendships, human sexuality, family life, and parenting

Helping students to develop healthy self-images and self-worth are integral to the learning and development experiences. Learning for students who are experiencing negative self-image and peer isolation is not necessarily the top priority, when students are feeling bullied or negated in the school community. When a student is attending school from a homeless shelter or is lost in the middle of a parent's divorce or feeling a need to conform to fit into a certain student group, the student is being compromised and may be unable to effectively navigate the educational process or engage in the required academic expectations towards graduation or promotion to the next grade level or subject core level.

Most schools will offer health classes that address teen issues around sexuality, self-image, peer pressure, nutrition, wellness, gang activity, drug engagement and a variety of other relevant teen experiences. Students are required to take a health class as a core class requirement and graduation requirement, so the incentive from the District and school's standpoint is that students are exposed to issues that directly affect them. The fact that one health class is not enough to effectively appreciate the multiplicity of issues that could create a psychological or physiological trauma for a teenager is lost in today's era of school budgets and financial issues that provide the minimum educational experience for students, but loses the student in the process.

Some schools have contracted with outside agencies to develop collaborative partnerships to bring in after school tutorial classes; gender and cultural specific groupings where students can deal authentically with integration of cultural and ethic experiences and lifestyles. Drug intervention programs and speakers on gang issues have created dynamic opportunities for school communities to bring the "undiscussable" issues to the forefront and alleviate fears that are rampant in schools that are afraid to say "No to Drugs and Gangs." Both students and teachers must be taught about the world of teenagers and understand the social, psychological and learning implications that underscore the process of academic acquisition for societies most vulnerable citizens.

TEACHER CERTIFICATION STUDY GUIDE

SUBAREA IV. `WORKING IN A COLLABORATIVE LEARNING COMMUNITY

COMPETENCY 18.0 UNDERSTAND HOW TO ESTABLISH PARTNERSHIPS WITH OTHER MEMBERS OF THE SCHOOL AND THE COMMUNITY TO ENHANCE LEARNING OPPORTUNITIES FOR STUDENTS WITH MILD/MODERATE DISABILITIES.

SKILL 18.1 Demonstrate awareness of consultation, collaboration, and communication strategies for working with others in the school community to solve problems and promote student achievement

Effective communication -Effective communication must occur between teacher and students, as well as among students. Clarity of expression as well as appropriate feedback is essential to successful teaching.

Thus, the special educator needs to be able to teach students who require varying techniques and approaches. They must be able to recognize specific needs, t possess diagnostic capabilities, and make the necessary environment and instruction adaptations, on an individual basis.

Teachers must be able to diagnose individual learning styles because the way in which students learn differs just as abilities vary. Learning can be affected by environmental elements like sound, room arrangement, and physical elements such as time of day or mobility. Coupled with the concern for learning styles is the use of sensory channels such as visual, auditory, and haptic. The special needs teacher must identify modality channels through which students process information most proficiently.

Special techniques are needed in order to teach the basics, due to the fact that students vary in their rate of learning, need for routine, ability to memorize or retain what they learn, and ability to generalize newly acquired concepts. Students must be able to learn from simple to more complex levels within a task hierarchy in order to experience success, and become independent learners to the greatest extent possible.

UNDERSTAND THAT THE TEACHER MAY NEED TO RESPOND TO FEELINGS AS WELL AS WORDS

Not all communication is delivered in a verbal manner. Indeed, words spoken are not always true indicators of what a person means and feels. Non-verbal communication, such as body language, facial expression, tone of voice, and speaking patterns, are all clues to the underlying message the student is attempting to deliver. The teacher demonstrates her willingness to listen by sitting close, leaning forward, making eye-to-eye contact, and showing understanding by nodding or smiling. By so doing, she is sending the message that she cares, is concerned about the student's feelings, and will take the time necessary to understand what is really being communicated.

To facilitate further communication, the teacher must become an active listener. This involves much more than just restating what the person has said. Her responses must reflect his feelings rather than the spoken language. It is essential that the teacher say back what she understands the student's message to mean, as well as the feelings she perceives, and ask for correctness of interpretation.

Often, teachers enter into active listening, with body language conveying a willingness to listen, but respond in such a way that judgment or disapproval of the underlying message is conveyed. Evaluative responses from the listener will decrease attempts to communicate. Encouragement toward communicative efforts is enhanced by use of statements rather than questions, spoken in the present tense and with use of personal pronouns, reflective of current feelings about the situation, and offering self-disclosure of similar experiences or feelings if the teacher feels inclined to do so.

Response to the child's feelings is particularly important since his message may not convey what he really feels. For example, a student who has failed a test may feel inadequate and have the need to blame someone else, such as his teacher, for his failure. He might say to her, "You didn't tell me that you were including all the words from the last six weeks on the spelling test." The teacher, if she were to respond solely to the spoken message might say, "I know I told you that you would be tested over the entire unit. You just weren't listening!" The intuitive, sensitive teacher would look beyond the spoken words by saying, "You're telling me that it feels bad to fail a test." By responding to the child's feelings, the teacher lets him know her understanding of his personal crisis, and the student is encouraged to communicate further.

Please refer to skill 14.2 about lesson plan collaboration.

SUPPORT AND PROFESSIONAL SERVICES

When making eligibility, program, and placement decisions about a student, the special education teacher serves as a member of a multidisciplinary team. Teachers are involved in every aspect regarding the education of individual students; therefore, they need to be knowledgeable not only about teaching and instructional techniques, but also know about support services. These services will need to be coordinated, and teachers must be able to work in a collaborative manner.

The concept of mainstreaming special needs students, that is integrating them with their classmates in as many living and learning environments as possible, caught hold about the time that provisions for the Individuals with Disabilities Education Act (IDEA) were formulated in the early to mid-70s. Even though mainstreaming is not specifically addressed in this legislation, the education of all children and youth with disabilities in their least restrictive environment is mandated. In addition, this important legislation defines special education, identifies related services that may be required if special education is to be effective, and requires the participation of parents and other persons involved in the education of children and youth with disabilities.

Close contact and communication must be established and maintained between the school district staff, each base school, and the various specialists (or consultants) providing ancillary services. These persons often serve special needs students in auxiliary (i.e., providing help) and supplementary (i.e., in addition to) ways. Thus, the principles and methods of special education must be shared with regular educators, and tenets and practices of regular education must be conveyed to special educators. Job roles and unique responsibilities and duties of support specialists like speech/language therapists, physical and occupational therapists, social workers, school psychologists and nurses, and others need to be known by all teachers.

Furthermore, the services that can be provided by community resources, and the support that can be given by parents and professional organizations, must be known to all in order for maximum education for exceptional students to occur. Professional services are offered on a local, state, and national level for most areas of disability. Teachers are able to stay abreast of most current practices and changes by reading professional journals, attending professional conferences, and maintaining membership in professional organizations.

TEACHER CERTIFICATION STUDY GUIDE

RECOGNIZING APPROPRIATE COLLABORATIVE TECHNIQUES FOR ENSURING THE POSITIVE AND EFFECTIVE FUNCTIONING OF CLASSROOM PARAPROFESSIONALS, AIDES, AND VOLUNTEERS

This section will specifically address the working relationship teachers should have with those they work with in their classroom environment. There are six basic steps to having a rewarding collaborative relationship with those whom you share a working environment, whether they are paraprofessionals, aides or volunteers.

While it is understood that there are many titles to those who may be assisting in your room, this section will summarize their titles as "Classroom Assistant."

1) *Get to know each other-*The best way to start a relationship with anyone is to find time alone to get to know each other. Give your new classroom assistant the utmost respect and look at this as an opportunity to share your talents and learn those of your co-worker. Remember that this is your opportunity to find places you agree and disagree, which can help maintain and build your working relationship. Good working relationships require the knowledge of where each other's strengths and weaknesses are. So share what your strengths and weaknesses are and listen to theirs. This knowledge may create one of one of the best working relationships you have ever had.

2) *Remember Communication is a two way street.-*As a professional educator it is important to remember that you must actively communicate with others. This is especially important with your classroom assistant. Let them see you listening. Pay attention and make sure that your classroom assistant sees that you care what he/she thinks. Encourage them to engage you in conversation by asking for more information. When you ask for clarification of what a student said, you are also displaying interest and active listening. Remember also that asking your classroom assistant for details and insights may help you further meet the needs of your students.

It is also your responsibility to remove and prevent communication barriers in your working relationship. You are the professional! You must be the one to avoid giving negative criticism or put downs. Do not "read" motivations into the actions of your classroom assistant. Learn about them through communicating openly.

3) *Establish Clear Roles and Responsibilities*-The Access Center for Improving Outcomes of All Students K-8, has defined these roles in the chart below.

	Teacher Role	Classroom Assistant Role	Areas of Communication
Instruction	• Plan all instruction, including what goals/objectives you expect in your small groups. • Provide instruction in whole-class settings.	• Work with small groups of students on specific tasks, including review or re-teaching of content • Work with one student at a time to provide intensive instruction or remediation on a concept or skill	• Teachers provide specific content and guidance about curriculum, students, and instructional materials • Classroom Assistants note student progress and give feedback to teachers
Curriculum & Lesson Plan Development	• Develop all lesson plans and instructional materials • Ensure alignment with standards, student needs, and IEPs	• Provide assistance in development of classroom activities, retrieval of materials, and coordination of activities	• Mutual review of lesson plan components prior to class • Teachers provide guidance about specific instructional methods
Classroom Management	• Develop and guide class-wide management plans for behavior and classroom structures • Develop and monitor individual behavior management plans	• Assist with the implementation of class-wide and individual behavior management plans • Monitor hallways, study hall, and other activities outside normal class	• Teachers provide guidance about specific behavior management strategies & student characteristics • Classroom Assistants note student progress and activities and give feedback to teachers

("Working Together: Teacher-Paraeducator Collaboration" The Access Center for Improving Outcomes of All Students K-8, http://www.k8accesscenter.org/documents/RESOURCELIST3-1.doc)

While the graph is nice and understandable by both parties, it is often helpful for the teacher to write out what roles and expectations they have for the Classroom Assistant together in a contract type fashion.

4) *Plan Together*-Planning together lets the paraprofessional know that the teacher considers them valuable and provides a timeline of expectations that will aide both teacher and parapro in their classroom delivery to the students. This also gives the impression to the students that the teacher and the parapro are on the same page and that both know what is going to happen next.

TEACHER CERTIFICATION STUDY GUIDE

5) *Show a united front*-It is essential to let the students know that both adults in the room deserve the same amount of respect. Have a plan in place on how to address negative behaviors individually, and together. Teachers should not make statements in front of the students indicating that the Classroom Assistant is wrong. Take time to address issues you may have regarding class time privately, not in front of the class.

6) *Reevaluate the relationship*-Feedback is wonderful! Stop every now and then and discuss how you are working as a team. Be willing to listen to suggestions. Taking this time may be your opportunity to improve your working relationship.

Additional Reading:
"Creating a Classroom Team" http://www.aft.org/pubs-reports/psrp/classroom_team.pdf

"Working Together: Teacher-Paraeducator Collaboration" The Access Center for Improving Outcomes of All Students K-8,
http://www.k8accesscenter.org/documents/RESOURCELIST3-1.doc

SKILL 18.2 Understand strategies for providing services in a variety of educational contexts (e.g., co-teaching, coordinating instruction with other teaching professionals)

Inclusion-Inclusion is both a concept and a method of service delivery. It includes both indirect and direct services rendered by the special education teacher. With indirect services, the special education teacher consults with the regular classroom teacher about the type of instruction and instructional materials that would best meet the needs of a particular student. Through direct services, the special education teacher comes into the regular classroom and team-teaches with the general education teacher. The special education teacher works with individuals, small groups, and large groups of students who are experiencing similar educational difficulties.

Composite Scenario of an Inclusive Educational Setting-The following composite scenario, published in the ERIC Clearinghouse Views (1993 pp. 66-67), provides a brief description of how regular and special teachers work together to address the individual needs of all of their students.

Jane Smith teaches 3rd grade at Lincoln Elementary School. Three days a week, she co-teaches the class with Lynn Vogei, a special education teacher. Their 25 students include four who have special needs due to disabilities, and two others who currently need special help in specific curriculum areas. Each of the students with a disability has an IEP that was developed by a team that included both teachers. The teachers, paraprofessionals, and the school principal believe that these students have a great deal to contribute to the class and that they will achieve their best in the environment of a general education classroom.

MILD-MODERATE DISABILITIES

All of the school personnel have attended in-service training designed to develop collaborative skills for teaming and problem solving. Mrs. Smith and the two professionals who work in the classroom also received special training on disabilities and how to create an inclusive classroom environment. The school's principal, Ben Parks, worked in special education many years ago and has received training on the impact of new special education developments and instructional arrangements on school administration. Each year, Mr. Parks works with the building staff to identify areas in which new training is needed. For specific questions that may arise, technical assistance is available through a regional special education cooperative.

Mrs. Smith and Miss Vogel share responsibility for teaching and for supervising their two paraprofessionals. In addition to the time they spend together in the classroom, they spend two hours each week planning instruction, plus additional planning time with other teachers and support personnel who work with their students.

The teachers use their joint planning time to problem-solve and discuss the use of special instructional techniques for all students who need special assistance. Monitoring and adapting instruction for individual students is an ongoing activity. The teachers use curriculum-based measurement in systematically assessing their students' learning progress. They adapt curricula so that lessons begin at the edge of the students' knowledge, adding new material at the students' pace, and presenting it in a style consistent with the students' learning style. For some students, preorganizers or chapter previews are used to bring out the most important points of the material to be learned; for other students new vocabulary words may need to be highlighted or reduced reading levels may be required. Some students may use special activity worksheets, while others may learn best by using audiocassettes.

In the classroom, the teachers group students differently for different activities. Sometimes, the teachers and paraprofessionals divide the class, each teaching a small group, or tutoring individuals. They use cooperative learning projects to help the students learn to work together and develop social relationships. Peer tutors provide extra help to students who need it. Students without disabilities are more than willing to help their friends' who have disabilities, and vice versa.

While the regular classroom may not be the best learning environment for every child with a disability, it is highly desirable for all who can benefit. It provides contact with age-peers and prepares all students for the diversity of the world beyond the classroom.

Successful Inclusion -Listed are activities and support systems that are commonly found where successful inclusion has occurred.

- **Attitudes and Beliefs**
    - The regular teacher believes that the student can succeed.
    - The school personnel are committed to accepting responsibility for the learning outcomes of students with disabilities.
    - School personnel and the students in the class have been prepared to receive a student with disabilities.
- **Services and Physical Accommodation**
    - Services needed by the student are available (e.g. health, physical, occupational, or speech therapy).
    - Adequate numbers of personnel, including aides and support personnel, are available.
    - Adequate staff development and technical assistance, based on the needs of the school personnel, are being provided (e.g. information on disabilities, instructional methods, and awareness and acceptance activities for students, and team-building skills.
    - Appropriate policies and procedures for monitoring individual students progress, including grading and testing, are in place.
- **Collaboration**
    - Special educators are part of the instructional or planning team.
    - Teaming approaches are used for problem solving and program implementation.
    - Regular teachers, special education teachers, and other specialists collaborate (e.g. co-teach, team teach, work together on teacher assistance teams).
- **Instructional Materials**
    - Teachers have the knowledge and skills needed to select and adapt curricula and instructional methods according to individual student needs.
    - A variety of instructional arrangements is available (e.g. team teaching, cross-grade grouping, peer tutoring, and teacher assistance teams).
    - Teachers foster a cooperative learning environment and promote socialization.

Source: ERJC Clearing House Views. Teaching Exceptional *Children. Fall 1993 pp.66*

DEMONSTRATE AN UNDERSTANDING OF THE CONCEPT OF THE RESOURCE ROOM

The resource room has been described as a regularly scheduled (specialized) instructional setting to which students go during the day for brief periods of special work. The emphasis is on teaching specific skills that the student needs. For the remainder of the school day, the student is in his regular classroom. It is important that the resource room teacher consults with the regular teacher, and cooperatively develops a program that is intended eventually to eliminate the need for resource room assistance.

The school population of students with mild disabilities is comprised of approximately 75 to 87 percent of all school-age students with disabilities. The majority of these students are enrolled in the regular classroom with resource room services. Causes of mild intellectual, learning, and behavioral disabilities are virtually unknown, and physical appearance is like that of the normal population.

Students with mild learning and behavior disorders are characterized as unable to meet the academic or behavioral standards of the regular education program. Therefore, the resource room provides a means of instructional programming to meet unique needs, even though these students remain in the regular classroom during the greater portion of the day. They may be seen as discipline problems, slow learners, or poorly motivated. After exiting formal schooling, these students appear to assume a better adaptive fit into society. Most are not perceivably different when they enter the world of work.

SKILL 18.3 Understand strategies for enhancing integration and coordination of related services for educational benefit

Students with disabilities will receive high quality therapeutic and related services aimed at enhancing their educational performance.

Related services can include services from physical therapists, occupational therapists, speech pathologists, counselors, and other specialists. The caseload for the specialists should be reviewed occasionally to ensure that they have the time to provide the necessary services. The specialist's should participate in team meetings, support integrated services, interact with teachers and parents, and take part in professional development activities and pre-referrals.

To the extent possible, the therapy and other related services should be integrated with the regular curriculum. This can be done by providing increased opportunities for specialists to be involved in curriculum development and implementation; providing appropriate services in the classroom as part of the school day, which should eliminate the need for separate pull-outs; and working with classroom staff to carry over therapeutic practices to other classroom activities.

There will be times when students will need individual attention from a therapist to focus on specific skills. An example of this could be an occupational therapist working on establishing a proper pencil holding technique.

Whenever possible, an individual therapist's caseload should be limited to one or a few schools, in order to encourage integration of services and decrease travel time of specialist's.

The educational opportunities of students with disabilities will be enhanced through active use of computers and related technology.

A comprehensive strategy for the use of technology in educating children with disabilities should be utilized. Students with disabilities should be provided with specialized augmentative or assistive technology equipment or devices.

See skill areas 6 for more information on related services.

SKILL 18.4 Demonstrate knowledge of strategies for assisting general education teachers in integrating students with disabilities into general education classes

Please refer to Skill 18.2.

SKILL 18.5 Demonstrate knowledge of local, state, and federal agencies and services that can help meet the needs of students with mild/moderate disabilities

KNOW COMMUNITY SERVICES AVAILABLE FOR INDIVIDUALS WITH DISABILITIES AND THEIR FAMILIES

School personnel, particularly special educators, need to possess knowledge about community resources available to special education students and to their parents. Federal and state laws guarantee a number of services for any resident whose situation meets specified criteria. Additional services are available to persons with disabling conditions. Some of the agencies perform enforcement, some provide rehabilitative services, and some are rehabilitative (e.g., large print library books), but the special education professional uses parts of each of these. Parent groups provide support for the parents of youngsters with disabilities to share their problems. These groups are not community service agencies per se, but utilize community services to be fully effective.

Health Services-An array of services is offered to families through their state department of health. Services are usually tailored to meet specific disability areas, and are available on a sliding-fee scale basis (i.e., fees priced at a family's ability to pay or income level). The Handicapped Children's Services Division, or the Crippled Children's Services, provides services directly, or contracts services, for all severe, chronic, or disabling forms of disorders (e.g., orthopedic, cerebral palsy, birth defects, heart and kidney diseases, and eye or ear conditions). Other areas in which services might be obtained from the state health department are: (1) family planning, (2) genetic counseling, (3) infant stimulation, (4) maternal and infant care, (5) nutrition counseling, (6) screening and treatment, and (7) provision of supplemental foods.

Financial Services-Financial assistance is provided through various sources; however, the major source is that of Social Security Disability (SSD) benefits. Recipients must be determined "unable to engage in gainful employment as a result of some severe physical or mental impairment" (Hardman, Drew, & Egan, 1984, p. 449). State rehabilitation agencies handle these claims and provide other pertinent services such as financial counseling, health and restoration services, training, job placement, post employment services, and transportation and maintenance allowances.

Individuals with disabilities may also receive assistance in rent subsidies; funding for participation in conjugate housing (e.g., social services assistance with meals, housekeeping, and personal hygiene or grooming needs); insured loans for purchasing or repairing housing; and insured loans for building group homes, conjugate housing, and sheltered workshop facilities.

Social Services-Families with special needs children can obtain assistance from state social service agencies. The Social Security Act (Title IV-B) is a funding service for the referral or special care of children with physical disabilities and mental retardation, foster care, day care, homemaker services, adoptive placements of children, and assistance to youth in transition from institutional to community living.

The Developmental Disabilities Assistance and Bill of Rights Act allocated federal funding for clients who qualify under the state criteria. "A developmental disability, as defined in the Act, refers to an individual who has a severe, chronic, or physical impairment that (1) began at birth or emerged during childhood, (2) is expected to continue indefinitely, and (3) substantially restricts the individual's capacity to perform many functional life skills" (Hardman, Drew, & Egan, 1984, p. 449). Though the Department of Social Services most frequently administers the developmental disabilities funds for each state, the state Departmental Disabilities Planning Council (DDPC) is responsible for selecting the programs that will receive funding. Families should be advised to contact their state DDPC.

Furthermore, subsequent amendments to the Developmental Disabilities Assistance and Bill of Rights Act made funding possible for case management, child development, alternative community living, and other services for those with disabilities of a social-developmental nature. There are many programs under the auspices of the Social Services Department that can assist youth with disabilities and their families.

Employment Services-Employability training is crucial in helping individuals with disabilities to become self-sufficient members of society. The Rehabilitation Services in each state assumes primary responsibility for assisting persons with disabilities to acquire occupational training, and later to secure employment. Fortunately, many postsecondary educational and training institutions have made accommodations for students with special needs, thus enabling employability skills to be acquired in a variety of settings. Sheltered workshop training and employment sites continue to serve persons with more severe disabling conditions.

Accessibility and affirmative action programs have been mandated by several federal acts. Access to employment is made possible through equal hiring opportunities (i.e., if, with accommodations, a person with a disability is able to perform the job as well as a person with a disability) in a physical environment with barriers removed. Affirmative action programs include employment-related aspects such as hiring and firing practices, job assignments and their locations, promotions and advancements, working conditions, and training. Legalities specifying these mandates are contained within Section 503 and 504 of the Rehabilitation Act Amendments (i.e., Public Law 93-112) and Section 402 of the Vietnam Era Veterans Readjustment Assistance Act. They mandate terms to employers who hold contracts with the government in excess of ten thousand dollars so that persons with physical and mental disabilities will be considered for job openings. Employers are encourages to hire qualified individuals with disabilities and, in turn, individuals with disabilities are encouraged to enter the labor force.

SKILL 18.6 Understand how to work with community agencies and services to promote students' successful transitions to community living

IDEA 2004 requires those receiving special education services to have transition plans. Planning for transition into the world after school needs the input of the student, parents, teacher and others involved in delivering services. It should be based on the student's individual strengths, preferences and interests. The goals of the students are often referred to as post-school outcomes. Ideally post-school outcomes/objectives of the students seek realistic goals. Unfortunately this is not always true and some guidance towards "alternatives" for the future should be provided.

Transition planning must look into providing instruction/training in vocational programming when possible and where related services outside the school environment can be tied into making a student's transition successful. It is also possible that transition planning could provide job opportunities that may lead beyond the school years, and possibly to the ability to achieve what may be considered "normal" independence.

Teachers in Oklahoma often refer those students finishing their school careers to their established departments for Vocational and Educational Services for Individuals with Disabilities (VESID) which will coordinate the delivery of additionally needed services beyond secondary level of education. State departments such as these offer continued support in college environments, training schools and assist those with disabilities to find jobs. Other community resources should be pointed out to the student and parent that can assist with the transition to the "real world" environment to provide some continuity as the emerging adult leaves the protective school environment.

COMPETENCY 19.0 UNDERSTAND HOW TO PROMOTE POSITIVE SCHOOL-HOME RELATIONSHIPS AND ENCOURAGE FAMILIES' INVOLVEMENT IN THEIR CHILDREN'S EDUCATION.

SKILL 19.1 Understand how to establish and maintain effective communication with all families, including culturally and linguistically diverse families, and to overcome communication barriers

One of the responsibilities of the special education teacher is to be the contact point for parents. The parents of your students will expect you to be the unique professional that understands their child better than anyone else in the building. They expect that you will make and maintain contact with others in the educational setting who will interact with their child.

When parents/guardians know they can talk to one teacher that teacher will share the information that will benefit their child throughout the educational setting they are confident in your ability and learn to respect you at a higher level. As a special education teacher you should also utilize your knowledge to discover community resources which may prove beneficial to the parents/guardians during and after their child's time in your educational setting.

There are various reasons parents may not be happy with the school. Sometimes they feel their child is not receiving the services he/she has on the IEP. Your professional manner in addressing this situation will foster confidence that your school is the best place for their child. Sometimes a parent needs to "vent" their anger because they too become frustrated and are looking for how best to help their child at home. Suggesting a strategy or an alternative person to provide the professional help needed also fosters the parent's view of you as a teacher and the school that you work for.

IDENTIFYING WAYS TO ADDRESS ONE'S OWN CULTURAL BIASES AND DIFFERENCES TO ENSURE POSITIVE REGARD FOR THE CULTURE, RELIGION, GENDER, AND SEXUAL ORIENTATION OF INDIVIDUAL STUDENTS

The role of the special education teacher is to advocate for the most appropriate education for their students and to guide them in discovering new knowledge and developing new skills to the best of their potential. According to IDEA 2004 (Individual's with Disabilities Education Act) the teacher is to prepare them for future, purposeful work in the society with the possibility of post-secondary education or training.

Although each special educator is also a person with a set of experiences, opinions and beliefs, it is important that they remain unbiased and positive in their professional role with students, parents, administration, and the community. Differences in culture, religion, gender, or sexual orientation should not influence the teacher's approach to instruction, student goals, expectations, or advocacy.

In order to remain unbiased, the special educator should avail themself of opportunities to learn about various cultures, religions, genders, and sexual orientations. This can be accomplished through reading, classroom awareness activities as appropriate, and teacher inservice.

Reading to increase awareness and acceptance of cultural differences may be done through professional, adult literature as well as through books read with the class.

Cultural activities in the classroom are especially well-received as foods, dress, and games are easily added to curriculum and often address learning standards.

The special educator is charged with academic, social, communicative, and independent skills instruction. Education or influence in other areas is not appropriate.

When the special educator remains unbiased, they are better able to meet the needs of their students and not react to additional factors. The students and their families are also more open to school-related suggestions.

The teacher's reaction to differences with their students and their families, models the commonly taught character education trait of respect. When the teacher demonstrates respect for all individuals in the program, it is likely that respect will also be practiced by students, parents, and administration.

SKILL 19.2 Understand how to design special education programs that are consistent with the beliefs and values of the individuals served and their families

In order for a special education teacher to design and implement programs that are consistent with the beliefs and values of the individuals is for the teacher to get to know the student and information about their cultures. This will be helpful when determining the needs of the child. The teacher needs to be informed so she will not offend anyone or culture while implementing a program.

In providing services to students with disabilities and their families, teachers need to be involved in a wide range of professional and multicultural activities that will help improve their instruction and their effectiveness in the classroom. This should include self-reflection and self-assessment. Self-reflection involves reflecting on one's practice to improve instruction and guide professional growth. In the area of special education, this would entail evaluating how successful one is in ensuring that student's are meeting their short and long-term goals in the classroom. When teacher's reflects on their own performance then they can evaluate what they are doing right and where improvements should be made.

The teacher should participate in professional activities and organizations that benefit individuals with exceptional needs, their families, and their colleagues. This will ensure that they are on the cutting edge of any new legislation that applies to special education teachers, as well as ensuring that they are aware of the best practices that are being implemented in teaching students with disabilities. They should also ensure that they incorporate the research into their daily teaching practice and implementing programs that are consistent with the beliefs and values of the cultures represented in the school system.

Other activities that improve teacher effectiveness include using available and innovative resources and technologies to enhance personal productivity and efficiency; using methods to remain current regarding evidence-based practices; and maintaining student, familial, and collegial confidentiality.

The special education teacher needs to be aware of how personal cultural biases and differences impact one's teaching and learning. They should also be aware of professional organizations relevant to practice.

The self-assessment and reflection process should form the basis for decisions about programs and instructional strategies. After the teacher has reflected and assessed his performance in the classroom, he should work to improve his teaching practice, as professional growth is the practitioner's responsibility.

SKILL 19.3 Understand the role of families in supporting students' learning and development

The discovery at birth or initial diagnosis of a child's disabling condition(s) has a strong impact upon the family unit. Though reactions are unique to individuals, the first emotion generally felt by a parent of a child with disabilities is shock, followed by disbelief, guilt, rejection, shame, denial, and helplessness. As parents finally accept the realization of their child's condition, many report feelings of anxiety or fearfulness about their personal ability to care for and rear their exceptional child. Many parents will doctor shop, hoping to find answers, while others will reject or deny information given them by health care professionals.

Role of the Family-The presence of a child with a disability within the family unit creates changes and possible stresses that will need addressing. Many will feel parenting demands greatly in excess of a non-disabled child's requirements. "A child (with a disability) frequently needs more time, energy, attention, patience, and money than the child (without a disability), and frequently returns less success, achievement, parent pride-inducing behavior, privacy, feelings of security and well-being" (Paul, 1981, p.6).

The family as a microcosmic unit in a society plays a vital role in many ways. The family assumes a protective and nurturing function, is the primary unit for social control, and plays a major role in the transmission of cultural values and mores. This role is enacted concurrently with changes in our social system at large. Paradoxically, the parents were formerly viewed as the cause of their children's disability who is now depended upon to enact positive changes in their children's lives.

Siblings play an important role in fostering the social and emotional developments of a brother or sister with a disability. A wide range of feelings and reactions will evolve as siblings interact. Some experience guilt over being the normal child, and try to over compensate by being the successful, perfect child for their parents. Others react in a hostile, resentful manner toward the amount of time and care the disabled sibling receives, and frequently creates disruption as a way of obtaining parental attention.

The extended family, especially grandparents, can provide support and assistance to the nuclear family unit if they live within a manageable proximity. Childcare services for an evening or a few days, can provide a means of reprieve for heavily involved parents.

Parents as Advocates-Ironically, the possibility for establishing the partnership, which is now sought by educators with parents of children with disabilities, came about largely through the advocacy efforts of parents. The state compulsory education laws began in 1918 and were adopted across the nation with small variances in agricultural regions. However, due to the fact that these children did not fit in with the general school curriculum, most continued to be turned away at the schoolhouse door, leaving the custodial services at state or private institutions as the primary alternative placement site for parents.

Educational policies reflected the litigation and legislation of the times, which overwhelmingly sided with the educational system and not with the family. After all, the educational policies reflected the prevailing philosophies of the times, such as Social Darwinism (i.e. survival of the fittest). Thus, persons with disabilities were set apart from the rest of society - literally out of sight, out of mind. Those with severe disabilities were placed in institutions, and those with moderate disabilities were kept at home to do family or farm chores.

Following the two world wars, the realization that a member of any family could incur disabling conditions came to the forefront. Several celebrity families allowed stories to be published in national magazines about a family member with an identified disability, thus taking the entire plight of this family syndrome out of the closet. The 1950s brought about the founding of many parent and professional organizations, and the movement continued into the next decade. Learning groups included the National Association of Parents and Friends of Mentally Retarded Children founded in 1950, later called the National Association for Retarded Children, and now named the National Association of Retarded Citizens; the International Parents Organization in 1957, as the parents' branch of the Alexander Graham Bell Association for Parents of the Deaf in 1965. The Epilepsy Foundation of America was founded in 1967. The International Council for Exceptional Children had been established by faculty and students at Columbia University as early as 1922, and the Council for Exceptional Children recognized small parent organizations in the late 1940s.

During the 1950s, Public Law 85-926 brought about support for the preparation of teachers to work with children with disabilities so that these children might receive educational services.

The 1960s was the first period in time during which parents received tangible support from the executive branch of the national government. In 1960, the White House Conference on Children and Youth made the declaration that a child should only be separated from his family as a last resort. This gave vital support to parents' efforts toward securing a public education for their youngsters with disabilities.

Parent as Partners-Parent groups are a major component in assuring appropriate services for children with disabilities, co-equal with special education and community service agencies. Their role is individual and political advocacy, and socio-psychological support. Great advances in services for children with disabilities have been made through the efforts of parent advocacy groups, which have been formed to represent almost every type of disabling condition.

SKILL 19.4 Understand roles and relationships within families and ways to involve families in the assessment of and service delivery to their children

The best resource a teacher has in reaching a student is having contact with his/her parents/guardians. Good teaching recognizes this fact and seeks to strengthen this bound through communication.

The first contact a teacher has with parents should be before the school year starts. While the teacher may be required to send a letter out stating the required supplies for the class, this does not count as an initial contact.

Parents are used to hearing their child has done something bad/wrong when they receive a phone call from a teacher. Parents should be contacted whenever possible to give positive feedback. When you call John's mother and say, "John got an A on the test today," you have just encouraged her to maintain open communication lines with you. Try to give 3 positive calls for every negative call you must give.

Parent-Teacher Conferences are scheduled at regular intervals throughout the school year. These provide excellent opportunities to discuss their children's progress, what they are learning and how it may relate to your future plans for their academic growth. It is not unusual for the parent or teacher to ask for a conference outside of the scheduled Parent-Teacher Conference days. These meetings should be looked at as opportunities to provide assistance to that student's success.

Modern technology has opened two more venues for communicating with parents. School/ Classroom websites are written with the intent of sharing regularly with parents/guardians. Many teachers now post their plans for the marking period and provide extra-credit/homework from these websites. Email is now one of the major modes of communication in the world today. Most parents now have email accounts and are more than willing to give you their email address to be kept appraised of their child's academic progress.

Special events also provide opportunities for parental contact. Poetry readings, science fairs, ice-cream socials, etc. are such events.

PARENTAL INVOLVEMENT IN ASSESSMENT PROCESS

The assessment process is an essential part of developing an individualized program for students. The needs of the whole child must be considered in order to address all of the needs of each child. Therefore information should be gathered by using various sources of information.

Besides the general education teacher, a vital person or persons in the assessment process should be the parent. The parent can provide needed background information on the child, such as a brief medical, physical, and developmental history. Paraprofessionals, doctors, and other professionals are also very helpful in providing necessary information about the child.

Ways of gathering information and involving parents:
- Interview: Interviews can be in person or on paper. The related parties can be invited to a meeting to conduct the interview, if the parent does not respond after several attempts, the paper interview may be sent or mailed home.
- Questionnaires: Questionnaires are also a good way of gathering information. Some questionnaires may be open ended questions and some may be several questions that are to be answered using a rating scale. The answerer is to circle ratings ranging from 1 to 5 or 1 to 7 meaning Strongly Disagree to Strongly Agree.
- Conference/ Meeting: With parents' permission, it may be useful to conduct a meeting, one on one, or in a group setting, to gather information about the child and the child's family. Everyone involved with the child that may be able to offer any information about the child, the child's academic progress, physical development, social skills, behavior, or medical history and/or needs should be invited to attend.

SKILL 19.5 Understand how to provide information, training, support, counseling, and referrals to families of students with mild/moderate disabilities

See skill 19.4 for information on ways to provide information to parents.

An educator must get to the child and the family because issues with the family maybe causing problems with the child and his or her learning. After the needs have been determine the educator must have knowledge of available resources to refer to the family. There are a variety of community agencies that are available to provide an array of needed services. Before referring any services the educator must speak with the parent or guardian to completely understand the need. lease see the resource guide at the end of this study guide for more information about outside resources.

COMPETENCY 20.0 UNDERSTAND THE HISTORY AND PHILOSOPHY OF SPECIAL EDUCATION AND KEY ISSUES AND TRENDS, ROLES AND RESPONSIBILITIES, AND LEGAL AND ETHICAL ISSUES RELEVANT TO SPECIAL EDUCATION.

SKILL 20.1 Demonstrate knowledge of historical, theoretical, and philosophical foundations of and current issues and trends in special education.

LEGAL MANDATES AND HISTORICAL ASPECTS

Special education is precisely what the term denotes: education of a special nature for students who have special needs. The academic and behavioral techniques that are used today in special education are a culmination of "best practices" and evolved from a number of disciplines (e.g. medicine, psychology, sociology, language, ophthalmology, otology) to include education. Each of these disciplines contributed uniquely to their field so that the needs of special students might be better met in the educational arena.

Unfortunately, during the earlier part of the 1900s and mid-1950s, too many educators placed in positions of responsibility, refused to recognize their professional obligation for assuring all children a free, appropriate, public education. Today, doors can no longer be shut, eyes cannot be closed, and heads cannot be turned since due process rights have been established for special needs students and their caregivers. Specific mandates are now stated in national laws, state regulations, and local policies. These mandates are the result of many years of successful litigation and politically advocacy, and they govern the delivery of special education.

What special educators do is one thing; how services are delivered is yet another. The concept of **inclusion** stresses the need for educators to rethink the continuum of services, which was designed by Evelyn Deno and has been in existence since the early 1970s. Many school districts developed educational placement sites, which contain options listed on this continuum. These traditional options extend from the least restrictive to the most restrictive special education settings. The least restrictive environment is the regular education classroom. The present trend is to team special education and regular classroom teachers in regular classrooms. This avoids pulling out students for resource room services, and provides services by specialists for students who may be showing difficulties similar to those of special education students.

The competencies in this section include the mandates (i.e. laws, regulations, policies) that apply to or have a bearing upon the respective states and local districts, as well as the major provisions of federal laws implemented twenty or more years ago, such as Public Laws 94-142 (1975), 93-112 (1973) and 101-476 (1990). These laws culminated into the comprehensive statute, IDEA (Individuals with Disabilities Education Act), which requires the states to offer comprehensive special education service programs to students with disabilities, and to plan for their transition into the work world. Most local districts have elaborately articulated delivery systems, which are an extension of national or state policies.

KNOW THE MAJOR DEVELOPMENTS IN THE HISTORY OF SPECIAL EDUCATION

The Early Years: The Beginning

Although the origin of special education services for youngsters with disabilities is relatively recent, the history of public attitude toward people with disabling conditions was recorded as early as 1552. The Spartans practiced infanticide, the killing or abandonment of malformed or sickly babies. The ancient Greeks and Romans thought people with disabilities were cursed and forced them to beg for food and shelter. Those who could or could not fend for themselves were allowed to perish. Some with mental disabilities were employed as fools for the entertainment of the Roman royalty.

In the time of Christ, people with disabilities were thought to be suffering the punishment of God. Those with emotional disturbances were considered to be possessed by the devil, and although early Christianity advocated humane treatment of those who were not normal physically or mentally, many remained outcasts of society, sometimes pitied and sometimes scorned.

During the Middle Ages, persons with disabilities were viewed within the aura of the unknown, and were treated with a mixture of fear and reverence. Some were wandering beggars, while others were used as jesters in the courts. The Reformation brought about a change of attitude, however, individuals with disabilities were accused of being possessed by the devil, and exorcism flourished. Many innocent people were put in chains and cast into dungeons.

The early seventeenth century was marked by a softening of public attitude toward persons with disabilities. Hospitals began to provide treatment for those with emotional disturbances and mental retardation. A manual alphabet for those with deafness was developed, and John Locke became the first person to differentiate between persons who were mentally retarded and those who were emotionally disturbed.

In America, however, the colonists treated people with severe mental disorders as criminals, while those who were harmless were left to beg or were treated as paupers. At one time, it was common practice to sell them to the person who would provide for them at the least cost to the public. When this practice was stopped, persons with mental retardation were put into poorhouses, where conditions were often extremely squalid.

The Nineteenth Century: The Beginning of Training
In 1799, Jean Marc Itard, a French physician, found a 12-year old boy who had been abandoned in the woods of Averyron, France. His attempts to civilize and educate the boy, Victor, established many of the educational principles presently in use in the field of special education, including developmental and multisensory approaches, sequencing of tasks, individualized instruction, and a curriculum geared toward functional life skills.

Itard's work had an enormous impact upon public attitude toward individuals with disabilities. They began to be seen as educable. During the late 1700s, rudimentary procedures were devised by which those with sensory impairments (i.e. deaf, blind) could be taught, closely followed in the early 1800s by attempts to teach students with mild intellectual disabilities and emotional disorders (i.e. at that time thought of as the "idiotic" and "insane"). Throughout Europe, schools for students with visual and hearing impairments were erected, paralleled by the founding of similar institutions in the United States. In 1817, Thomas Hopkins Gallaudet founded the first American school for students who were deaf, known today as Gallaudet University in Washington, D.C., one of the world's best institutions of higher learning for those with deafness. Gallaudet's work was followed closely by that of Samuel Gridley, who was instrumental in the founding of the Perkins Institute for students who were blind in 1829.

The mid-1800s saw the further development of Itard's philosophy of education of students with mental disabilities. Around that time, his student, Edward Seguin, immigrated to the United States, where he established his philosophy of education for persons with mental retardation in a publication entitled <u>Idiocy and Its Treatment by the Physiological Method</u> in 1866. Seguin was instrumental in the establishment of the first residential school for individuals with retardation in the United States.

State legislatures began to assume the responsibility for housing people with physical and mental disabilities - the institutional care was largely custodial. Institutions were often referred to as warehouses due to the deplorable conditions of many. Humanitarians like Dorthea Dix helped to relieve anguish and suffering in institutions for persons with mental illnesses.

1900 - 1919: Specific Programs

The early twentieth century saw the publication of the first standardized test of intelligence by Alfred Binet of France. The test was designed to identify educationally substandard children, but by 1916, the test was revised by an American Louis Terman, and the concept of the intelligence quotient (IQ) was introduced. Since then the IQ test has come to be used as a predictor of both retarded (delayed) and advanced intellectual development.

At approximately the same time, Italian physician Maria Montessori was concerned with the development of effective techniques for early childhood education. Although she is known primarily for her contributions to this field, her work included methods of education for children with mental retardation as well, and the approach she developed is used in preschool programs today.

Ironically, it was the advancement of science and the scientific method that led special education to its worst setback in modern times. In 1912, psychologist Henry Goddard published a study based on the Killikak family, in which he traced five generations of the descendants of a man who had one legitimate child and one illegitimate child. Among the descendants of the legitimate child were numerous mental defectives and social deviates. This led Goddard to conclude that mental retardation and social deviation were inherited traits, and therefore that mental and social deviates were a threat to society, an observation that he called the Eugenics Theory.

Reinforcing the concept of retardation as hereditary deviance was a popular philosophy called positivism, under which these unscientific conclusions were believed to be fixed, mechanical laws that were carrying mankind to inevitable improvement. Falling by the wayside was seen as the natural, scientific outcome for the defective person in society. Consequently, during this time mass institutionalization and sterilization of person with mental retardation and criminals were practiced.

Nevertheless, public school programs for persons with retardation gradually increased during this same period. Furthermore, the first college programs for the preparation of special education teachers were established between 1900 and 1920.

1919 - 1949: Professional and Expansion of Services

As awareness of the need for medical and mental health treatment in the community, was evidenced during the 1920s. Halfway houses became a means for monitoring the transition from institution to community living; outpatient clinics were established to provide increased medical care. Social workers and other support personnel were dispensed into the community to coordinate services for the needy. The thrust toward humane treatment within the community came to an abrupt halt during the 1930s and 1940s, primarily due to economic depression and widespread dissatisfaction toward the recently enacted social programs.

Two factors related to Word Wars I and II helped to improve public opinion toward persons with disabilities. First, the intensive screening of the population of young men with physical and mental disabilities that were present in the United States. Second, patriotism caused people to regard the enormous number of young men who returned from the wars with physical and emotional disabilities in a different light than they would have been regarded with before that time. People became more sensitive to the problems of the veterans with disabilities, and this acceptance generalized to other groups in the special needs population.

With increased public concern for people with disabilities came new research. John B. Watson introduced behaviorism, which shifted the treatment emphasis from psychoanalysis to learned behavior. He demonstrated in 1920 that maladaptive (or abnormal) behavior was learned by Albert, an 11-month old boy, through conditioning. B.F. Skinner followed with a book entitled the Behavior of Organisms, which outlined principles of operant behavior (i.e. voluntary) behavior.

In 1922, the Council for Exceptional Children (first called the International Council for Exceptional Children) was founded. During the 1920s, many comprehensive statewide programs were initiated. The number of special education programs in public schools increased at a rapid rate until the 1930s, when the push for humane and effective treatment of people with disabilities began to diminish once again.

The period of the Depression was marked by large-scale institutionalization and lack of treatment. Part of the cause was inadequately planned programs and poorly trained teachers. WW II did much to swing the pendulum back in the other direction, however, and inaugurated the most active period in the history of the development of special education.

1950 - 1969: The Parents, the Legislators, and the Courts Become Involved
The first two decades of the second half of this century was characterized by increased federal involvement in general education, gradually extending to special education.

In 1950, came the establishment of the National Association of Retarded Children, later renamed the National Association of Retarded Citizens (NARC). It was the result of the efforts among concerned parents who felt the need of an appropriated public education. Increased media coverage exposed the miserable conditions in some of the institutions devoted to caring for people with disabilities, especially those with intellectual and emotional disabilities, and treatment consequently became more humane.

> [1]The first cluster of two digits of each public law represents the congressional session during which the law, numbered by the last three digits, was passed.. Congressional sessions begin every two years on the odd numbered year. The first biennial session sat in 1787-88. Bills may be passed and signed into law during either of the two years during which the congressional session is being held. For example, Public Law 94-142 was the 142nd law passed by the Ninety-fourth Congress, which was in session in 1975-76 and was passed and signed in 1975.

It was at about this time that parents of children with disabilities discovered the federal courts as a powerful agent on behalf of their children. The 1954 decision in the Brown v. the Topeka Board of Education case guaranteed equal opportunity rights to a free public education for all citizens, and the parents of children and youth with disabilities insisted that their children be included in that decision. From this point on, court cases and public laws enacted[1] as a result of court decisions, are too numerous to include in their entirety.

Only those few, which had the greatest impact on the development of special education, as we know it today, are listed. Collectively, they are part of a movement in U.S. Supreme Court history known as the Doctrine of Selective Incorporation, under which the states are compelled to honor various substantive rights under procedural authority of the 14th Amendment.

1954: The Cooperative Research Act was passed, the first designation of general funds for the use of students with disabilities.

1958: Public Law 85-926 provided grants to institutions of higher learning and to state education agencies for training professional personnel who would, in turn, train teachers of students with mental retardation.

1963: Public Law 88-164 (Amendment to Public Law 85-926) extended support to the training of personnel for teaching those with other disabling conditions (i.e. hard of hearing, speech impaired, visually impaired, seriously emotionally disturbed, crippled and other health impaired.

1965: Elementary and Secondary Education Act provided funds for the education of children who were disadvantaged and disabled (Public Law 89-10).

Public Law 89-313 (Educational Consolidation and Improvement Act -State Operated Programs) provided funds for children with disabilities who are or have been in state-operated or state-supported schools.

1966: Public Law 89-750 authorized the establishment of the Bureau Education for the Handicapped (BEH) and a National Advisory Committee on the Handicapped.

1967: Hanson v. Hobson ruled that ability grouping (tracking) based on student performance on standardized tests is unconstitutional.

1968: Public Law 80-538 (Handicapped Children's Early Education Assistance Act) funded model demonstration programs for preschool students with disabilities

1968: Public law 90-247 included provisions for deaf-blind centers, resource centers and expansion of media services for students with disabilities.

Public Law 90-576 specified that ten percent of vocational education funds be earmarked for youth with disabilities.

1969: Public Law 91-230 (Amendments to Public Law 89-10). Previous enactment relating to children with disabilities was consolidated into one act: Education of the Handicapped.

1970-Present: Federal Involvement in the Education of Children and Youth with Disabilities

During early involvement of the government in the education of individuals with disabilities, states were encouraged to establish programs, and they were rewarded with monetary assistance for compliance. Unfortunately, this assistance was often abused by those in control of services and funds.

Therefore, a more dogmatic attitude arose, and the states were mandated to provide education for those with disabilities, or else experience the cutoff of education funds from the federal government. Federal legal authority for this action was the 14th Amendment due process denial, paralleling enforcement of the 1954 Brown v. Topeka desegregation decision.

High proportions of minority students in programs for mental retardation resulted in a mandatory reexamination of placement procedures, which in turn brought about a rigid legal framework for the provision of educational services for students with disabilities.

1970: Diana v. the State Board of Education resulted in the decision that all children must be tested in their native language.

1971: Wyatt v. Stickney established the right to adequate treatment (education) for institutionalized persons with mental retardation.

The decision in Pennsylvania Association for Retarded Children (PARC) v. the Commonwealth of Pennsylvania prohibited the exclusion of students with mental retardation from educational treatment at state schools.

1972: Mills v. the Board of Education of the District of Columbia asserted the right of children and youth with disabilities to a constructive education, which includes appropriate specialized instruction.

1973: Public Law 93-112 (Rehabilitation Amendments of 1973) was the first comprehensive federal statute to address specifically the rights of disabled youth. It prohibited illegal discrimination in education, employment, or housing on the basis of a disability.

1974: Public Law 93-380 (Education Amendments of 1974. Public Law 94-142 is the funding portion of this act). It requires the states to provide full educational opportunities for children with disabilities. It addressed identification, fair evaluation, alternative placements, due process procedures, and free, appropriate public education.

1975: Public Law 94-142 (Education for all Handicapped Children Act) provided for a free, appropriate public education for all children with disabilities, defined special education and related services, and imposed rigid guidelines on the provisions of those services. (Refer to Objectives 2 and 3 in this section). It paralleled the provision for a free and appropriate public education in Section 504 of Public Law 94-142, and extended these services to preschool children with disabilities (ages 3-5) through provisions to preschool incentive grants.

1975: Goss v. Lopez ruled that the state could not deny a student education without following due process. While this decision is not based on a special education issue, the process of school suspension and expulsion is obviously critical in assuring an appropriate public education to children with disabilities.

1978: Public Law 95-56 (Gifted and Talented Children's Act) defined the gifted and talented population, and focused upon this exceptionality category, which was not included in Public Law 94-142.

1979: Larry P. v. Riles ordered the reevaluation of black students enrolled in classes for educable mental retardation (EMR) and enjoined the California state department of education from the use of intelligence tests in subsequent EMR placement decisions.

1980: Parents in Action on Special Education (PASE) v. Hannon ruled that IQ tests are necessarily biased against ethnic and racial subcultures.

1982: The appeal for services of an interpreter during the school day for a deaf girl was denied by the Supreme Court in Hendrick Hudson Board of Education v. Rowley. Established that an "appropriate" education does not mean the "best" education has to be provided. What is required is that individuals benefit and those due process procedures are followed in developing the educational program.

1983: Public Law 98-199 (Education of the Handicapped Act [EHA] Amendments). Public Law 94-142 was amended to provide added emphasis on parental education and preschool, secondary, and post-secondary programs for children and youth with disabilities.

1984: Irving Independent School District v. Tarro (468 U.S. 883) established that catheterization and similar health-type services are "related services" when they are relatively simple to provide and medical assistance is not needed in providing them.

1985: Public Law 99-457 mandated service systems for infants and young children.

1986: Public Law 99-372 (Handicapped Children's Protection Act of 1985). This law allowed parents who are unsuccessful in due process hearings or reviews to seek recovery of attorney's fees.

Public Law 99-457 (Education of the Handicapped Act Amendments of 1986). It re-authorized existing EHA, amended Public Law 94-142 to include financial incentives for states to educate children 3 to 5 years of age by the 1990-1991 school years, and established incentive grants to promote programs serving infants with disabilities (birth to 2 years of age).

Public Law 99-506 (Rehabilitation Act Amendments of 1986). It authorized formula grant funds for the development of supported employment demonstration projects.

1987: School Board of Nassau County v. Arline established that contagious diseases are a disability under Section 504 of the Rehabilitation Act and that people with them are protected from discrimination, if otherwise qualified (actual risk to health and safety to others may render persons unqualified).

1988: Honig v. Doe established that expulsion from school programs for more than ten days constitutes a change in placement for which all due process provisions must be met; temporary removals permitted in emergencies.

1990: Public Law 101-336 (American with Disabilities Act – (ADA) gives civil rights protection to individuals with disabilities in private sector employment, all public services, public accommodations, transportation, and telecommunications. Patterned after Section 504 of the Rehabilitation Act of 1973.

The U.S. House of Representatives opened for citizen comment the issue of a separate exceptionality category for students with attention deficit disorders. The issue was tabled without legislative action.

Public Law 101-476 (Individuals with Disabilities Education Act IDEA) reauthorized and renamed existing EHA. This amendment to EHA changed the term "handicapped" to "disability," expanded related services, and required individual education programs (IEPs) to contain transitional goals and objectives for adolescents (ages 16 and above, special situations).

1993: Florence County School District Four v. Shannon Carter established that when a school district does not provide FAPE for a student with disability, the parents may seek reimbursement for private schooling. This decision has encouraged districts to be more inclusive of students with Autism who receive ABA/Lovaas therapy.

1994: Goals 2000: Educate America Act, Pub. L. 103-227, established national education goals to help guide state and local education systems

1997: Reauthorization of IDEA—required involvement of a regular education teacher as part of the IEP team. Provided additional strength to school administrators for the discipline of students with special needs.

2002: No Child Left Behind Act (NCLB) read the NCLB section below time line

2004: M.L. v. Federal Way School District (WA) in the Ninth Circuit Court of Appeals ruled that absence of a regular education teacher on an IEP team was a serious procedural error.

Reauthorization of IDEA—Required all Special Education Teachers on a Secondary Level to be no less qualified than other teachers of the subject areas.

DEMONSTRATE AN UNDERSTANDING OF THE PHILOSOPHY OF SPECIAL EDUCATION THAT LED TO THE PASSAGE OF PUBLIC LAW 94-142

The passage of Public Law (PL) 94-142 , signed in 1975 and renamed Individuals with Disabilities Education Act (IDEA) in 1990, was a culmination of many years' struggle to achieve equal educational opportunity for children and youth with disabilities.

The 1960s was an era when much national emphasis was placed upon civil rights of the U.S. citizenry. Special education was supported by such leaders President John F. Kennedy, Vice-President Hubert Humphrey, President Lyndon B. Johnson, and many more in Congress.

Unlike rights legislation of a racial or ethnic nature, the reform laws for persons with disabilities mostly enjoyed bipartisan support. From the late 1960s to the mid-1970s, much legislation and litigation from the courts included decisions supporting the need to assure an appropriate education to all persons, regardless of race, creed, or disabling conditions. Much of what was stated in separate court rulings and mandated legislation was brought together into what is now considered to be the "backbone" of special education. PL 94-142, was formally signed into law by President Gerald R. Ford in 1975.

Three important political forces were instrumental in obtaining the forerunner legislation and litigation, which is now within PL 94-142. These important forces included: (1) parent and professional support groups, (2) reform legislation, and (3) adversary litigation. These three were compacted to provide public education programs, which by law, are required to meet each child's unique educational needs.

NO CHILD LEFT BEHIND - No Child Left Behind, Public Law 107-110, was signed on January 8, 2002. It addresses accountability of school personnel for student achievement with the expectation that every child will demonstrate proficiency in reading, math, and science.

The first full wave of accountability will be in 12 years when children who attended school under NCLB graduate, but the process to meet that accountability begins now. In fact, as student's progress through the school system, testing will show if an individual teacher has effectively met the needs of her students. Through testing, each student's adequate yearly progress or lack thereof will be tracked.

NCLB affects regular and special education students, gifted students and slow learners, and children of every ethnicity, culture and environment. NCLB is a document that encompasses every American educator and student.

Educators are affected as follows:
- Elementary teachers (K-3) are responsible for teaching reading and using different, scientific-based approaches as needed.
- Elementary teachers of upper grades will teach reading, math and science.
- Middle and high school teachers will teach to new, higher standards. Sometimes, they will have the task of playing catch up with students who did not have adequate education in earlier grades.
- Special educators are responsible for teaching students to a level of comparable proficiency as their non-disabled peers. This will raise the bar of academic expectations throughout the grades. For some students with disabilities, the criteria for getting a diploma will be more difficult. Although a small percentage of students with disabilities will need alternate assessment, they will still need to meet grade appropriate goals.

In order for special education teachers to meet the professional criteria of this act, they must be *highly qualified*, that is certified or licensed in their area of special education and show proof of a specific level of professional development in the core subjects that they teach.

MAJOR COMPONENTS RETAINED AND CHANGES OF IDEA 2004

The second revision of IDEA occurred in 2004, IDEA was re-authorized as the Individuals with Disabilities Education Improvement Act of 2004 (IDEIA 2004). It is commonly referred to as IDEA 2004(effective July 1, 2005).

It was the intention to improve IDEA by adding the understanding that special education students need preparation for further study beyond the high school setting by teaching compensatory methods. Accordingly, IDEA 2004 provided a close tie to PL 89-10, the Elementary and Special Education Act of 1965, and stated that students with special needs should have maximum access to the general curriculum. This was defined as the amount for an individual student to reach his fullest potential. Full inclusion was stated not to be the only option by which to achieve this, and specified that skills should be taught to compensate students later in life, in cases where inclusion was not the best setting.

IDEA 2004 added a new requirement for special education teachers on the secondary level enforcing NCLB's "Highly Qualified" requirements in the subject area of their curriculum. The rewording in this part of IDEA states that they shall be "no less qualified" than teachers in the core areas.

Free and Appropriate Public Education (FAPE), was revised by mandating that students have maximum access to appropriate general education. Additionally, LRE placement for those students with disabilities must have the same school placement rights as those students who are not disabled.

IDEA 2004 recognizes that due to the nature of some disabilities, appropriate education may vary in the amount of participation / placement in the general education setting. For some students, FAPE will mean a choice as to the type of educational institution they attend (private school for example), any of which must provide the special education services deemed necessary for the student through the IEP.

The definition of *assistive technology devices* was amended to exclude devices that are surgically implanted (i.e. cochlear implants), and clarified that students with assistive technology devices shall not be prevented from having special education services. Assistive technology devices may need to be monitored by school personnel, but schools are not responsible for the implantation or replacement of such devices surgically. An example of this would be a cochlear implant.

The definition of *Child with a disability* is the term used for children ages 3-9 with a developmental delay. Additionally, the term disability has been changed to allow for the inclusion of Tourettes Syndrome.

IDEA 2004 recognized that all states must follow the National Instructional Materials Accessibility Standards which states that students who need materials in a certain form will get those at the same time their non-disabled peers receive their materials. Teacher recognition of this standard is important.

Changes in Requirements for Evaluations -The clock/time allowance between the request for an initial evaluation and the determination if a disability is present has been changed to state the finding/determination must occur within 60 calendar days of the request. This is a significant change as previously it was interpreted to mean 60 school days. Parental consent is also required for evaluations and prior to the start of special education services.

No single assessment or measurement tool may now be used to determine special education qualification. Assessments and measurements used should be in the *language and form* that will give the most accurate picture of the child's abilities.

IDEA 2004's recognized that there exists a disproportionate representation of minorities and bilingual students and that pre-service interventions that are *scientifically based on early reading programs, positive behavioral interventions and support, and early intervening services)* may prevent some of those children from needing special education services. This understanding has led to a child not being considered to have a disability if he/she has not had appropriate education in math or reading, nor shall a child be considered to have a disability if the reason for his/her delays is that English is a second language.

When determining a specific learning disability, the criteria may or may not use a discrepancy between *achievement and intellectual ability* but whether or not the child responds to scientific research-based intervention. In general, children who may not have been found eligible for special education (via testing) but are known to need services (via functioning, excluding lack of instruction) are still eligible for special education services. This change now allows input for evaluation to include state and local testing, classroom observation, academic achievement, and *related developmental needs*. This is known as a Response to Intervention (RTI) model.

Changes in Requirements for IEPs -Individualized Education Plans (IEP's) continue to have multiple sections. One section, *present levels,* now addresses *academic achievement and functional performance.* Annual IEP goals must now address the same areas.

IEP goals should be aligned to state standards, thus short term objectives are not required on every IEP. Students with IEPs must not only participate in regular education programs to the fullest extent possible, they must show progress in those programs. This means that goals should be written to reflect academic progress.

For students who must participate in alternate assessment, there must be alignment to *alternate achievement standards*.

Significant change has been made in the definition of the IEP team as it now includes *not less than one* teacher from each of the areas of special education and regular education be present.

IDEA 2004 recognized that the amount of required paperwork placed upon teachers of students with disabilities reduced if possible, for this reason a pilot program has been developed in which some states will participate using multi-year IEPs. Individual student inclusion in this program will require consent by both the school and the parent.

Parent and Professional Advocacy Activity and Parent Organization-There have always been, and will always be, exceptional children with special needs, but special education services have not always been in existence to provide for those needs.

Private school and state institutions were primary sources of education for individuals with retardation in earlier years. The 9th and 10th amendments to the U.S. Constitution leave education as an unstated power, and therefore vested in the states. As was the practice in Europe, government funds in America were first appropriated to experimental schools to determine whether students with disabilities actually could be educated.

MILD-MODERATE DISABILITIES

During the mid-twentieth century, legislators and governors in control of funds, faced with evidence of need and the efficacy of special education programs, refused to expend funds adequately, thus creating the ultimate need for federal guidelines in PL 94-142 to mandate flow-through money.

Concurrently, due process rights and procedures were outlined, based on litigation and legislation enacted by parents of children with disabilities, parent organizations, and professional advocacy groups. "Public support in the form of legislation and appropriation of funds has been achieved and sustained only by the most arduous and persevering efforts of individuals who advocate for exceptional children." (Hallahan & Kauffman, 1986 p. 26).

Parents, professionals, and other members of advocacy groups and organizations finally succeeded in bringing to the attention of legislators astounding data about the population of youth with disabilities in our country. Among the findings revealed, Congress noted that: (1) there were more than eight million children with disabilities in the United States, and more than half were not receiving an appropriate education; (2) more than one million children with disabilities were excluded from the educational system, and many other children with disabilities were enrolled in regular education classes where they were not benefiting from the educational services provided because of their undetected conditions; and (3) due to inadequate educational services within the public school systems, families were forced to seek services outside the public realm. Years of advocacy effort resulted in the current laws and court decisions mandating special education at a federal level.

Litigation-Over the years, court decisions have reflected different opinions about whether public school attendance should be: "(1) a privilege that may be awarded or withheld from an individual child at the discretion of local school officials; (2) the right of every child, regardless of his or her handicap; or (3) a means of assuring that every child receives an education appropriated for his or her individual needs." (Hallahan & Kauffman, 1986, p.27).

Around the turn of the twentieth century, courts aided in the protection of the school-aged majority from the minority who were disabled. Other children were spared the pain of seeing those with disabilities, and teachers were protected from being overburdened by them. The 1950s and 1960s brought about equal protection rights in the field of education, and in 1975, Congress passed the most comprehensive legislation in history to assure appropriate education and treatment of students with disabilities.

A series of landmark legal decisions laid the foundation for the passage of Public Law 94-142. The Brown v. Topeka (1954) case guaranteed equal resources through equal ethnic and racially nonsegregated educational environments. This case, based upon ethnic and racial issues with socioeconomic outcomes, set the precedent for civil rights in the area of special education.

Pennsylvania (1971) resulted in a consent agreement that ensured (1) a free and appropriate public education for all mentally retarded children, (2) education in the least restrictive educational environment appropriate to the learner, (3) periodic review and evaluation of the educational program, and (4) procedural due process.

Mills v. Board of Education of the District of Columbia extended this mandate to include, not only those with mental retardation, but also all children and youth with disabilities. Institutionalized persons with disabilities were secured the right to education through the ruling, which occurred in Wyatt v. Stickney (1972). Diana v. State Board of Education (1970) and later, Larry P. v. Riles (1979), guaranteed the use of proper evaluation procedures that led to appropriate placement of learners with disabilities.

Along with equalization suits, litigation has more recently included legal suits filed for inclusionary and exclusionary reasons, the former by parents who contended their children were not being provided with appropriate special education services, and the latter by parents whose children were considered by the schools in need of special education services, but the parents believed their children not to be in need of them. Courts have been asked to make decisions based on children's physical, intellectual, and emotional characteristics. Schools and teachers are increasingly being held accountable for providing every child with an appropriate education.

Legislation-The court rulings have comprised the framework for the comprehensive legislation passed on behalf of students with disabilities. Collectively, these landmark rulings paved the way to significant legislation assuring education for those with disabilities, and ultimately to the Education of all Handicapped Children Act of 1975.

Other significant legislation acted as a forerunner to PL 94-142. Congress passed the Elementary and Secondary Education Act (ESEA) in 1965. Shortly thereafter, Title I of ESEA was amended to establish grants to state agencies, enabling them to provide a free, appropriate public education for students with disabilities. Funds were authorized to facilitate recruitment of personnel, as well as to disseminate information about special education services.

Funding for model demonstration programs for preschool students with disabilities was obtained through the Handicapped Children's Early Education Act of 1968. Provisions for students determined gifted and talented were made as amendments to ESEA in 1970.

The vocational Rehabilitation Act of 1973 extended funds, which had been granted ten years before. Section 503 of this act mandated affirmative action in personnel practices (e.g. interviewing, hiring, promoting, and retention) for those with disabilities, while Section 504 authorized the inclusion of persons with severe disabilities in federally supported programs and facilities through non-barrier, as well as schedule accessibility.

All these driving forces culminated in the formation of a major comprehensive act, considered by many to be the "backbone" of special education. The results of litigation, legislative authorization, and principles advocated by parent groups resulted in the provisions of Public Law 94-142.

Present and Future Perspectives-What is the state of special education today? What can we anticipate as far as changes that might occur in the near future? It has been two decades since the passage of the initial Individuals with Disabilities Education Act as Public Law 93-142 in 1975.

So far, mandates stand with funding intact. The clients are still here, and in greater numbers due to improved identification procedures and due to medical advances that have left many, who might have died in the past, with conditions considered disabling. Among the disabling conditions afflicting the population with recently discovered lifesaving techniques are blindness, deafness, amputation, central nervous system or neurological impairments, brain dysfunction, and mental retardation from environmental, genetic, traumatic, infectious, and unknown etiologies.

Despite challenges to the principles underlying PL 94-142 in the early 1980s, total federal funding for the concept increased as new amendments were passed throughout the decade. These amendments expanded services to infants, preschoolers, and secondary students. (Rothstein, 1995).

Following public hearings, Congress voted in 1990 not to include Attention Deficit Disorders (ADD) as a new exceptionality area. Determining factors included the alleged ambiguity of the definition and eligibility criteria for students with ADD, the large number of students who might be identified if it became a service delivery area, the subsequent cost of serving such a large population, and the fact that many of these students are already served in the exceptionality areas of learning disabilities and behavior disorders.

The revision of the original law that we now call IDEA included some other changes. These changes were primarily in language (terminology), procedures (especially transition), and the addition of new categories (autism and traumatic brain injury).

Thus, we can see that despite challenges to federal services and mandates in special education as an extension of the Fourteenth Amendment since 1980, there has actually been growth in mandated categories and net funding.

The Doctrine of Selective Incorporation is the name for one major set of challenges to this process. Lobbyists and activists representing coalition and advocacy groups for those with disabilities have combined with bi-partisan congressional support to avert the proposed changes, which would have meant drastic setbacks in services for persons with disabilities.

Nevertheless, there remain several philosophical controversies in special education for the late 1990s. The need for labels for categories continues to be questioned. Many states are serving special needs students by severity level rather than by the exceptionality category.

Presently, special educators are faced with possible changes in what is considered to be the least restrictive environment for educating students with special needs. Following upon the heels of the Regular Education Initiative, the concept of **inclusion** has come to the forefront.

Both of these movements were, and are, an attempt to educate special needs students in the mainstream of the regular classroom. Both would eliminate pulling out students from regular classroom instructional activities, and both would incorporate the services of special education teachers in the regular classroom in collaboration with general classroom teachers.

See Objective 9 in this section for a discussion of current service delivery options.

SKILL 20.2 **Understand roles and responsibilities of teachers of students with mild/moderate disabilities and relationships of special education to the organization and functions of schools and school systems**

The Teacher's Role-Teaching consists of a multitude of roles. Teachers must plan and deliver instruction in a creative and innovating way so that students find learning both fun and intriguing.

The teacher must also research various learning strategies, decide which to implement in the classroom, and balance that information according to the various learning styles of the students. Teachers must facilitate all aspects of the lesson including preparation and organization of materials, delivery of instruction, and management of student behavior and attention.

Simultaneously, the teacher must also observe for student learning, interactions, and on-task behavior while making mental or written notes regarding what is working in the lesson and how the students are receiving and utilizing the information. This will provide the teacher with immediate feedback as to whether to continue with the lesson, or if it is necessary to slow the instruction or present the lesson in another way. Teachers must also work collaboratively with other adults in the room and utilize them to maximize student learning. The teacher's job requires the teacher to establish a delicate balance among all these factors.

How the teacher handles this balance depends on the teaching style of the teacher and/or lesson. Cooperative learning will require the teacher to have organized materials ready, perhaps even with instructions for the students as well. The teacher should conduct a great deal of observations during this type of lesson. Direct instruction methods will require the teacher to have an enthusiastic, yet organized, approach to the lesson. When teaching directly to students, the teacher must take care to keep the lesson student-centered and intriguing while presenting accurate information.

Collaborator-The role of the special education teacher and the general education teacher is to work together to ensure that student's with disabilities are able to attain their educational objectives in the least restrictive environment. Some students are best served in the general education setting with additional accommodations, while other students may be best served in the special education setting. The educators must work together to decide what educational program is best suited for the student and where the student can best meet his goals and objectives.

These decisions should be made during the student's IEP meeting. It is important that the special education teacher, the general education teacher, and other interested professionals, such as speech teacher, are in attendance at the meeting so they can discuss and collaborate on their role in helping the student.

Students with disabilities often experience insufficient access to and a lack of success in the general education curriculum. To promote improved access to the general curriculum for all learners, information should be presented in various formats using a variety of media forms; students should be given numerous methods to express and demonstrate what they have learned; and students should be provided with multiple entry points to engage their interest and motivate their learning.

Teachers as advocates-Because of the unique needs of each student with disabilities, special education teachers are frequently advocates for their students and the special education program in general.

In order to be an effective advocate, the teacher must be knowledgeable in a number of areas. First, the special educator must understand the general education program that is the counterpart of her program. Factors such as student expectations (learning standards), materials used, and teacher training and in-service provide a starting point. If the special educator is familiar with the goals and overall program for all students at her grade level, she will have a clear picture of the direction she should be working with her students with disabilities.

The special educator should also have a clear understanding of each student's strengths and needs. She must consider how can each student participate in the general education curriculum to the extent that it is beneficial for that student (IDEA 2004). When should services and instruction take place outside of the general education classroom?

In addition, special educators should have an understanding of alternate materials that would be useful or necessary for her students and what resources or materials are available to her.

Knowledge of the Individual's with Disabilities Education Act (IDEA 2004) and NCLB (No Child Left Behind) provide an outline of legislative mandates for special education.

A clear understanding of the above points will allow the special educator to most effectively advocate for the most appropriate placement, programming, and materials for each student. They will be able to advocate for research-based methods with measurable outcomes.

Often advocacy happens between regular and special education teachers. A special educator may see modification or accommodation possibilities that could take place in the general education classroom. It is his or her responsibility to advocate those practices. The special education teacher may also offer to make supplementary materials or to work with a group of students in the general education setting to achieve that goal. When students with disabilities are in an inclusion classroom, give and take on the part of both teachers as a team is crucial.

The special education teacher may need to be an advocate for her program (or the needs of an individual student) with the administration. Although success for all students is important to administration, often the teacher must explain the need for comparable materials written at the different reading level, the need for assistance in the classroom, or the offering of specific classes or therapies.

Occasionally, the local school district cannot provide an appropriate educational setting. The special educator must advocate with the school district for appropriate placement of the child in another, more suitable environment.

Teach self-advocacy-The teacher should not only be an advocate but she should also be a teacher of self-advocacy. The role of the teacher in promoting self-advocacy should include encouraging the student to participate in the IEP process as well as other key parts of their educational development.

Self-advocacy issues and lessons are effective when they are incorporated into the student's daily life. Teachers should listen to the student's problems and ask the student for input on possible changes that he may need. The teacher should talk with the student about possible solutions, discussing the pros and cons of doing something. A student who self-advocates should feel supported and encouraged. Good self-advocates know how to ask questions and get help from other people. They do not let other people do everything for them.

Students need to practice newly acquired self-advocacy skills. Teachers should have student's role play various situations, such as setting up a class schedule, moving out of the home, and asking for accommodations needed for a course.

SKILL 20.3 Demonstrate knowledge of rights and responsibilities of students, parents/guardians, classroom teachers, and other professionals related to exceptional learning needs

Like the teacher, the student has more than one role in a child-centered classroom. In collaborative settings, each student is expected to participate in class or group discussions. Through participation, students begin to realize their contributions have a place in a comprehensive discussion of a topic. Participation engages students in active learning, while increasing their self-confidence as they realize their ideas are necessary for group success.

Students also play the role of observer. As previously stated, behavioral theorists believe that through observation, a human's mind begins to make sense of the world around them as they decide to mimic or avoid certain behaviors. In a classroom, students observe many positive outcomes from behavior, as well as questioning, discussion and hands-on activities.

An important goal for students should be to become self-directed in their learning. Teachers help students obtain this goal by providing them with ample opportunities to seek out their academic interests with various types of projects and assignments.

Self-directed learners gain a lot from their inquiries since the topic usually interests them, and when student's take over certain aspects of their own education, they gain a sense of empowerment and ownership over their learning. This is an important role in the classroom because the sense of ownership promotes a sense of lifelong learning in students.

Please refer to Skill 10.1 about roles of members and skill 6.4.

SKILL 20.4 Demonstrate knowledge of mediation techniques and crisis prevention/ intervention

Please refer to Skill 16.3.

SKILL 20.5 Demonstrate knowledge of sources of specialized materials, services, curricula, and resources for individuals with disabilities and organizations and publications relevant to individuals with disabilities

Please refer to the list of resources at the end of this document and the state website **HTTP://WWW.SDE.STATE.OK.US/HOME/DEFAULTIE.HTML** for information to answer this skill.

SKILL 20.6 Demonstrate knowledge of legal and ethical issues in special education (e.g., eligibility, equity, least restrictive environment, confidentiality, due process) and special-education-related laws, regulations, and guidelines (e.g., Section 504 of the Rehabilitation Act, the Americans with Disabilities Act [ADA], the Individuals with Disabilities Education Act [IDEA])

Please refer to Skill 20.1 for more information.

IDENTIFY THE MAJOR PRINCIPLES OF PUBLIC LAW 101-476 AND EXPLAIN THE SPECIFIC REGULATIONS PERTAINING TO EACH PRINCIPLE

Public Law 94-142 was enacted by Congress in 1975. This law was reauthorized as Public Law 101-476 in 1990, and at that time renamed Individuals with Disabilities Education Act (IDEA). Six basic principles are specified in the regulations. These principles are: zero reject, nondiscriminatory testing, individualized education programs, least restrictive environment, due process, and parent participation. Knowledge of these interrelated principles enables educators to understand better the cornerstone of the Act, which is the provision of a free, appropriate public education for student with disabilities.

Zero Reject-The principle of zero reject requires that <u>all</u> children with disabilities be provided with a free, appropriate public education. This legal requirement was made for all school-age children, and for those in the 3 to 5 and 18 to 21 age groups, unless a state law or a court order makes an exception to the extended age ranges.

A documented report is filed annually by each local education agency (LEA) reporting all attempts to locate, identify, and evaluate children with disabilities residing within jurisdiction. Priorities identified in the legislation for the delivery of services and appropriation of federal funds is: (1) children with disabilities not receiving any education, and (2) children with the most severe disabilities receiving an inappropriate education.

Ethically, zero reject exists to guard against both total and functional exclusion. "<u>Total exclusion</u> refers to past situations in which children with disabilities have been denied access to any educational services at all. <u>Functional exclusion</u> occurs in cases in which educational services have been provided, but they have been inappropriate to the needs of the student with a disability." (Turnbull, Strickland, & Brantley, 1978, p. 4).

Please refer to skills 6.3 and 10.4 for more information on LRE, due process, identification, intervention, and nondiscriminatory evaluations.

Sample Test

1. One technique that has proven especially effective in reducing self-stimulation and repetitive movements in autistic or severely retarded children is:

   A. Shaping
   B. Overcorrection
   C. Fading
   D. Response cost

2. In math class, Mary talked out without raising her hand. Her teacher gave her a warning and asked her to state the rule for being recognized to speak. However, Mary was soon talking out again and lost a point from her daily point sheet. This is an example of:

   A. Shaping
   B. Overcorrection
   C. Fading
   D. Response cost

3. Which body language would not likely be interpreted as a sign of defensiveness, aggression, or hostility?

   A. Pointing
   B. Direct eye contact
   C. Hands on hips
   D. Arms crossed

4. The minimum number of IEP meetings required per year is:

   A. As many as necessary
   B. One
   C. Two
   D. Three

5. Satisfaction of the LRE requirement means that:

   A. A school is providing the best services it can offer there.
   B. The school is providing the best services the district has to offer.
   C. The student is being educated in the least restrictive setting that meets his or her needs.
   D. The student is being educated with the fewest special education services necessary.

6. A review of a student's eligibility for an exceptional student program must be done:

   A. At least once every 3 years.
   B. At least once a year.
   C. Only if a major change occurs in academic or behavioral performance.
   D. When a student transfers to a new school.

7. Crisis intervention methods are above all concerned with:

A. Safety and well-being of the staff and students.
B. Stopping the inappropriate behavior.
C. Preventing the behavior from occurring again.
D. The student learning that outbursts are inappropriate.

8. Ricky, a third grade student, runs out of the classroom and onto the roof of the school. He paces around the roof, looks around to see who is watching, and laughs at the people on the ground. He appears to be in control of his behavior. What should the teacher do?

A. Go back inside and leave him up there until he decides he is ready to come down.
B. Climb up to get Ricky so he doesn't fall off and get hurt.
C. Notify the crisis teacher and arrange to have someone monitor Ricky.
D. Call the police.

9. Judy, a fourth grader, is often looking around the room or out of the window. She does not disturb anyone, but has to ask for directions to be repeated and does not finish her work. Her teacher decides to reinforce Judy when she is on task. This would be an example of which method of reinforcement?

A. Fading
B. DRO
C. DRI
D. Shaping

10. An appropriate time out for a ten-year-old would be:

A. Ten minutes
B. Twenty minutes
C. No more than one-half hour.
D. Whatever time it takes for the disruptive behavior to stop.

11. During the science lesson Rudy makes remarks from time to time but his classmates are not attending to them. The teacher reinforces the students who are raising their hand to speak, but ignores Rudy. The teacher reinforces Rudy when he raises his hand. This technique is an example of:

A. Fading
B. Response Cost
C. Extinction
D. Differential Reinforcement of Incompatible behavior

12. Mike was caught marking graffiti on the walls of the bathroom. His consequence was to clean all the walls of the bathroom. This type of overcorrection would be:

A. Response cost
B. Restitution
C. Positive Practice
D. Negative Practice

13. Which of these would probably not be a result of implementing an extinction strategy?

A. Maladaptive behavior gets worse before it gets better.
B. Maladaptive behavior stops, then starts up again for a brief time.
C. Aggression may occur for a brief period following implementation of extinction.
D. The length of time and patience involved to implement the strategy might tempt the teacher to give up.

14. Witholding or removing a stimulus that reinforces a maladaptive behavior is:

A. Extinction
B. Overcorrection
C. Punishment
D. Reinforcing an incompatible Behavior.

15. Which of these would not be used to strengthen a desired behavior?

A. Contingency contracting
B. Tokens
C. Chaining
D. Overcorrection

16. If the arrangement in a fixed-ratio schedule of reinforcement is 3, when will the student receive the reinforcer?

A. After every third correct response.
B. After every third correct response in a row.
C. After the third correct response in the time interval of the behavior sample.
D. After the third correct response even if the undesired behavior occurs in between correct responses.

17. Wesley is having trouble ignoring distractions. At first you have him seated at a carrel which is located in a corner of the room. He does well so, you eventually move him out of the carrel for increasing portions of the day. Eventually he is able to sit in a seat with the rest of his classmates. This is an example of:

A. Shaping
B. Extinction
C. Fading
D. Chaining

18. Laura is beginning to raise her hand first instead of talking out. An effective schedule of reinforcement would be:

A. Continuous
B. Variable
C. Intermittent
D. Fixed

19. As Laura continues to raise her hand to speak, the teacher would want to change this schedule of reinforcement in order to wean her from reinforcement:

A. Continuous
B. Variable
C. Intermittent
D. Fixed

20. Laura has demonstrated that she has mastered the goal of raising her hand to speak, reinforcement during the maintenance phase should be:

A. Continuous
B. Variable
C. Intermittent
D. Fixed

21. An integral part of ecological interventions are consequences that:

A. Are natural and logical.
B. Include extinction and overcorrection.
C. Are immediate and consistent.
D. Involve fading and shaping.

22. Examples of behaviors that are appropriate to be measured for their duration, include all EXCEPT:

A. Thumb-sucking
B. Hitting
C. Temper tantrums
D. Maintaining eye contact

23. Examples of behaviors that are appropriate to be monitored by measuring frequency include all EXCEPT:

A. Teasing
B. Talking out
C. Being on time for class
D. Daydreaming

24. Criteria for choosing behaviors to measure by frequency include all but those that:

A. Have an observable beginning.
B. Last a long time.
C. Last a short time.
D. Occur often.

25. Criteria for choosing behaviors to measure by duration include all but those that:

A. Last a short time.
B. Last a long time.
C. Have no readily observable beginning or end.
D. Do not happen often.

26. Data on quiet behaviors (e.g. nail biting or daydreaming) are best measured using a:

A. Interval or time sample.
B. Continuous sample.
C. Variable sample.
D. Fixed-ratio sample.

27. Mr. Jones wants to design an intervention for reducing Jason's sarcastic remarks. He wants to find out who or what is reinforcing Jason's remarks, so he records data on Jason's behavior as well as the attending behavior of his peers. This is an example of collecting data on:

A. Reciprocal behaviors
B. Multiple behaviors for single subjects
C. Single behaviors for multiple subjects
D. Qualitative data on Jason

28. Ms. Beekman has a class of students who frequently talk out. She wishes to begin interventions with the students who are talking out the most. She monitors the talking behavior of the entire class for 1 minute samples every half hour. This is an example of collecting data on:

A. Multiple behaviors for single subjects
B. Reciprocal behaviors
C. Single behaviors for multiple subjects
D. Continuous behaviors for fixed intervals

29. Mark got a B on his social studies test. Mr. Wilner praised him for his good grade but he replies, "I was lucky this time. It must have been an easy test." Mark's statement is an example of:

A. External locus of control
B. Internal locus of control
C. Rationalization of his performance
D. Modesty

30. Mr. Smith is on a field trip with a group of high school EH students. On the way they stop at a fast food restaurant for lunch, and Warren and Raul get into a disagreement. After some heated words, Warren stalks out of the restaurant and refuses to return to the group. He leaves the parking lot, continues walking away from the group, and ignores Mr. Smith's directions to come back. What would be the best course of action for Mr. Smith?

A. Leave the group with the class aide and follow Warren to try to talk him into coming back.
B. Wait a little while and see if Warren cools off and returns.
C. Telephone the school and let the crisis teacher notify the police in accordance with school policy.
D. Call the police himself.

31. Which is the least effective of reinforcers in programs for mildly to moderately handicapped learners?

A. Tokens
B. Social
C. Food
D. Activity

32. Tyrone likes to throw paper towards the trash can instead of getting up to throw it away. After several attempts of positive interventions, Tyrone has to serve a detention and continue to throw balls of paper at the trash can for the entire detention period. This would be an example of:

A. Negative practice
B. Overcorrection
C. Extinction
D. Response cost

33. A student may have great difficulty in meeting a target goal if the teacher has not first considered:

A. If the student has external or internal locus of control.
B. If the student is motivated to attain the goal.
C. If the student has the essential prerequisite skills to perform the goal.
D. If the student has had previous success or failure meeting the goal in other classes.

34. The Premack principle of increasing the performance of a less-preferred activity by immediately following it with a highly-preferred activity is the basis of:

A. Response cost
B. Token systems
C   Contingency contracting
D. Self-recording management

35. Mr. Brown finds that his chosen consequence does not seem to be having the desired effect of reducing the target misbehavior. Which of these would LEAST LIKELY account for Mr. Brown's lack of success with the consequence?

A. The consequence was aversive in Mr. Brown's opinion, but not the students'.
B. The students were not developmentally ready to understand the connection between the behavior and the consequence.
C. Mr. Brown was inconsistent in applying the consequence.
D. The intervention had not previously been shown to be effective in studies.

36. Teaching techniques that stimulate active participation and understanding in the mathematics class include all but which of the following?

A. Having students copy computation facts for a set number of times.
B. Asking students to find the error in an algorithm.
C. Giving immediate feedback to students.
D. Having students chart their progress.

37. Justin, a second grader, is reinforced if he is on task at the end of each 10-minute block of time that the teacher observes him. This is an example of what type of reinforcement schedule?

A. Continuous
B. Fixed-interval
C. Fixed ratio
D. Variable ratio

38. Addressing a student's maladaptive behavior right away with a "time out" should be reserved for situations where:

A. The student has engaged in the behavior continuously throughout the day.
B. Harm might come to the student or others.
C. Lesser interventions have not been effective.
D. The student displayed the behavior the day before.

39. At the beginning of the school year, Annette had a problem with being late to class. Her teacher reinforced her each time she was in her seat when the bell rang. In October, her teacher decided to reward her every other day when she was not tardy to class. The reinforcement schedule appropriate for making the transition to maintenance phase would be:

A. Continuous
B. Fixed interval
C. Variable ratio
D. Fixed ratio

40. By November, Annette's teacher is satisfied with her record of being on time and decides to change the schedule of reinforcement. The best type of reinforcement schedule for maintenance of behavior is:

A. Continuous
B. Fixed interval
C. Variable ratio
D. Fixed Ratio

41. Which of these groups is not comprehensively covered by IDEA?

A. Gifted and talented
B. Mentally retarded
C. Specific learning disabilities
D. Speech and language impaired

42. Organizing ideas by use of a web or outline is an example of which writing activity?

A. Revision
B. Drafting
C. Prewriting
D. Final Draft

43. When a teacher is choosing behaviors to modify, the issue of social validity must be considered. Social validity refers to:

A. The need for the behavior to be performed in public.
B. Whether the new behavior will be considered significant by those who deal with the child.
C. Whether there will be opportunities to practice the new behavior in public.
D. Society's standards of behavior.

44. Dena, a second grader, is a messy eater who leaves her lunch area messy as well. Dena's teacher models correct use of eating utensils and napkins for her. As Dena approximates the target behavior of eating neatly and leaving her area clean, she receives praise and a token. Finally, Dena reaches her target behavior goal and redeems her tokens. Dena's teacher used the strategy of:

A. Chaining
B. Extinction
C. Overcorrection
D. Shaping

45. Educators who advocate educating all children in their neighborhood classrooms and schools, propose the end of labeling and segregation of special needs students in special classes, and call for the delivery of special supports and services directly in the classroom may be said to support the:

A. Full Service Model
B. Regular Education Initiative
C. Full Inclusion Model
D. Mainstream Model

46. In Ellis's ABC model, maladaptive behavior in response to a situation results from:

A. Antecedent events
B. Stimulus events
C. Thinking about the consequences
D. Irrational beliefs about the event

47. Section 504 differs from the scope of IDEA because its main focus is on:

A. Prohibition of discrimination on the basis of disability.
B. A basis for additional support services and accommodations in a special education setting.
C. Procedural rights and safeguards for the individual.
D. Federal funding for educational services.

48. Public Law-457 amended the IDEA to make provisions for:

A. Education services for "uneducable" children.
B. Educational services for children in jail settings.
C. Procedural rights and safeguards for the individual.
D. Federal funding for educational services

49. A holistic approach to stress management should include all of the following EXCEPT:

A. Teaching a variety of coping methods.
B. Cognitive modification of feelings.
C. Teaching the flight or fight response.
D. Cognitive modification of behaviors.

50. Marisol has been mainstreamed into a ninth grade language arts class. Although her behavior is satisfactory and she likes the class, Marisol's reading level is about two years below grade level. The class has been assigned to read "Great Expectations" and write a report. What intervention would be LEAST successful in helping Marisol complete this assignment?

A. Having Marisol listen to a taped recording while following the story in the regular text.
B. Giving her a modified version of the story.
C. Telling her a modified version of the story.
D. Showing a film to the entire class and comparing and contrasting it to the book.

51. Fractions may be thought of in each of these ways EXCEPT:

A. Part of a whole
B. Part of a parent set
C. Ratio
D. An exponent

52. Many special education students may have trouble with the skills necessary to be successful in algebra and geometry for all but one of these reasons:

A. Prior instruction focused on computation rather than understanding.
B Unwillingness to problem solve.
C. Lack of instruction in prerequisite skills.
D. Large amount of new vocabulary.

53. Which of these processes is NOT directly related to the meaningful development of number concepts in young children:

A. Describing
B. Classifying
C. Grouping
D. Ordering

54. Mr. Ward wants to assess Jennifer's problem-solving skills in mathematics. Which question would not address her use of strategies?

A. Does Jennifer check for mistakes in computation?
B. Does Jennifer use trial and error to solve problems?
C. Does Jennifer have an alternative strategy if the first one fails?
D. Does Jennifer become easily frustrated if she doesn't immediately get an answer?

55. Ryan is working on a report about dogs. He uses scissors and tape to cut and rearrange sections and paragraphs, then photocopies the paper so he can continue writing. Ryan is in which stage of the writing process?

A. Final Draft
B. Prewriting
C. Revision
D. Drafting

56. Talking into a tape reorder is an example of which writing activity?

A. Prewriting
B. Drafting
C. Final Draft
D. Revision

57. Publishing a class newsletter, looking through catalogues and filling out order forms and playing the role of secretaries and executives are activities designed to teach:

A. Expressive writing
B. Transactional writing
C. Poetic writing
D. Creative writing

58. Under the provisions of IDEA, the student is entitled to all of these EXCEPT:

A. Placement in the best environment
B. Placement in the least restrictive environment
C. Provision of educational needs at no cost
D. Provision of individualized, appropriate educational program

59. Teacher modeling, student-teacher dialogues, and peer interactions are part of which teaching technique designed to provide support during the initial phases of instruction?

A. Reciprocal teaching
B. Scaffolding
C. Peer tutoring
D. Cooperative learning

60. Modeling of a behavior by an adult who verbalizes the thinking process, overt self-instruction, and covert self-instruction are components of:

A. Rational-Emotive Therapy
B. Reality Therapy
C. Cognitive Behavior Modification
D. Reciprocal Teaching

61. Standards of accuracy for a student's spelling should be based on the student's:

A. Grade level spelling list
B. Present reading book level
C. Level of spelling development
D. Performance on an informal assessment

62. Which of these techniques is least effective in helping children correct spelling problems?

A. The teacher models the correct spelling in a context.
B. Student sees the incorrect and the correct spelling together in order to visualize the correct spelling.
C. Positive reinforcement as the child tests the rules and tries to approximate the correct spelling.
D. Copying the correct word 5 times.

63. The single most important activity for eventual reading success of young children is:

A. Giving them books.
B. Watching animated stories.
C. Reading aloud to them.
D. Talking about pictures in books.

64. Skilled readers use all but which one of these knowledge sources to construct meanings beyond the literal text:

A. Text Knowledge
B. Syntactic Knowledge
C. Morphological Knowledge
D. Semantic Knowledge

65. The cooperative nature of Glasser's Reality Therapy in which the problem-solving approach is used to correct misbehavior is best signified by:

A. Minimal punishment
B. Its similar approach to methods that teach students how to deal with academic mistakes.
C. Students' promises to use the alternative behavior plan to help them reach their goals.
D. Procedure sheets used during conflict situations.

66. Diaphragmatic breathing, progressive relaxation training, and exercises are examples of which type of stress coping skills?

A. Rational-emotive
B. Cognitive-psychological
C. Somatic-physiological
D. Stress inoculation

67. The stress that we experience when we win a race or accomplish a difficult task is called:

A. Stressor
B. Stresses
C. Eustress
D. Distress

68. Jane is so intimidated by a classmate's teasing that she breaks down in tears and cannot stand up for herself. The feelings she is experiencing is:

A. Stressors
B. Stresses
C. Eustress
D. Distress

69. The movement towards serving as many children with disabilities as possible in the regular classroom with supports and services is known as:

A. Full service Model
B. Regular Education Initiative
C. Full Inclusion Model
D. Mainstream Model

70. Which of the following is NOT a feature of effective classroom rules?

A. They are about 4 to 6 in number.
B. They are negatively stated.
C. Consequences for infraction are consistent and immediate.
D. They can be tailored to individual classroom goals and teaching styles.

71. A suggested amount of time for large-group instruction lesson for a sixth or seventh grade group would be:

A. 5 to 40 minutes
B. 5 to 50 minutes
C. 5 to 30 minutes
D. 5 to 15 minutes

72. Sam is working to earn half an hour of basketball time with his favorite P E teacher. At the end of each half-hour Sam marks his point sheet with an X if he reached his goal of no call-outs. When he has received 25 marks, he will receive his basketball free time. This behavior management strategy is an example of:

A. Self-recording
B. Self-evaluation
C. Self-reinforcement
D. Self-regulation

73. Mark has been working on his target goal of completing his mathematics class work. Each day he records on a scale of 0 to 3 how well he has done his work and his teacher provides feedback. This self-management technique is an example of:

A. Self-recording
B. Self-reinforcement
C. Self-regulation
D. Self-evaluation

74. When Barbara reached her target goal, she chose her reinforcer and softly said to herself, "I worked hard and I deserve this reward." This self-management technique is an example of:

A. Self-reinforcement
B. Self-recording
C. Self-regulation
D. Self-evaluation

75. Grading should be based on all of the following EXCEPT:

A. Clearly defined mastery of course objectives
B. A variety of evaluation methods
C. Performance of the student in relation to other students
D. Assigning points for activities and basing grades on a point total

76. The following words describe an IEP objective EXCEPT:

A. Specific
B. Observable
C. Measurable
D. Criterion-referenced

77. Teacher feedback, task completion, and a sense of pride over mastery or accomplishment of a skill are examples of:

A. Extrinsic reinforcers
B. Behavior modifiers
C. Intrinsic reinforces
D. Positive feedback

78. Social approval, token reinforcers, and rewards such as pencils or stickers are examples of:

A. Extrinsic reinforcers
B. Behavior modifiers
C. Intrinsic reinforcers
D. Positive feedback

79. Aggression, escape, and avoidance are unpleasant side effects which can be avoided by using:

A. Time out
B. Response cost
C. Overcorrection
D. Negative practice

80. Josie forgot that it was school picture day and did not dress up for the pictures. In the media center, Josie notices some girls in the line waiting to have their pictures taken. They appear to be looking over at her and whispering. Josie feels certain that they are making fun of the way her hair and clothes look and gets so upset that she leaves the line and hides out in the bathroom. Josie did not think to ask when the makeup day for pictures would be. According to Ellis's ABC Model, Jodie's source of stress is:

A. Her forgetting to dress appropriately for picture day.
B. The girls in the library who appear to be whispering about her.
C. Her belief that they are making fun of her appearance.
D. The girls' insensitive behavior.

81. Token systems are popular for all of these advantages EXCEPT:

A. The number needed for rewards may be adjusted as needed.
B. Rewards are easy to maintain.
C. They are effective for students who generally do not respond to social reinforcers.
D. Tokens reinforce the relationship of desirable behavior and reinforcement.

82. Which would not be an advantage of using a criterion-referenced test?

A. Information about an individual's ability level is too specific for the purposes of the assessment.
B. It can pinpoint exact areas of weaknesses and strengths.
C. You can design them yourself.
D. You do not get comparative Information.

83. Which is NOT an example of a standard score?

A. T Score
B. Z Score
C. Standard deviation
D. Stanine

84. The most direct method of obtaining assessment data and perhaps the most objective is:

A. Testing
B. Self-recording
C. Observation
D. Experimenting

85. The basic tools necessary to observe and record behavior include all BUT:

A. Cameras
B. Timers
C. Counters
D. Graphs or charts

86. Which of these characteristics is NOT included in the P.L. 94-142 definition of emotional disturbance:

A. General pervasive mood of unhappiness or depression
B. Social maladjustment manifested in a number of settings
C. Tendency to develop physical symptoms, pains, or fear associated with school or personal problems
D. Inability to learn which is not attributed to intellectual, sensory, or health factors

87. Of the various factors that contribute to delinquency and antisocial behavior, which has been found to be the weakest?

A. Criminal behavior and/or alcoholism in the father
B. Lax mother and punishing father
C. Socioeconomic disadvantage
D. Long history of broken home or marital discord among parents

88. Poor moral development, lack of empathy, and behavioral excesses such as aggression are the most obvious characteristics of which behavioral disorder?

A. Autism
B. ADD-H
C. Conduct disorder
D. Pervasive development disorder

89. School refusal, obsessive-compulsive disorders, psychosis, and separation anxiety are also frequently accompanied by:

A. Conduct disorder
B. ADD-H
C. Depression
D. Autism

90. Signs of depression do not typically include:

A. Hyperactivity
B. Changes in sleep patterns
C. Recurring thoughts of death or suicide
D. Significant changes in weight or appetite

91. Children who are characterized by impulsivity, generally:

A. Do not feel sorry for their actions.
B. Blame others for their actions.
C. Do not weigh alternatives before acting.
D. Do not out grow their problem.

92. Which of these is listed as only a minor scale on the Behavior Problem Checklist?

A. Motor Excess
B. Conduct Disorder
C. Socialized Aggression
D. Anxiety Withdrawal

93. The extent that a test measures what it claims to measure is called:

A. Reliability
B. Validity
C. Factor Analysis
D. Chi Square

94. Which is not a goal of collaborative consultation?

A. Prevent learning and behavior problems with mainstreamed students.
B. Coordinate the instructional programs between mainstream and ESE classes.
C. Facilitate solutions to learning and behavior problems.
D. Function as an ESE service model.

95. An important goal of collaborative consultation is:

A. Mainstream as many ESE students as possible
B. Guidance on how to handle ESE students from the ESE teacher
C. Mutual empowerment of both the mainstream and the ESE teacher.
D. Document progress of mainstreamed students.

96. Knowledge of evaluation strategies, program interventions, and types of data are examples of which variable for a successful consultation program?

A. People
B. Process
C. Procedural implementation
D. Academic preparation

97. Skills as an administrator, and background in client, consulter, and consultation skills are examples of which variable in a successful consultation program?

A. People
B. Process
C. Procedural implementation
D. Academic preparation

98. The ability to identify problems, generate solutions, and knowledge of theoretical perspectives of consultation are examples of which variable in a successful consultation program?

A. People
B. Process
C. Procedural implementation
D. Academic preparation

99. A serious hindrance to successful mainstreaming is:

A. Lack of adapted materials
B. Lack of funding
C. Lack of communication among teachers
D. Lack of support from administration

100. Which of the following statements was not offered as a rationale for the REI?

A. Special education students are not usually identified until their learning problems have become severe.
B. Lack of funding will mean that support for the special needs children will not be available in the regular classroom.
C. Putting children in segregated special education placements is stigmatizing.
D. There are students with learning or behavior problems who do not meet special education requirements but who still need special services.

101. The key to success for the exceptional student placed in a regular classroom is:

A. Access to the special aids and Materials.
B. Support from the ESE teacher.
C. Modifications in the curriculum.
D. The mainstream teacher's belief that the student will profit from the placement.

102. Lack of regular follow-up, difficulty in transporting materials, and lack of consistent support for students who need more assistance are disadvantages of which type of service model?

A. Regular classroom
B. Consultant with Regular Teacher
C. Itinerant
D. Resource Room

103. Ability to supply specific instructional materials, programs, and methods, and to influence environmental learning variables are advantages of which service model for exceptional students?

A. Regular Classroom
B. Consultant Teacher
C. Itinerant Teacher
D. Resource Room

104. An emphasis on instructional remediation and individualized instruction in problem areas, and a focus on mainstreaming students are characteristics of which model of service delivery?

A. Regular Classroom
B. Consultant Teacher
C. Itinerant Teacher
D. Resource Room

105. Which of these would not be considered a valid attempt to contact a parent for an IEP meeting?

A. Telephone
B. Copy of correspondence
C. Message left on an answering machine
D. Record of home visits

106. A best practice for evaluating student performance and progress on IEP is:

A. Formal assessment
B. Curriculum based assessment
C. Criterion based assessment
D. Norm-referenced evaluation

107. Guidelines for an Individualized Family Service Plan (IFSP) would be described in which legislation?

A. PL 94-142
B. PL 99-457
C. PL 101-476
D. ADA

108. In a positive classroom environment, errors are viewed as:

A. Symptoms of deficiencies
B. Lack of attention or ability
C. A natural part of the learning process
D. The result of going too fast

109. Recess, attending school social or sporting events, and eating lunch with peers are examples of:

A. Privileges
B. Allowances
C. Rights
D. Entitlements

110. Free time, shopping at the school store, and candy are examples of:

A. Privileges
B. Allowances
C. Rights
D. Entitlements

111. Eating lunch, access to a bathroom, and privacy are examples of:

A. Privileges
B. Allowances
C. Rights
D. Entitlements

112. Cheryl is a 15-year-old student receiving educational services in a full-time EH classroom. The date for her IEP review will take place two months before her 16th birthday. According to the requirements of IDEA, what must ADDITIONALLY be included in this review?

A. Graduation plan
B. Individualized transition plan
C. Individualized Family Service Plan
D. Transportation planning

113. Hector is a 10th grader in a program for the severely emotionally handicapped. After a classmate taunted him about his mother, Hector threw a desk at the other boy and attacked him. As a crisis intervention team attempted to break up the fight, one teacher hurt his knee. The other boy received a concussion. Hector now faces disciplinary measures. How long can he be suspended without the suspension constituting a "change of placement"?

A. 5 days
B. 10 days
C. 10 + 30 days
D. 60 days

114. The concept that a handicapped student cannot be expelled for misconduct which is a manifestation of the handicap itself is not limited to students which were labeled "seriously emotionally disturbed." Which reason does NOT explain this concept?

A. Emphasis on individualized evaluation.
B. Consideration of the problems and needs of handicapped students.
C. Right to a free and appropriate public education.
D. Putting these students out of school will just leave them on the streets to commit crimes.

115. An effective classroom behavior management plan includes all but which of the following?

A. Transition procedures for changing activities
B. Clear consequences for rule infractions
C. Concise teacher expectations for student behavior
D. Copies of lesson plans

116. Statements like "Darrien is lazy," are not helpful in describing his behavior for all but which of these reasons?

A. There is no way to determine if any change occurs from the information given.
B. The student and not the behavior becomes labeled.
C. Darrien's behavior will manifest itself clearly enough without any written description.
D. Constructs are open to various interpretations among the people who are asked to define them.

117. Mercie often is not in her seat when the bell rings. She may be found at the pencil sharpener, throwing paper away, or fumbling through her notebook. Which of these descriptions of her behavior can be described as a "pinpoint"?

A. Is tardy a lot
B. Is out of seat
C. Is not in seat when late bell rings
D. Is disorganized

118. When choosing behaviors for change, the teacher should ask if there is any evidence that the behavior is presently or potentially harmful to the student or others. This is an example of which test?

A. Fair-Pair
B. "Stranger" Test
C. Premack Principle
D. "So-What Test

119. Ms. Taylor takes her students to a special gymnastics presentation that the P.E. coach has arranged in the gym. She has a rule against talk-outs and reminds the students that they will lose 5 points on their daily point sheet for talking out. The students get a chance to perform some of the simple stunts. They all easily go through the movements except for Sam, who is known as the class klutz. Sam does not give up, and finally completes the stunts. His classmates cheer him on with comments like "Way to go!" their teacher, however, reminds them that they broke the no talking rule and will lose the points. What mistake was made here?

A. The students forgot the no-talking rule.
B. The teacher considered talk-outs to be maladaptive in all school settings.
C. The other students could have distracted Sam with talk-outs and caused him to get hurt.
D. The teacher should have let the P. E. coach handle the discipline in the gym.

120. Which of the following should be avoided when writing objectives for social behavior?

A. Nonspecific adverbs
B. Behaviors stated as verbs
C. Criteria for acceptable performance
D. Conditions where the behavior is expected to be performed

121. Criteria for choosing behaviors that are in the most need of change involve all but the following:

A. Observations across settings to rule out certain interventions.
B. Pinpointing the behavior that is the poorest fit in the child's environment.
C. The teacher's concern about what is the most important behavior to target.
D. Analysis of the environmental reinforcers.

122. Ms. Wright is planning an analysis of Audrey's out-of-seat behavior. Her initial data would be called:

A. Pre-referral phase
B. Intervention phase
C. Baseline phase
D. Observation phase

123. To reinforce Audrey each time she is on-task and in her seat, Ms. Wright decides to deliver specific praise and stickers, which Audrey may collect and redeem for a reward. The data collected during the time Ms. Wright is using this intervention is called:

A. Referral phase
B. Intervention phase
C. Baseline phase
D. Observation phase

124. Indirect requests and attempts to influence or control others through one's use of language is an example of:

A. Morphology
B. Syntax
C. Pragmatics
D. Semantics

125. Kenny, a fourth grader, has trouble comprehending analogies, using comparative, spatial, and temporal words, and multiple meanings. Language interventions for Kenny would focus on:

A. Morphology
B. Syntax
C. Pragmatics
D. Semantics

126. Celia, who is in fourth grade, asked, "Where are my ball?" She also has trouble with passive sentences. Language interventions for Celia would target:

A. Morphology
B. Syntax
C. Pragmatics
D. Semantics

127. Scott is in middle school, but still says statements like "I gotted new high-tops yesterday," and, "I saw three mans in the front office." Language interventions for Scott would target:

A. Morphology
B. Syntax
C. Pragmatics
D. Semantics

128. Which is not indicative of a handwriting problem?

A. Errors persist over time.
B. Little improvement on simple handwriting tasks.
C. Fatigue after writing for a short time.
D. Occasional letter reversals, word omissions, and poor spacing.

129. All of these are effective in teaching written expression EXCEPT:

A. Exposure to various styles and direct instruction in those styles.
B. Immediate feedback from the teacher with all mistakes clearly marked.
C. Goal setting and peer evaluation of written products according to set criteria.
D. Incorporating writing with other academic subjects.

130. Mr. Mendez is assessing his student's written expression. Which of these is not a component of written expression?

A. Vocabulary
B. Morphology
C. Content
D. Sentence Structure

131. Ms. Tolbert is teaching spelling to her students. The approach stresses phoneme-grapheme relationships within parts of words. Spelling rules, generalizations, and patterns are taught. A typical spelling list for her third graders might include light, bright, night, fright, and slight. Which approach is Ms. Tolbert using?

A. Rule-based instruction
B. Fernald Method
C. Gillingham Method
D. Test-Study-Test

132. At the beginning of the year, Mr. Johnson wants to gain an understanding of his class' social structure in order to help him assess social skills and related problems. The technique that would best help Mr. Johnson accomplish this is:

A. Personal interviews with each student
B. Parent rating form
C. Sociometric techniques
D. Self-reports

133. In assessing a group's social structure, asking a student to list the classmates whom he or she would choose to be his or her best friend, and preferred play partners is an example of:

A. Peer nomination
B. Peer rating
C. Peer assessment
D. Sociogram

134. Naming classmates who fit certain behavioral descriptions such as smart, disruptive, or quiet, is an example of which type of sociometric assessment?

A. Peer nomination
B. Peer rating
C. Peer assessment
D. Sociogram

135. Mr. Johnson asks his students to score each of their classmates in areas such as who they would prefer to play with and work with. A likert-type scale with nonbehavioral criteria is used. This is an example of:

A. Peer nomination
B. Peer rating
C. Peer assessment
D. Sociogram

136. Which of these explanations would not likely account for the lack of a clear definition of behavior disorders?

A. Problems with measurement
B. Cultural and/or social influences and views of what is acceptable
C. The numerous types of manifestations of behavior disorders
D. Differing theories that use their own terminology and definitions

137. Ryan is 3, and her temper tantrums last for an hour. Bryan is 8, and he does not stay on task for more than 10 minutes without teacher prompts. These behavior differ from normal children in terms of their:

A. Rate
B. Topography
C. Duration
D. Magnitude

138. All children cry, hit, fight, and play alone at different times. Children with behavior disorders will perform these behaviors at a higher than normal:

A. Rate
B. Topography
C. Duration
D. Magnitude

139. The exhibition of two or more types of problem behaviors across different areas of functioning is known as:

A. Multiple maladaptive behaviors
B. Clustering
C. Social maladjustment
D. Conduct disorder

140. Children with behavior disorders often do not exhibit stimulus control. This means that they have not learned:

A. The right things to do
B. Where and when certain behaviors are appropriate
C. Right from wrong
D. Listening skills

141. Social withdrawal, anxiety, depression, shyness, and guilt are indicative of:

A. Conduct disorder
B. Personality disorders
C. Immaturity
D. Socialized aggression

142. Short attention span, daydreaming, clumsiness, and preference for younger playmates are associated with:

A. Conduct disorder
B. Personality disorders
C. Immaturity
D. Socialized aggression

143. Truancy, gang membership, and feeling of pride in belonging to a delinquent subculture are indicative of:

A. Conduct disorder
B. Personality disorders
C. Immaturity
D. Socialized aggression

144. Temper tantrums, disruption of class, disobedience, and bossiness are associated with:

A. Conduct disorder
B. Personality disorders
C. Immaturity
D. Socialized aggression

145. Which of these is not true for most children with behavior disorders?

A. Many score in the "slow learner" or "mildly retarded" range on IQ tests.
B. They are frequently behind their classmates in terms of academic achievement.
C. They are bright, but bored with their surroundings.
D. A large amount of time is spent in nonproductive, nonacademic behaviors.

146. Echolalia, repetitive stereotype actions, and a severe disorder of thinking and communication are indicative of:

A. Psychosis
B. schizophrenia
C. Autism
D. Paranoia

147. Teaching children functional skills that will be useful in their home life and neighborhoods is the basis of:

A. Curriculum-based instruction
B. Community-based instruction
C. Transition planning
D. Functional curriculum

148. Disabilities caused by fetal alcohol syndrome are many times higher for which ethnic group?

A. Native Americans
B. Asian Americans
C. Hispanic Americans
D. African Americans

149. Which of these would be the least effective measure of behavioral disorders?

A. Projective test
B. Ecological assessment
C. Standardized test
D. Psychodynamic analysis

150. Which behavioral disorder is difficult to diagnose in children because the symptoms are manifested quite differently than in adults?
A. Anorexia
B. Schizophrenia
C. Paranoia
D. Depression

Answer Key

1) B	31) C	61) C	91) C	121) C
2) D	32) A	62) D	92) A	122) C
3) B	33) C	63) C	93) B	123) B
4) B	34) C	64) C	94) D	124) C
5) D	35) D	65) C	95) C	125) D
6) A	36) A	66) C	96) B	126) B
7) A	37) B	67) C	97) A	127) A
8) C	38) B	68) D	98) C	128) D
9) C	39) B	69) C	99) C	129) B
10) A	40) C	70) B	100) B	130) B
11) C	41) C	71) C	101) D	131) A
12) C	42) C	72) A	102) C	132) C
13) B	43) D	73) D	103) B	133) A
14) A	44) A	74) A	104) D	134) C
15) D	45) C	75) C	105) C	135) A
16) B	46) D	76) D	106) B	136) C
17) A	47) A	77) C	107) B	137) C
18) A	48) C	78) A	108) C	138) A
19) D	49) C	79) B	109) D	139) B
20) C	50) C	80) C	110) A	140) B
21) A	51) D	81) B	111) C	141) B
22) B	52) A	82) D	112) B	142) C
23) D	53) C	83) C	113) B	143) D
24) B	54) D	84) C	114) D	144) A
25) A	55) C	85) A	115) D	145) C
26) A	56) C	86) B	116) C	146) C
27) A	57) B	87) C	117) C	147) B
28) C	58) A	88) C	118) D	148) A
29) A	59) B	89) C	119) D	149) C
30) C	60) C	90) A	120) A	150) D

Rationales with Sample Questions

1. One technique that has proven especially affective in reducing self-stimulation and repetitive movements in autistic or severely retarded children is:
   a. Shaping
   b. Overcorrection
   c. Fading
   d. Response Cost

A Shaping: To change a person's behavior gradually using rewards as the person comes closer to the desired behavior, or punishment for moving away from it.
B Overcorrection: a form of punishment, e.g. cleaning of a marked surface.
C Fading: gradual lessening of a reward or punishment.
D Response cost a form of punishment, e.g. loss of privileges

b. is correct.
Rationale: All behavior is learned

2. In math class, Mary talked out without raising her hand. Her teacher gave her a warning and asked her to state the rule for being recognized to speak. However, Mary was soon talking again, and lost a point from her daily point sheet. This is an example of:
   a. Shaping
   b. Overcorrection
   c. Fading
   d. Response cost

d. is correct.
Rationale: Mary lost a point in response to the undesirable behavior.

3. Which body language would not likely be interpreted as a sign of defensiveness, aggression, or hostility?
   a. Pointing
   b. Direct eye contact
   c. Hands on hips
   d. Arms

b. is correct.
Rationale: In our culture, A, C, and D are considered nonverbal acts of defiance. Direct eye contact is not considered an act of defiance.

4. The minimum number of IEP meetings required per year is:
   a. as many as necessary
   b. one
   c. two
   d. three

b. is correct.
Rationale: P. L. 99-457 (1986) grants an annual IEP

5. Satisfaction of the LRE requirement means:
   a. The school is providing the best services it can offer
   b. The school is providing the best services the district has to offer
   c. The student is being educated with the fewest special education services necessary
   d. The student is being educated in the least restrictive setting that meets his or her needs

d. is correct.
Rationale: The legislation mandates **LRE** Least Restrictive Environment

6. A review of a student's eligibility for an exceptional student program must be done:
   a. At least once every three years
   b. At least once a year
   c. Only if a major change occurs in academic or behavioral performance
   d. When a student transfers to a new school

a. is correct.
 Rationale: P. L. 95-56 1978, (Gifted and Talented Children's Act)

7. Crisis intervention methods are above all concerned with:
   a. Safety and well-being of the staff and students
   b. Stopping the inappropriate behavior
   c. Preventing the behavior from occurring again
   d. The student learning that out bursts are inappropriate

a. is correct.
Rationale: It encompasses B, C, and D.

8. Ricky, a third grade student, runs out of the classroom and onto the roof of the school. He paces around the roof, looks around to see who is watching, and laughs at the person standing on the ground. He appears to be in control of his behavior. What should the teacher do?
   a. Go back inside and leave him up there until he decides he is ready to come down
   b. Climb up to get Ricky so he does not fall off and get hurt
   c. Notify the crisis teacher and arrange to have someone monitor Ricky
   d. Call the police

c. is correct.
Rationale: The teacher cannot be responsible for both Ricky and his or her class. He must pass the responsibility to the appropriate person.

9. Judy, a fourth grader, is often looking around the room or out the window. She does not disturb anyone, but has to ask for directions to be repeated and does not finish her work. Her teacher decides to reinforce Judy when she is on task. Which method of reinforcement is she using?
   a. Fading
   b. DRO
   c. DRI
   d. Shaping

c. is correct.
Rationale: This is an example of Direct Reinforcement (Individual)

10. An appropriate time out for a ten-year old would be:
    a. Ten minutes
    b. Twenty minutes
    c. No more than one half-hour
    d. Whatever time it takes for the disruptive behavior to stop

a. is correct.
Rationale: An appropriate time-out is no more than 10 minutes.

TEACHER CERTIFICATION STUDY GUIDE

11. During the science lesson Rudy makes remarks from time to time, but his classmates are not attending to them. the teacher reinforces the students who are raising their hand to speak, but ignores Rudy. The teacher reinforces Rudy when he raises his hand. This technique is an example of:
    a. Fading
    b. Response cost
    c. Extinction
    d. Differential reinforcement of incompatible behavior

c. is correct.
Rationale: By ignoring the behavior, the teacher hopes it will become extinct.

12. Mike was caught marking up the walls of the bathroom with graffiti. His consequence was to clean all the walls of the bathroom. This type of overcorrection would be:
    a. Response cost
    b. Restitution
    c. Positive practice
    d. Negative practice

c. is correct.
Rationale: This is a positive form of over correction in which the student is learning another skill.

13. Which of these would probably not be a result of implementing an extinction strategy?
    a. Maladaptive behavior gets worse before it gets better
    b. Maladaptive behavior stops, then starts up again for a brief time
    c. Aggression may occur for a brief period following implementation of extinction
    d. The length of time and patience involved to implement the strategy might tempt the teacher to give up

b. is correct.
Rationale: The student responds in A, B, and C. In B, he ignores the teacher's action.

14. Withholding or removing a stimulus that reinforces a maladaptive behavior is:
    a. Extinction
    b. Overcorrection
    c. Punishment
    d. Reinforcing an incompatible behavior

a. is correct.
Rationale: There is no stimulus involved in this strategy.

15. Which of these would not be used to strengthen a desired behavior?
    a. Contingency contracting
    b. Tokens
    c. Chaining
    d. Overcorrection

d. is correct.
Rationale: A, B, and C are all used to strengthen a desired behavior. D is punishment.

16. If the arrangement in a fixed-ratio schedule of reinforcement is 3, when will the student receive the reinforcer?
    a. After every third correct response
    b. After every third correct response in a row
    c. After the third correct response in the time interval of the behavior sample
    d. After the third correct response even if the undesired behavior occurs in be between correct responses

b. is correct.
Rationale: This is the only one that follows a pattern. A fixed ratio is a pattern.

17. Wesley is having difficulty ignoring distractions. At first you have him seated at a carrel which is located in a corner of the room. He does well, so you eventually move him out of the carrel for increasing portions of the day. Eventually, he is able to sit in a seat with the rest of his classmates. This is an example of:
    a. Shaping
    b. Extinction
    c. Fading
    d. Chaining

a. is correct.
Rationale: The teacher is shaping a desired behavior.

18. Laura is beginning to raise her hand first instead of talking out. An effective schedule of reinforcement should be:
    a. Continuous
    b. Variable
    c. Intermittent
    d. Fixed

a. is correct.
Rationale: The pattern of reinforcement should not be variable, intermittent or fixed. It should be continuous.

19. As Laura continues to raise her hand to speak, the teacher would want to change to this schedule of reinforcement in order to wean her from the reinforcement:
    a. Continuous
    b. Variable
    c. Intermittent
    d. Fixed

d. is correct.
Rationale: The pattern should be in a fixed ratio.

20. Laura has demonstrated that she has mastered the goal of raising her hand to speak; reinforcement during the maintenance phase should be:
    a. Continuous
    b. Variable
    c. Intermittent
    d. Fixed

c. is correct.
Rationale: Reinforcement should be intermittent, as the behavior should occur infrequently.

21. An integral part of ecological interventions are consequences that:
    a. Are natural and logical
    b. Include extinction and overcorrection
    c. Are immediate and consistent
    d. Involve fading and shaping

a. is correct.
Rationale: The student must understand both the behavior and the consequence. The consequence should fit the infraction.

22. Examples of behaviors that are appropriate to be monitored by measuring frequency include all EXCEPT:
    a. Thumb sucking
    b. Hitting
    c. Temper tantrums
    d. Maintaining eye contact

b. is correct.
Rationale: Hitting takes place in an instant. This should be measured by frequency.

23. Examples of behaviors that are appropriate to be monitored by measuring frequency include all EXCEPT:
    a. Teasing
    b. Talking out
    c. Being on time for class
    d. Daydreaming

d. is correct.
Rationale: Daydreaming cannot be measured by frequency. It should be measured by duration.

24. Criteria for choosing behaviors to measure by frequency include all but those that:
    a. Have an observable beginning
    b. Last a long time
    c. Last a short time
    d. Occur often

b. is correct.
Rationale: We use frequency to measure behaviors that do not last a long time.

25. Criteria for choosing behaviors to measure by duration include all but those that:
    a. Last a short time
    b. Last a long time
    c. Have no readily observable beginning or end
    d. Don't happen often

a. is correct.
Rationale: We use duration to measure behavior that do not last a short time.

26. Data on quiet behaviors e.g., nail biting or daydreaming, are best measured using a (an):
    a. Interval or time sample
    b. Continuous sample
    c. Variable sample
    d. Fixed-ratio sample

a. is correct.
Rationale: An interval or time sample is best to measure the duration of the behavior.

27. Mr. Jones wants to design an intervention for reducing Jason's sarcastic remarks. He wants to find out who or what is reinforcing Jason's remarks, so he records data on Jason's behavior as well as the attending behavior of his peers. This is an example of collecting data on:
    a. Reciprocal behaviors
    b. Multiple behaviors for single subjects
    c. Single behaviors for multiple subjects
    d. Qualitative data on Jason

a. is correct.
Rationale: Jason's peers' behaviors are in response to Jason's disruptive behaviors.

28. Ms Beekman has a class of students who frequently talk out. She wishes to begin interventions with the students who are talking out the most. She monitors the talking behavior of the entire class for 1-minute samples every half-hour. This is an example of collecting data on:
    a. Multiple behaviors for single subjects
    b. Reciprocal behaviors
    c. Single behaviors for multiple subjects
    d. Continuous behaviors for fixed intervals

c. is correct.
Rationale: Talking out is the only behavior being observed.

29. Mark got a B on his social studies test. Mr. Wilner praised him for his good grade but he replies, "I was lucky this time. It must have been an easy test." Mark's statement is an example of:
    a. External locus of control
    b. Internal locus of control
    c. Rationalization of his performance
    d. Modesty

a. is correct.
Rationale: Locus of control refers to the way a person perceives the relation between his or her efforts and the outcome of an event. A person who has an external orientation anticipates no relation between his or her efforts and the outcome of an event.

TEACHER CERTIFICATION STUDY GUIDE

29. Mr. Smith is on a field trip with a group of high school EH students. On the way, they stop at a fast-food restaurant for lunch, and Warren and Raul get into an argument. After some heated words, Warren stalks out of the restaurant and refuses to return to the group. He leaves the parking lot, continues walking away from the group, and ignores Mr. Smith's directions to come back. What would be the best course of action for Mr. Smith?
    a. Leave the group with the class aide and follow Warren to try to talk him into coming back.
    b. Wait a little while and see if Warren cools off and returns.
    c. Telephone the school and let the crisis teacher notify the police in accordance with school policy.
    d. Call the police himself.

c. is correct.
Rationale: Mr. Smith is still responsible for his class. This is his only option.

31. Which is the least effective of reinforcers in programs for mildly to moderately handicapped learners?
    a. Tokens
    b. Social
    c. Food
    d. Activity

c. is correct.
Rationale: Food is the least effective reinforcer for most handicapped children. Tokens, social interaction or activity is more desirable. Food may have reached satiation.

32. Tyrone likes to throw paper towards the trashcan instead of getting up to throw it away. After several attempts at positive interventions, Tyrone has to serve a detention and continue to throw balls of paper at the trashcan for the entire detention period. This would be an example of:
    a. Negative practice
    b. Overcorrection
    c. Extinction
    d. Response cost

a. is correct.
Rationale: Tyrone has to continue to practice the negative behavior.

MILD-MODERATE DISABILITIES 338

33. A student may have great difficulty in meeting a target goal if the teacher has not first considered:
    a. If the student has external or internal locus of control.
    b. If the student is motivated to attain the goal.
    c. If the student has the essential prerequisite skills to perform the goal.
    d. If the student has had previous success or failure meeting the goal in other classes.

c. is correct.
Rationale: Prerequisite skills are essential in both setting goals and attaining goals.

34. The Premack Principle of increasing the performance of a less-preferred activity by immediately following it with a highly preferred activity is the basis of:
    a. response cost
    b. token systems
    c. contingency contracting
    d. self-recording management

c. is correct.
Rationale: The student eagerly completes the less desirable activity, to obtain the reward of the more desirable activity, in an unwritten contract.

35. Mr. Brown finds that his chosen consequence does not seem to be having the desired effect of reducing the target misbehavior. Which of these would LEAST LIKELY account for Mr. Brown's lack of success with the consequence?
    a. The consequence was aversive in Mr. Brown's opinion but not the students'.
    b. The students were not developmentally ready to understand the connection.
    c. Mr. Brown was inconsistent in applying the consequence.
    d. The intervention had not previously been shown to be effective in studies.

d. is correct.
Rationale: A, B, and C, might work if applied in the classroom, but research, is the least of Mr. Brown's options.

36. Teaching techniques that stimulate active participation and understanding in the mathematics class include all but which of the following?
    a. Having student's copy computation facts for a set number of times.
    b. Asking students to find the error in an algorithm.
    c. Giving immediate feedback to students.
    d. Having students chart their progress.

a. is correct.
Rationale: Copying does not stimulate participation or understanding.

37. Justin, a second grader, is reinforced if he is on task at the end of each 10-minute block of time that the teacher observes him. This is an example of what type of schedule?
    a. Continuous
    b. Fixed interval
    c. Fixed-ratio
    d. Variable ratio

b. is correct.
Rationale: 10 minutes is a fixed interval of time.

38. Addressing a student's maladaptive behavior right away with a "time out" should be reserved for situations where:
    a. The student has engaged in the behavior continuously throughout the day.
    b. Harm might come to the student or others.
    c. Lesser interventions have not been effective.
    d. The student displayed the behavior the day before.

b. is correct.
Rationale: The best intervention is to move the student away from the harmful environment.

39. At the beginning of the school year, Annette had a problem with being late for class. Her teacher reinforced here each time she was in her seat when the bell rang. In October, her teacher decided to reward her every other day when she was not tardy to class. The reinforcement schedule appropriate for making the transition to maintenance phase would be:
    a. Continuous
    b. Fixed interval
    c. Variable ratio
    d. Fixed ratio

b. is correct.
Rationale: Every other day is a fixed interval of time.

40. By November, Annette's teacher is satisfied with her record of being on time and decides to change the schedule of reinforcement. The best type of reinforcement schedule for maintenance or behavior is:
    a. Continuous
    b. Fixed interval
    c. Variable ratio
    d. Fixed ratio

c. is correct.
Rationale: The behavior will occur infrequently. Variable ratio is the best schedule.

41. Which of these groups is not comprehensively covered by IDEA?
    a. Gifted and talented
    b. Mentally retarded
    c. Specific learning disabilities
    d. Speech and language impaired

c. is correct.
Rationale: IDEA: Individuals with Disabilities Education Act 101-476 (1990) did not cover all exceptional children. The Gifted and Talented Children's Act, P. L. 95-56 was passed in 1978.

42. Organizing ideas by use of a web or outline is an example of which writing activity?
    a. Revision
    b. Drafting
    c. Prewriting
    d. Final draft

c. is correct.
Rationale: Organizing ideas come before Drafting, Final Draft and Revision.

43. When a teacher is choosing behaviors to modify, the issue of social validity must be considered. Social validity refers to:
    a. The need for the behavior to be performed in public.
    b. Whether the new behavior will be considered significant by those who deal with the child.
    c. Whether there will be opportunities to practice the new behavior in public.
    d. Society's standards of behavior.

d. is correct.
Rationale: Validity has to do with the appropriateness of the behavior. Is it age appropriate? Is it culturally appropriate?

44. Dena, a second grader, is a messy eater who leaves her lunch area messy as well. Dena's teacher models correct use of eating utensils, and napkins for her. As Dena approximates the target behavior of neatly and leaving her area clean, she receives praise and a token. Finally, Dena reaches her target behavior goal and redeems her tokens. Dena's teacher used the strategy of:
   a. Chaining
   b. Extinction
   c. Overcorrection
   d. Shaping

a. is correct.
Rationale: Chaining is a procedure in which individual responses are reinforced when occurring in sequence to form a complex behavior. Shaping, however, targets single behaviors.

45. Educators who advocate educating all children in their neighborhood classrooms and schools, propose the end of labeling and segregation of special needs students in special classes, and call for the delivery of special supports and services directly in the classroom may be said to support the:
   a. Full service model
   b. Regular education initiative
   c. Full inclusion model
   d. Mainstream model

c. is correct.
Rationale: All students must be included in the regular classroom.

46. In Ellis' ABC model, maladaptive behavior in response to a situation results from:
   a. Antecedent events
   b. Stimulus events
   c. Thinking about the consequences
   d. Irrational beliefs about the event

d. is correct.
Rationale: All behavior is learned. This behavior is different from the norm. It is different because of something the child has experienced or learned.

TEACHER CERTIFICATION STUDY GUIDE

47. Section 504 differs from the scope of IDEA because its main focus is on:
    a. Prohibition of discrimination on the basis of disability.
    b. A basis for additional support services and accommodations in a special education setting.
    c. Procedural rights and safeguards for the individual.
    d. Federal funding for educational services.

a. is correct.
Rationale: Section 504 prohibits discrimination on the basis of disability.

48. Public Law 99-457 amended the EHA to make provisions for:
    a. Education services for "uneducable" children
    b. Education services for children in jail settings
    c. Special education benefits for children birth to five years
    d. Education services for medically fragile children

c. is correct.
Rationale: P.L. 99-457 amended EHA to provide Special Education programs for children 3-5 years, with most states offering outreach programs to identify children with special needs from birth to age 3.

49. A holistic approach to stress management should include all of the following EXCEPT:
    a. Teaching a variety of coping methods
    b. Cognitive modification of feelings
    c. Teaching the fight or flight response
    d. Cognitive modification of behaviors

c. is correct.
Rationale: A, B, and D are coping interventions. C is not.

50. Marisol has been mainstreamed into a ninth grade language arts class. Although her behavior is satisfactory and she likes the class, Marisol's reading level is about two years below grade level. The class has been assigned to read "Great Expectations" and write a report. What intervention would be LEAST successful in helping Marisol complete this assignment?
    a. Having Marisol listen to a taped recording while following the story in the regular text.
    b. Giving her a modified version of the story.
    c. Telling her to choose a different book that she can read.
    d. Showing a film to the entire class and comparing and contrasting it with the book.

c. is correct.
Rationale: A, B, and D, are positive interventions. C is not an intervention.

51. Fractions may be thought of in each of these ways EXCEPT:
    a. Part of a whole
    b. Part of a parent set
    c. Ratio
    d. An exponent

d. is correct.
Rationale: An exponent can never be a fraction

52. Many special education students may have trouble with the skills necessary to be successful in algebra and geometry for all but one of these reasons:
    a. Prior instruction focused on computation rather than understanding
    b. Unwillingness to problem solve
    c. Lack of instruction in prerequisite skills
    d. Large amount of new vocabulary

a. is correct.
Rationale: In order to build skills in math, students must be able to understand math concepts.

53. Which of these processes is NOT directly related to the meaningful development of number concepts in younger children?
    a. Describing
    b. Classifying
    c. Grouping
    d. Ordering

c. is correct.
Rationale: Grouping does not involve the meaningful development of number concepts.

54. Mr. Ward wants to assess Jennifer's problem-solving skills in mathematics. Which question would not address her use of strategies?
    a. Does Jennifer check for mistakes in computation?
    b. Does Jennifer use trial and error to solve problems?
    c. Does Jennifer have an alternative strategy if the first one fails?
    d. Does Jennifer become easily frustrated if she doesn't get an answer immediately?

d. is correct.
Rationale: A, B, and C, are problem-solving skills Jennifer needs to develop.

55. Ryan is working on a report about dogs. He uses scissors and tape to cut and rearrange sections and paragraphs, then photocopies the paper so he can continue writing. In which stage of the writing process is Ryan?
    a. Final draft
    b. Prewriting
    c. Revision
    d. Drafting

c. is correct.
Rationale: Ryan is revising and reordering before final editing.

56. Talking into a tape recorder is an example of which writing activity?
    a. Prewriting
    b. Drafting
    c. Final Draft
    d. Revision

c. is correct.
Rationale: Ryan is preparing his final draft.

57. Publishing a class newsletter, looking through catalogues, and filling out order forms and playing the role of secretaries are activities designed to teach:
    a. Expressive writing
    b. Transactional writing
    c. Poetic writing
    d. Creative writing

b. is correct.
Rationale: Transactional writing includes expository writing, descriptive writing and persuasive writing. It does not include any of the other three types of writing listed.

58. Under the provisions of IDEA, the student is entitled to all of these EXCEPT:
    a. Placement in the best environment
    b. Placement in the least restrictive environment
    c. Provision of educational needs at no cost
    d. Provision of individualized, appropriate educational program

a. is correct.
Rationale: IDEA mandates a **least restrictive environment, an IEP, (individual education plan) and a free public education.**

TEACHER CERTIFICATION STUDY GUIDE

59. Teacher modeling, student-teacher dialogues, and peer interactions are part of which teaching technique designed to provide support during the initial stages of instruction?
    a. Reciprocal teaching
    b. Scaffolding
    c. Peer tutoring
    d. Cooperative learning

b. is correct.
Rationale: Scaffolding provides support.

60. Modeling of a behavior by an adult who verbalizes the thinking process, overt self-instruction, and covert self-instruction are components of:
    a. Rational-emotive therapy
    b. Reality therapy
    c. Cognitive behavior modification
    d. Reciprocal teaching

c. is correct.
Rationale: Neither A, B, nor D, involves modification or change of behavior.

61. Standards of accuracy for a student's spelling should be based on the student's:
    a. Grade level spelling list
    b. Present reading book level
    c. Level of spelling development
    d. Performance on an informal assessment

c. is correct.
Rationale: Spelling instruction should include words misspelt in daily writing, generalizing spelling knowledge and mastering objectives in progressive stages of development.

62. Which of these techniques is least effective in helping children correct spelling problems?
    a. The teacher models the correct spelling in a context
    b. Student sees the incorrect and the correct spelling together in order to visualize the correct spelling
    c. Positive reinforcement as the child tests the rules and tries to approximate the correct spelling
    d. Copying the correct word five times

d. is correct.
Rationale: Copying the word is least effective.

TEACHER CERTIFICATION STUDY GUIDE

63. The single most important activity for eventual reading success of young children is:
    a. Giving them books
    b. Watching animated stories
    c. Reading aloud to them
    d. Talking about pictures in books

c. is correct.
Rationale: Reading aloud exposes them to language.

64. Skilled readers use all but which one of these knowledge sources to construct meanings beyond the literal text:
    a. Text knowledge
    b. Syntactic knowledge
    c. Morphological knowledge
    d. Semantic knowledge

c. is correct.
Rationale: The student is already skilled so morphological knowledge is already in place.

65. The cooperative nature of Glasser's Reality Therapy, in which problem-solving approach is used to correct misbehavior, is best signified by:
    a. Minimal punishment
    b. It's similar approach to methods that teach students how to deal with academic mistakes
    c. Student's promises to use the alternative behavior plan to help them reach their goals
    d. Procedure sheets used during conflict situations

c. is correct.
Rationale: Glasser's Reality Therapy makes use of an alternative behavior plan, a form of group therapy.

66. Diaphragmatic breathing, progressive relaxation training, and exercises are examples of which type of stress coping skills?
    a. Rational-emotive
    b. Cognitive-psychological
    c. Somatic-physiological
    d. Stress inoculation

c. is correct.
Rationale: When we analyze the expression, somatic-physiological, we find, somatic: relating to the body physiological: relating to nature and natural phenomena.

MILD-MODERATE DISABILITIES

67. The stress that we experience when we win a race or experience a difficult task is called:
    a. Stressor
    b. Stresses
    c. Eustress
    d. Distress

c. is correct.
Rationale: Eustress is a sort of elation, or release of anxiety. It is the opposite of distress.

68. Jane is so intimidated by a classmate's teasing that she breaks down in tears and cannot stand up for herself.
    a. Stressors
    b. Stresses
    c. Eustress
    d. Distress

d. is correct.
Rationale: Jane is in a state of distress.

69. The movement towards serving as many children with disabilities as possible in the regular classroom with supports and services is known as:
    a. Full service model
    b. Regular education initiative
    c. Full inclusion model
    d. Mainstream model

c. is correct.
Rationale: It is the movement to include all students in the regular classroom.

70. Which of the following is NOT a feature of effective classroom rules?
    a. They are about 4 to 6 in number
    b. They are negatively stated
    c. Consequences are consistent and immediate
    d. They can be tailored to individual teaching goals and teaching styles

b. is correct.
Rationale: Rules should be positively stated and they should follow the other three features listed.

71. A suggested amount of time for large-group instruction lesson for a sixth or seventh grade group would be:
    a. 5 to 40 minutes
    b. 5 to 20 minutes
    c. 5 to 30 minutes
    d. 5 to 15 minutes

c. is correct.
Rationale: The recommended time for large group instruction is 5 - 15 minutes for grades 1-5 and 5 – 40 minutes for grades 8-12.

72. Sam is working to earn half an hour of basketball time with his favorite PE teacher. At the end of each half-hour, Sam marks his point sheet with an X, if he reached his goal of no call-outs. When he has received 25 marks, he will receive his basketball free time. This behavior management strategy is an example of:
    a. Self-recording
    b. Self-evaluation
    c. Self-reinforcement
    d. Self-regulation

***Self-Management*-**This is an important part of social skills training, especially for older students preparing for employment. Components for self-management include:
    1. *self-monitoring:* choosing behaviors and alternatives and monitoring those actions.
    2. *self-evaluation:* deciding the effectiveness of the behavior in solving the problem.
    3. *self-reinforcement:* telling oneself that one is capable of achieving success.

a. is correct.
Rationale: Sam is recording his behavior.

73. Mark has been working on his target goal of completing his mathematics class work. Each day he records on a scale of 0 to 3 how well he has done his work and his teacher provides feedback. This self-management technique is an example of:
    a. Self-recording
    b. Self reinforcement
    c. Self-regulation
    d. Self-evaluation

d. is correct.
Rationale: Sam is evaluating his behavior, not merely recording it.

74. When Barbara reached her target goal, she chose her reinforcer and said softly to herself, "I worked hard and I deserve this reward". This self-management technique is an example of:
   a. Self-reinforcement
   b. Self recording
   c. Self-regulation
   d. Self-evaluation

a. is correct.
Rationale: Barbara is reinforcing her behavior.

75. Grading should be based on all of the following EXCEPT:
   a. Clearly defined mastery of course objectives
   b. A variety of evaluation methods
   c. Performance of the student in relation to other students
   d. Assigning points for activities and basing grades on a point total

c. is correct.
Rationale: Grading should never be based on the comparison of performance of other students. It should always be based on the student's mastery of course objectives, the methods of evaluation and the grading rubric (how points are assigned).

76. The following words describe an IEP objective EXCEPT:
   a. Specific
   b. Observable
   c. Measurable
   d. Criterion-referenced

d. is correct.
Rationale: An Individual Education Plan should be specific, observable, and measurable.

77. Teacher feedback, task completion, and a sense of pride over mastery or accomplishment of a skill are examples of:
   a. Extrinsic reinforcers
   b. Behavior modifiers
   c. Intrinsic reinforcers
   d. Positive feedback

Motivation may be achieved through intrinsic reinforcers or extrinsic reinforcers. Intrinsic reinforcer are usually intangible and extrinsic reinforcers are usually tangible rewards and from an external source.

c. is correct.
Rationale: These are intangibles.

78. Social approval, token reinforcers, and rewards such as pencils or stickers are examples of:
    a. Extrinsic reinforcers
    b. Behavior modifiers
    c. Intrinsic reinforcers
    d. Positive feedback reinforcers

a. is correct.
Rationale: These are rewards from external sources

79. Aggression, escape and avoidance are unpleasant side effects, which can be avoided by using:
    a. Time-out
    b. Response cost
    c. Overcorrection
    d. Negative practice

b. is correct.
Rationale: In response cost, students know that there will be consequences for these undesirable behaviors.

80. Josie forgot that it was school picture day and did not dress up for the pictures. In the media center, Josie notices some girls in the line waiting to have their pictures taken. They appear to be looking over at her and whispering. Josie feels certain that they are making fun of the way her hair and clothes look and gets so upset that she leaves the line and hides out in the bathroom. Josie did not think of asking when the make-up day for pictures would be. According to Ellis' ABC model, Josie's source of stress is:
    a. Her forgetting to dress appropriately for picture day
    b. The girls in the library who appear to be whispering about her
    c. Her belief that they are making fun of her appearance
    d. The girls' insensitive behavior

c. is correct.
Rationale: Josie is responding to her belief.

TEACHER CERTIFICATION STUDY GUIDE

81. Token systems are popular for all of these advantages EXCEPT:
    a. The number needed for rewards may be adjusted as needed
    b. Rewards are easy to maintain
    c. They are effective for students who generally do not respond to social reinforcers
    d. Tokens reinforce the relationship between desirable behavior and reinforcement

b. is correct.
Rationale: The ease of maintenance is not a valid reason for developing a token system.

82. Which would not be an advantage of using a criterion-referenced test?
    a. Information about an individual's ability level is too specific for the purposes of the assessment
    b. It can pinpoint exact areas of weaknesses and strengths
    c. You can design them yourself
    d. You do not get comparative information

d. is correct.
Rationale: Criterion-referenced tests measure mastery of content rather than performance compared to others. Test items are usually prepared from specific educational objectives and may be teacher-made or commercially prepared. Scores are measured by the percentage of correct items for a skill (e.g. adding and subtracting fractions with like denominators).

83. Which is NOT an example of a standard score?
    a. T score
    b. Z score
    c. Standard deviation
    d. Stanine

c. is correct.
Rationale: A, B, and D, are all standardized scores. Stanines are whole number scores from 1 to 9, each representing a wide range of raw scores. Standard deviation is **not a score.** It measures how widely scores vary from the mean.

84. The most direct method of obtaining assessment data and perhaps the most objective is:
    a. Testing
    b. Self-recording
    c. Observation
    d. Experimenting

c. is correct.
Rationale: Observation is often better than testing, due to language, culture or other factors.

85. The basic tools necessary to observe and record behavior include all BUT:
    a. Cameras
    b. Timers
    c. Counters
    d. Graphs or charts

a. is correct.
Rationale: The camera gives a snapshot. It does not record behavior.

86. Which of these characteristics is NOT included in the P.L. 94-142 definition of emotional disturbance?
    a. General pervasive mood of unhappiness or depression
    b. Social maladjustment manifested in a number of settings
    c. Tendency to develop physical symptoms, pains, or fear associated with school or personal problems
    d. Inability to learn which is not attributed to intellectual, sensory, or health factors

b. is correct.
Rationale: Social maladjustment is not considered a disability.

87. Of the various factors that contribute to delinquency, and anti-social behavior, which has been found to be the weakest?
    a. Criminal behavior and/or alcoholism in the father
    b. Lax mother and punishing father
    c. Socioeconomic disadvantage
    d. Long history of broken home and marital discord among parents

c. is correct.
Rationale: There are many examples of A, B, and C, where there is socio-economic advantage.

88. Poor moral development, lack of empathy, and behavioral excesses such as aggression are the most obvious characteristics of which behavioral disorder?
    a. Autism
    b. ADD-H
    c. Conduct disorder
    d. Pervasive developmental disorder

c. is correct.
Rationale: A student with conduct disorder or social maladjustment displays behaviors/values that are in conflict with the school, home, or community. The characteristics listed are all behavioral/social.

89. School refusal, obsessive-compulsive disorders, psychosis, and separation anxiety are also frequently accompanied by:
    a. Conduct disorder
    b. ADD-H
    c. depression
    d. autism

c. is correct.
Rationale: These behaviors are usually accompanied by depression in ADD-H.

90. Signs of depression do not typically include:
    a. Hyperactivity
    b. Changes in sleep patterns
    c. Recurring thoughts of death or suicide
    d. Significant changes in weight or appetite

a. is correct.
Rationale: depression is usually characterized by listlessness, brooding, low anxiety, and little activity. Hyperactivity, conversely is over activity.

91. Children who are characterized by impulsivity generally:
    a. Do not feel sorry for their actions
    b. Blame others for their actions
    c. Do not weigh alternatives before acting
    d. Do not outgrow their problem

c. is correct.
Rationale: They act without thinking, so they either cannot think or do not think before they act.

92. Which of these is listed as only a minor scale on the Behavior Problem Checklist?
    a. Motor Excess
    b. Conduct Disorder
    c. Socialized Aggression
    d. Anxiety/Withdrawal

a. is correct.
Rationale: Motor Excess has to do with over activity, or hyperactivity, physical movement. The other three items are disorders, all of which may be characterized by excessive activity.

93. The extent that a test measures what it claims to measure is called:
    a. Reliability
    b. Validity
    c. Factor analysis
    d. Chi Square

b. is correct.
Rationale: The degree to which a test measures what it claims to measure.

94. Which is not a goal of collaborative consultation?
    a. Prevent learning and behavior problems with mainstreamed students
    b. Coordinate the instructional programs between mainstream and ESE classes
    c. Facilitate solutions to learning and behavior problems
    d. Function as an ESE service model

d. is correct.
Rationale: A, B, and C are goals. Functioning as an Exceptional Student Education model is not a goal. Collaborative consultation is necessary for the classification of students with disabilities and provision of services to satisfy their needs.

95. An important goal of collaborative consultation is:
    a. Mainstream as many ESE students as possible
    b. Guidance on how to handle ESE students from the ESE teacher
    c. Mutual empowerment of both the mainstream and the ESE teacher
    d. Document progress of mainstreamed students

c. is correct.
Rationale: Empowerment of these service providers is extremely important.

96. Knowledge of evaluation strategies, program interventions, and types of data are examples of which variable for a successful consultation program?
    a. People
    b. Process
    c. Procedural implementation
    d. Academic preparation

b. is correct.
Rationale: Consultation programs cannot be successful without knowledge of the process.

97. Skills as an administrator and background in client, consulter, and consultation skills are examples of which variable in a successful consultation program?
    a. People
    b. Process
    c. Procedural implementation
    d. Academic preparation

a. is correct.
Rationale: Consultation programs cannot be successful without people skills.

98. The ability to identify problems, generate solutions, and knowledge of theoretical perspectives of consultation are examples of which variable in a successful consultation program?
    a. People
    b. Process
    c. Procedural implementation
    d. Academic preparation

c. is correct.
Rationale: Consultation programs cannot be successful without implementation skills.

99. A serious hindrance to successful mainstreaming is:
    a. Lack of adapted materials
    b. Lack of funding
    c. Lack of communication among teachers
    d. Lack of support from administration

c. is correct.
Rationale: All 4 choices are hindrances but lack of communication and consultation between the service providers is serious.

100. Which of the following statements was not offered as a rationale for REI?
    a. Special education students are not usually identified until their learning problems have become severe
    b. Lack of funding will mean that support for the special needs children will not be available in the regular classroom.
    c. Putting children in segregated special education placements is stigmatizing
    d. There are students with learning or behavior problems who do not meet special education requirements but who still need special services

b. is correct.
Rationale: All except lack of funding were offered in support of regular education intervention or inclusion.

101. The key to success for the exceptional student placed in a regular classroom is:
    a. Access to the special aids and materials
    b. Support from the ESE teacher
    c. Modification in the curriculum
    d. The mainstream teacher's belief that the student will profit from the placement

d. is correct.
Rationale: Without the regular teacher's belief that the student can benefit, no special accommodations will be provided.

102. Lack of regular follow-up, difficulty in transporting materials, and lack of consistent support for students who need more assistance are disadvantages of which type of service model?
a. Regular classroom
b. Consultant with regular teacher
c. Itinerant
d. Resource room

c. is correct.
Rationale: The itinerant model, as the name implies, is not regular.

103. Ability to supply specific instructional materials, programs, and methods and to influence environmental learning variables are advantages of which service model for exceptional students?
a. Regular classroom
b. Consultant teacher
c. Itinerant teacher
d. Resource room

b. is correct.
Rationale: Consultation is usually done by specialists.

104. An emphasis on instructional remediation and individualized instruction in problem areas, and a focus on mainstreaming are characteristics of which model of service delivery?
a. Regular classroom
b. Consultant teacher
c. Itinerant teacher
d. Resource room

d. is correct.
Rationale: The Resource room is usually a bridge to mainstreaming.

105. Which of these would not be considered a valid attempt to contact a parent for an IEP meeting?
   a. Telephone
   b. Copy of correspondence
   c. Message left on answering machine
   d. Record of home visits

c. is correct.
Rationale: A message left on an answering machine is not direct contact.

106. A best practice for evaluating student performance and progress on IEPs is:
   a. Formal assessment
   b. Curriculum based assessment
   c. Criterion based assessment
   d. Norm-referenced evaluation

b. is correct.
Rationale: This is a teacher-prepared test that measures the student's progress, but at the same time shows the teacher whether or not the accommodations are effective.

107. Guidelines for an Individualized Family Service Plan (IFSP) would be described in which legislation?
   a. P.L. 94-142
   b. P. L. 99 – 457
   c. P.L. 101 – 476
   d. ADA

b. is correct.
Rationale: P. L. 99-457, 1986 provides services for children of ages 3-5 and their families; P.L. 101 – 476 is IDEA; P.L. 94 – 142 Education for All Handicapped Children Act, was passed in the Civil Rights era. ADA is the Americans with Disabilities Act.

108. In a positive classroom environment, errors are viewed as:
a. Symptoms of deficiencies
b. Lack of attention or ability
c. A natural part of the learning process
d. The result of going too fast

c. is correct.
Rationale: We often learn a great deal from our mistakes and shortcomings. It is normal. Where it is not normal, fear develops. This fear of failure, inhibits children from working and achieving. Copying and other types of cheating, results.

109. Recess, attending school social or sporting events, and eating lunch with peers are examples of:
   a. Privileges
   b. Allowances
   c. Rights
   d. Entitlements

d. is correct.
Rationale: These are entitlements. They may be used as consequences.

110. Free time, shopping at the school store, and candy are examples of:
   a. Privileges
   b. Allowances
   c. Rights
   d. Entitlements

a. is correct.
Rationale: These are privileges or positive consequences.

TEACHER CERTIFICATION STUDY GUIDE

111. Eating lunch, access to a bathroom, and privacy are examples of:
    a. Privileges
    b. Allowances
    c. Rights
    d. Entitlements

c. is correct.
Rationale: These are rights. They may not be used as consequences.

112. Cheryl is a 15-year old student receiving educational services in a full-time EH classroom. The date for her IEP review is planned for two months before her 16th birthday. According to the requirements of IDEA, what must ADDITIONALLY be included in this review?
    a. Graduation plan
    b. Individualized transition plan
    c. Individualized family service plan
    d. Transportation planning

b. is correct.
Rationale: This is necessary, as the student should be transitioning from school to work.

113. Hector is 10th grader in a program for the severely emotionally handicapped. After a classmate taunted him about his mother, Hector threw a desk at the other boy and attacked him. A crisis intervention team tried to break up the fight, one teacher hurt his knee. The other boy received a concussion. Hector now faces disciplinary measures. How long can he be suspended without the suspension constituting a "change of placement?"
    a. 5 days
    b. 10 days
    c. 10 + 30 days
    d. 60 days

b. is correct.
Rationale: According to ***Honig versus Doe,*** 1988, *Where the student has presented an immediate threat to others, that student may be temporarily suspended for up to 10 school days to give the school and the parents time to review the IEP and discuss possible alternatives to the current placement.*

114. The concept that a handicapped student cannot be expelled for misconduct which is a manifestation of the handicap itself, is not limited to students which are labeled "seriously emotionally disturbed". Which reason does not explain this concept?
    a. Emphasis on individualized evaluation
    b. Consideration of the problems and needs of handicapped students
    c. Right to a free and appropriate public education
    d. Putting these students out of school will just leave them on the streets to commit crimes

d. is correct.
Rationale: A, B, and C are tenets of IDEA, and should take place in the least restrictive environment. D does not explain this concept.

115. An effective classroom behavior management plan includes all but which of the following?
    a. Transition procedures for changing activities
    b. Clear consequences for rule infractions
    c. Concise teacher expectations for student behavior
    d. Copies of lesson plans

d. is correct.
Rationale: D is not a part of any behavior management plan. A, B, and C are.

116. Statements like "Darren is lazy" are not helpful in describing his behavior for all but which of these reasons?
    a. There is no way to determine if any change occurs from the information given
    b. The student and not the behavior becomes labeled
    c. Darren's behavior will manifest itself clearly enough without any written description
    d. Constructs are open to various interpretations among the people who are asked to define them

c. is correct.
Rationale: 'Darren is lazy' is a label. It can be interpreted in a variety of ways and there is no way to measure this description for change. A description should be measurable.

117. Often, Marcie is not in her seat when the bell rings. She may be found at the pencil sharpener, throwing paper away, or fumbling through her notebook. Which of these descriptions of her behavior can be described as a pinpoint?
    a. Is tardy a lot
    b. Is out of seat
    c. Is not in seat when late bell rings
    d. Is disorganized

c. is correct.
Rationale: Even though A, B, and D describe the behavior, C is most precise.

118. When choosing behaviors for change, the teacher should ask if there is any evidence that the behavior is presently or potentially harmful to the student or others. This is an example of which test?
    a. Fair-Pair
    b. "Stranger" Test
    c. Premack Principle
    d. "So – What?" Test

d. is correct.

119. Mrs. Taylor takes her students to a special gymnastics presentation that the P.E. coach has arranged in the gym. She has a rule against talk-outs and reminds the students that they will lose 5 points on their daily point sheet for talking out. The students get a chance to perform some of the simple stunts. They all easily go through the movements except for Sam, who is known as the class klutz. Sam does not give up and finally completes the stunts. His classmates cheer him on with comments like "Way to go". Their teacher, however, reminds them that they broke the no talking rule and will lose the points. What mistake was made here?
    a. The students forgot the no talking rule
    b. The teacher considered talk outs to be maladaptive in all school settings
    c. The other students could have distracted Sam with talk-outs and caused him to get hurt
    d. The teacher should have let the P.E. coach handle the discipline in the gym

d. is correct.
The gym environment is different from a classroom environment. The gym teacher should have been in control of a possibly hazardous environment.

120. Which of the following should be avoided when writing objectives for social behavior?
   a. Non-specific adverbs
   b. Behaviors stated as verbs
   c. Criteria for acceptable performance
   d. Conditions where the behavior is expected to be performed

a. is correct.
Behaviors should be specific. The more clearly the behavior is described, the less the chance for error.

121. Criteria for choosing behaviors that are in the most need of change involve all but the following:
   a. Observations across settings to rule out certain interventions
   b. Pinpointing the behavior that is the poorest fit in the child's environment
   c. The teacher's concern about what is the most important behavior to target
   d. Analysis of the environmental reinforcers

c. is correct.
Rationale: The teacher must take care of the criteria in A, B, and D. Her concerns are of the least importance.

122. Ms. Wright is planning an analysis of Audrey's out of seat behavior. Her initial data would be called:
   a. Pre-referral phase
   b. Intervention phase
   c. Baseline phase
   d. Observation phase

c. is correct.
Rationale: Ms Wright is a teacher. She should begin at the Baseline phase.

123. To reinforce Audrey each time she is on task and in her seat, Ms. Wright delivers specific praise and stickers, which Audrey may collect and redeem for a reward. The data collected during the time Ms. Wright is using this intervention is called:
    a. Referral phase
    b. Intervention phase
    c. Baseline phase
    d. Observation phase

b. is correct.
Rationale: Ms Wright is involved in behavior modification. This is the intervention phase.

124. Indirect requests and attempts to influence or control others through one's use of language is an example of:
    a. Morphology
    b. Syntax
    c. Pragmatics
    d. Semantics

c. is correct.
Rationale: Pragmatics involves the way that language is used to communicate and interact with others. It is often used to control the actions and attitudes of people.

125. Kenny, a fourth grader, has trouble comprehending analogies, using comparative, spatial and temporal words, and multiple meanings. Language interventions for Kenny would focus on:
    a. Morphology
    b. Syntax
    c. Pragmatics
    d. Semantics

d. is correct.
Rationale: Semantics has to do with word meanings. Semantic tests measure receptive and expressive vocabulary skills.

126. Celia, who is in first grade, asked, "Where are my ball"? She also has trouble with passive sentences. Language interventions for Celia would target:
    a. Morphology
    b. Syntax
    c. Pragmatics
    d. Semantics

b. is correct.
Rationale: Syntax refers to the rules for arranging words to make sentences.

127. Scott is in middle school, but still makes statements like "I gotted new high-tops yesterday," and "I saw three mans in the front office." Language interventions fro Scott would target:
   a. Morphology
   b. Syntax
   c. Pragmatics
   d. Semantics

a. is correct.
Rationale: Morphology is the process of combining phonemes into meaningful words.

128. Which is not indicative of a handwriting problem?
   a. Errors persisting over time
   b. Little improvement on simple handwriting tasks
   c. Fatigue after writing for a short time
   d. Occasional letter reversals, word omissions, and poor spacing

d. is correct.
Rationale: A, B, and C are physical, handwriting problems. D, however, is a problem with language development.

129. All of these are effective in teaching written expression EXCEPT:
   a. Exposure to various styles and direct instruction in those styles
   b. Immediate feedback from the teacher with all mistakes clearly marked.
   c. Goal setting and peer evaluation of written products according to set criteria
   d. Incorporating writing with other academic subjects

b. is correct.
Rationale: Teacher feedback is not always necessary. The student can have feedback from his peers, or emotional response, or apply skills learned to other subjects.

130. Mr. Mendez is assessing his students' written expression. Which of these is not a component of written expression?
   a. Vocabulary
   b. Morphology
   c. Content
   d. Sentence structure

b. is correct.
Rationale: Morphology is correct. Vocabulary consists of words, content is made up of ideas, which are expressed in words, and sentences are constructed from words. Morphemes, however, are not always words. They may be prefixes or suffixes.

131. Ms. Tolbert is teaching spelling to her students. The approach stresses phoneme-grapheme relationships within parts of words. Spelling rules, generalizations, and patterns are taught. A typical spelling list for her third graders might include light, bright, night, fright, and slight. Which approach is Ms. Tolbert using?
   a. Rule-based Instruction
   b. Fernald Method
   c. Gillingham Method
   d. Test-Study -Test

a. is correct.
Rationale: Rule-based Instruction employs a system of rules and generalizations. It may be taught using the linguistic or phonics approach.

132. At the beginning of the year, Mr. Johnson wants to gain an understanding of his class' social structure in order to help him assess social skills and related problems. The technique that would best help Mr. Johnson accomplish this is:
   a. Personal interviews with each student
   b. Parent rating form
   c. Sociometric techniques
   d. Self-reports

c. is correct.
Rationale: The issue of reliability and validity arises with A, B, and D. C is the best technique.
Sociometric Measures: There are three basic formats. (a) peer nominations based on non-behavioral criteria such as preferred playmates, (b) peer ratings in which students rate all of their peers on nonbehavioral criteria such as work preferences, and (c) peer assessments, in which peers are rated with respect to specific behaviors.

133. In assessing a group's social structure, asking a student to list a classmate whom he or she would choose to be his or her best friends, preferred play partners, and preferred work partners is an example of:
   a. Peer nomination
   b. Peer rating
   c. Peer assessment
   d. Sociogram

a. is correct.
Rationale: Students are asked to nominate their peers.

134. Naming classmates who fit certain behavioral descriptions such as smart, disruptive or quiet, is an example of which type of sociometric assessment?
    a. Peer nomination
    b. Peer rating
    c. Peer assessment
    d. Sociogram

c. is correct.
Rationale: Students are asked to assess their peers' behavior.

135. Mr. Johnson asks his students to score each of their classmates in areas such as whom they would prefer to play with and work with. A likert-type scale with non-behavioral criteria is used. This is an example of:
    a. Peer nomination
    b. Peer rating
    c. Peer assessment
    d. Sociogram

a. is correct.
Rationale: Students are asked for their preferences on non-behavioral criteria.

136. Which of these explanations would not likely account for the lack of a clear definition of behavior disorders?
    a. Problems with measurement
    b. Cultural and/or social influences and views of what is acceptable
    c. The numerous types of manifestations of behavior disorders
    d. Differing theories that use their own terminology and definitions

c. is correct.
Rationale: A, B, and D, are factors that account for the lack of a clear definition of some behavioral disorders. C is not a factor.

137. Ryan is 3, and her temper tantrums last for an hour. Bryan is 8, and he does not stay on task for more than 10 minutes without teacher prompts. These behaviors differ from normal children in terms of their:
    a. Rate
    b. Topography
    c. Duration
    d. Magnitude

c. is correct.
Rationale: It is not normal for temper tantrums to last an hour. At age eight, a normal student stays on task much longer than ten minutes without teacher prompts.

138. All children cry, hit, fight, and play alone at different times. Children with behavior disorders will perform these behaviors at a higher than normal:
   a. Rate
   b. Topography
   c. Duration
   d. Magnitude

a. is correct.
Rationale: Children with behavior disorders display them at a much higher rate than normal children.

139. The exhibition of two or more types of problem behaviors across different areas of functioning is known as:
   a. Multiple maladaptive behaviors
   b. Clustering
   c. Social maladjustment
   d. Conduct disorder

b. is correct.
Rationale: Children with behavior disorders do display a single behavior. They display a range of behaviors. These behaviors are usually clustered together, hence, clustering.

140. Children with behavior disorders often do not exhibit stimulus control. This means they have not learned:
   a. The right things to do
   b. Where and when certain behaviors are appropriate
   c. Right from wrong
   d. Listening skills

b. is correct.
Rationale: These children respond to stimuli at almost any place and time. They are not able to stop and think or control their responses to stimuli.

141. Social withdrawal, anxiety, depression, shyness, and guilt are indicative of:
   a. Conduct disorder
   b. Personality disorders
   c. Immaturity
   d. Socialized aggression

b. is correct.
 Rationale: These are all personality disorders.

142. Short attention span, daydreaming, clumsiness, and preference for younger playmates are associated with:
    a. Conduct disorder
    b. Personality disorders
    c. Immaturity
    d. Socialized aggression

c. is correct.
Rationale: These disorders show immaturity. The student is not acting age appropriately.

143. Truancy, gang membership, and a feeling of pride in belonging to a delinquent subculture are indicative of:
    a. Conduct disorder
    b. Personality disorders
    c. Immaturity
    d. Socialized aggression

d. is correct.
Rationale: The student is acting out by using aggression. This gives him a sense of belonging.

144. Temper tantrums, disruption or disobedience, and bossiness are associated with:
    a. Conduct disorder
    b. Personality disorders
    c. Immaturity
    d. Socialized aggression

a. is correct.
Rationale: These behaviors are designed to attract attention. They are conduct disorders.

145. Which of these is not true for most children with behavior disorders?
    a. Many score in the "slow learner"
    b. They are frequently behind classes in academic achievement
    c. They are bright but bored with their surroundings
    d. A large amount of time is spent in nonproductive, nonacademic behaviors

c. is correct.
Rationale: Most children with conduct disorders display the traits found in A, B, and D.

146. Echolalia, repetitive stereotyped actions, and a severe disorder of thinking and communication are indicative of:
    a. Psychosis
    b. Schizophrenia
    c. Autism
    d. Paranoia

c. is correct.
Rationale: The behaviors listed are indicative of autism.

147. Teaching children functional skills that will be useful in their home life and neighborhoods is the basis of:
    a. Curriculum-based instruction
    b. Community-based instruction
    c. Transition planning
    d. Functional curriculum

b. is correct.
Rationale: Teaching functional skills in the wider curriculum is considered community based instruction.

148. Disabilities caused by fetal alcohol syndrome are many times higher for which ethnic group?
    a. Native Americans
    b. Asian Americans
    c. Hispanic Americans
    d. African Americans

a. is correct.
Rationale: There is a very high incidence of this syndrome in Native American children on reservations.

149. Which of these would be the least effective measure of behavioral disorders?
    a. Projective test
    b. Ecological assessment
    c. Standardized test
    d. Psychodynamic analysis

c. is correct.
Rationale: These tests make comparisons, rather than measure skills.

150. Which behavioral disorder is difficult to diagnose in children because the symptoms are manifested quite differently than in adults?
   a. Anorexia
   b. Schizophrenia
   c. Paranoia
   d. Depression

d. is correct.
Rationale: In an adult, it may be displayed as age-appropriate behavior, and go undiagnosed. In a child, it may be displayed as not age appropriate, so it is easier to recognize.

References

AGER, C.L. & COLE, C.L. (1991). A review of cognitive-behavioral interventions for children and adolescents with behavioral disorders. Behavioral Disorders. 16(4), 260-275.

AIKEN, L.R. (1985). Psychological Testing and Assessment (5th ed.) Boston: Allyn and Bacon.

ALBERTO, P.A. & TROUTHMAN, A.C. (1990). Applied Behavior Analysis for Teachers: Influencing Students Performance. Columbus, Ohio: Charles E. Merrill.

ALGOZZINE, B. (1990) Behavior Problem Management. Educator's Resource Service. Gaithersburg, MD: Aspen Publishers.

ALGOZZINE, B., RUHL, K., 7 RAMSEY, R. (1991). Behaviorally Disordered? Assessment for Identification and Instruction CED Mini-library. Renson, VA: The Council for Exceptional Children.

AMBRON, S.R. (1981. Child Development (3rd ed.). New York: Holt, Rinehart and Winston.

ANERSON, V., & BLACK, L. (Eds.). (1987, Winter). National news: U.S. Department of Education releases special report (Editorial). GLRS Journal [Georgia Learning Resources System].

ANGUILI, r. (1987, Winter). The 1986 Amendment to the Education of the Handicapped Act. Confederation [A quarterly publication of the Georgia Federation Council for Exceptional Children].

ASHLOCK, R.B. (1976). Error Patterns in Computation: A Semi-programmed Approach (2nd ed.). Columbus, Ohio: Charles E. Merrill.

ASSOCIATION OF RETARDED CITIZENS OF GEORGIA (1987). 1986-87 Government Report. College Park, GA: Author.

AUSUBEL, D.P. & SULLIVAN, E.V. (1970) Theory and Problems of Child Development. New York: Grune & Stratton.

BANKS, J.A., & McGee Banks, C.A. (1993). Multicultural Education (2nd ed.). Boston: Allyn and Bacon.

BARRETT, T.C. (Ed.). (1967). The Evaluation of Children's Reading Achievement. In Perspectives in Reading No. 8. Newark, Delaware: International Reading Association.

BARTOLI, J.S. (1989). An ecological response to Cole's interactivity alternative. Journal of Learning Disabilities, 22(5). 292-297.

BASILE-JACKSON, J. The Exceptional Child in the Regular Classroom. Augusta, GA: East Georgia Center, Georgia Learning Resources System.

BAUER, A.M., & SHEA, T.M. (1989). Teaching Exceptional Students in Your Classroom. Boston: Allyn and Bacon.

BENTLEY, E.L. Jr. (1980). Questioning Skills [Videocassette & manual series]. Northbrook, IL. Hubbard Scientific Company. (Project STRETCH [Strategies to Train Regular Educators to Teach Children with Handicaps]. Module 1. ISBN 0-8331-1906-0).

BERDINE, W.H. & BLACKHURST, A.E. (1985). An Introduction to Special Education. (2nd ed.) Boston: Little, Brown and Company.

BLAKE, K. (1976). The Mentally Retarded: An Educational Psychology. Englewood Cliff, NJ: Prentice-Hall.

BOHLINE, D.S. (1985). Intellectual and Affective Characteristics of Attention Deficit Disordered Children. Journal of Learning Disabilities. 18 (10). 604-608.

BOONE, R. (1983). Legislation and litigation. In R.E. Schmid, & L. Negata (Eds.). Contemporary Issues in Special Education. New York: McGraw Hill.

BRANTLINGER, E.A., & GUSKIN, S.L. (1988). Implications of social and cultural differences for special education. In Meten, E.L. Vergason, G.A., & Whelan, R.J. Effective Instructional Strategies for Exceptional Children. Denver, CO: Love Publishing.

BREWTON, B. (1990). Preliminary identification of the socially maladjusted. In Georgia Psycho-educational Network, Monograph #1. An Educational Perspective On: Emotional Disturbance and Social Maladjustment. Atlanta, GA Psychoeducational Network.

BROLIN, D.E. & KOKASKA, C.J. (1979). Career Education for Handicapped Children Approach. Renton, VA: The Council for Exceptional Children.

BROLIN, D.E. (Ed). (1989) Life Centered Career Education: A Competency Based Approach. Reston, VA: The Council for Exceptional Children.

BROWN, J.W., LEWIS, R.B., & HARCLEROAD, F.F. (1983). AV instruction: Technology, Media, and Methods (6TH ED.). New York: McGraw-Hill.

BRYAN, T.H., & BRYAN, J.H. (1986). Understanding Learning Disabilities (3rd ed.). Palo Alto, CA: Mayfield.

BRYEN, D.N. (1982). Inquiries Into Child Language. Boston: Allyn & Bacon.

BUCHER, B.D. (1987). Winning Them Over. New York: Times Books.

BUSH, W.L., & WAUGH, K.W. (1982). Diagnosing Learning Problems (3rd ed.) Columbus, OH: Charles E. Merrill.

CAMPBELL, P. (1986). Special Needs Report [Newsletter]. 1(1). 1-3.

CARBO, M., & DUNN, K. (1986). Teaching Students to Read Through Their Individual Learning Styles. Englewood Cliffs, NJ. Prentice Hall.

CARTWRIGHT, G.P. & CARTWRIGHT, C.A., & WARD, M.E. (1984). Educating Special Learners (2nd ed.). Belmont, CA: Wadsworth.

CEJKA, J.M. (Consultant), & NEEDHAM, F. (Senior Editor). (1976). Approaches to Mainstreaming. [Filmstrip and cassette kit, units 1 & 2]. Boston: Teaching Resources Corporation. (Catalog Nos. 09-210 & 09-220).

CHALFANT, J. C. (1985). Identifying Learning Disabled Students: A Summary of the National Task Force Report. Learning Disabilities Focus. 1, 9-20.

CHARLES, C.M. (1976). Individualizing Instructions. St Louis: The C.V. Mosby Company.

CHRISPEELS, J.H. (1991). District Leadership in Parent Involvement - Policies and Actions in San Diego. Phi Delta Kappa, 71, 367-371.

CLARIZIO, H.F. (1987). Differentiating Characteristics. In Georgia Psychoeducational Network, Monograph #1, An educational Perspective on: Emotional Disturbance and Social Maladjustment. Atlanta, GA Psychoeducational Network.

CLARIZIO, H.F. & MCCOY, G.F. (1983) Behavior Disorders in Children (3rd ed.). New York: Harper & Row.

COLES, G.S. (1989). Excerpts from The Learning Mystique: A Critical Look at Disabilities. Journal of Learning Disabilities. 22 (5). 267-278.

COLLINS, E. (1980). Grouping and Special Students. [Videocassette & manual series]. Northbrook, IL: Hubbard Scientific Company. (Project STRETCH [Strategies to Train Regular Educators to Teach Children with Handicaps], Module 17, ISBN 0- 8331-1922-2).

CRAIG, E., & CRAIG, L. (1990). Reading In the Content Areas [Videocassette & manual series]. Northbrook, IL: Hubbard Scientific Company. (Project STRETCH [Strategies to Train Regular Educators to Teach Children with Handicaps].Module 13, ISBN 0-8331-1918-4).

COMPTON, C., (1984). A Guide to 75 Tests for Special Education. Belmont, CA., Pitman Learning.

COUNCIL FOR EXCEPTIONAL CHILDREN. (1976). Introducing P.L. 94-142. [Filmstrip-cassette kit manual]. Reston, VA: Author.

COUNCIL FOR EXCEPTIONAL CHILDREN. (1987). The Council for Exceptional Children's Fall 1987. Catalog of Products and Services. Renton, VA: Author.

COUNCIL FOR EXCEPTIONAL CHILDREN DELEGATE ASSEMBLY. (1983). Council for Exceptional Children Code of Ethics (Adopted April 1983). Reston, VA: Author.

CZAJKA, J.L. (1984). Digest of Data on Person With Disabilities (Mathematics Policy Research, Inc.). Washington, D.C.: U.S. Government Printing Office.

DELL, H.D. (1972). Individualizing Instruction: Materials and Classroom Procedures. Chicago: Science Research Associates.

DEMONBREUN, C., & MORRIS, J. Classroom Management [Videocassette & Manual series]. Northbrook, IL: Hubbard Scientific Company. Project STRETCH (Strategies to Train Regular Educators to Teach Children with Handicaps]. Module 5, ISBN 0-8331-1910-9).

DEPARTMENT OF EDUCATION. Education for the Handicapped Law Reports. Supplement 45 (1981), p. 102: 52. Washington, D.C.: U.S. Government Printing Office.

DEPARTMENT OF HEALTH, EDUCATION AND WELFARE, OFFICE OF EDUCATION. (1977, August 23). Education of Handicapped Children. Federal Register, 42, (163).

DIANA VS. STATE BOARD OF EDUCATION, Civil No. 70-37 R.F.P. (N.D.Cal. January, 1970).

DIGANGI, S.A., PERRYMAN, P., & RUTHERFORD, R.B., Jr. (1990). Juvenile Offenders in the 90's A Descriptive Analysis. Perceptions, 25(4), 5-8.

DIVISION OF EDUCATIONAL SERVICES, SPECIAL EDUCATION PROGRAMS (1986). Fifteenth Annual Report to Congress on Implementation of the Education of the Handicapped Act. Washington, D.C.: U.S. Government Printing Office.

DOYLE, B.A. (1978). Math Readiness Skills. Paper presented at National Association of School Psychologists, New York. K.J. (1978). Teaching Students Through Their Individual Learning Styles.

DUNN, R.S., & DUNN, K.J. (1978). Teaching Students Through Their Individual Learning Styles: A Practical Approach. Reston, VA: Reston.

EPSTEIN, M.H., PATTON, J.R., POLLOWAY, E.A., & FOLEY, R. (1989). Mild retardation: Student characteristics and services. Education and Training of the Mentally Retarded, 24, 7-16.

EKWALL, E.E., & SHANKER, J.L. 1983). Diagnosis and Remediation of the Disabled Reader (2nd ed.) Boston: Allyn and Bacon.

FIRTH, E.E. & REYNOLDS, I. (1983). Slide tape shows: A creative activity for the gifted students. Teaching Exceptional Children. 15(3), 151-153.

FRYMIER, J., & GANSNEDER, B. (1989). The Phi Delta Kappa Study of Students at Risk. Phi Delta Kappa. 71(2) 142-146.

FUCHS, D., & DENO, S.L. 1992). Effects of curriculum within curriculum-based measurement. Exceptional Children 58 (232-242).

FUCHS, D., & FUCHS, L.S. (1989). Effects of examiner familiarity on Black, Caucasian, and Hispanic Children. A Meta-Analysis. Exceptional Children. 55, 303-308.

FUCHS, L.S., & SHINN, M.R. (1989). Writing CBM IEP objectives. In M.R. Shinn, Curriculum-based Measurement: Assessing Special Students. New York: Guilford Press.

GAGE, N.L. (1990). Dealing With the Dropout Problems? Phi Delta Kappa. 72(4), 280-285.

GALLAGHER, P.A. (1988). Teaching Students with Behavior Disorders: Techniques and Activities for Classroom Instruction (2nd ed.). Denver, CO: Love Publishing.

GEARHEART, B.R. (1980). Special Education for the 80s. St. Louis, MO: The C.V. Cosby Company.

GEARHART, B.R. & WEISHAHN, M.W. (1986). The Handicapped Student in the Regular Classroom (2nd ed.). St Louis, MO: The C.V. Mosby Company.

GEARHART, B.R. (1985). Learning Disabilities: Educational Strategies (4th ed.). St. Louis: Times Mirror/ Mosby College of Publishing.

GEORGIA DEPARTMENT OF EDUCATION, PROGRAM FOR EXCEPTIONAL CHILDREN. (1986). Mild Mentally Handicapped (Vol. II), Atlanta, GA: Office of Instructional Services, Division of Special Programs, and Program for Exceptional Children. Resource Manuals for Program for Exceptional Children.

GEORGIA DEPARTMENT OF HUMAN RESOURCES, DIVISION OF REHABILITATION SERVICES. (1987, February). Request for Proposal [Memorandum]. Atlanta, GA: Author.

GEORGIA PSYCHOEDUCATIONAL NETWORK (1990). An Educational Perspective on: Emotional Disturbance and Social Maladjustment. Monograph #1. Atlanta, GA Psychoeducational Network.

GEREN, K. (1979). Complete Special Education Handbook. West Nyack, NY: Parker.

GILLET, P.K. (1988). Career Development. Robinson, G.A., Patton, J.R., Polloway, E.A., & Sargent, L.R. (eds.). Best Practices in Mild Mental Disabilities. Reston, VA: The Division on Mental Retardation of the Council for Exceptional Children.

GLEASON, J.B. (1993). The Development of Language (3rd ed.). New York: Macmillan Publishing.

GOOD, T.L., & BROPHY, J.E. (1978). Looking into Classrooms (2nd Ed.). New York: Harper & Row.

HALL, M.A. (1979). Language-Centered Reading: Premises and Recommendations. Language Arts, 56 664-670.

HALLLAHAN, D.P. & KAUFFMAN, J.M. (1988). Exceptional Children: Introduction to Special Education. (4th Ed.). Englewood Cliffs, NJ; Prentice-Hall.

HALLAHAN, D.P. & KAUFFMAN, J.M. (1994). Exceptional Children: Introduction to Special Education 6th ed.). Boston: Allyn and Bacon.

HAMMILL, D.D., & BARTEL, N.R. (1982). Teaching Children With Learning and Behavior Problems (3rd ed.). Boston: Allyn and Bacon.

HAMMILL, D.D., & BARTEL, N.R. (1986). Teaching Students with Learning and Behavior Problems (4th ed.). Boston and Bacon.

HAMILL, D.D., & BROWN, L. & BRYANT, B. (1989) A Consumer's Guide to Tests in Print. Austin, TX: Pro-Ed.

HANEY, J.B. & ULLMER, E.J. ((1970). Educational Media and the Teacher. Dubuque, IA: Wm. C. Brown Company.

HARDMAN, M.L., DREW, C.J., EGAN, M.W., & WOLF, B. (1984). Human Exceptionality: Society, School, and Family. Boston: Allyn and Bacon.

HARDMAN, M.L., DREW, C.J., EGAN, M.W., & WORLF, B. (1990). Human Exceptionality (3rd ed.). Boston: Allyn and Bacon.

HARGROVE, L.J., & POTEET, J.A. (1984). Assessment in Special Education. Englewood Cliffs, NJ: Prentice-Hall.

HARING, N.G., & BATEMAN, B. (1977). Teaching the Learning Disabled Child. Englewood Cliffs, NJ: Prentice-Hall.

HARRIS, K.R., & PRESSLEY, M. (1991). The Nature of Cognitive Strategy Instruction: Interactive strategy instruction. Exceptional Children, 57, 392-401.

HART, T., & CADORA, M.J. (1980). The Exceptional Child: Label the Behavior [Videocassette & manual series], Northbrook, IL: Hubbard Scientific Company. (Project STRETCH [Strategies to Train Regular Educators to Teach Children with Handicaps], Module 12, ISBN 0-8331-1917-6). HART, V. (1981) Mainstreaming Children with Special Needs. New York: Longman.

HENLEY, M., RAMSEY,R.S., & ALGOZZINE, B. (1993). Characteristics of and Strategies for Teaching Students with Mild Disabilities. Boston: Allyn and Bacon.

HEWETT, F.M., & FORNESS, S.R. (1984). Education of Exceptional Learners. (3rd ed.). Boston: Allyn and Bacon.

HOWE, C.E. (1981) Administration of Special Education. Denver: Love.

HUMAN SERVICES RESEARCH INSTITUTE (1985). Summary of Data on Handicapped Children and Youth. (Digest). Washington, D.C.: U.S. Government Printing Office.

JOHNSON, D.W. (1972) Reaching Out: Interpersonal Effectiveness and Self-Actualization. Englewood Cliffs, NJ: Prentice-Hall.

JOHNSON, D.W. (1978) Human Relations and Your Career: A Guide to Interpersonal Skills. Englewood Cliffs, NJ: Prentice-Hall.

JOHNSON, D.W., & JOHNSON, R.T. (1990). Social Skills for Successful Group Work. Educational Leadership. 47 (4) 29-33.

JOHNSON, S.W., & MORASKY, R.L. Learning Disabilities (2nd ed.) Boston: Allyn and Bacon.

JONES, F.H. (1987). Positive Classroom Discipline. New York: McGraw-Hill Book Company.

JONES, V.F., & JONES, L. S. (1986). Comprehensive Classroom Management: Creating Positive Learning Environments. (2nd ed.). Boston: Allyn and Bacon.

JONES, V.F. & JONES, L.S. (1981). Responsible Classroom Discipline: Creating Positive Learning Environments and Solving Problems. Boston: Allyn and Bacon.

KAUFFMAN, J.M. (1981) Characteristics of Children's Behavior Disorders. (2nd ed.). Columbus, OH: Charles E. Merrill.

KAUFFMAN, J.M. (1989). Characteristics of Behavior Disorders of Children and Youth. (4th ed.). Columbus, OH: Merrill Publishing.

KEM, M., & NELSON, M. (1983). Strategies for Managing Behavior Problems in the Classroom. Columbus, OH: Charles E. Merrill.

KERR, M.M., & NELSON, M. (1983) Strategies for Managing Behavior Problems in the Classroom. Columbus, OH: Charles E. Merrill.

KIRK, S.A., & GALLAGHER, J.J. (1986). Educating Exceptional Children (5th ed.). Boston: Houghton Mifflin.

KOHFELDT, J. (1976). Blueprints for construction. Focus on Exceptional Children. 8 (5), 1-14.

KOKASKA, C.J., & BROLIN, D.E. (1985). Career Education for Handicapped Individuals (2nd ed.). Columbus, OH: Charles E. Merrill.

LAMBIE, R.A. (1980). A systematic approach for changing materials, instruction, and assignments to meet individual needs. Focus on Exceptional Children, 13(1), 1-12.

LARSON, S.C., & POPLIN, M.S. (1980). Methods for Educating the Handicapped: An Individualized Education Program Approach. Boston: Allyn and Bacon.

LERNER, J. (1976) Children with Learning Disabilities. (2nd ed.). Boston: Houghton Mifflin.

LERNER, J. (1989). Learning Disabilities,: Theories, Diagnosis and Teaching Strategies (3rd ed.). Boston: Houghton Mifflin.

LEVENKRON, S. (1991). Obsessive-Compulsive Disorders. New York: Warner Books.

LEWIS, R.B., & DOORLAG, D.H. (1991). Teaching Special Students in the Mainstream. (3rd ed.). New York: Merrill.

LINDSLEY, O. R. (1990). Precision Teaching: By Teachers for Children. Teaching Exceptional Children, 22. (3), 10-15.

LINDDBERG, L., & SWEDLOW, R. (1985). Young Children Exploring and Learning. Boston: Allyn and Bacon.

LONG, N.J., MORSE, W.C., & NEWMAN, R.G. (1980). Conflict in the Classroom: The Education of Emotionally Disturbed Children. Belmont, CA: Wadsworth.

LOSEN, S.M., & LOSEN, J.G. (1985). The Special Education Team. Boston: Allyn and Bacon.

LOVITT, T.C. (1989). Introduction to Learning Disabilities. Boston: Allyn and Bacon.

LUND, N.J. * DUCHAN, J.F. (1988)/ Assessing Children's Language in Naturalist Contexts. Englewood Cliffs, NJ: Prentice Hall

MALE, M. (1994) Technology for Inclusion: Meeting the Special Needs of all Children. (2nd ed.). Boston: Allyn and Bacon.

MANDELBAUM, L.H. (1989). Reading. In G.A. Robinson, J.R., Patton, E.A., Polloway, & L.R. Sargent (eds.). Best Practices in Mild Mental Retardation. Reston, VA: The Division of Mental Retardation, Council for Exceptional Children.

MANNIX. D. (1993). Social Skills for Special Children. West Nyack, NY: The Center for Applied Research in Education.

MARSHALL, ET AL, VS. GEORGIA U.S. District court for the Southern District of Georgia. C.V. 482-233. June 28, 1984.

MARSHALL, E.K., KURTZ, P.D., & ASSOCIATES. Interpersonal Helping Skills. San Francisco, CA: Jossey-Bass Publications.

MARSTON, D.B. (1989) A curriculum-based measurement approach to assessing academic performance: What it is and why do it. In M. Shinn (Ed.). Curriculum-Based Measurement: Assessing Special Children. New York: Guilford Press.

MCDOWELL, R.L., ADAMSON, G.W., & WOOD, F.H. (1982). Teaching Emotionally Disturbed Children. Boston: Little, Brown and Company.

MCGINNIS, E., GOLDSTEIN, A.P. (1990). Skill Streaming in EarlyChildhood: Teaching Prosocial Skills to the Preschool and Kindergarten Child. Champaign, IL: Research Press.

MCLOUGHLIN, J.A., & LEWIS, R.B. (1986). Assessing Special Students (3rd ed.). Columbus, OH: Charles E. Merrill.

MERCER, C.D. (1987). Students with Learning Disabilities. (3rd. ed.). Merrill Publishing.

MERCER, C.D., & MERCER, A.R. (1985). Teaching Children with Learning Problems (2nd ed.). Columbus, OH: Charles E. Merrill.

MEYEN, E.L., VERGASON, G.A., & WHELAN, R.J. (Eds.). (1988). Effective Instructional Strategies for Exceptional Children. Denver, CO: Love Publishing.

MILLER, L.K. (1980). Principles of Everyday Behavior Analysis (2nd ed.). Monterey, CA: Brooks/Cole Publishing Company.

MILLS VS. THE BOARD OF EDUCATON OF THE DISTRICT OF COLUMBIA, 348F. Supp. 866 (D.C. 1972).

MOPSICK, S.L. & AGARD, J.A. (Eds.) (1980). Cambridge, MA: Abbott Associates.

MORRIS, C.G. (1985). Psychology: An Introduction (5th ed.). Englewood Cliffs, NJ: Prentice-Hall.

MORRIS, J. (1980). Behavior Modification. [Videocassette and manual series]. Northbrook, IL: Hubbard Scientific Company. (Project STRETCH [Strategies to Train Regular Educators to Teach Children with Handicaps,] Module 16, Metropolitan Cooperative Educational Service Agency.). MORRIS, J. & DEMONBREUN, C. (1980). Learning Styles [Videocassettes & Manual series]. Northbrook, IL: Hubbard Scientific Company. (Project STRETCH [Strategies to Train Regular Educators to Teach Children with Handicaps], Module 15, ISBN 0-8331-1920-6).

MORRIS, R.J. (1985). Behavior Modification with Exceptional Children: Principles and Practices. Glenview, IL: Scott, Foresman and Company.

MORSINK, C.V. (1984). Teaching Special Needs Students in Regular Classrooms. Boston: Little, Brown and Company.

MORSINK, C.V., THOMAS, C.C., & CORREA, V.L. (1991). Interactive Teaming, Consultation and Collaboration in Special Programs. New York: MacMillan Publishing.

MULLSEWHITE, C.R. (1986). Adaptive Play for Special Needs Children: Strategies to Enhance Communication and Learning. San Diego: College Hill Press.

NORTH CENTRAL GEORGIA LEARNING RESOURCES SYSTEM/CHILD SERVE. (1985). Strategies Handbook for Classroom Teachers. Ellijay, GA.

PATTON, J.R., CRONIN, M.E., POLLOWAY, E.A., HUTCHINSON, D., & ROBINSON, G.A. (1988). Curricular considerations: A life skills orientation. In Robinson, G.A., Patton, J.R., Polloway, E.A., & Sargent, L.R. (Eds.). Best Practices in Mental Disabilities. Des Moines, IA: Iowa Department of Education, Bureau of Special Education.

PATTON, J.R., KAUGGMAN, J.M., BLACKBOURN, J.M., & BROWN, B.G. (1991). Exceptional Children in Focus (5th ed.). New York: MacMillan.

PAUL, J.L. (Ed.). (1981). Understanding and Working with parents of Children with Special Needs. New York: Holt, Rinehart and Winston.

PAUL, J.L. & EPANCHIN, B.C. (1991). Educating Emotionally Disturbed Children and Youth: Theories and Practices for Teachers. (2nd ed.). New York: MacMillan.

PENNSYLVANIA ASSOCIATION FOR RETARDED CHILDREN VS. COMMONWEALTH OF PENNSYLVANIA, 334 F. Supp. 1257 (E.D., PA., 1971), 343 F. Supp. 279 (L.D. PA., 19972).

PHILLIPS, V., & MCCULLOUGH, L. (1990). Consultation based programming: Instituting the Collaborative Work Ethic. Exceptional Children. 56 (4), 291-304.

PODEMSKI, R.S., PRICE, B.K., SMITH, T.E.C., & MARSH, G.E., IL (1984). Comprehensive Administration of Special Education. Rockville, MD: Aspen Systems Corporation.

POLLOWAY, E.A., & PATTON, J.R. (1989). Strategies for Teaching Learners with Special Needs. (5th ed.). New York: Merrill.

POLLOWAY, E.A., PATTON, J.R., PAYNE, J.S., & PAYNE, R.A. 1989). Strategies for Teaching Learners with Special Needs, 4th ed.). Columbus, OH: Merrill Publishing.

PUGACH, M.C., & JOHNSON, L.J. (1989a). The challenge of implementing collaboration between general and special education. Exceptional Children, 56 (3), 232-235.

PUGACH, M.C., & JOHNSON, L.J. (1989b). Pre-referral interventions: Progress, Problems, and Challenges. Exceptional Children, 56 (3), 217-226.

RADABAUGH, M.T., & YUKISH, J.F. (1982). Curriculum and Methods for the Mildly Handicapped. Boston: Allyn and Bacon.

RAMSEY, R.S. (1981). Perceptions of disturbed and disturbing behavioral characteristics by school personnel. (Doctoral Dissertation, University of Florida) Dissertation Abstracts International, 42(49), DA8203709.

RAMSEY, R.S. (1986). Taking the practicum beyond the public school door. Journal of Adolescence. 21(83), 547-552.

RAMSEY, R.S., (1988). Preparatory Guide for Special Education Teacher competency Tests. Boston: Allyn and Bacon, Inc.

RAMSEY, R.S., DIXON, M.J., & SMITH, G.G.B. (1986) Eyes on the Special Education: Professional Knowledge Teacher Competency Test. Albany, GA: Southwest Georgia Learning Resources System Center.

RAMSEY R.W., & RAMSEY, R.S. (1978). Educating the emotionally handicapped child in the public school setting. Journal of Adolescence. 13(52), 537-541.

REINHEART, H.R. (1980). Children I Conflict. Educational Strategies for the Emotionally Disturbed and Behaviorally Disordered. (2nd ed.). St Louis, MO: The C.V. Mosby Company.

ROBINSON, G.A., PATTON, J.R., POLLOWAY, E.A., & SARGENT, L.R. (Eds.). (1989a) Best Practices in Mental Disabilities. Des Moines, IA Iowa Department of Education, Bureau of Special Education.

ROBINSON, G.A., PATTON, J.R., POLLOWAY, E.A., & SARGENT, L.R. (Eds.). (1989b). Best Practices in Mental Disabilities. Renton, VA: The Division on Mental Retardation of the Council for Exceptional Children.

ROTHSTEIN, L.F. (1995). Special education Law (2nd ed.). New York: Longman Publishers.

SABATINO, D.A., SABATION, A.C., & MANN, L. (1983). Management: A Handbook of Tactics, Strategies, and Programs. Aspen Systems Corporation.

SALVIA, J., & YSSELDYKE, J.E. (1985). Assessment in Special Education (3rd. ed.). Boston: Houghton Mifflin.

SALVIA J., & YSSELDYKE, J.E. (1991). Assessment (5th ed.). Boston: Houghton Mifflin.

SALVIA, J. & YSSELDYKE, J.E. (1995) Assessment (6th ed.). Boston: Houghton Mifflin.

SATTLER, J.M. (1982). Assessment of Children's Intelligence and Special Abilities (2nd ed.). Boston: Allyn and Bacon.

SCHLOSS, P.J., HARRIMAN, N., & PFIEFER, K. (in press). Application of a sequential prompt reduction technique to the independent composition performance of behaviorally disordered youth. Behavioral Disorders.

SCHLOSS, P.J.., & SEDLAK, R.A.(1986). Instructional Methods for Students with Learning and Behavior Problems. Boston: Allyn and Bacon.

SCHMUCK, R.A., & SCHMUCK, P.A. (1971). Group Processes in the Classroom. Dubuque, IA: William C. Brown Company.

SCHUBERT, D.G. (1978). Your teaching - the tape recorder. Reading Improvement, 15(1), 78-80.

SCHULZ, J.B., CARPENTER, C.D., & TURNBULL, A.P. (1991). Mainstreaming Exceptional Students: A Guide for Classroom Teachers. Boston: Allyn and Bacon.

SEMMEL, M.I., ABERNATHY, T.V., BUTERA G., & LESAR, S. (1991). Teacher perception of the regular education initiative. Exceptional Children, 58 (1), 3-23.

SHEA, T.M., & BAUER, A.M. (1985). Parents and Teachers of Exceptional Students: A Handbook for Involvement. Boston: Allyn and Bacon.

SIMEONSSON, R.J. (1986). Psychological and Development Assessment of Special Children. Boston: Allyn and Bacon.

SMITH, C.R. (1991). Learning Disabilities: The Interaction of Learner, Task, and Setting. Boston: Little, Brown, and Company.

SMITH, D.D., & LUCKASSON, R. (1992). Introduction to Special Education: Teaching in an Age of Challenge. Boston: Allyn and Bacon.

SMITH, J.E., & PATTON, J.M. (1989). _A Resource Module on Adverse Causes of Mild Mental Retardation._ (Prepared for the President's Committee on Mental Retardation).

SMITH, T.E.C., FINN, D.M., & DOWDY, C.A. (1993). _Teaching Students With Mild Disabilities._ Fort Worth, TX: Harcourt Brace Jovanovich College Publishers.

SMITH-DAVIS, J. (1989a April). _A National Perspective on Special Education._ Keynote presentation at the GLRS/College/University Forum, Macon, GA.

STEPHENS, T.M. (1976). _Directive Teaching of Children with Learning and Behavioral Disorders._ Columbus, OH Charles E. Merrill.

STERNBURG, R.J. (1990). _Thinking Styles: Key to Understanding Performance._ Phi Delta Kappa, 71(5), 366-371.

SULZER, B., & MAYER, G.R. (1972). _Behavior Modification Procedures for School Personnel._ Hinsdale, IL: Dryden.

TATEYAMA-SNIEZEK, K.M. (1990.) Cooperative Learning: Does it improve the academic achievement of students with handicaps? _Exceptional Children, 57_(2), 426-427.

THIAGARAJAN, S. (1976). Designing instructional games for handicapped learners. _Focus on Exceptional Children._ 7(9), 1-11.

THOMAS, O. (1980). _Individualized Instruction_ [Videocassette & manual series]. Northbrook, IL: Hubbard Scientific Company. (Project STRETCH [Strategies to Train Regular Educators to Teach Children with Handicaps]. Module 14, ISBN 0- 8331-1919-2).

THOMAS, O. (1980). _Spelling_ [Videocassette & manual series]. (Project STRETCH [Strategies to Train Regular Educators to Teach Children with Handicaps]. Module 10, ISBN 0-83311915-X).

THORNTON, C.A., TUCKER, B.F., DOSSEY, J.A., & BAZIK, E.F. (1983). _Teaching Mathematics to Children with Special Needs._ Menlo Park, CA: Addison-Wesley.

TURKEL, S.R., & PODEL, D.M. (1984). Computer-assisted learning for mildly handicapped students. _Teaching Exceptional Children._ 16(4), 258-262.

TURNBULL, A.P., STRICKLAND, B.B., & BRANTLEY, J.C. (1978). _Developing Individualized Education Programs._ Columbus, OH: Charles E. Merrill.

U.S. DEPARTMENT OF EDUCATION. (1993). To Assure the Free Appropriate Public Education of all Children with Disabilities. (Fifteenth annual report to Congress on the Implementation of The Individuals with Disabilities Education Act.). Washington, D.C.

WALKER, J.E., & SHEA, T.M. (1991). Behavior Management: A Practical Approach for Educators. New York: MacMillan.

WALLACE, G., & KAUFFMAN, J.M. (1978). Teaching Children with Learning Problems. Columbus, OH: Charles E. Merrill.

WEHMAN, P., & MCLAUGHLIN, P.J. (1981). Program Development in Special Education. New York: McGraw-Hill.

WEINTRAUB, F.J. (1987, March). [Interview].

WESSON, C.L. (1991). Curriculum-based measurement and two models of follow-up consultation. Exceptional Children. 57(3), 246-256.

WEST, R.P., YOUNG, K.R., & SPOONER, F. (1990). Precision Teaching: An Introduction. Teaching Exceptional Children. 22(3), 4-9.

WHEELER, J. (1987). Transitioning Persons with Moderate and Severe Disabilities from School to Adulthood: What Makes it Work? Materials Development Center, School of Education, and Human Services. University of Wisconsin-Stout.

WHITING, J., & AULTMAN, L. (1990). Workshop for Parents. (Workshop materials). Albany, GA: Southwest Georgia Learning Resources System Center.

WIEDERHOLT, J.L., HAMMILL, D.D., & BROWN, V.L. (1983). The Resource Room Teacher: A Guide to Effective Practices (2nd ed.). Boston: Allyn and Bacon.

WIIG, E.H., & SEMEL, E.M. (1984). Language Assessment and Intervention for the Learning Disabled. (2nd ed.). Columbus, OH: Charles E. Merrill.

WOLFGANG, C.H., & GLICKMAN, C.D.(1986). Solving Discipline Problems: Strategies for Classroom Teachers (2nd ed.). Boston: Allyn and Bacon.

YSSELKYKE, J.E., ALGOZZINE, B., (1990). Introduction to Special Education (2nd ed.). Boston: Houghton Mifflin.

YSSELDYKE, J.E., ALGOZZINE, B., & THURLOW, M.L. (1992). Critical Issues in Special Education (2nd ed.). Boston: Houghton Mifflin Company.

YSSEDLYKE, J.E., THURLOW, M.L., WOTRUBA, J.W., NANIA, PA.A (1990). Instructional arrangements: Perceptions From General Education. Teaching Exceptional Children, 22(4), 4-8.

ZARGONA, N., VAUGHN, S., 7 MCINTOSH, R. (1991). Social Skills Interventions and children with behavior problems: A review. Behavior Disorders, 16(4), 260-275.

ZIGMOND, N., & BAKER, J. (1990). Mainstream experiences for learning disabled students (Project Meld): Preliminary report. Exceptional Children, 57(2), 176-185.

ZIRPOLI, T.J., & MELLOY, K.J. (1993). Behavior Management. New York: Merrill.

Resource Guide

Organization	Members	Mission
Alexander Graham Bell Association for the Deaf and Hard of Hearing 3417 Volta Place, N.W. Washington, D.C. 27.0 www.agbell.org	Teachers of the deaf, speech-language pathologists, audiologists, physicians, hearing aid dealers	To promote the teaching of speech, lip reading, and use of residual hearing to persons who are deaf; encourage research; and work to further better education of persons who are deaf.
Alliance for Technology Access 1304 Southpoint Blvd., Suite 240, Petaluma, CA 94954 www.Ataccess.org Email: ATAinfo@ATAccess.org • Phone: 707.778.3011 Fax 707.765.2080 TTY 707.778.3015	People with disabilities, family members, and professionals in related fields, and organizations with work in their own communities and ways to support our mission.	To increase the use of technology by children and adults with disabilities and functional limitations.
American Council of the Blind 1155 15th Street, NW, Suite 1004, Washington, DC 25.0 Acb.org (202) 467-5081 (800) 424-8666 FAX: (202) 467-5085		To improve the well-being of all blind and visually impaired people by: serving as a representative national organization of blind people and conducting a public education program to promote greater understanding of blindness and the capabilities of blind people.

Organization	Members	Mission
American Council on Rural Special Education (ACRES) Utah State University 2865 Old Main Hill Logan, Utah 84322 E-mail: inquiries at acres-sped.org Phone: (435)797 3728	Open to anyone interested in supporting their mission	To provide leadership and support that will enhance services for individuals with exceptional needs, their families, and the professionals who work with them, and for the rural communities in which they live.
American Society for Deaf Children 3820 Hartzdale Drive, Camp Hill, PA 17011 www.deafchildren.org Phone: (717) 703-0073 1-866-895-4206 FAX: (717) 909-5599 Email: asdc@deafchildren.org	Open to everyone	To provide support, encouragement and information to families raising children who are deaf or hard of hearing.

Organization	Members	Mission
Asperger Syndrome Education Network (ASPEN) 9 Aspen Circle Edison, NJ 08820 (732)321-0880 www.aspennj.org Email: info@AspenNJ.org		Provides families and individuals whose lives are affected by Autism Spectrum Disorders (Asperger Syndrome, Pervasive Developmental Disorder-NOS, High Functioning Autism), and Nonverbal Learning Disabilities with:<ul><li>Education about the issues surrounding the disorders.</li><li>Support in knowing that they are not alone, and in helping individuals with ASD's and NLD achieve their maximum potential.</li><li>Advocacy in areas of appropriate educational programs, medical research funding, adult issues and increased public awareness and understanding</li></ul>

Organization	Members	Mission
Autism Society of America 7910 Woodmont Avenue, Suite 300 Bethesda, Maryland 20814 www.autism-society.org 1-800-328-8476	Open to all who support the mission of ASA	To increase public awareness about autism and the day-to-day issues faced by individuals with autism, their families and the professionals with whom they interact. The society and its chapters share a common mission of providing information and education, and supporting research and advocating for programs and services for the autism community.
Brain Injury Association of America 8201 Greensboro Drive Suite 611 McLean, VA 22102 www.biausa.org/ Phone: (703) 761-0750	Open to all	Provides information, education and support to assist the 5.3 million Americans currently living with traumatic brain injury and their families.
National Mental Health Information Center P.O. Box 42557 Washington, DC 215.0 http://www.mentalhealth.samhsa.gov/ 1-800-789-2647	Government Agency	Developed for users of mental health services and their families, the general public, policy makers, providers, and the media.

Organization	Members	Mission
Children and Adults with Attention Deficit/Hyperactive Disorder (CHADD) 8181 Professional Place - Suite 150 Landover, MD 20785 www.chadd.org Tel: 301-306-7070 / Fax: 301-306-7090 Email: national@chadd.org	Open to all	Providing resources and encouragement to parents, educators and professionals on a grassroots level through CHADD chapters
Council for Exceptional Children 1110 N. Glebe Road Suite 300 Arlington, VA 22201 www.cec.sped.org 1-888-232-7733 TTY: 1-866-915-5000 FAX 703-264-9494	Teachers, administrators, teacher educators, and related service personnel	Advocate for services for [disabled] and gifted individuals. A professional organization that addresses service, training, and research relative to exceptional persons.
Epilepsy Foundation of America 8301 Professional Place Landover, MD 20785 www.epilepsyfoundation.org/ (800) 332-1000	A non-membership organization	Works to ensure that people with seizures are able to participate in all life experiences; and to prevent, control and cure epilepsy through research, education, advocacy and services

Organization	Members	Mission
Hands and Voices P.O. Box 371926 Denver CO 80237 www.handsandvoices.org Toll Free: (866) 422-0422 parentadvocate@handsandvoices.org	families, professionals, other organizations, pre-service students, and deaf and hard of hearing adults who are all working towards ensuring successful outcomes for children who are deaf and hard of hearing.	Supporting families and their children who are deaf or hard of hearing, as well as the professionals who serve them.
The International Dyslexia Association Chester Building, Suite 382 8600 LaSalle Road Baltimore, Maryland 21286 http://www.interdys.org/ 410-296-0232 Fax: 410-321-5069	Anyone interested in IDA and its mission can become a member	Provides information and referral services, research, advocacy and direct services to professionals in the field of learning disabilities.

Organization	Members	Mission
Learning Disabilities Association of America 4156 Library Road Pittsburgh, PA 15234 http://www.ldanatl.org/ Phone (412) 341-1515 Fax (412) 344-0224	Anyone interested in LDA and its mission can become a member	• Provides cutting edge information on learning disabilities, practical solutions, and a comprehensive network of resources. • Provides support to people with learning disabilities, their families, teachers and other professionals.
American Psychological Association 1200 17th St., N.W. Washington, D.C. 20036 (Especially Divisions of Child and Youth Services, Clinical Psychology, Educational Psychology, School Psychology, Mental Retardation, Counseling Psychology, and Developmental Psychology)	Psychologists and educators	Scientific and professional society working to improve mental health services and to advocate for legislation and programs that will promote mental health; facilitate research and professional development.

Organization	Members	Mission
American Speech-Language-Hearing Association 10801 Rockville Pike Rockville, MD 20852	Specialists in speech-language pathology and audiology	Advocate for provision of speech-language and hearing services in school and clinic settings; advocate for legislation relative to the profession; and work to promote effective services and development of the profession.
Association for Children and Adults with Learning Disabilities 4156 Library Road Pittsburgh, PA 15234 http://www.acldonline.org/	Parents of children with learning disabilities and interested professionals	Advanced the education and general well-being of children with adequate intelligence who have learning disabilities arising from perceptual, conceptual, or subtle coordinative problems, sometimes accompanied by behavior difficulties.
The Association for the Gifted 1920 Association Drive Reston, VA 22091	Members of the Council for Exceptional Children who teach gifted students or educate professionals to work with students who are gifted	Disseminate information, encourage research and scholarly investigation on education of gifted students, encourage professional development for teachers and others who work with gifted students.

Organization	Members	Mission
Association for Retarded Citizens 2501 Avenue J Arlington, TX 76011	Parents, professionals, and others interested in individuals with mental retardation	Work on local, state, and national levels to promote treatment, research, public understanding, and legislation for persons with mental retardation; provide counseling for parents of students with mental retardation.
The Association for the Severely Handicapped 7010 Roosevelt Way, N.E. Seattle, WA 98115	Teachers, therapists, parents, administrators, university faculty, and advocates involved in all areas of service to persons with severe disabilities	Advocate quality education for persons with disabilities, and work to ensure a dignified, autonomous lifestyle for all persons with disabilities; disseminate information and promote research on education of and service to individuals with severe disabilities.
Council for Children with Behavioral Disorders 1920 Association Drive Reston, VA 22091	Members of the Council for Exceptional Children who teach children with behavior disorders or who train teachers to work with those children	Promote education and general welfare of children and youth with behavior disorders or serious emotional disturbances. Promote professional growth and research on students with behavior disorders and severe emotional disturbances.

Organization	Members	Mission
Council for Educational Diagnostic Services 1920 Association Drive Reston, VA 22091	Members of the Council for Exceptional Children who are school psychologists, educational diagnosticians, [and] social workers who are involved in diagnosing educational difficulties	Promote the most appropriate education of children and youth through appraisal, diagnosis, educational intervention, implementation, and evaluation of a prescribed educational program. Work to facilitate the professional development of those who assess students. Work to further development of better diagnostic techniques and procedures.
Council for Exceptional Children 1920 Association Drive Reston, VA 22091	Teachers, administrators, teacher educators, and related service personnel	Advocate for services for [disabled] and gifted individuals. A professional organization that addresses service, training, and research relative to exceptional persons.
Council for Learning Disabilities Dept. of Special Education University of Louisville Louisville, KY 40292 (originally est. in 1968 as a division of Council for Exceptional Children)	Teachers who work with students with specific learning disabilities, teacher trainers who educate professionals to work with those students, and researchers who conduct research of students with learning disabilities	Promote the general welfare and education of individuals with specific learning disabilities through improving teacher preparation programs, local special education programs, and research.

Organization	Members	Mission
Council of Administrators of Special Education 1920 Association Drive Reston, VA 22091	Members of the Council for Exceptional Children who are administrators, directors, coordinators, or supervisors of programs, schools, or classes for exceptional children; college faculty who train administrators	Promote professional leadership; provide opportunities for the study of problems common to its members; communicate through discussion and publications information that will facilitate improved services for children with exceptional needs.
Division for Children with Communication Disorders 1920 Association Drive Reston, VA 22091	Members of the Council for Exceptional Children who are speech-language pathologists, audiologists, teachers of children with communication disorders, or educators of professionals who plan to work with children who have communication disorders	Promote the education of children with communication disorders. Promote professional growth and research.
Division for Early Childhood 1920 Association Drive Reston, VA 22091	Members of the Council for Exceptional Children who teach preschool children and infants or educate teachers to work with young children	Promote effective education for young children and infants. Promote professional development of those who work with young children and infants. Promote legislation and research.

Organization	Members	Mission
Division for the Physically Handicapped 1920 Association Drive Reston, VA 22091	Members of the Council for Exceptional Children who work with individuals who have physical disabilities or educate professionals to work with those individuals	Promote closer relationships among educators of students who have physical impairments or are homebound. Facilitate research and encourage development of new ideas, practices, and techniques through professional meetings, workshops, and publications.
Division for the Visually Handicapped 1920 Association Drive Reston, VA 22091	Members of the Council for Exceptional Children who work with individuals who have visual disabilities or educate professionals to work with those individuals	Work to advance the education and training of individuals with visual impairments. Work to bring about better understanding of educational, emotional, or other problems associated with visual impairment. Facilitate research and development of new techniques or ideas in education and training of individuals with visual problems.
Division on Career Development 1920 Association Drive Reston, VA 22091	Members of the Council for Exceptional Children who teach or in other ways work toward career development and vocational education of exceptional children	Promote and encourage professional growth of all those concerned with career development and vocational education. Promote research, legislation, information dissemination, and technical assistance relevant to career development and vocational education.

Organization	Members	Mission
Division on Mental Retardation 1920 Association Drive Reston, VA 22091	Members of the Council for Exceptional Children who work with students with mental retardation or educate professionals to work with those students	Work to advance the education of individuals with mental retardation, research mental retardation, and the training of professionals to work with individuals with mental retardation. Promote public understanding of mental retardation and professional development of those who work with persons with mental retardation.
Gifted Child Society P.O. Box 120 Oakland, NJ 07436	Parents and educators of children who are gifted	Train educators to meet the needs of students with gifted abilities, offer assistance to parents facing special problems in raising children who are gifted, and seek public recognition of the needs of these children.
National Association for the Education of Young Children 1834 Connecticut Ave., N.W. Washington, D.C. 29.0	Teachers and directors of nursery schools, day care centers, cooperatives, church schools, play groups, and others interested in preschool education	Promote service and action on behalf of the needs and rights of young children, with emphasis on provision of educational services and resources.

Organization	Members	Mission
National Association of School Psychologists 1929 K Street, Suite 520 Washington, D.C. 26.0	School psychologists	Serve the mental health and educational needs of all children and youth. Encourage and provide opportunities for professional growth for school psychologists. Inform the public about the services and practice of school psychology. Work to advance the standards of the profession of school psychology.
National Association for Retarded Citizens 5101 Washington Ave., N.W. Washington, D.C www.thearc.org	People with mental retardation and related developmental disabilities, parents and other family members, and friends of people with mental retardation and professionals who work with them.	Work to promote the general welfare of persons with mental retardation; facilitate research and information dissemination relative to causes, treatment, and prevention of mental retardation.
National Association of Social Workers 1425 H St., N.W., Suite 600 Washington, D.C. 25.0	Persons with a minimum of a bachelor's degree in social work	Promote the quality and effectiveness of social work practice by advancing sound social policies and programs and using the professional knowledge and skills of social work to "alleviate sources of deprivation, distress, and strain;" set professional standards; conduct research; and work to improve professional practice.

Organization	Members	Mission
National Easter Seal Society 2023 W. Ogden Avenue Chicago, IL 60612	State units (49) and local societies (951); no individual members	Establish and run programs for individuals with physical impairments, usually including diagnostic services, speech therapy, preschool services, physical therapy, and occupational therapy.
National Federation of the Blind 1800 Johnson Street Baltimore, MD 21230	State and local organizations of people with blindness	Work to facilitate equality of opportunity for people with blindness and their integration into society. Monitor legislation affecting persons who are blind, evaluate services, and work to improve policies toward these individuals. Conduct leadership training for people with blindness and work to stimulate research on blindness.
Orton Society 8415 Bellona Lane, Suite 113 Towson, MD 21204	Members of the profession of neurology, pediatrics, psychiatry, education, social work, psychology; parents and others interested in study, treatment and prevention of the problems of specific language disability, often called dyslexia	Provide a focal point for activities and ideas generated in various fields as they relate to problems of language development and learning; specific reference to students with dyslexia.

Organization	Members	Mission
Teacher Education Division 1920 Association Drive Reston, VA 22091	Members of the Council for Exceptional Children who are teacher educators	Stimulate and actively assist in development of programs to educate professionals who will work with exceptional students. Promote research on teacher education.

XAMonline, INC. 21 Orient Ave. Melrose, MA 02176

Toll Free number 800-509-4128

TO ORDER Fax 781-662-9268 OR www.XAMonline.com

<u>CERTIFICATION EXAMINATION FOR OKLAHOMA EDUCATORS - CEOE - 2007</u>

PO#   Store/School:

Address 1:

Address 2 (Ship to other):

City, State Zip

Credit card number ____-____-____-____   expiration_____
EMAIL _____
PHONE   FAX

13# ISBN 2007	TITLE	Qty	Retail	Total
978-1-58197-781-3	CEOE OSAT Advanced Mathematics Field 11			
978-1-58197-775-2	CEOE OSAT Art Sample Test Field 02			
978-1-58197-780-6	CEOE OSAT Biological Sciences Field 10			
978-1-58197-776-9	CEOE OSAT Chemistry Field 04			
978-1-58197-778-3	CEOE OSAT Earth Science Field 08			
978-1-58197-794-3	CEOE OSAT Elementary Education Fields 50-51			
978-1-58197-795-0	CEOE OSAT Elementary Education Fields 50-51 Sample Questions			
978-1-58197-777-6	CEOE OSAT English Field 07			
978-1-58197-779-0	CEOE OSAT Family and Consumer Sciences Field 09			
978-1-58197-786-8	CEOE OSAT French Sample Test Field 20			
978-1-58197-798-1	CEOE OGET Oklahoma General Education Test 074			
978-1-58197-792-9	CEOE OSAT Library-Media Specialist Field 38			
978-1-58197-787-5	CEOE OSAT Middle Level English Field 24			
978-1-58197-789-9	CEOE OSAT Middle Level Science Field 26			
978-1-58197-790-5	CEOE OSAT Middle Level Social Studies Field 27			
978-1-58197-788-2	CEOE OSAT Middle Level-Intermediate Mathematics Field 25			
978-1-58197-791-2	CEOE OSAT Mild Moderate Disabilities Field 29			
978-1-58197-782-0	CEOE OSAT Physical Education-Health-Safety Field 12			
978-1-58197-783-7	CEOE OSAT Physics Sample Test Field 14			
978-1-58197-793-6	CEOE OSAT Principal Common Core Field 44			
978-1-58197-796-7	CEOE OPTE Oklahoma Professional Teaching Examination Fields 75-76			
978-1-58197-784-4	CEOE OSAT Reading Specialist Field 15			
978-1-58197-785-1	CEOE OSAT Spanish Field 19			
978-1-58197-797-4	CEOE OSAT U.S. & World History Field 17			
			SUBTOTAL	
FOR PRODUCT PRICES GO TO WWW.XAMONLINE.COM			Ship	$8.25
			TOTAL	

www.ingramcontent.com/pod-product-compliance
Lightning Source LLC
Chambersburg PA
CBHW080533300426
44111CB00017B/2703